Europe in Law and Literature

Law & Literature

Edited by
Daniela Carpi and Klaus Stierstorfer

Volume 23

Europe in Law and Literature

Transdisciplinary Voices in Conversation

Edited by
Laura A. Zander and Nicola Kramp-Seidel

DE GRUYTER

ISBN 978-3-11-107202-9
e-ISBN (PDF) 978-3-11-107569-3
e-ISBN (EPUB) 978-3-11-107646-1
ISSN 2191-8457

Library of Congress Control Number: 2023930424

Bibliographic information published by the Deutsche Nationalbibliothek
The Deutsche Nationalbibliothek lists this publication in the Deutsche Nationalbibliografie; detailed bibliographic data are available on the internet at http://dnb.dnb.de.

Typesetting: Integra Software Services Pvt. Ltd.
Printing and binding: CPI books GmbH, Leck

www.degruyter.com

Europa

You tell me I'm safe
though the wind is wailing
with winter at my back everything's unwieldy
the cold is deceitful, excuses abound
time heals, time heals, the scars stay around

and I touch it,
I touch it to give it a name
it evades my grasp and is all just the same,
the name is Stockholm, London, Manchester, Copenhagen,
the name is Srebrenica, Dresden and Mariupol,
Guernica and Kharkiv, a strategic military goal
the name is Budapest, Paris, Sarajevo, Prague, Bordeaux
the name is arbeit macht frei and iron curtain also

Isn't that right Europe,
I'll just try to understand
'cause in the mirror I see
that I own you, Europe
it's etched in my skin
a tattered little continent I've worn very thin
where I'm fairly mobile, can choose where to live
but Europe – you're supposed to be a place
so why do you act like mother?
Like a blood tie
a family
the relations I never claimed

I touch it I touch it
I want to know to have it named

the name is Congo, Algeria,
the name is Utøya, Berlin
the name is East India Company
the name is racial biology
the name is Brussels, Warsaw, Kyiv,
Stalingrad, Madrid
the name is Nice and Lampedusa
time heals time heals
though we skid

You tell me, Europe,
you say: look where I live
all these beautiful churches, bridges, castles, cities there

https://doi.org/10.1515/9783111075693-202

Mine, too, my birthright
these borders, these seas
But how can they be mine if they are not mine to share?

Es tut mir Leid, Europe,
desolée, forgive
rubber rafts, life jackets, holes like a sieve

so we choose our own abuses
and then we choose our shame
the map's not hard to read, but it's tough going just the same
when words become language and languages law
I looked in the mirror and here's what I saw:
You own me, Europe!
Christen me daughter or son
and no matter how I shout
that is where I am from

so I touch it touch it
'cause I need to know the name

the name is Leopold and Ludwig
the name is Charles and George and Peter
You said never again
You said of course no more walls
No you don't use the word race,
but you say culture
the name is Orbàn,
the name is Putin,
the name is Pegida and Le Pen
like a golden dawn
though you said never ever again

but it is still Jesus always Jesus
it's Columbus and Linnaeus
it's my body in the looking glass
'cause since I pass as European
the name is Hitler, the name is Stalin, the name is Franco, Mussolini
the name is Dublin
the name is Schengen,
the name is Bossi-Fini

That is you, Europe,
you who could have been a dream
And I know that you can hear me 'cause your gaze has a soft sheen
So Europe, *j'accuse* . . . I deny you and I know

you give me all the world except generosity
so I christen you Hypocrite
Killer Miller Wild

And then – you shrug your shoulders
as at one you love, your problem child

Since you know that I am safe it feels
you leave these winds to weep
the shield I have is skin and name
time heals time heals
but how can I forgive
that I am in the safe securest place
when I rest in your embrace

Olivia Bergdahl
Translated by Linda Schenck

Acknowledgements

The conceptual origin for this volume derives from a symposium on “Law and Literature in Europe” held at Villa Vigoni from September 13–16, 2021 by the Collaborative Research Center (CRC) “Law and Literature” at the University of Münster. Many of the contributions are based on input statements delivered during the symposium and the ensuing discussions. We owe to the Vigoni participants many of the thematic foci and the contours that later found their way into and came to shape the volume. We are also grateful to those contributors – both inside and outside the CRC – for enriching the volume with their own, different, and new perspectives, thus further broadening the scope of the collection. What all these contributions have in common is that they, much like the discussions at the Villa Vigoni, are not limited to a single discipline or field, but envision new paths beyond the boundaries of conventional, in-field approaches. Even though our discussions of Europe, Law, and Literature did not begin in the Villa, but started almost two years before the symposium and continue to this day, the lively conversations in this unique atmosphere have certainly led to a diversification and intensification of the different research perspectives. The volume is thus a tangible product of the particular institutional context and would not have been possible without the unique environment and the interdisciplinary collaboration within the Collaborative Research Center as well as the Vigoni Symposium.

Even though the volume is inherently a collaborative effort, there are some people in addition to the contributors to whom we owe special thanks, as the volume would not have been possible without their help. This is especially true for Jesper Reddig, whose continuous and expert support in producing the final manuscript was invaluable and highly appreciated. We are also very grateful for Marina Böhmer’s indispensable practical wisdom and effective hands-on approach to the nitty-gritty of editing. We would like to express our gratitude to Cynthia Brown and her team, Christopher M. Darby and Jason Fisher, for the final polishing touches they put on the volume. Very special thanks also goes to our two poets, Olivia Bergdahl and Julia Cimafiejeva, who have allowed us to frame our volume with their both timely and topical poems. Last but not least, we would like to thank Klaus Stierstorfer, the speaker of the CRC, who initiated the Vigoni Symposium and suggested the original format of the *conversazioni*, which in turn inspired us not only to include individual contributions “in conversation,” but to render the entire volume as a dialog of the disciplines – transdisciplinary voices in conversation indeed.

https://doi.org/10.1515/9783111075693-203

Contents

Borders

Part III: **Concerns**

Human Rights

Migration

Citizenship

Digital Self-Determination

Epilogue

Laura A. Zander and Nicola Kramp-Seidel

Introduction

1 Origins

In September 2021, a small group of scholars from our Collaborative Research Center “Law and Literature” (CRC) and selected guests – from various subdisciplines ranging from Law, Slavistics, Jewish Studies, Islamic Studies, and English Studies – came together under Vigoni’s scenic colonnade with marvelous views of the Lago Di Como to discuss law and literature in Europe. The program alternated between keynote lectures on European literature, comparative law, and human rights discourse as well as panel discussions on Europe from the different subdisciplines, from a global perspective, and as it is represented in various German and English legal and literary texts. The open format of the symposium also made it possible to link to the Conference on the Future of Europe, allowing participants worldwide to listen to the input statements and contribute to the panel discussions on human rights and some major challenges in this field in Europe, such as the (dis)integration of Europe, migration, or informational self-determination.

Since then, our *conversazioni* on law and literature in Europe have continued – a fact that this very volume bears written testimony to – and as we are keen to replicate the conversational nature for our discussions, we decided to give this collection the title *Europe in Law and Literature: Transdisciplinary Voices in Conversation*. We invited experts from various fields from within and beyond the CRC to contribute to a highly topical and interdisciplinary study. Whether in a short input statement, a longer essay, or a proper article, we wanted to bring together various disciplines and perspectives on Europe as well as discuss Europe’s representation in legal and literary texts while also highlighting the ongoing and dynamic nature of these discussions.

Shortly after the conference – as a source for inspiration and invitation for further debate on law and literature in Europe – we posted a brief essay on Olivia Bergdahl’s poem “Europa” on our CRC blog, a poem that centers on the Union not only in title, but also very much in its literary trajectory.[1] The poem serves as an

1 Swedish performance poet Bergdahl won the Swedish poetry slam when only 17 years old and took fourth place in the subsequent World Slam Cup in the following year. Her poem “Europa” can be found at <https://www.lyrikline.org/en/poems/europe-13512> in both a written and a performance format. An updated version of the poem can be found at <https://swedishbookreview.org/europe>. Our blog entry on the Villa Vigoni Symposium and Bergdahl’s poem can be accessed on <https://sfb1385.hypotheses.org/69>. The report to the CRC panel at the Conference on the

https://doi.org/10.1515/9783111075693-001

epigraph for this volume, as it seems highly appropriate in the context of the concerns the collection seeks to address.

What is particularly interesting about Bergdahl's poem in light of the conceptualization of this volume is that the persona throughout the course of the poem longs to pin down a reliable vision of Europe, but this attempt seems a futile one as Europe constantly eludes the poet's grasp. So, while the lyrical I ultimately fails to render Europe tangible, she instead succeeds in capturing the complexity and plurality of Europe in geographical, historical, political, cultural, and moral terms. Negotiating various conceptualizations of Europe and questioning one's self-positioning towards Europe, Bergdahl's poem contains a heightened sense of alienation and reproach towards Europe and its allegedly failed promises; she paints a picture of a Europe that trades supposed safety for a hostile environment towards those who are less fortunate or are not thought to belong.[2] It is in this confrontation of the individual with Europe that legal aspects become particularly significant. What appears to be at stake here is the dubious accountability for legal demarcation in terms of place as well as people, but also linguistic or narrative framing and its possible impact on legal discourse, which subsequently facilitates both inclusions and exclusions. Ultimately, the underlying argument seems to span the discursive space between a necessary and also justified Eurocentric perspective and an international ethical human rights discourse. The poem – just like this volume – ultimately asks how much self-preservation, how much privilege an ethical consciousness allows for. More than anything, the poem speaks to the evanescence and complexity of Europe, an evasiveness that is mirrored in the difficulty of framing or defining European literature at large and that is contrasted by the realm of a much more clearly demarcated European law.

Future of Europe can be accessed at <https://futureu.europa.eu/processes/ValuesRights/f/11/meetings/27292>. For more information on the Collaborative Research Center "Law and Literature," please visit <https://www.uni-muenster.de/SFB1385/en/index.html>.

2 On the notion of false promises and the disintegration of Europe see, for instance, Cvete Koneska, "The Vanishing European Dream: The Double Crisis of Migration and European (Dis)Integration" in *A European Crisis: Perspectives on Refugees, Solidarity, and Europe*, ed. Timofey Agarin and Nevena Nancheva (Stuttgart: ibidem P, 2017), 149–167.

2 Europe

As already indicated, Europe is a broad and multifaceted construct, variously understood as a geographical,[3] political, legal,[4] institutional,[5] social, or cultural formation.[6] In this context, the question arises as to when and why actors of certain processes, structures, or norms understand themselves as specifically European. Furthermore, it is unclear which assumptions, claims, or even endeavors at demarcation are associated with Europe, and on which social, legal, or moral processes of negotiation these are based.

From a historical perspective, the allegedly solid borderline between countries and cultures has always been an artificial construct. Individual territories were never isolated spaces; spatial and social transfer processes took place at will, for instance in the field of trade and economy, aesthetics, rules, normative orders, and languages.[7] The historical position of Europe, therefore, was initially defined *ex negativo* in relation to Asia, and for centuries, no further sharpening of the concept took place. The idea of "Europe" did not emerge until modern times. While Europe appears to be a "cosmopolitan project" through the supranational union of the European Union, it is still largely defined by segregation and

---

3 This is usually not in isolation but in combination with a cultural or political mindset, thus defining Western or Eastern Europe. See, for instance, Frithjof Benjamin Schenk, "Mental Maps: Die Konstruktion von geographischen Räumen in Europa seit der Aufklärung," *Geschichte und Gesellschaft* 28.3 (2002): 493–514. With regard to the various changes in EU territory due to different steps of enlargement, see Stefan Seidendorf, "Von welchem Europa reden wir? Reichweiten nationaler Europadiskurse," *Integration* 29.3 (2006): 243–249, 246.

4 Cf. Alec Stone Sweet, *The Judicial Construction of Europe* (Oxford: Oxford UP, 2004).

5 See Joseph Weiler, *The Constitution of Europe* (Cambridge: Cambridge UP, 1999).

6 Cf. Rodolphe Gasche, *Europe, or: The Infinite Task: A Study of a Philosophical Concept* (Stanford: Stanford UP, 2009); Robert Shannan Peckham, *Rethinking Heritage: Cultures and Politics in Europe* (London: I. B. Tauris, 2003). With regard to the cultural formation of Europe, see Wolfgang Schmale, "Europa: Kulturelle Referenz – Zitatensystem – Wertesystem" in *Europäische Geschichte Online*, ed. Institut für Europäische Geschichte (Mainz: IEG, 2010) <http://www.ieg-ego.eu/schmalew-2010-de> (acc. August 6, 2022), 1–29, 10–29. On the relationship between culture and EU law, see Thomas Kearns, "Culture and EU Law: The Exploration of an Interface" in *Culture and European Law*, ed. Rachael Craufurd Smith (Oxford: Oxford UP, 2004), 385–403.

7 Cf. Francesca Fauri, *The History of Migration in Europe: Perspectives from Economics, Politics and Sociology* (London: Routledge, 2015); Peter Gatrell, *The Unsettling of Europe: The Great Migration, 1945 to the Present* (London: Allen Lane, 2019); Nicholas de Genova, ed., *The Borders of "Europe": Autonomy of Migration, Tactics of Bordering* (Durham: Duke UP, 2017).

demarcation – this has become evident, for instance, with Brexit or the continuous debate on the role of Turkey.[8]

In this respect, an understanding of Europe as a geographical space (with more or less clear nation-state allocations and fixed territorial borders) must also necessarily be distinguished from an understanding of Europe as a social space that creates identities[9] and enables interactions.[10] After all, Europe is also a community of values,[11] a cultural concept, a space of closely interconnected common history, similar social systems, and languages.[12]

Consequently, contemporary Europe, like this volume, is characterized by numerous conflicts and processes of negotiation that have accompanied or sustained the development of normative orders and divergent conceptions of law, both in relation to individual states and to Europe as a whole. The same applies, of course, to the field of literature, language, and aesthetics. Ultimately, numerous myths and ideologies have also shaped today's understanding of Europe and still support it today.[13] In this regard, this volume also wants to ask how such processes

---

8 Aleida Assmann, *Der europäische Traum: Vier Lehren aus der Geschichte* (Munich: C.H. Beck, 2018), 14.

9 In such a vein, Sabine Penth acknowledges the lack of a shared identity in Europe, more specifically in the EU. According to Penth, the emergence of such an identity requires a process of becoming aware of one's own in demarcation from the other, the foreign. Integration and disintegration, identity formation, and demarcation are two sides of the same coin, according to Penth's argument. Sabine Penth, "Einführung: Die Grenzen Europas" in *Europas Grenzen*, ed. Penth et al. (St. Ingbert: Röhrig, 2006), 9. Cf. also Claus Altmayer, "Auf dem Weg zur Einheitssprache? Europäische Sprachenpolitik und die Grenzen der europäischen Identität" in *Europas Grenzen*, 229–258, 248–251. See also Jeffrey T. Checkel and Peter J. Katzenstein, *European Identity: Contemporary European Politics* (Cambridge: Cambridge UP, 2009); Bo Stråth, "A European Identity," *European Journal of Social Theory* 5.4 (2002): 387–401.

10 Cf. Neil Fligstein, "Who Are the Europeans" in *Euroclash, The EU, European Identity, and the Future of Europe* (New York: Oxford UP, 2008), 123–164.

11 Grosse Hüttmann uses the term "politische Wertegemeinschaft" to refer to a community of shared political values. Martin Grosse Hüttmann, "Die Osterweiterung der Europäischen Union," *Bürger im Staat* 54.1 (2004): 4–10, 5.

12 With regard to the EU, Seidendorf highlights the divergent shared histories as a result of the various stages of enlargement. See Seidendorf, "Von welchem Europa," 246.

13 Cf. Brook Thomas' discussion of the myths that sustain nation states as well as his exploration of non-territorial citizenship in *Civic Myths: A Law-and-Literature Approach to Citizenship* (Chapel Hill: U of North Carolina P, 2007); see also Mattias Kumm on Europe's relation to constitutionalism, "The Idea of Thick Constitutional Patriotism and its Implications for the Role and Structure of European Legal History" in *Dialogues on Justice: European Perspectives on Law and Humanities*, ed. Helle Porsdam and Thomas Elmholm (Berlin: De Gruyter, 2012), 108–137; Jeanne Gaakeer, "European Law and Literature: Forever Young. The Nomad Concurs" in *Dialogues on Justice*, 44–72.

were legally structured, and literarily negotiated, criticized, and complemented. Whereas Europe, from a legal perspective, appears to be endowed with a clearly determined scope, this seems to be less the case with literature. As a result, it is not always easy to find literature that concerns or is concerned with Europe specifically, but as can be seen from various contributions in this volume, Europe more often than not features on an implicit level.

3 Conversazioni

The particular format of this volume aims at providing a space for reflection, a space that certainly does not prescribe meaning, direction, or instruction, but instead may offer intricate possibilities for contributing to the ongoing discussion on law and literature in Europe.[14] In continuation of the Vigoni symposium in September 2021, we intended to keep a comparatively dynamic, open, and informal format. Some of the contributions were developed based on input statements delivered at Vigoni, and we deliberately decided to preserve a degree of that vibrant and lively character in the spirit of "thinking out loud" for this volume. Nevertheless, other contributions are of a longer, denser, and more formal nature, as they were based on some of the keynote lectures, or the respective scholars did not feel a shorter essay would do justice to the complexity of their topic.

This varied, diverse, and perhaps also somewhat unusual format was deliberately chosen to replicate our discussions at Villa Vigoni, but more importantly, it is also intended to mirror the varied, diverse, and unparalleled nature of Europe as such. What we at any rate sought to avoid was giving the impression that we could exhaustively capture Europe's complexity and contradictions or force them into reliable, coherent categories. To stress the dialogical and dialectical nature of the ongoing discussion on Europe, we have arranged all contributions into pairs, a formal choice intended to resemble *conversazioni*. This structure highlights absences in and conflicts between individual contributions and renders each as continuous, non-final, and non-definitive. They are to be seen as part of an intricate whole, a fragmented, sometimes conflicting, but always productive mosaic of

14 For an introduction to law and literature, cf., for instance, Greta Olsen and Martin Kayman, "Introduction: From 'Law-and-Literature' to 'Law, Literature, and Language': A Comparative Approach," *European Journal of English Studies* 11.1 (2007): 1–15; Elisabeth S. Anker and Bernadette Meyler, "Introduction to New Directions in Law and Literature," in *New Directions in Law and Literature*, ed. Anker and Meyler (Oxford: Oxford UP, 2017), 1–33; Robert Weisberg, "The Law-Literature Enterprise," *Yale Journal of Law & the Humanities* 1.1 (1989): 1–67.

voices, ideas, and concepts. To illustrate more poignantly how the respective contributions in each of these sections relate to each other and to highlight their interconnection, each section is preceded by a brief introduction that will hopefully provide an additional link to help embed each individual contribution in the larger debate about law and literature in and beyond Europe.

Europe's complexity and contradictions are also replicated in the vast variety of contributions from a wide range of various subdisciplines such as legal studies, Slavistics, Jewish Studies, Islamic Studies, German Studies, American Studies, and British Studies, to name just a few. This diverse and interdisciplinary approach seeks to bring together various disciplines as well as perspectives on Europe and its versatile representation in legal and/or literary texts. Many of the issues discussed are highly topical in terms of Europe's immediate future and constituted key issues in the debate at Vigoni, such as human rights, migration, or digital self-determination.[15] It is therefore no surprise that many of the contributions address the future and impending challenges of Europe, for instance the aftermath of Brexit, discrimination in migration and border policy, or the possibility and need to defend alleged "European" values.

Rather than simply approaching this vast range of issues solely from a European perspective, we found it essential to broaden the view and address Europe from beyond its geographical and political boundaries. We are therefore thrilled that the volume includes contributions on Russian literature, Belarusian poetry, and poetry by the Rohingyas instead of merely being confined to a European perspective. The necessity of discussing Europe, European values, and the future of Europe beyond a Eurocentric vision has become even more acute than we would have thought possible since the egregious Russian attack and invasion of Ukraine on February 24, 2022. This willingness to think beyond Eurocentric visions of Europe is, however, not only mirrored in the range of topics and regions covered by this volume, but also in some of their propositions to "think Europe, anew" for instance in Matteo Nicolini's proposal "to pluralise the debate" in the eyes of climate change or Thomas Gutmann's suggestion for dissolving the distinction between internal and external mobility into a global society.

The volume is divided into three parts, entitled Concepts, Commitments, and Concerns. The first section is dedicated to the constitution of Europe, to its conceptualization, classification, significance, and representation across multiple disciplines. Four key areas – Constructing Europe, Constituting Europe, Contrasting Europe, and Defending Europe – attempt to approximate Europe as a concept

15 For Europe's questionable future, cf. Ivan Krastev, *After Europe*. (Philadelphia: U of Pennsylvania P, 2017).

and examine its underlying principles from a broad perspective. In the second part, entitled Commitments, key aspects and agents of Europe are explored, namely the Rule of Law, Legal Actors, Justice, and Borders. Last but certainly not least, the final section, Concerns, zooms in on some highly topical and contentious areas of the ongoing debate on Europe, i.e., Citizenship,[16] Migration,[17] Human Rights,[18] and Digital Self-Determination.[19]

Ultimately, this volume does not intend to resolve any of the complexities and contradictions that characterize the continuous discussions on law, literature, and Europe, but it aims to mark the dawn of further engagement and continuous confrontations with new and alternative negotiations of Europe. Even after our work on this Vigoni volume is complete, we are certain that the exploration of Europe will be all but finished, and thus welcome each and every contribution that adds new ideas on the various topics discussed in this volume, as well as on the larger debate on Europe in law and literature. As we stated in our concluding remarks in the blog entry on the Vigoni conference of 2021, this is only the beginning!

16 Cf., for instance, Klaus Eder and Bernhard Giesen, *European Citizenship: Between National Legacies and Postnational Projects* (New York: Oxford UP, 2001).

17 Cf. Gasche, *Europe*; Cvete "The Vanishing European Dream."

18 On Human Rights in the EU context, see Philip Alston, *The EU and Human Rights* (New York: Oxford UP, 1999); Nanette A. Neuwahl, *The European Union and Human Rights* (Leiden: Martinus Nijhoff, 1995).

19 Cf. Julia Pohle, "Digital Sovereignty: A New Key Concept of Digital Policy in Germany and Europe" (Berlin: Konrad-Adenauer-Stiftung, 2020); Antoinette Rouvroy and Yves Poullet, "The Right to Informational Self-Determination and the Value of Self-Development: Reassessing the Importance of Privacy for Democracy" in *Reinventing Data Protection?*, ed. Serge Gutwirth, Poullet, Paul Hert, Cécile Terwangne, and Sjaak Nouwt (Dordrecht: Springer, 2009), 45–76.

Part I: **Concepts**

Constructing Europe

The broad scope and conceptual complexity of Europe is evident not only, but perhaps particularly obviously, in the difficulty of circumscribing, defining, and delimiting what is distinctively European. Europe incidentally presents itself as multi-layered and often inconsistent, yet this is exactly why it represents a particularly rich and very promising field of research. Whereas Europe from a legal perspective appears to be endowed at least with a clearly determined scope, this seems to be less the case with literature – and there seem to be only a few literary works that are dedicated to Europe or European concerns specifically. Law in Europe, in a similar vein, is certainly also not a self-contained whole, but an equally contested and permeable legal realm.

But even if Europe defies simple and definite categorizations, this does not mean that the attempt to delineate its character is in vain or unproductive. In fact, the special character of Europe emerges in the futile attempt to capture it, and numerous approaches to approximate its substance allow it to be painted ever more distinctively, while – at the same time – providing space for uncertainties and permitting the necessary openness for dynamic development in the future. In this regard, both contributions in this section are dedicated to constructing Europe in the respective fields of law and literature.

Pier Giuseppe Monateri and Walter Cohen both offer a broad comparative perspective that places the European legal and literary traditions within and in contrast to their global development, thereby illustrating that these are by no means isolated phenomena; the two contributions thus highlight the numerous connections as well as the fact that such classifications are invariably artificial and thus consist of particular lines of inquiry or preconceived perspectives.

In "Comparative Law and the Style of Legal Systems," Monateri presents different theories and approaches in comparative law, such as those from Zweigert and Kötz, while also drawing attention to their respective deficiencies. The intricate connection between law and literature is conveniently charted by Zweigert and Kötz, since their analysis has achieved "a greater granularity by focusing on the overwhelming importance of 'style' and its role in shaping a cultural tradition and also a legal system," according to Monateri.[1] In contrast, Cohen presents three major conditions "that render *European* literature distinctively *European*," namely the intra-vernacular, its particular expansion, and the competitive system; he thereby rejects earlier views about the characteristics of European literature by juxtaposing them with parallels in the literature of other continents.[2] Ultimately, both contributions make use of comparison and demarcation in their respective prolific attempts to further contour and construct Europe.

1 Pier Giuseppe Monateri, this volume, 25.

2 Walter Cohen, this volume, 30.

https://doi.org/10.1515/9783111075693-002

Pier Giuseppe Monateri

Comparative Law and the Style of Legal Systems

1 Traditions and Originality

At the beginning of the twentieth century, Adhémar Esmein proposed a first theory to subdivide the world of law into a Roman, a Germanic, an Anglo-Saxon, a Slavic, and an Islamic group.[3] He explicitly adopted as the principle for this classification that of originality.

Each of Esmein's groups is singled out by its original conception of the law. The Roman, Germanic, Islamic, Anglo-Saxon, and Slavic conceptions of the law were characterized as ideal types representing different occurrences of the law to be taken into account for mapping the various legal systems of the world.

Though presented as the outcome of a scientific theory of the law, Esmein's whole conception derives from an implicit Romantic aesthetic, as the very concept of "originality" gained its full modern meaning in Romanticism. Originality, for Romanticism, is that which marks a work of art with the imprint of genius. For Esmein, the genius of the Romans for the law is undeniable as it is different, and sometimes opposite to that of the Anglo-Saxons. The insistence on origins, as that which is not only original but also connected with the beginnings of something, was typically Romantic, and resulted in a flux of research on folklore and the original Indo-Germanic roots of modern European languages.

The way comparatists capture the differences between one legal culture and the others derives, therefore, from their capacity to perceive the singularity of different legal styles. If one adopts such methods of inquiry, current legal systems become *tableaux vivants* of a variety of notions of justice and can be characterized mainly through their aesthetics. One critical conclusion is then inescapable – either aesthetics is a pivotal field in legal scientific inquiries, or comparative classifications have been shaped by analogy and impression more than by scientific method.

It is intriguing that, though not a theory conforming to contemporary scientific standards, Esmein's classification had a strong grip. It captured, beyond the veil of its aesthetic ideology, a deep structure of the global space as it was politically organized at the beginning of the twentieth century.

3 Adhémar Esmein, *Eléments de droit constitutionnel français et comparé* (Paris: Sirey, 1909).

https://doi.org/10.1515/9783111075693-003

Esmein's theory had a political meaning because it depicted the condition of the world space as it was shaped by European interstate law and politics. As the legal world of Esmein was divided into five great families, so the world space was subdivided among five major groups of European powers: France with her empire and her culturally dominated Latin sisters (Italy and Spain) with Roman codifications; the German and Austrian Empires, having their own codes; the Russian (Slavic) Empire; the British Empire; and the Ottoman (Islamic) Empire.

In essence, from a political point of view, Esmein's Romantic attitude reflected the concert of European powers in their geopolitical subdivision of the planet into spheres of political and cultural influence, their practice of international conferences among the European powers that characterized the development of international law, and their efforts to reach legal uniformity in many areas of commerce and finance.

These observations indicate that in comparative law, there is narrative on one side, and the meaning of it in geopolitical terms on the other. The gist of Esmein's narrative is that of originality and an aesthetic of legal styles, but its meaning is a portrait of power relations among empires and spheres of influence.

As is clear to see, in the case of Esmein, the marker of a group is its "originality," which renders the whole of his theory rather subjective and almost surely aesthetic. The more scientific a marker is, the more it would resist subjective interpretations.[4] The marker of originality can hardly pass a test of objectivity as it really depends on an interpretation.

If one were to interpret the available characteristics of these traditions in just a slightly different way, for instance in comparison to English common law, one could well affirm that Russian, German, and French laws are but three variants of the same Romanic tradition. They have different stories and differ on many details, they possess different legal styles, but they share common concepts and categories that are much more similar to each other than they are to English legal concepts.

The main point of analyzing Esmein's classification is to reflect on how to construct a classification that does not depend heavily on the mere viewpoint of the observer, and which does not rely on concerns for the ranking of the observer's legal tradition.

Moreover, in Esmein's classification there was no place for Africa or the Far East. Islamic law was considered due to the enduring importance of the Ottoman Empire. But, for instance, in spite of its patent originality, the Chinese conception

4 Franco Moretti, *Canon/Archive: Studies in Quantitative Formalism* (New York: N+1 Foundation, 2018).

of the law was never properly considered as China was not an international power at the time. Japan plays no role as it was only just about to be counted among the great powers. Since Europeans saw European nations as the main actors of international law, Esmein's theory was correct in depicting that world, but not for the reasons he gave.

From the standpoint of methods, Esmein's use of the Romantic device of originality was significant. The claim to dominion in the field of law did not only pass through the material world of hard power relations, but also through the soft power represented by the capacity to mount a narrative. Through comparative law, some legal systems may assume a cultural legitimacy derived from their representing original stages in the "history of the spirit." Though perhaps not evident at first glance, there may be implicit in comparative legal theories an effort toward legitimation and the exercise of soft power in the field of law.

2 Language, Religion, and Space

The nexus of geopolitical relevance and comparative methods may also be discovered in the tentative classification of legal systems purported by Henri Lévy-Ullmann. The main distinction traced in his work was between a continental group, a group of English-speaking countries, and a group of Islamic jurisdictions.[5]

In his classification, a first group of systems is clearly identified based on a spatial feature: the continent. In this way, the laws of Europe can be thought as related because of geography. Here, it is not so much tradition or ancestry which is presented as the key factor for grouping as it is the element of earth. It is worth noting that Esmein's different Slavic, German, and French-Roman groups become unified into one group as an expression of a "law of the earth," as opposed to a "law of the sea," thus reflecting two great spaces and modes of dominance whose opposition to one another could have had a deep political meaning at a time when the British Empire still enveloped the entire Euro-Asian continental mass through its African, Indian, and Far Eastern possessions – dominions that were effectively connected by control of the seas.

At the same time, Lévy-Ullmann does not follow his premise to the end. Rather than using a geographical characteristic such as "the continent," he uses different markers, such as language and religion. He creates one classification based on three different benchmarks for each group. While he combines considerations in a

5 Henri Lévy-Ullmann and Boris Mirkine-Guetzévitch, *La vie juridique des peuples* (Paris: Librairie Delagrave, 1931).

way that would not pass current scientific standards, his classification may have captured something relevant about the world order. Through the use of disparate categories, such as "continental" on one side and "language" or "religion" on another, Lévy-Ullmann sketches an outline of a European bloc, an Anglo-sphere, and an Islamic space. Once again, the structure of the theory can be unsound, but its content can be meaningful in unintended ways.

The use of "religion" in this context reveals the difficulties of dealing with the Islamic space from a European geographical perspective – the characteristics of the Islamic space being profoundly different from the European spatial subdivisions of the world. The conception of the world space may greatly vary from a cultural strategic vision to another. Here, religion becomes a key to understanding legal institutions that can effectively be explained in other ways. Polygamy preceded Islam, rather than following it. The prohibition of usury derived from Roman times and had parallels in the West. The "Islamic veil" was diffused in the Mediterranean basin before Islam. Political theology – the assumption of importance of theological concepts to account for political institutions – is mainly of Byzantine origin.

Using religion as a marker and as a strong divisive factor obscures these parallels, and reproduces the stereotype of a lay modern world, the West, as opposed to a world still anchored to faith. Religion becomes part of an orientalist strategy of exoticization, so much so that some of the main terms of Islamic religion are left untranslated even when they could be easily translated, contributing to the representation of these terms as different. The best example is the term *Allah*, whose meaning is "the one unique God," but which is left untranslated, thereby generating the impression that it is a particular name of a particular god different from God in Christianity or Judaism.

A peak in bias was reached by Georges Sauser-Hall when he classified legal systems on the basis of the problematic concept of "race," making apparent to what extent comparative law may serve projects of differentiation and hegemony more than of cooperation and openness.[6] In his work, "race" explicitly implies the idea of a different "genius" of different races for the law. This slippery approach led Sauser-Hall to distinguish Indo-European, Semitic, and Mongolian legal models. Within the Indo-European family, he further distinguished the subgroups of Hindu, Iranian, Celtic, Greek-Latin, Germanic, Anglo-Saxon, and Latvian-Slavic law. The template for such classification may also be found in early comparative linguistics.

---

6 Georges Sauser-Hall, *Fonction et méthode du droit comparé* (Geneva: Kuendig, 1913), 59–63.

He identified the notion of "race" on the basis of "geography," "language," and "cultural affinity," rendering apparent how this concept of race was used as a proxy for other factors. While language and geography have a reference, cultural affinity depends rather entirely on the observer's judgment. Consequently, it is biased not only from a political point of view, but also from the standpoint of methods. Lévy-Ullmann's theory arbitrarily renders race as the locus of difference, defining it as based on a set of factors that are ultimately linked to a subjective perception of affinity.

This discussion raises a key issue of comparative legal studies, which is where to locate diversity. To say that two systems differ because their cultures are different is not saying much. Culture is a rather prescientific concept. Like "race," "culture" is often used as a proxy for an unknown black box where differences are originated or dissolved. The fact that, even today, reasons for divergent legal systems based on culture still appeal to some only exhibits the poor evolution of the discipline.

This first review of European theories on the grouping of legal systems shows a few things. First, comparative theories have been built on rather vague notions of originality or affinity when not being based on a mixture of markers such as space, language, or religion. Second, comparative law theories may have a loose structure, but they also may retain meaning as ideological constructs of the world and of the struggle for supremacy fought among different conceptions of justice. As such, these theories tend to be essentially biased, based on the standpoint of the author, as they also tend to coalesce around a mysterious locus of difference which remains unscientifically described as culture. Finally, there have been strong inconsistencies in methods which have marked early European efforts to reach a meaningful classification of legal traditions.

3 A Panorama of the World's Legal Systems

A turn to the United States reveals that methodological problems continued, but in a slightly different way. In 1928, John Henry Wigmore attempted to devise a classification of legal traditions explicitly based on a method which he called "pictorial."[7] His enterprise was more consciously affirmed as aesthetic than those of previous European scholars, underlining the subjective and artistic nature of sketching different legal traditions. Wigmore identified five groups of legal cultures based on

7 John H. Wigmore, *A Panorama of the World's Legal Systems* (St. Paul: West Publishing Company, 1928).

their different "cultural contexts": (1) primitive laws, (2) ancient laws, (3) Euro-American law, (4) religious systems, and (5) Afro-Asian systems.

Two points deserve immediate attention. First, all European subdivisions among French, German, or Slavic were removed and a single legal family was created with the explicit introduction of the United States on the front stage, as part of the Euro-American law classification. Second, Wigmore marked a deep historical divide between the past and present.

In a European classification, Roman law would always remain as the origin of modern systems. In Wigmore's model, a deep line is traced that would place Roman law distant from current jurisdictions into the group of "ancient laws." This would make the law of the Romans closer, for instance, to ancient Egyptian or Greek law, and rather distant from current French or German laws.

Of course, Wigmore's classification, with its total disregard of European differentiations and its marked historical breaks, sounds rather American and is indeed equally as biased as those of his European predecessors, although in a different sense. First, he presumed that all primitive legal systems are similar, that all ancient societies are comparable, and that all religious systems can be ranked in one big family. In addition, he placed the "Afro-Asiatic" systems into a single group without any clear connection. In a way, this classification adopted the truism that everything that is not Euro-American is Afro-Asiatic. His unique conception was that of the existence of a Euro-American law, which featured the inclusion of America in a context that was otherwise European. For his time, this was certainly an invention.

In short, Wigmore made the first attempt to consider American culture on an equal footing with Europe in terms of the law and its ability to contribute to the legal evolution. Moreover, the problem of "primitives" acquired in Wigmore a specifically American dimension in relation to the "Indian" rights – that is, the rights of Native Americans as an autonomous field of study, an undertaking that American scholars had already embarked on since Hoebel to Llewellyn.[8] After all, for these authors – and the question must have seemed like a real metaphorical gauntlet – the distinction between Cheyenne and Sioux law began to appear more relevant than the one between a "Slavic" and a "Germanic" model.

Methodologically, Wigmore's work attempted to capture the essence of legal conceptions through a method that, as we have said, he himself described as pictorial. His book contained 25 pictures which represented in his view the most emblematic conceptions of justice, legal actors, and the contents of the law among

8 David Luban, *Legal Modernism: A Critique and Defense of Modern Legal Theory* (Ann Arbor: U of Michigan P, 1994).

Egyptians, Chinese, Greeks, Jews, and many other peoples. In particular, its sub-classifications also included Roman law described as Romanesque, and English law labeled as "Anglican," providing a very particular key to interpret these traditions. Above all, Wigmore also included a section dedicated to maritime law, or the law of the sea, which he considered an autonomous system of justice.

What emerges from this new intellectual framework is the strong conception of a single, large Euro-American family spatially dislocated beyond the standard European borders, where modern societies are clearly separated from ancient laws. Wigmore innovated from a double point of view: he grouped together all modern Euro-American legal models and separated them from their historical origins.

4 History, Ideology, and Styles

After the Second World War, the European spatial order of the world began to fade in favor of new conceptions which were only formally linked to previous European conceptions of the international order. In this context, Pierre Arminjon, Boris Emanuelovič Nolde, and Martin Wolff tried to make a defense of law's autonomy in the field of comparison. These authors proposed making a distinction between legal systems based on their intrinsic characteristics.[9]

This premise was combined with the usual search for genealogies following diffusionist theories looking at relations of derivation and similarity springing from common centers of influence. The approach called diffusionism, which prevailed in anthropological studies, purported that similar practices of different cultures or peoples are solely or primarily the result of diffusion as opposed to independent discovery or development. The theory thus effectively supported the idea that in human history there are few original models and a variety of imitations. There are few leading and innovative systems and many followers, with imitation being the normal way of legal evolution. Thus, the study of it can be profitably limited to an "important" few and supposedly pure centers of diffusion. This approach would lead the authors to a classification based on seven different spheres of influence: French, Germanic, Scandinavian, English, Russian, Islamic, and Hindu.

Again, Eurocentric distinctions were brought back. In this taxonomy the usual triple consisting of France, Germany, and England is, as always, placed

9 Pierre Arminjon, Boris Emanuelovič Nolde, and Martin Wolff, *Traité de droit comparé* (Paris: LGDJ, 1950).

prominently, with – in addition – a new emphasis on the Nordic subdivisions, so that the difference between Sweden and Germany is closely parallel in magnitude to that between France and Islam. England, in particular, regained a leading role while the United States almost disappeared. The Hindu element, which held great importance in comparative linguistics, reappeared as a distinct legal family, all the more noteworthy given the complete obliteration of China and Japan. The authors' three volumes of refined erudition could not, however, compensate for the old-fashioned character of a classification which tried to renew worn out conceptions as they were starting to fade.

René David contributed a fresh start in a process of elaboration which began with his *Traité élémentaire* and culminated in his *Les Grands systems de droit,* which is still today the most-widely used textbook on comparative law.[10] The key element considered by David in the *Traité* was "ideology." An explicit consideration of ideology made this a considerable move toward an approach to law and politics which was a major departure from traditional searches for pure structural or genealogical connections. By ideology, David meant a complex of ideas or ideals which can form the basis for policy considerations, so that a legal system could be analyzed as embedding political conceptions "frozen" in legal rules and principles. With this consciousness, David singled out a "Western Law" subdivided into two groups: the French and the Anglo-American. In contrast to a Western ideology of the law, he classified a Socialist, Islamic, Hindu, and Chinese law as embodying complexes of ideas different from the values of the West.

This new conception of Western law represented an Atlantic duality of the West with clear geopolitical consequences, and quite naturally obliterated any strong reference to Germany or Sweden, putting France on the same level as the United States. Any reference to the old label of an Anglo-Saxon family was transformed into a reference to an Anglo-American group following a suggestion that we have already seen at work in Wigmore's conception.

David elaborated his ideological approach to legal systems in *Les grands systems,* where he combined it with the traditional search for similarity of legal techniques and concepts. David offered a great simplification with a complex mechanism. Combining legal techniques and ideology, or worldview, David created a classification based on only three major legal systems: Romano-Germanic Law, Common Law, and Socialist Law. All other systems in the world would be classified under the broad category of other conceptions of law and justice. Among these, Muslim law stands out in terms of analysis as there was a more detailed consideration of its breadth and singularity.

10 René David, *Les grands systèmes de droit contemporains* (Paris: Dalloz, 1964).

It is worth noting that David set aside the previous label of Western law in favor of a more traditional distinction between the Romano-Germanic group and the common law group. Germany was revitalized in the process of revision and the West lost its unity. In his taxonomy David would use traditional considerations, based on legal concepts and techniques, to distinguish Romano-Germanic legal systems from common law systems. At the same time he would instead use the 'political' element to distinguish socialist systems from others. That is, socialist systems would not be distinguished on account of having different techniques or concepts, but via different politics. From a genealogical viewpoint, socialist countries inherited the apparatus of Roman law, but this form of the law became almost entirely connoted by the different political orientation of those countries.

As already stated in regard to Esmein, David refers to the device of representation to illustrate the characteristics of a large group of systems through the analysis of the most representative of the family. France, the country of the Napoleonic Code, epitomized the Roman-Germanic family. As it gained power in the world following the Second World War, the United States became more representative of common law than England, and socialist countries were represented by the Soviet Union (USSR).

If we look for parallels between comparative law classifications and the geopolitical setting of the world at the time, David's classification itself had an ideology: that of the French Fifth Republic in the context of the Cold War – two superpowers, the United States and the USSR, and a third pole with France as the leader of European countries and its influence in Asia, Africa, Latin America, and wherever the respective codes would have been imitated if not explicitly adopted.

The rest of the world seems like an immense "overseas department." Room is obviously made for Chinese and Japanese traditions but more for their "exotic" past than their present. Africa is considered too, but mainly through legal anthropology. More importance, as mentioned, is given to Islamic law with a detailed analysis of Islamic legal techniques and concepts, but where the Islamic space remains torn between relevance and traditionalism.

Methodologically, the mapping strategy of David is of particular importance, and received great approval, because it succeeded in combining history, legal analysis, and policy considerations into a picture capturing the essence of the world order in its age. David's world was effectively the legal world we lived in.

A legal system is rooted in its origins, but becomes oriented by its current political values. The style of a system is given by its practices and techniques as established by experience. These techniques change slowly over time. Each system has its own particular institutions, like trust in English law or *waqf* (whereby property is entrusted to God and administered by a representative) in the Islamic tradition.

Each system also shares with other systems common features, and especially common values, which allow for larger groupings. Each system's importance is determined by its relevance in world affairs. Politics is no longer independent and can only develop within and through the constraints of one legal tradition.

If we, then, reconsider the various classifications that we have encountered, there is a point that can emerge with a certain clarity, and that is the instability of the "Germanic" element. From time to time, the Germanic tradition represents a family, or a subgroup of a larger family. It is opposed to or combined with Roman law.

This instability also found expression in debates between German academics and the rival theories of Germanists and Romanists. The former stressed the relevance of German customs, and the latter that of Roman studies in the formation of a learned German legal tradition. Friedrich Carl von Savigny succeeded in combining these conflicting views in his theory of popular law, or *Volksgeist*. He theorized that law develops through popular practices, but to express them with scientific precision we need the refined apparatus which is offered by Roman legal studies. He became the standard bearer of the mainstream, but minority schools always contested the packaging of classic legal thought with, in particular, the legal formalism implied by the use of Roman concepts to describe new realities.

The instability of the Germanic element in comparative analysis was reflected in Germany's shifting political power. Before 1870, Germany was divided into many sovereign states and did not represent a political unity. From 1870/71 to 1914, the German Empire became a dominant power on the continent and an emerging world power. Defeated and humiliated after the First World War, it jolted the entire world in the Second World War, and after a second fall, re-emerged as a strong power in the European Union. It is no coincidence, then, that starting at the end of the 1960s, German authors reconsidered the renewed European importance of German law, criticizing David's classification and his almost tacit but pervasive downgrading of its relevance.

A newer classification proposed by Konrad Zweigert and Hein Kötz can indeed be interpreted as a specific response to René David. In their treatise, these authors clearly re-distinguished between a "Romanist system," which still saw France as its most important offspring in that historical moment, and a "Germanic model," which culminated in the Austrian, Swiss, and German systems.[11] France and Germany, in short, no longer constituted a single family, but represented two distinct models. Germany was placed at the same level as France, and both were at the same level as the Anglo-American legal system. On a par with these models was the

11 Konrad Zweigert and Hein Kötz, *Introduction to Comparative Law* (Oxford: Oxford UP, 1998).

Scandinavian system and that of the fading socialist countries. Finally, Islamic law, Hindu law, and a "Far Eastern legal family" would complete the picture.

Zweigert and Kötz adopted a method based on the styles of legal systems. The style of a legal tradition can be reconstructed through a combined study of history, modes of thought, distinctive institutions, legal sources, and ideology. The tool Zweigert and Kötz used to achieve this result is extremely important and must be properly underscored. The German authors employed an explicit literary notion of "style" to identify the different modes of expression of the law. In a fairly direct way, Zweigert and Kötz provided a clarification of what they meant. According to them, the study of style must include: 1) the historical origin and evolution of a legal system; 2) the predominant and characteristic way of expressing the law; 3) the particular characteristics of some legal institutions; 4) the sources of law and their interpretation; and 5) other ideological factors.

According to Zweigert and Kötz, there is a complex interrelation between style, logic, and rules. A "way of thinking" appears to emerge here. By integrating considerations of style into the ideological approach of David, Zweigert and Kötz added an important element to comparative analysis. David's project combined French, German, and common law to form a single Western legal family, an approach that was rather different from the process of investigating the technicalities by which each legal system works. David's approach stressed general principles and aimed at a broad map of the world's basic conceptions of justice. Zweigert and Kötz's analysis has achieved a greater granularity by focusing on the overwhelming importance of 'style' and its role in shaping a cultural tradition and also a legal system.

In this way, a typically literary, or if you will, aesthetic notion such as style becomes a central notion in the science of comparative law. This combination of literary concepts and aesthetic ideas to classify such technical objects as jurisdictions has – in my opinion – not yet been sufficiently noticed. On the authority of Zweigert and Kötz it has been given for granted, just as it has been given for granted what can be meant by style.

What I wish to emphasize is that from Esmein to the present, in various ways, literary notions, such as originality and style, have exerted a very influential role in comparative law theory. This fact must be taken into account, for indeed these notions capture something about the law that we cannot express in any other way. They, after all, point to an aesthetic dimension of law and jurisdiction. In this sense the study of law and literature goes far beyond the study of how law is represented in literary texts, for in effect what happens is that we explain the difference between laws on the basis of literary notions.

In particular, I am emphasizing how style, the literary notion par excellence, has actually become a key factor in legal taxonomies. What we can then ask is whether, after all, the articulation of law is a literary enterprise. Is our way of thinking about justice more literary than philosophical?

The aesthetics of law, far from being the ornament of refined discourse, is perhaps indeed an appeal to a *gnoseologia major* – higher form of knowledge that we seek to exorcise, but by which we are in fact deeply governed.

Walter Cohen

The Europe of European Literary History

1 Introduction

Making sense of the connection between literature and law in Europe is a daunting task. This essay, originally presented at a conference on the same topic, has little more than an oblique, preparatory relationship to that subject. Its emphasis, as proposed by the conference organizer, Klaus Stierstorfer, is on how Europe has evolved out of its literary history. Such a focus ought to raise suspicions, however. This is true regardless of which of the two main, antithetical stances one takes on the matter. If you argue that the literature of Europe is too diverse to allow for significant generalization, the risk is banality. But if you adopt the adventurous alternative – that European literary history displays distinctive patterns – you are guaranteed to produce one counterchallenge after another. For better and worse, it is the second line of inquiry that is followed here.

Most of the great accounts of European literary history that remain influential today were composed between the 1920s and 1950s, primarily in German. I am thinking of Erich Auerbach above all, but also of Ernst Robert Curtius, Georg Lukács, Leo Spitzer, and, in Russian, Mikhail Bakhtin. Comparable philosophical investigations include works by Max Horkheimer and Theodor Adorno and, later, by Jacques Derrida. With the exception of Derrida, these writers were in part responding to Communism, Fascism, or both. Their problems are therefore not our problems, although the recent rise of authoritarian politics may render this claim optimistic. Second, and more importantly for what follows, these are all intra-European accounts of the history of European literature.

What happens instead, then, if we register both the differentiation within European literature and the relationship of European literature to the literatures of other continents? This is the path I intend to take. I will be making three main claims. First, European literature is uniquely defined by intra-vernacular leadership. Literary dominance has long belonged less to a prestigious Classical literary language than to a succession of vernaculars. Second, European literature may be differentiated by its expansionist vocation – an assertion intended to include, but not be limited to, imperial power. Third, European literature may be understood

Note: Documentation for the claims made in this essay may be found in Walter Cohen, *A History of European Literature: The West and the World from Antiquity to the Present* (Oxford: Oxford UP, 2017).

https://doi.org/10.1515/9783111075693-004

as a competitive system, with equal emphasis on competition and systematicity. As we shall see, these categories often blend into each other.

2 European Literature's Typicality

To make this case, I will begin by looking at the features of European literature often wrongly taken to be distinctive. In fact, European literature often resembles literature from other parts of the world. It is only when set against these areas of commonality that its distinctive features emerge.

Most Europeans have long spoken, and more recently written, Indo-European languages. But by the beginning of the Common Era, if not much earlier, this language group had already spread through Turkey and Central Asia, south to India and, probably, east to Western China (Tokharian in present-day Xinjiang Province). For almost a millennium – from the conquests first of Alexander in the fourth century BCE and subsequently of Rome beginning in the third, to those of the Arabs in the seventh and eighth centuries CE – Indo-European also dominates urban North Africa in the form of Greek in the East and Latin in the West, just as on the northern shores of the Mediterranean. Today, it remains the spoken and written language group of Iran and parts of Central Asia, of most of South Asia, and, of course, of the European settler colonies. Again, European languages are written alphabetically – long the global norm, with the important exception of East Asia. Even if we look at linguistic pressure on Europe, it is easy to find a crucial analogue. "Barbarian" invaders from the north bring down the Han Dynasty in China more than 200 years before their Germanic-speaking counterparts put an end to the Western Roman Empire – in both instances with a lasting impact on the subjugated civilization and its language. Finally, if we consider which language prevails following a foreign invasion – that of the conqueror or that of the conquered – Europe conforms to the cross-continental pattern. The conquerors are forced to relinquish their language unless women are able to raise a substantial percentage of subsequent generations in the newly arrived tongue.

If we instead turn our attention to characteristic literary forms, similar overlaps are evident. Short poetry is ubiquitous and provides no basis for differentiation. Even the European love lyric, which *is* relatively distinctive, has multiple analogues elsewhere in the world and is likely, in its initial stages, to have drawn on Semitic literature, above all the Arabic of al-Andalus, medieval Spain. The Old High German *Hildebrandslied* shares with epic traditions across Eurasia the unwitting, and often-fatal, military conflict between father and son. This appears to be the result of both structural parallelism and the influence of narratives originating from Iran. Medieval chivalric romance, particularly the tale of Tristan and Isolde, also has significant parallels and, I believe, source material in Iranian narrative. Further, Western literate and often literary drama, invented first in ancient Greece and then again in the medieval Church, finds its equivalents in Sanskrit theater of the first millennium CE and in Chinese and Japanese theater of the second.

Even the novel, often taken to be uniquely European, looks less distinctive when compared with its Japanese and Chinese counterparts. One method is to opt for a more capacious definition of the form by redefining all works of prose fiction as novels. I will take the opposite stance, however. My claim is that any definition of the European novel able to incorporate not just eighteenth- and nineteenth-century realist fiction but also, say, the texts of Henry James and Marcel Proust has no conceptual basis for excluding Murasaki Shikibu's *Tale of Genji* (by 1020, Japanese) or Cao Xueqin's and, perhaps, Gao E's *Story of the Stone* (also known as *The Dream of the Red Chamber*, pub. 1792, Chinese). Further, both the East Asian and the Western European novelistic traditions can be traced back to South Asian oral narratives of the first millennium BCE. If we then move forward chronologically once more, the co-presence of great ages of both drama and prose fiction in early modernity at the opposite ends of Eurasia seems to point to both the modernizing impulse behind these forms and the parallel steps toward modernity.

This last point enables a smooth transition to thematic concerns, where, once again, analogues are widespread. The emphasis on the serious treatment of everyday reality (Auerbach), often coupled with popular alternatives to elite culture (Bakhtin), finds equivalents in early-modern Eurasia in masterpieces of Chinese fiction such as Wu Cheng'en's *Journey to the West* (often known as *Monkey*, pub. 1592) or the pseudonymous Lanling Xiaoxiao Sheng's *Plum in the Golden Vase* (pub. c. 1618, the title in the original, *Jin Ping Mei*, being an elaborate, obscene pun that can be rendered as: *The Glamor of Entering the Vagina*). The same popular dimension applies to the roughly contemporaneous devotional *bhakti* lyric poetry in various South Asian vernaculars; along multiple axes, some of it can be compared to the writings of the Protestant Reformation. Religious parallels may also be found between Western European satire on the *Christian* clergy and Chinese satire on the *Buddhist* clergy. In a different vein, Curtius's *European Literature and the Latin Middle Ages* clearly refers to a phenomenon unique to European, mainly Western European, literature. But one could just as easily speak of South Asian literature and the Sanskrit Middle Ages (where "middle ages" is meant as a purely temporal, rather than conceptual, marker). In the case of both regions, the ancient high literary language is also the bearer of the dominant religion – respectively Catholicism or Hinduism.

To reiterate: everything said so far might seem to work against the avowed aim of this paper to delineate the unique features of European literature. My objective, of course, is simply to exclude those features that contribute to European *literature* but also to other world *literatures*, in favor of focusing specifically on the former – those aspects that render *European* literature distinctively *European*. Let me recall, then, my three central categories – intra-vernacular leadership, expansionist vocation, and organization into a competitive system. I will take each of these up in turn.

3 Intra-Vernacular Leadership

Compared with China, Europe is marked by the failure of empire. Although the continuity of Chinese civilization or even of Chinese imperial rule is routinely overstated, it nonetheless offers a striking contrast. To be sure, a strong army and an effective political bureaucracy matter a lot in the maintenance of domination over a broad territorial expanse. But consider an alternative angle. The Han Dynasty, the most important imperial contemporary of Ancient Rome, becomes concerned about the proliferation of increasingly divergent *written* versions of the increasingly divergent Chinese *spoken* languages of its realm. It mandates uniformity, based on the literary practice of the capital. The mandate succeeds – more or less permanently.

A thousand years later, Charlemagne faces the same problem with the increasingly divergent *written* Latin in different parts of *his* empire – a divergence that, as in China, is a response to the increasing divergence among the *spoken* languages, in this case the nascent Romance tongues. Charlemagne, too, issues an order for uniformity. He essentially succeeds with Latin. But, in contrast to the earlier Chinese experience, he fails in the long run to prevent the development of multiple written languages in the lands where Latin was once spoken. That is, he fails to prevent the development of the *written* Romance languages. On the other hand, China does not see even a remotely comparable emergence of multiple, regionally marked, *written* Sinitic languages. Why should there be these almost antithetical outcomes? Partly because Charlemagne's empire was short-lived. But also partly because European writing is alphabetical rather than character-based, is hence more tied to the phonetic rendering of spoken syllables and words, and is therefore more likely to encourage differentiation.

This encouragement is not limited to the forms of literacy. Language and writing (including literature) are at times important social forces – a phenomenon obscured partly by an exclusive focus on admittedly important economic or environmental factors (feudalism and capitalism; the plagues of Late Antiquity or the Black Death) but also by almost-always self-discrediting claims for the world-changing impact of this or that individual text or author. There are better pickings to be had at a higher level of generality: for instance, the crucial role of Dante, Petrarch, and Boccaccio in causing the Florentine dialect to be elevated into the official language of a newly-united Italy 500 years later – despite the fact that Florence, unlike Paris in France or London in England, was very much not the center of political power.

To return to the contrast with China, however: the failure of empire, though a promising point of departure, is in itself an inadequate interpretive lens. Empire has faltered in many places. Thus, we need to seek other explanations. The earliest post-classical vernacular European literatures – in which literature retains its etymological sense of writing – are overwhelmingly composed in the Celtic and Germanic languages during the second half of the first millennium in the Northwest part of the continent, largely beyond the boundaries of the former Roman Empire. Why should the continent's periphery have gotten there first? Because its spoken languages are almost entirely unrelated to Latin. A cleric in what is now Italy, France, Spain, or Portugal could long preach in Latin to his illiterate parishioners and expect to be understood. Such a practice would not have occurred to his contemporaries to the Northwest, where Latin, rather than serving as a barrier to vernacular innovation because *it* was considered the literary version of popular speech, was a completely foreign language and hence incapable of being thought of in the way that it was understood in the emerging zone of Romance speech. Instead, Latin might function as a model for vernacular literary creativity.

Accordingly, only beginning around 1100 do the Romance-language literatures appear. Their belatedness is a consequence of their greater proximity to Latin. Note that here, language and literature might be considered both effect and cause – the effect of the rise of independent medieval monarchies and city states but also perhaps a condition of their emergence and certainly a contributor to their consolidation. In the territory of modern-day France, what are sometimes considered the two main themes of European literature are introduced – love in the South (Occitan lyric), adventure in the North (Old French romance). It is at this point that one can truly begin to speak of European literature as more than a collection of heterogeneous products united only by the fact of having been composed in what is now Europe. One can instead start contemplating European literature in the strong sense – as a category marked by shared forms and themes. Although I prefer medieval romances in German to those in French, and Renaissance plays in English to those in Italian, there is no doubt that literary leadership is the preserve of the Romance languages and hence of what is also the political, military, economic, and social core of Western Europe at least until 1750.

It is at this point, however, that the periphery strikes back: first in the form of the Scottish Enlightenment and especially in that of German letters (previously important in the Reformation but not as literature). These movements are followed in the nineteenth century by the American Renaissance, by the great age of Russian literature, and, later, by Scandinavian drama. Around the turn of the century, one can point initially to Anglophone Irish literature, then, and more problematically, to a relatively non-nationalist Jewish writing in Yiddish and many national vernaculars, subsequently to the American South, and even more recently to Latin American, global Anglophone, and just plain global literature – albeit still in a somewhat subordinate position with respect to publishing centers such as New York, London, Paris, and Barcelona. What explains this partial return to the periphery? I shall observe only the obvious: that in the face of an ever-encroaching modernization, these increasingly far-flung, previously marginal regions seem to have possessed the comparative advantage of rendering the clash of contemporary innovation with traditional culture – an option unavailable in France or England.

Yet as striking as this trajectory is, it is certainly not unique. South Asia, for instance, witnesses a development of vernacular literature remarkably similar to that of Western Europe. The earliest vernaculars influenced by Sanskrit arise not among the Indo-European spoken vernaculars of the North but in the Dravidian languages of the South and, to a lesser extent, in the various languages of Southeast Asia. This occurs for the same reason as in Western Europe: the qualitative difference between popular speech and the high Classical literary language, in this case Sanskrit. Given the similarity of the two regions, where then does European literary distinctiveness lie? The answer, of course, is in vernacular literary leadership. From 1100 onwards, the model of Latin is challenged, then displaced, by the norm of whatever the preeminent Romance vernacular happens to be – first Old French and Occitan, next Tuscan, subsequently Renaissance Castilian, then Classical French. Even the return to Latin and, still more, to Greek in the Renaissance is mediated through Italian – both as the founding example of how this recovery is to be carried out and as a body of writing to be emulated in its own right (most strikingly, perhaps, in the Petrarchan sonnet). In South Asia, by contrast, Sanskrit usually remains at the center, with the different vernaculars – both Indo-European and Dravidian – acting more like independent spokes on a bicycle wheel than as a European-style mesh of cross-linguistic interactions. This distinction enables us to see the specificity of European literature. Finally, though the comparisons here have been limited to China and South Asia, a wider inquiry that encompassed Byzantine Greek, Arabic, and Persian would only confirm this conclusion.

4 The Expansion of European Literature

European literature, in its pre-history, is the western periphery of ancient Near Eastern literacy and literature. This is true of Linear B, in use at least as early as the fifteenth century BCE to write Greek, as well as of the Classical Greek alphabet beginning perhaps 700 years later. Similarly, the Olympian gods as rendered soon after in Homer and especially Hesiod have Near Eastern antecedents. The same goes for the intellectual traditions of pre-Socratic philosophy, or, much later, of the religion that eventually dominates what in time becomes Europe. These claims, some of them once controversial, are now routinely accepted, thanks to the pioneering work of primarily German and British scholars. Culturally, then, the West is mainly on the receiving end until, as already suggested, the upheaval of Alexander's victories. Those conquests produce a reversal of the prior pattern of influence. For the next millennium, up to the Arab conquests, Classical civilization (Greece and then Rome) is a net exporter of language and literature – to the interior of Western Europe, to North Africa, and to Greek-influenced Western and Central Asia as far south as northern South Asia. In other words, during this period, literary expansion *is* tied to imperial expansion.

Following the rise of Islam, however, we see a reversion to the status quo ante for almost a thousand years, with European literature borrowing from elsewhere, above all from Arabic. It should not be assumed, however, that the influence of European literature recedes. It *does* so in Muslim lands, though not entirely: Arabic letters absorb much of ancient Greek culture, elements of which are then passed on to Western Europe. Even more important is the geographical expansion of what constitutes literary Europe. Some of this constitutes Europeanization by the sword (parts of Germany; much of Spain – albeit gradually), but most is not. Instead, missionary work spreads Christianity and, in its wake, literature in Latin to Celtic and Germanic lands in the West; and literature in Greek to primarily Slavic lands in the East

This era is, of course, the Middle Ages, a term properly reserved only for Europe – and for Western Europe at that. The region is not unique in its demographic decline and long-term stagnation during the first millennium CE: this phenomenon is widespread in Eurasia at the time, perhaps owing to the completion of the Silk Roads and the resulting prevalence of pandemics. What *is* unparalleled is the collapse of urban civilization and consequently of literary culture in the Latin West. But this regression also opens the way, eventually, for innovation and, a millennium later, the recovery of Classical Antiquity. Again, this is a specifically European phenomenon for the simple reason that you can't recover something that has never been lost – the "problem," as it were, elsewhere.

The region has an additional uniqueness in that it draws on not one (as is the norm elsewhere) but two Classical predecessor literatures, long geographically divided but ultimately cultivated together, within the same locales. I am referring, of course, to a relatively familiar Latin and an initially far more remote Greek, understood as late as 1400 by only a tiny percentage of the learned elite of Western Europe. The two languages are at times treated as a more or less homogeneous whole but often placed in shifting hierarchical relations to one another – differences that can play out over time or at any given moment within and across languages. For instance, while in the nineteenth century Alfred, Lord Tennyson places Virgil at the top of the pyramid, his German contemporaries, including Marx, clearly favor Greek, a preference that ultimately prevails. In one sense, the recovery of the Classics merely enables Europe to catch up with other regions, where the Classical literary language had been a living presence all along. But this is not the whole story: the Classics enter European literature as something partly alien, even hostile to its ruling Christian ideologies. Here, ironically, is a literary expansion linked not to imperial gain but to its opposite. The Ottoman conquest of Constantinople puts an end to the last of the Byzantine Empire and drives scholars West, where they aid in the mastery of Classical Greek by the region's intellectual elite.

It is during the Renaissance, with the overseas expansion of the Atlantic economies beginning in the fifteenth century, that the poles of cross-continental cultural impact again reverse, though for a long time at a modest rate. Only in the European settler colonies is there any major European literary influence before the nineteenth or, in many cases, even the twentieth century. Global empire is clearly something new under the sun – without either historical precedent or, *a fortiori*, contemporary analogue. Ultimately, the consequences for the rest of the world are many-faceted and profound. If I had to single out one distinctively literary outcome, it would be the spread of literatures composed in European languages across large swaths of the rest of the planet – above all, in the Americas.

But what does global expansion signify for Europe itself? The obvious outcome is the huge gain in European wealth and power, both a cause and effect of European imperialism, as well as a material benefit to the continent's literature. I am interested, however, in more specific issues. In Renaissance studies, there has been considerable effort dedicated to showing literary engagement with the Americas, Africa, and Asia. The pickings are pretty slim, however. Only a small number of the most admired works of the era pay much attention to other continents, and only a tiny percentage of those are actually set in real overseas locales. The *oeuvre* of the Portuguese epic and lyric poet Luís Vaz de Camões is the most prominent exception. But things look rather different when we observe that overseas contact inspires numerous literary thought experiments, "what-if" scenarios – most obviously in utopian writing, but also in a wide range of other genres as well, especially in the languages of the Atlantic economies, but also in Italian literature.

In the eighteenth century, this practice is reinvented as, loosely speaking, the Oriental tale – in, for instance, Montesquieu, Voltaire, and Samuel Johnson. But after 1800, a striking generic bifurcation is evident. Scholarship in English has been much preoccupied with the realist novel's complicity with colonialism. But if we ask ourselves a simple question – how many of the most esteemed European realist novels of the century set even a single scene overseas? – we will have almost nothing to say in reply. Characters may come and go, to and from distant climes, but the novelist rarely follows them. This is the case for a simple reason: realism runs the risk of exoticism once it leaves the streets of London, Paris, and even St. Petersburg, or equally familiar rural regions. Realism's avoidance of the exotic has the unintended consequence of undermining the otherwise apparent totalizing vocation of the form – until, that is, the genre is taken up on other continents. Nevertheless, we may detect a partial deviation from the Western European norm in the two land-based empires occupying, in different ways, the periphery of Europe – Tsarist Russia and the republican U.S. There, terrestrial expansion results in direct contact with the indigenous population (Cooper, Tolstoy) or imported slaves (Stowe).

But is the general absence of such representation in standard Western European realist novels actually a formal constraint rather than a sign of bad faith, of a refusal to confront the ugly overseas conduct of their nations? The refutation of this politically skeptical hypothesis is provided by lyric poetry, which has no trouble engaging with the rest of the world – as the work of Goethe, Coleridge, Byron, Pushkin, Mickiewicz, Leopardi, Hugo, Baudelaire, and many others reveals. Only when European settler colonies acquire significant density toward the end of the nineteenth century, in areas that have not yet broken away from their metropolitan masters, do important novels of the period resort to overseas settings. This is the age of Kipling, of Conrad, of Gide, and, more surprisingly (at least to me), of Kafka.

Over the past century, this multicontinental perspective has of course become more common, while remaining, however, a distinctly minority phenomenon. To pursue this point to what I take to be its conclusion, I need to return to my scattered earlier comments on the influence of European literature beyond Europe. Since 1900, increasingly after 1945, and still more so in the present century, European literary forms have become the norm around the world. The novel provides the clearest evidence, but a similar pattern can be detected across a wide variety of genres. What difference does this make for Europe? One could profitably point to the prominence, especially in recent decades, of immigrant literature, composed by former residents, or the descendants of former residents, of colonies or neo-colonies. I prefer a different approach, however.

As we have seen, European, as opposed to Western literature, emerges in the Middle Ages. What counts as part of the history of European literature today? Pagan literature from Iceland always does. So, too, does pagan or pagan-influenced literature from Ireland and Wales. Greek Eastern Orthodox literature from the Balkans and European Constantinople, Arabic Muslim literature from Spain, and Hebrew Jewish literature from Spain, France, and Germany often do not. In other words, geographical proximity matters less than religion, and religion less than language. Accordingly, European literature may be defined as the literatures of medieval Latin Christendom's self-constitution as such (at first in the former Western Roman Empire), of their chosen predecessors (initially, portions of Classical Latin), of the cultures deeply influenced by Latin Christendom (initially, Celtic and Germanic lands), of the chosen predecessors of those influenced cultures (pagan literature in the Northwest), of newly chosen predecessors of an expanded Latin Christendom (the rest of ancient Latin, together with ancient Greek), of the cultures subsequently influenced by Western Europe (Slavic Europe, the settler colonies), and so on (the rest of the world). It may be easier to follow this statement if it is repackaged as a list.

European literature consists of the literatures of, successively:

1. medieval Latin Christendom's self-constitution as such (initially, in the former Western Roman Empire);
2. their chosen predecessors (initially, portions of Classical Latin);
3. the cultures deeply influenced by Latin Christendom (initially, Celtic and Germanic lands);
4. the chosen predecessors of those influenced cultures (pagan literature in Northwest Europe);
5. the newly chosen predecessors of an expanded Latin Christendom (the rest of ancient Latin, together with ancient Greek);
6. the cultures subsequently influenced by Western Europe (Slavic Europe, the settler colonies);
7. and so on (the rest of the world).

If this is still a little difficult to digest, do not worry. My points are simply these: First, this is a model to explain European literature's self-understanding, its self-fashioning. Second, it has the potential, and in time the reality, of infinite expansion – an expansion that long predates the era of overseas imperialism beginning in early modernity and is not limited to the colonial enterprise.

We can infer, then, that when we include its prehistory, European literature begins and ends (if this is the end) as part of world literature. That is, it is initially a spinoff of ancient Near Eastern literature, a literature that for a time may well be all there is of world literature. Today, European literature is the dominant influence on world literature. To understand the continent's relationship to global developments, visualize, if you will, an hourglass tipped over onto its side, with the larger parts representing world literature, at the two ends of this process, while European literature is the narrower neck connecting the two.

If, however, through the globalization of European forms European literary influence has become pervasive and European literature has increasingly come to mean all literature, then what exactly is the distinctiveness of European literature today? Does the trajectory of European literature issue in a self-abolishing contradiction? In response, we can contrast this notion to a simpler one: European literature consists of all the literature ever written in what is now Europe. Which alternative is preferable? Neither and both. The blander, second formulation has the advantage of inclusiveness; it has the disadvantage of failing to provide any handle on how European literature came to be what it is. For this reason, one must recognize the reality of illusion, embracing both the ideology of European self-fashioning and the critique of that ideology. But the point is not to find a plausible medial position between these partially opposed acts of reconstruction. European literature most nearly comes into focus if one explains, rather than explains away, the relationship of non-identity between its self-definition and, as far as it is possible to tell, its actuality. I realize that this is an unsatisfying conclusion. It leaves blurry what I would prefer to have sharply defined. My defense of having it both ways, however, is simply that not doing so is worse.

5 The Competitive System

The two previous categories – intra-vernacular leadership and an expansionist vocation – may usefully be reframed as evidence of the competitive system of European literature. We see intra-vernacular competition in the borrowings from the dominant literary culture by more peripheral ones – not just Gottfried and Wolfram drawing on French romance, Shakespeare on Italian drama, or Renaissance sonneteers on Petrarch, but also Corneille turning to Spanish theater, eighteenth-century British novelists to Spanish and French fiction, nineteenth-century historical novelists to Sir Walter Scott, or twentieth-century novelists around the world to Kafka and Joyce, among numerous other examples. The very historical succession of centers of innovation and influence noted earlier attests to the same phenomenon. In recent centuries this would include first German and then Russian writers defining themselves against French culture, U.S. writers against

British letters (for instance, Melville's displaced autobiographical railing against Anglophilia on the grounds that another Shakespeare may be born on the banks of the Ohio River at any moment), or, more recently, Latin American authors against literature from the U.S., Spain, and France.

Such is also the case with expansion: its complex, arguably contorted, logic of predecessors and successors entails the absorption of ever-more literatures into the system. The competitive side of this might be seen in the Renaissance appropriation of Classical Antiquity, first in the service of Italian civic humanism, then in the adornment of Italy's petty principalities vying for both cultural and military preeminence, and thereafter in the comparable strategies of the new absolute monarchies beyond the Alps. It can also be detected in the nineteenth century's recovery of its previously uninfluential epic past – for instance, *Beowulf* in the UK – in the service of an aggressive nationalism from which the realist novel is likewise inseparable. Beginning in the fifteenth century but especially in the nineteenth, European conflicts are projected overseas as well, such that all the inhabited continents become a playground, a terrain on which intra-European leadership may be contested.

More systematically, we might ask: what were the consequences of the competitive system for Western Europe beginning in the early modern period? It is clear that these consequences extend well beyond literature. In pursuit of maritime empire, a Spanish king might employ Italian or Portuguese sailors (Columbus, Vespucci, Magellan). An English monarch can turn to a Dutch sailor, from whom the river that runs through New York City gets its name. A Polish astronomer argues for a heliocentric system; his work is taken up and advanced by Danish, German, Italian, and English successors. On the eve of industrialization, Western Europe's competitive system is thus one of its comparative advantages.

These examples suggest the efficacy of such a model, but they say little about the role of language, much less literature, beyond what I have anecdotally noted above. Here, the German-led Reformation provides an interesting case in point. Protestantism gains adherents in Italy, France, Poland, Hungary, and Bohemia (today's Czech Republic) – in none of which it ultimately triumphs. Why not? Except for Calvin's Geneva, the locales where the Reformation still remains entrenched at the end of the seventeenth century are either Germanic-speaking lands or their colonies. Perhaps Church Latin's greater distance from Germanic than from Romance languages makes it feel more remote, less intimate, and hence less effective at inspiring attachment. This argument does not help explain the eventual defeat of the Reformation in Eastern Europe, however: Slavic languages are at least as remote from Latin as Germanic languages are, Hungarian more so. What is more, such a hypothesis does not explain Ireland's fidelity to Rome. Perhaps an intra-Germanic communications network, a network that includes competent translators, enables the rapid spread of Luther's views beginning in 1517. Speed is crucial here. Most of the lands where Protestantism prevails see printed vernacular translations of the Bible before 1530.

The claim here is for the causal force of a Germanic print network in the triumph of Protestantism. The split in Latin Christendom occurs more than a millennium after Christianity's establishment in Western Europe. In this respect, the religion's history differs from that of Islam, where the Sunni-Shiite schism exists from the beginning. It also stands apart from South Asia, where Islam, as a result of both conquest and voluntary conversion, provides an escape valve, as it were, for those experiencing the caste constraints of Hinduism. Put another way, the confinement of Arab conquests largely to Spain and the gradual rollback there mean that no alternative religion or version of the religion is readily available. Religious conflict must come largely from within Western European Christianity: it is not a bug but a feature of the competitive system.

What has this to do with literature in the narrower sense? The answer is not straightforward. Despite the presence of some religiously-generated divergences, European literature from the sixteenth century onward does not reveal a clear distinction between the Protestant and Catholic realms (or, later, between both of them, on one hand, and Eastern Orthodox regions, on the other) – partly owing to multidirectional influences. This is the systematic side of the competitive system at work. A contributing force to that end is a more specific shared heritage than the broad impact of the Bible across Christendom. The influence of Luther's writings on subsequent German-language literature or of the King James Bible (1611) on subsequent Anglophone letters is routinely affirmed. But the same conclusion holds to a greater or lesser extent for Protestant translations of the Bible into vernaculars where the Reformation does not succeed – French (1535), Czech (1564–1568), Basque (1571), Hungarian (1590), and Castilian (1602).

If, however, we confine ourselves to secular literature, the development of the European novel offers a paradigmatic case. The novella form is given high literary expression for the first time by Boccaccio in the fourteenth century. *The Decameron* sets off a quarter of a millennium of frame-tale collections in various vernaculars. But the decisive step forward is taken by Cervantes, to a limited extent in his own novellas but far more importantly in *Don Quixote*. I take the unoriginal view that he began that work as a novella, before discovering new possibilities, above all in Quixote's squire, Sancho Panza. The resulting novel is by far the most influential literary work in the world over the past 400 years. Nevertheless, for a long period, its key impact is not in Spain. It is instead found in France in the seventeenth and eighteenth centuries, and in England in the first two-thirds of the eighteenth, before Cervantes's masterpiece becomes a European-wide and then a global phenomenon. Finally, in a related development, the novella itself is reinvented above all in nineteenth-century Germany.

A similar, if less consequential pattern, can be discerned following the emergence of Shakespeare as an internationally recognized artist, also in the nineteenth century – thanks, above all, to the contributions of German writers and scholars. One result at the time is the appropriation of Shakespearean tragedy by the novel, as part of the effort of practitioners of that genre to underscore the high seriousness of their upstart form. Just as the Cervantine legacy is most significant outside Spain, so, too, are the leading instances of the Shakespearean legacy located not in England, but in Germany (Goethe), France (Balzac), the U.S. (Melville), and Russia (Turgenev and Leskov). The uptake of Sterne's *Tristram Shandy* in the late eighteenth and nineteenth centuries conforms to the same pattern. While a case can be made for a modest influence of Sterne on Dickens, the main impact again occurs abroad. *Tristram Shandy*'s legacy can be found in France (Diderot, Balzac), Germany (Jean Paul and Hoffmann), Italy (Manzoni), Russia (Pushkin, Gogol, Leskov), the U.S. (Melville), Brazil (Machado de Assis), and perhaps the Netherlands (Multatuli/Dekker) and the Philippines (Rizal). This is of interest because Sterne offers the leading high-cultural alternative to realism in the novel during this era.

Overall, the inference seems clear. An advance in one nation or language may reach a dead end. Further innovation may be blocked. But the enterprise can then be taken up in a new literature, sometimes with the avowed intent of surpassing the original. This is how the competitive system has long worked – and continues to work.

6 Conclusion

I will end with two points – one ideological, the other literary. In discussing the competitive system of European literature, I have said little about the violence – both European and global – attendant upon this system. I have not dwelt upon suffering and exploitation because I take it for granted that the reader is already well aware that the vast majority of people in Europe and the world have, until very recently, gotten the short end of the stick – a reality even now only partially mitigated and then only in a limited number of areas, most obviously in Western Europe.

My literary observation is that I have placed less emphasis on ideas than on forms – represented here primarily by genres, though potentially extendable to literary institutions. What then does such a choice have to do with the topic of this volume – Europe in law and literature? It would be possible to analyze the presentation of law in the literature of Europe and of its predecessors – in

Aeschylus and Cicero, in the *Poem of the Cid* and in Shakespeare, in Dickens and Dostoevsky, in Kafka and Camus, and so on. I have not pursued this path partly out of ignorance but partly because I do not believe that a thematic approach is the most useful way to go. Instead, in my remarks on Renaissance responses to the New World or the nineteenth-century realist novel's non-response to global empire, I have emphasized the non-mimetic dimensions of European literature. Another line of inquiry I have not pursued is into the importance of interpretation to both fields. Of course, this is hardly a complete list of my omissions.

Nonetheless, my emphasis on a conceptualized historical account and especially on the notion of a competitive system seems to me to have possible relevance to the European Union. Seen through American eyes, where the political system is a mess and the future of even a highly circumscribed democracy seems very uncertain, much of the juridical challenge in Europe lies in the fact that it is not one nation. Thus, the task is to find a way for a series of independent countries to act in concert. It is certainly the case that the differences among European countries, and especially Western European ones, have greatly declined since I first visited the continent in 1970. There are many causes for this, one of them being the emergence of English as a global *lingua franca* particularly useful in Europe – the result of the historical concatenation of the formal British Empire and the informal American one. The irony of Brexit at this very moment only highlights the challenges of a competitive system. The problem is not how to suppress disagreements within such a system. It is how to progress in a way that honors those differences, manages them and even turns them where possible into advantages (as has often been the case in the history of European literature), and above all avoids further outbreaks of violence. I wrote these words before the Russian invasion of Ukraine – a catastrophic turn of events that, depending on your outlook, either underscores the importance of finding a peaceful resolution to the antagonisms inherent in a competitive system or, alternatively, reveals the vacuity of any such aspiration. It is on this terrain that I would like to think about the relationship of law and literature in Europe.

Constituting Europe

While the first dialogue in this volume was dedicated to the conceptualization and demarcation of European literary and legal traditions, the second section now turns to the "inner" constitution of Europe, especially in its manifestation as a community of values. In this respect, the question arises as to what sustains Europe, what unites it, as well as what might come to threaten its unity. In such a vein, the articles in this section illuminate how conceptions and ideas of Europe are expressed via literary means, but also how the impact of Brexit is negotiated in literature.

Martina Wagner-Egelhaaf dedicates her contribution to the *European Constitution in Verse* and compares it with the *Treaty Establishing a Constitution for Europe* in order to examine the question of a potential literary surplus value of the lyrical rendering of the Constitution, of how the *European Constitution in Verse* benefits from its legal counterpart, and which idea of Europe becomes apparent in the text. The *European Constitution in Verse* is evidently a broad, multilingual project performed by different groups and thus consistent with a "multi-voiced" rendering of Europe.[1]

Sidia Fiorato highlights and analyzes how the impact of Brexit is expressed in children's literature, namely, *Alice in Brexitland*, an exploration that she embeds within the larger framework of juridical critique in literature in general and children's literature in particular, as well as in the context of what has come to be known as "Brexlit." According to Fiorato, the former "engage our collective and individual legal imagination, as their narratives give expression to the concrete experience of individuals and communities within a specific juridical context," while the latter focuses "on the process of identity formation of its young readers as the future constituent members of society, and, for this reason," has "often portrayed acknowledged models of social and political behaviour."[2] Fiorato also broaches the issue of Britain's allegedly limited role in Europe and resulting fears in view of immigration, framing Britain's exit from the EU as that of a nation alienated from the original ideal of a European Union.

Both authors also touch upon Europe's defects and deficiencies, for instance by emphasizing the naive idealistic vision of the EU, problematic political figures, or the limited recognition in contemporary politics of the significance of working-class and ordinary people in sustaining Europe. What in particular unites both contributions, however, is their specific emphasis on the relation, mutual influences, and reciprocal effects of the literary and the legal discourse, whether in terms of narrative, conceptualization, or the imaginative constitution of law and literature in Europe.

1 Martina Wagner-Egelhaaf, this volume, 67.
2 Sidia Fiorato, this volume, 71.

https://doi.org/10.1515/9783111075693-005

Martina Wagner-Egelhaaf

Constituting Europe in Verse?

A constitutional text in verse? This sounds unusual, provocative, and perhaps a little weird. The idea behind the project, initiated by Flemish author David Van Reybrouck, was to substitute the *Constitution for Europe*, which unfortunately did not come into force, with an alternative text that presents European values but would reach more people than a dry legal text could. In their introduction to the English translation of *The European Constitution in Verse*, the artistic co-ordinators, Peter Vermeersch and David Van Reybrouck, explain the project as follows:

> If the present European institutions cannot manage to inspire, charm, stir or touch the people, or if necessary anger them, then we shall have to do it. Europe is currently stumbling from one crisis to another, is floating somewhere high above the heads of its citizens, and at certain times suffers from arrogance and hypocrisy, at others from confusion and anxiety.
>
> In this situation, we would like to reflect on who and what Europe *might* be. We wonder which past we should recall and of what future we can still dream. How proud we are, and how sorrowful we can still be.[3]

Fifty-four authors from various European and non-European countries took part in the project including "[p]oets who were born here and others who fled here."[4]

---

3 Peter Vermeersch and David Van Reybrouck, "Introduction" in *The European Constitution in Verse* (Brussels: Passa Porta, 2009), 5–7, 5. The initial multilingual text of *The European Constitution in Verse* and a Dutch translation of all articles/poems can be found in Van Reybrouck and Vermeersch, *Neem bijvoorbeeld granite: De Europese grondwet in verzen* (Amsterdam: De Bezige Bij, 2011); further references in the text, abbreviated as "EGV." Passa Porta (Brussels, Cahier 1) has provided complete translations into Dutch, French, and English in three monolingual booklets. In the following analysis, the poems/articles will be cited in their original language with an English translation. I thank Geert van Istendael for providing further information about the project.

4 Vermeersch and Van Reybrouck, "Introduction," 5. The poets involved were Eugenijus Alisanka, Clare Azzopardi, Faraj Bayrakdar, Tahar Bekri, Petr Borkovec, Narcís Comadira, Eva Cox, Francis Dannemark, Jacques Darras, Mircea Dinescu, Theo Dorgan, Franzobel, Antonio Gamoneda, Michal Habaj, Seamus Heaney, Tsjêbbe Hettinga, Chenjerai Hove, Easterine Kire Iralu, Péter Kántor, Ekaterina Karabasheva, Gerrit Komrij, Abdellatif Laâbi, Liāna Langa, Manza, Niki Marangou, Patrick McGuinness, Kamran Mir Hazar, José Ovejero, Agda Bavi Pain, Jean Portante, Artur Punte, Xavier Queipo, Louise Rosengreen, Kateřina Rudčenková, Eva Runefelt, Saila Susiluoto, Fabio Scotto, Kader Sevinç, Aleš Šteger, Ulf Stolterfoht, Leszek Szaruga, Hedina Tahirović Sijerčić, Jüri Talvet, Paulo Teixeira, Carles Torner, Geert van Istendael, David Van Reybrouck,

https://doi.org/10.1515/9783111075693-006

The European Constitution in Verse was presented during the Passa Porta Festival 2009 in Flagey[5] and nominated for the Third European Book Prize Award. The poems are written in various languages[6] and, in the initial version, stand next to or among each other without translation.

The European Constitution in Verse has been performed in a variety of personalized configurations throughout Europe (see Figure 1). The selection of poems and performers vary and people who did not contribute to any of the poems have also appeared as performers.

The questions this essay undertakes to answer are as follows:

1. How does *The European Constitution in Verse* relate to the *Treaty Establishing a Constitution for Europe*?
2. What is the literary surplus of *The European Constitution in Verse* compared to the *Constitution for Europe*?
3. In what way do the poems benefit from their juridical reference?
4. What idea of Europe is conveyed by *The European Constitution in Verse*?

Jean-Pierre Verheggen, Peter Vermeersch, Laurence Vielle, Haris Vlavianos, Bart Vonk, Torild Wardenær, and Salem Zenia. For a critical view of putting constitutions in verse see Jean-Claude Alexandre Ho, "Recht poetisch: Eine Charta in Versen und andere Ungereimtheiten," (May 17, 2010), *Legal Tribune Online* <https://www.lto.de/recht/feuilleton/f/recht-poetisch-eine-charta-in-versen-und-andere-ungereimtheiten/> (acc. January 20, 2022), n. pag. Ho refers to various projects from the nineteenth century that put legal texts into verse, mostly for didactic reasons, such as Joseph-Henri Flacon and Benoît-Michel Decomberousse, who authored lyrical versions of the *Code Napoléon*, or a judge with the descriptive name Versemann, who is said to have undertaken the same task for the *Bürgerliches Gesetzbuch*. I am grateful to Stefan Arnold for drawing my attention to these projects.

5 See Van Reybrouck, "The European Constitution in Verse," (n.d.), *Werk* <https://www.davidvanreybrouck.be/?q=en/content/european-constitution-verse> (acc. January 11, 2022), n. pag.

6 The languages used are: Albanian, Amhaars, Arabic, Armenian, Bambara, Basque, Belarusian, Bengali, Bosnian, Breton, Bulgarian, Catalan, Chinese, Croatian, Czech, Danish, Dutch, English, Esperanto, Estonian, Ewe, Filipino/Tagalog, Finnish, French, Frisian, Gaelic, German, Greek, Hebrew, Hungarian, Icelandic, Italian, Japanese, Korean, Latvian, Lingala, Lithuanian, Luxembourgish, Macedonian, Malay, Maori, Norwegian, Occitan, Urdu, Quechua, Papiamento, Persian/Farsi, Polish, Portuguese, Punjabi, Romani, Romanian, Russian, Sepedi/Northern Sotho, Serbian, Sesotho/Southern Sotho, Slovakian, Slovene, Sorbian, Spanish, Swahili, Swedish, Turkish, Ukrainian, Wolof, Xhosa, Yiddish, Zulu.

Fig. 1: The Brussels Poets Collective performing *The European Constitution in Verse* (September 18, 2021, Nordkolleg, Rendsburg, Germany); © M. Wagner-Egelhaaf.

1 A Constitution for Europe – And its Lyrical Counterpart

The *Treaty Establishing a Constitution for Europe*[7] begins with a "Preamble" followed by "Part I" which is divided into several descriptively titled sections. Title I provides a definition and explains the objectives of the Union. Title II sets out the fundamental rights and citizenship of the Union whereas Title III covers the "Union Competencies." The Union's institutions and bodies are set out in Title IV. Title V

7 European Union, "*Treaty Establishing a Constitution for Europe*," *Official Journal of the European Union* 47 (2004): 1–474, <http://publications.europa.eu/resource/cellar/7ae3fd7e-8820-413e-8350-b85f9daaab0c.0005.02/DOC_1> (acc. June 23, 2022); further references in the text, abbreviated as "CE." On the history and structure of the *Treaty*, see Thomas Läufer, "Einführung" in *Verfassung der Europäischen Union: Verfassungsvertrag vom 29. Oktober 2004. Protokolle und Erklärungen zum Vertragswerk*, ed. Läufer (Bonn: Bundeszentrale für politische Bildung, 2005), 7–26.

discusses the exercise of Union competencies while Title VI explores the democratic life of the Union. The Union's finances are the subject of Title VII and the relations between the Union and its neighbours are outlined in Title VIII. Title IX covers Union membership. Part II of the *Treaty Establishing a Constitution for Europe* contains "The Charter of Fundamental Rights of the Union." The *Charter* is broken down into another "Preamble" followed by seven titles: Title I highlights "Dignity," Title II "Freedoms," Title III "Equality," Title IV "Solidarity," Title V "Citizens' Rights," Title VI "Justice," and Title VII gives the "General Provisions Governing the Interpretation and Application of the Charter." The "Policies and Functioning of the Union" is the focus of Part III, which is comprised of Title I, regarding the "Provisions of General Application"; Title II, covering "Non-Discrimination and Citizenship"; and Title III, summarizing the "Internal Policies and Action." Title IV discusses the "Association of the Overseas Countries and Territories," while Title V explains "The Union's External Action," Title VI outlines "The Functioning of the Union" and Title VII concludes with an overview of the "Common Provisions." Part IV, under the heading of "General and Final Provisions," lists the protocols and annexes. A "Final Act" assembles various declarations concerning the provisions of the Constitution itself and the Protocols annexed to it. Thus, even a first glance at the work conveys the impression that the European constitutional architecture is highly complex and not at all easy to present in a simple overview.[8]

The textual structure of *The European Constitution in Verse* reflects the juridical framework of its official counterpart in many ways. However, it is, of course, not identical to it. The poetic version also begins with a "Preamble," followed, in the original version, by the "Constitution." The "Constitution" is composed of six "Articles," followed by "Part I," which introduces the "Principles" (Articles 7 to 18); "Part II" sets out the "fundamental rights" (Articles 19 to 48), and "Part III" presents the "Declarations," specifically the "Declarations Concerning Musea" (Article 49 to 55) and the "Declarations Concerning Landscapes" (Articles 56 to 58). "Part IV" addresses "Policy and Operation" (Articles 59 to Article 77; in the English version, the title is given as "Policies and Action"), whereas "Part V" contains a "European Hymn." Part IV also contains a "Final Provision."

While the *Treaty Establishing a Constitution for Europe*, in sum, consists of 448 articles, the lyrical version contains only seventy-seven articles. One might think that, in the real world, a constitution must consider the complexity of regulations and, therefore, needs to be more carefully differentiated than its artistic counterpart. In other words, the 'real' constitution should be as clear as possible;

8 Chapters, sections, and subsections have not been mentioned in this initial overview.

every individual regulation should be unambiguous and, therefore, the document should cover all essential juridical aspects separately. In contrast, the literary version of a constitution may provide differentiation through its fundamentally poetic language, with ambiguity being of productive lyrical value. However, even lawyers hold that a constitution should be short and open to various readings.[9]

Comparing the preambles provides a first impression of how both constitutions conceive of Europe. After naming the representatives of each of the European Union's member states (the 'Majesties' and the 'Presidents'), the Preamble of the *Treaty Establishing a Constitution for Europe* states that it draws its inspiration "from the cultural, religious and humanist inheritance of Europe, from which have developed the universal values of the inviolable and inalienable rights of the human person, freedom, democracy, equality and the rule of law" (CE, 3). The next paragraph highlights the belief "that Europe, reunited after bitter experiences, intends to continue along the path of civilisation, progress and prosperity, for the good of all its inhabitants, including the weakest and most deprived; that it wishes to remain a continent open to culture, learning and social progress; and that it wishes to deepen the democratic and transparent nature of its public life, and to strive for peace, justice and solidarity throughout the world" (CE, 3). The signatories are "[c]onvinced that, while remaining proud of their own national identities and history, the peoples of Europe are determined to transcend their former divisions and, united ever more closely, to forge a common destiny" (CE, 3). They are also "[c]onvinced that, thus 'United in diversity,' Europe offers them the best chance of pursuing, with due regard for the rights of each individual and in awareness of their responsibilities towards future generations and the Earth, the great venture which makes of it a special area of human hope" (CE, 3). Furthermore, the Preamble refers to the determination "to continue the work accomplished within the framework of the Treaties Establishing the European Communities and the Treaty on European Union, by ensuring the continuity of the Community *acquis*" (CE, 3). It concludes with the assertion of gratefulness

9 Napoleon Bonaparte is credited with the dictum that a constitution must be short and obscure ("courte et obscure"). See Martin Morlok and Lothar Michael, *Staatsorganisationsrecht* (Baden-Baden: Nomos, 2021), 48. And there has been a debate on whether the Constitution for Europe is too long or not. See Jürgen Meyer and Sven Hölscheidt, "Die Europäische Verfassung des Europäischen Konvents," *Europäische Zeitschrift für Wirtschaftsrecht* 20 (2003): 613–621, 614; Franz C. Mayer, "Die Rückkehr der Europäischen Verfassung? Ein Leitfaden zum Vertrag von Lissabon," *Zeitschrift für ausländisches öffentliches Recht und Völkerrecht* 4 (2007): 1141–1217, 1186. I thank Marcus Schnetter for providing me with this background.

"to the members of the European Convention for having prepared the draft of this Constitution on behalf of the citizens and States of Europe" (CE, 3).[10]

These are strong words and it is a big vision indeed that is presented with an emotional and emphatic gesture: every individual statement is introduced with capital letters that reflect the statement's intended status.[11] Whereas the *Treaty*'s Preamble can be read in the language of each member state,[12] the Preamble of *The European Constitution in Verse*, in its initial version, combines languages: in fact, it even mixes languages within individual poems. Peter Vermeersch and David von Reybrouck explain how such a text came into being. The members of the Brussels Poetry Collective wrote their first draft and sent it to their colleagues around Europe who shared their reactions and also added and amended verses. They allowed the coordinators to use their contributions freely noting that "[w]e could make silent poems talk to each other and loud ones be lyrically lonely."[13] Thus, *The European Constitution in Verse* is a genuinely collective work.

The Preamble of *The European Constitution in Verse* consists of five poems, the titles of which are "[Nothing]," "[Beginning]," "[We]," "[Mornings]," and "[Voices]."[14] The first poem reads as follows:

---

10 For a critical comment on the Preamble of the *Constitution for Europe*, see Georg Kristian Kampfer, "Präambel" in *Verfassung für Europa: Der Taschenkommentar für Bürgerinnen und Bürger*, ed. Carsten Berg and Georg Kampfer (Bielefeld: Bertelsmann, 2004), 48–53.

11 The pathos of the Preamble was reduced in the *Consolidated Version of the Treaty on European Union* and the *Treaty on the Functioning of the European Union*. These preambles are much more technical and pragmatic as they also separately address the "Functioning of the Institutions," "Strengthening and the Convergence of [. . .] Economies," "Economic and Social Progress," "Common Foreign and Security Policy." "Free Movement of Persons," "Safety and Security," "Subsidiarity" (*Consolidated Version of the Treaty of European Union*), "Balanced Trade and Fair Competition," "Reducing the Differences Existing Between the Various Regions and Backwardness of the Less Favoured Regions," and "Progressive Abolition of Restrictions on International Trade" (*Consolidated Version of the Treaty on the Functioning of the European Union*). The *Treaty of Lisbon* does not have its own Preamble. Instead, it makes technical amendments to the Preamble and individual articles of the *Treaty on European Union* and to the *Treaty Establishing the European Community*. For the purposes of this essay, it is appropriate to compare the *Treaty Establishing a Constitution for Europe* and *The European Constitution in Verse* as the latter is a reaction to the former – and its ultimate failure.

12 *The Treaty Establishing a Constitution for Europe* can be downloaded in the languages of all EU member states.

13 Vermeersch and van Reybrouck, "Introduction," 6.

14 The use of square brackets has not yet been clarified. They probably indicate titles chosen by the coordinators. The poems are not attributed to individual authors in the text itself. However, the poets can be identified for each article in the Index of Titles.

[Nothing]

nie mówcie Europa mówią mówcie Śmierć

Ik zit in een verkoolde woestenij
Te kijken naar een roze wolkenrand
(De sporen van een gloed, voorgoed voorbij)
En oude sintels uit een oude brand,

nie mówcie Europa mówią mówcie Śmierć

Europa dat flakkert en bloedt en versmacht,
Karwatsen en brandstapels, galgen en gas,
Europa, geschiedenis, troebel filtraat,
Slagvelden, klaprozen, grafzerken, haat.

nie mówcie Europa mówią mówcie Śmierć

Veo lana sangrienta y, en los alimentos, grasa mortal, pústulas negras y, bajo ramas inmoviles, números infecciosos.
Arden los huesos, oigo la fermentación del rocio : lloran los árboles torturados.
Hay llagas sucias en la luz, veo el temblor de las últimas aguas

nie mówcie Europa mówią mówcie Śmierć (EGV, 12)

[(Nothing)

don't say Europe they say say Death

Amid a charred wasteland I sit and gaze
At a pink-fringed cloud that's billowing higher
(The remnants of a long extinguished blaze)
And ancient embers from an ancient fire,

don't say Europe they say say Death

Europe that flickers and stifles and bleeds,
Horsewhips and burning, gas chambers, gallows,
Europe, history, turbid filtration,
Battlefields, poppies, gravestones, hatred.

don't say Europe they say say Death

I see bloody wool, deadly grease in the food, black sores, and under motionless branches numerous infections.

Bones burn, I hear the dew fermenting: tortured trees weep.
In the light I see unclean wounds, the tremor of expiring water.

don't say Europe they say say Death][15]

The Polish lines are by Leszek Szaruga, the Dutch ("Ik zit") by Gerrit Komrij and Geert van Istendael ("Europa dat flakkert"), while Antonio Garmoneda composed the Spanish verses.[16] While the Preamble of the *Treaty* only briefly refers to the "bitter experiences" that preceded the unification of Europe, the Preamble in verse delves much more deeply into the dreadful European experiences that emerged after the devastation of World War II. Indeed, to sing about pain was a conscious objective of the project, as is pointed out by the coordinators in their introduction.[17] It is death, the death of the gas chambers and battlefields, gravestones and hatred that stand at the beginning of the new Europe. Preambles usually highlight something that applies to the entire work that follows and should be kept in mind for the following. The refrain line, which is repeated over and over again, is particularly emphatic but also irritating: "nie mówcie Europa mówią mówcie Śmierć" ["don't say Europe they say say Death"]. "[M]ówią" ["they say"] indicates quoted speech. However, who is being cited here? The speakers being quoted may be those who lost their lives in the horrors of Europe's past and to whom the verses are giving voice. We can debate whether the "roze wolkenrand" ["pink-fringed cloud"] which is reminiscent of "een gloed, voorgoed voorbij" ["a long extinguished blaze"] and "een oude brand" ["an ancient fire"] refers to the former flames of Europe's wars or to a slim glimmer of hope for a better Europe sometime in the future. The second meaning, however, may be seen as a handover to the next poem "[Beginning]."[18]

"[Beginning]" leads the reader back to an ancient time when men, still unconscious of themselves, "first created music" (ECV, 14) and thus began to articulate themselves. At the end of the poem, which is also written in English, Dutch, and Polish, Europeans are gathering:

Wij die hier komen vanuit alle landen, kerken en krotten, hoeken en panden,
Wij van Europa verlaten de bergen, bezoeken de dalen, benaderen de dorpen,

15 Vermeersch and Van Reybrouck, *The European Constitution in Verse*, 13; further references in the text, abbreviated as "ECV."

16 The English translations were provided by Peter Vermeersch, Paul Vincent, Gregory Ball, Frank Bergon and Holly St John Bergon.

17 Vermeesch and Van Reybrouck, "Introduction," 5.

18 Unfortunately, for reasons of space, not all poems can be fully cited.

> Verdwalen in steden. Wij, ja, wij allen, verzoeken de burgers, luister toch, luister,
> Wil horen de zorgen, het branden, het sneeuwen van onze verhalen. (EGV, 14)[19]
>
> [We who come here from every country, church and slum, nooks and crannies,
> We in Europe, we leave the mountains, visit the valleys, approach the villages,
> Get lost in cities. We, yes, all of us, we entreat the citizens, listen, please, listen,
> Now hear the worries, the fires, the snows of our stories.] (ECV, 14)

The people of Europe are joining together as a group. Yet it seems important to listen to the people's worries – it is a well-known anti-European stereotype that Europe is oblivious to the concerns of the real people.[20]

Individual 'real' people are named in the following poem entitled "[We]":

> Ole, de windingenieur, uit Roskilde,
> Ines van de vis uit Figueira da Foz,
> Dimitriu, die paarden verkoopt, in Suceava,
> Benazir, aan de kassa bij Woolworths in Slough,
> Armand, de vuurmeester, uit de Famenne (EGV, 16)[21]
>
> [Ole, the wind engineer, from Roskilde,
> Ines and her fish from Figueira da Foz,
> Dimitriu, who sells horses in Suceava,
> Benazir, at the till at the drug store in Slough,
> Armand, the pyrotechnician from Famenne] (ECV, 14)[22]

The poem mentions twenty-two more individuals, naming their specific occupations and locations, thereby creating a powerful impression of the 'real' people who form the 'real' Europe. The Preamble of the *Treaty Establishing a Constitution for Europe* states that it was Europe's Majesties and Presidents, as the representatives of their countries, who having designed their plenipotentiaries and "exchanged their full powers, found in good and due form, [that] have agreed" to the treaty (CE, 10). In contrast, in *The European Constitution in Verse*, it is Ole, Ines, Dimitriu, Benazir, Armand, Caitlin, Paavo, Maja, France, Elena, Juan, Marija, Heinz, Claude, Linda, Jaan, Madlo, Rudolfs, Ute, Domínic, Ceija, Joop, Battista,

---

19 The Dutch verses are by Geert van Isendael who is second from the left in the above-given photo (see Figure 1). The English translation was provided by Gregory Ball.

20 See, for instance, Petra Pinzler, "Wo bleiben die kleinen Leute? Die EU kümmert sich um alles, nur die Sozialpolitik sollen die Mitglieder allein gestalten – können sie aber nicht," (April 21, 2005), *Die Zeit* https://www.zeit.de/2005/17/Argument_17> (acc. February 2, 2022), n. pag.

21 The author of these verses is, again, Geert van Istendael.

22 The translation is by Gregory Ball.

Erzsébet, Henryk, Thérèse, and Melissa who are identified as "Wij, soeverein, wij volk van Europa" (EGV, 18) ["We, the sovereign people of Europe"] (ECV, 14).

"[Mornings]," written in Galician, Italian, and Turkish, calls for a comprehensive dialogue of all musical instruments and a powerful rhythm instead of the organized musical accompaniment programmes usually found at official public events; and "Acordar. Acordar" ["Awake. Awake"][23] is the emphatic message delivered here. The last poem in the preamble, "[Voices]," forcefully affirms the united chorus of European voices and stresses the power of ink, writing, and the word. It is written in French, Galician, Dutch, and Greek.[24] The verses refer to a sensual experience of Europe ("Geurig als verzen en brood uit Europa." ["As fragrant as verses from Europe"]) and appeal for peace before concluding with a 'realistic vision':

> Για να φανεί το χάλασμα το ρήγμα η απουσία.
> Για να εκτιμηθεί η προσπάθεια η αποτυχία το έργο. (EGV, 20)
>
> [That the ruin, the rift, the absence may be revealed.
> That the strife, the fall, the work may be appraised.] (ECV, 17)

Compared with the Preamble of the *Treaty*, the verse version not only allows the 'ordinary' people of Europe to speak; it performs the very process of articulating the Constitution's objectives. Although its language is much more visual than its official counterpart, it seems to be even more 'realistic' as it also considers abysses, problems, and differences.

2 The Legal and the Lyrical

The question raised at the beginning of this essay about the additional lyrical value of a project that draws on the Constitution for Europe in its legal form will now be discussed by looking more closely at Part I "Principles" and Part II "Fundamental Rights" of the lyrical project.[25] However, Part I is preceded by six articles, in verse, that revolve around a beginning out of chaos. Whereas Article I-1 of the *Treaty* presents the "Establishment of the Union" in well-ordered and

23 The authors are Xavier Queipo, Fabio Scotto, and Kader Sevinç; Gregory Ball, Judith Baumel, and Kader Sevinç translated the verses into English.
24 The poem was composed by Manza, Xavier Queipo, Geert van Istendael, and Haris Vlavianos. It was translated into English by Griffin Translations, Gregory Ball, and Mina Karavanta.
25 Obviously, this essay can in no way do justice to the richness of the poems. At best, it can provide a bridge to a better understanding of this multi-layered work of art.

constructive terms,[26] the six verse articles are an outburst of creative will and power that pretends to set up their own non-regulative order. As "Article 3" states: "Sempre hai unha orde que xurde do magma da desorde" (EGV, 25) ["Order emerges again and again from the magma of chaos"] (ECV, 21).[27] Subversion of any formalized order seems to be the guiding poetic principle performatively demonstrated by "Article 6." This poem is a parody of the biblical story of creation; thus it counts down the days from the seventh day, which is not respected as a day of rest ("Kerítést mázoltunk a hetedik napon"; EGV, 26 ["We painted the fence on the seventh day"]; ECV, 22), to the first day proclaiming again the force of beginning anew ("kezdtük elölről az első napon"; EGV, 26 ["We began from the beginning on the first day"]; ECV, 22).[28] Breaking established laws and emphasizing the power of a new start seem to be the aims of the verse project, a stark contrast to the orderly accordance to all the rules of constitutional law in the drafted legal framework.

Title I, Part I of the *Treaty Establishing a Constitution for Europe* speaks about the foundations of the proposed European constitution. Article I-2, for example, names "The Union's Values"; Article I-3 "The Union's Objectives" and Article I-6 explains the status of "Union Law," specifically, stipulating that it shall have primacy over the law of the member states. Part I of *The European Constitution in Verse* also deals with "Principles." The most striking difference, at first glance, is that while the legal document speaks *about* values, objectives, fundamental freedoms, non-discrimination, and the status of the law etc. from the perspective of the formal legislator, the lyrical constitution allows a collective "we" to speak and sometimes even an individual "I." The lyrical voices do not so much speak *about* the themes, but rather *through* the lyrical act of speaking. While Article I-1 of the *Treaty* mentions "freedom," among other values, "Article 11" of *The European Constitution in Verse* dedicates a whole poem to freedom and reflects on what 'freedom' fundamentally means:

Artikel 11: Vrijheid
het is bekend:
vergeefs ben je op zoek
naar een houvasts

26 "Establishment of the Union. 1. Reflecting the will of the citizens and States of Europe to build a common future, this Constitution establishes the European Union, on which the Member States confer competences to attain objectives they have in common. The Union shall coordinate the policies by which the Member States aim to achieve these objectives, and shall exercise on a Community basis the competences they confer on it" (CE, 11).

27 The Galician version is by Xavier Quipo and was translated into English by Gregory Ball.

28 The author of the Hungarian lines is Péter Kántor; the text was translated into English by Michael Blumenthal.

naar cijfers in het wrakhout
structuur in de confetti

je mag ook dieper zwemmen in het zwart

je bent vrij
dit is geen strand
dit is niet het einde van de zee dit is een horizon met meeuwen, dit is nacht en leegte
die lichtheid is een aarzeling

je mag ook dieper zwemmen in het zwart

leg me nu niet neer
ik leg jou niet neer (EGV, 37)

[**Article 11: Freedom**
it is known:
in vain you search
for something to hold on

for numbers in the wreckage
structure in the confetti

you may also swim deeper in the blackness

you are free
this is no beach
this is not the end of the sea
this is a horizon with gulls, this is night and emptiness
the lightness is a hesitation

you may also swim deeper in the blackness

don't put me down now
I won't put you down] (ECV, 28)

This poem by Dutch poet Peter Vermeersch, which has been translated into English by Kate Ashton, also highlights what freedom means: namely, a lack of support, insecurity, and doubt. It also reflects that, in their search for freedom, men need each other – as is descriptively staged in the little dialogue at the end of the poem. Similarly, verses in "Article 13" and "Article 13bis" reflect on "L'État de droit" (EGV, 40) ["The Rule of Law"] (ECV, 30)[29] considering the relationships between law and

29 "Article 13" on "L'État de droit" is by the French author Manza and "Article 13bis" by the Galician poet Queipo, while the English versions are by Griffin Translations and Gregory Ball.

truth, law and reality, thoughts and needs, habits and customs, and love and capital. The poems question the common understanding of the seemingly clear notions that are used in legal texts such as the *Treaty Establishing a Constitution for Europe,* and they offer – sometimes in a humorous way – their own and unexpected interpretations, for example, in "Article 18: Respect for Minorities: Genier er også en minoritet! [Geniuses are also a minority!]" (EGV, 48 [ECV, 34]).[30]

Both constitutions, the *Treaty* and the verse constitution, place a strong emphasis on fundamental rights. Part II of the *Treaty Establishing a Constitution for Europe* contains "The Charter of Fundamental Rights of the Union," in which 'dignity,' 'freedom,' 'equality,' 'solidarity,' 'citizens' rights,' and 'justice' are explicitly mentioned and elaborated upon in the subsections which follow. Overall, there are forty-five articles concerning fundamental rights.[31] In contrast, *The European Constitution in Verse* has thirty articles on "Fundamental Rights" and, correspondingly, they are also to be found in Part II. Some of them loosely correspond to the articles of the *Treaty,* such as "Article 21: The Right to Citizenship," "Article 23: The Right to Work," "Article 25: The Right to Housing" and "Article 44: The Right to Marriages of Convenience." However, even these articles contain unexpected content, for example:

Article 23: The Right to Work
dal si život kladivu aj sekere, zohol si chrbát na nákovu
z blata si umiesil chlieb, džbán s vodou, poličku plnú bohov.
vdýchol si smer zástavám, objavil teplú vodu.
túto zem odjakživa brázdili pluhy, kosáky a kladivá. celé pluky
zlaté časy doby železnej. na koberci mapy. v očiach púšť.
práca oslobodzuje. práca to je klasa. zas a znova a zasa
krutá bohyňa, ku ktorej sa spínajú tvoje ruky (EGV, 56)[32]

[**Article 23: The Right to Work**
you gave life to hammer and axe too, you bent your back for an anvil
you kneaded the mud for a bread, jug with the water, shelf full of gods.
you breathed direction to the flags, discovered warm water.
from time immemorial this land was furrowed by ploughs, sickles and hammers
whole regiments
golden ages of the iron age. Maps on the carpet, eyes full of sands.

30 This is by Danish author Louise Rosengreen (pictured in the middle in the above-given photo; see Figure 1) and translated by John Irons.
31 Stephan Korte welcomes the fact that the *Constitution for Europe* has included a catalogue of fundamental rights, but criticizes it for stopping halfway, because no clear way is outlined as to how Union citizens can sue against a violation of their fundamental rights. Stephan Korte, "Grundrechte und Unionsbürgerschaft" in *Verfassung für Europa*, 65–73, 71.
32 "Article 23" was written by Slovakian writer Agda Bavi Pain.

> work sets free, work is a class act. A fact bare fact
> cruel goddess to whom you upraise your hands] (ECV, 39)[33]

While Article II-91 of the *Treaty* states, generally speaking, that "[e]very worker has the right to working conditions which respect his or her health, safety and dignity" and that "[e]very worker has the right to limitation of maximum working hours, to daily and weekly rest periods and to an annual period of paid leave" (CE, 48), "Article 23" of the verse constitution addresses a specific and personal "you" and in doing so makes the individual worker visible and meaningful. At the same time, the verses show the hardness and social injustice of work and what bad working conditions inflict upon people. The statement that "[w]ork sets free" is, then, an ultimately ironic comment that recollects the cruel perversion of the concept of work enacted by the national socialist regime. Impressively, the poem/article indicates how ideologies of work have suppressed and destroyed people.

In contrast, most of the other articles hold themes that one would not have expected in a 'legal' framework as fundamental rights. Here are just a few examples: "Article 20: The Right to Be In-Between," "Article 22: The Right to Remember," "Article 27: The Right to Walk," "Article 29: The Right to Slowness," "Article 31: The Right to Language," "Article 33: "The Right to Exile in Art," "Article 37: "The Right to Complexity and to Slow and Deep Understanding," "Article 39: The Right to Rage" and "Article 40: The Right to Disconnect." At first glance, these articles appear somehow displaced and absurd, yet upon further consideration, they identify elements of human life that are indispensable for human well-being. The added lyrical value of these poems brings into reflection what we may consider the essentials of man's existence and living together – within and beyond Europe. In addition, there is, of course, a strong aesthetic surplus, an amazing reservoir of creativity, visuality, and wit, as "Article 24: The Right to Laziness" demonstrates in the representation of others:

> **Article 24: The Right to Laziness**
> El buen jardinero aprecia la sombra del manzano.
>
> **Article 24bis: Recht op appelbomen**
> Hier heeft eenieder recht op appelbomen,
> Op hoge stammen uit verloren dromen
> Ramboer en goudrenet en grauw rabauw,
> Rins vlees zal over de papillen komen. (EGV, 56–57)[34]

33 The translation is by Dasha Brandtner.

34 Spanish author José Ovejero wrote "Article 24" and Geert van Istendael amended the Dutch "Article 24bis."

[**Article 24: The Right to Laziness**
The good gardener prizes the shadow of the apple tree.

Article 24bis: The Right to Apple Trees
Here, everyone has the right to apple trees,
On mighty trunks from long forgotten dreams.
Bramley and knotty russet, golden noble,
Tart flesh from now on shall the palate please.] (ECV, 39)[35]

3 The Legal Subtext

Whereas the previous section of this paper considered the lyrical, literary surplus created by the project of setting a pan-European constitution to verse, this section investigates the benefit the poetic form may find in choosing, *specifically*, a legal subtext. The articles/poems of Part III "Declarations" and Part IV "Policy and Operation" provide good examples through which this issue can be tackled. There is a specific legal meaning of 'declaration,' for instance, in international law:

> Declaration is the means by which subjects of international law express their will, intention, or opinion when acting in the field of international relations. [. . .] If used in a formal sense, the notion *declaration* generally indicates some degree of solemnity and the intention of public notice. [. . .] If subjects of international law refer to a document as a declaration, this might generally suggest that they do not want it to have legal effect. Therefore, most of the statements published as declarations only have a political character and, if at all, political consequences. By operation of legal norms, however, even those declarations may produce legal effects. Besides, some declarations, depending on their wording and the circumstances under which they are made, may actually be intended to alter a given legal situation. From a doctrinal point of view, therefore, immediate and indirect legal effects of declarations must be distinguished.[36]

According to this definition, the 'declarations' of *The European Constitution in Verse* are political declarations that express a 'will.' This meaning is enforced if one considers that, in speech act theory, declarative speech acts are strong speech acts usually embedded in an institutional framework. Furthermore, declarative speech acts have an immediate effect on the world, as for example, 'I hereby declare you husband and wife.'

35 "Article 24" was translated by Frank Bergon and Holly St John Bergon; "Article 24bis" was translated by Gregory Ball.
36 Oliver Dörr, "Declaration," *Max Planck Encyclopedias of International Law* (August 2019): n. pag., <https://opil.ouplaw.com/view/10.1093/law:epil/9780199231690/law-9780199231690-e1397?rskey=8QoahK&result=1&prd=MPIL> (acc. February 8, 2022).

The European Constitution in Verse has two different types of declaration: “Declarations concerning Museums” and “Declarations concerning Landscapes.” With “Article 49: nie mówcie Europa,” also written by Polish author Leszek Szarµga, the “Declarations concerning Museums” refer back to the very first poem of the Preamble.[37] Thus, we are again led back to a devastated Europe and, at first, do not quite understand what is being declared. All the poems in this section seem to look back to European history, remembering the Pilgrim Fathers, the “Гастарбайтеры” (EGV, 96) [“Gastarbeiters”] (ECV, 59), and migrants. The poems speak of “Het verdriet van Europa” (EGV, 97) [“The Sorrows of Europe”] (ECV, 59), but also of “Europa’s troost” (EGV, 99) [“The Consolation of Europe”] (ECV, 60).[38] Article 53, a poem written in Persian by Kamran Mir Hazar, is titled “Painting.”

شود یتو خوانده م یتمام سرودها برا
آوازها تمام
سِن اجرا خواهد شد یتمام رقص ها رو و
آدم هاست یمه یبرا اندوه
یآن ها پنهان شو یآنکه لا یبرا ایرو و
توست یبرا ایدر
کنند، یم بیرا تعق یعرشه اندام دختر یکه رو ینگاه ملوانان و
رود یم سیپار یکیتا نزد یکشت نیا
اورندیب شانیقصه ها یرا لا نیغمگ یدختر یسیپار سندگانینو تا
رود یم سیپار یکیتا نزد یکشت نیا
در لوور ینقاش کیراست ی گوشه
شود یپنهان م ینقاش یکه اندوه آدم ها لا ییجا
یآب یرنگ ها کنار

(EGV, 98)

[Every song is sung for you
every lyric
every dance performed on stage is for you
sorrow is everybody’s lot
and dreams are there to hide you in their folds
the sea is yours
as is the gaze of the sailors sizing up the contours of a girl’s body
this ship will berth near Paris

37 The translation into English is by Peter Vermeersch.
38 Both poems were written in Dutch by Gerrit Komrij and translated into English by Paul Vincent.

so the Parisian writers can usher a doleful girl into the folds of their tales
this ship will berth near Paris
somewhere in the right-hand corner of a painting at the Louvre
people's sorrow hides itself in the folds of a painting
next to the shades of blue] (ECV, 60–61)[39]

The Louvre was previously mentioned in "Article 52: Europa's Troost" as a tourist attraction. Here, in "Article 53," the Louvre is named as housing a non-specific painting, in the right-hand corner of which people's sorrow is hidden. This is a political statement speaking on behalf of museums which, on the one hand, store the sorrow by conserving the memory, and on the other hand, hide people's sorrow and thereby relieve it – at least for a time.

The "Declarations concerning Landscapes" bring together three poems/articles that all deal with work and suffering but also love and lust as embedded in landscapes full of life, natural power, and beauty. "Article 57: Under Harrier Hawks" is a long, hymn-like poem consisting of seventy-five verses written in Frisian by Tsjêbbe Hettinga. It is not quite clear what these articles 'declare.' If they do have a political message, it may be to save the beauty of nature for the well-being and happiness of animals and humankind. However, this would sound somewhat simplistic and is therefore not directly stated. The better argument would probably be to say that the poems declare themselves – they proclaim exactly what they claim to be saying, no more and no less. This means that they are using a legal claim to validity to claim their own poetic validity:

Want de zuiderzon die schamper toekijkt
Zwijgt; en hoe kleiner de kiekendief wordt, des te
Groter het verlangen dat schuilt in 't brekende
Koren (EGV, 109)

[Since the southern sun watches on in breezy
Silence; besides, the smaller the harrier gets,
The greater the desire concealed in the crushed
Grain] (ECV, 65)[40]

The titles of the poems/articles in the section "Part IV: Policies and Action" of *The European Constitution in Verse* clearly remind the reader of the corresponding articles in the *Treaty Establishing a Constitution for Europe*: "Article 59: Démocratie" (*Treaty*, Part I, Title VI: "The Democratic Life of the Union"); "Article 60: Representation" (evidently,

39 This article was translated by Judith Wilkinson.

40 Hettinga's Frisian poem was translated into English by Susan Massoty.

a frequently used notion in the *Treaty*[41]); “Artikel 62: De vrije markt” (*Treaty*, Part III, Title III, Chapter I: “Internal Market [. . .] Free movement [. . .] Freedom of establishment [. . .] Freedom to provide services”); “Article 63: Currency” (*Treaty*, Part III, Title III, Chapter II: “Economic and Monetary Policy”); “Article 64: Free Movement of Ideas”; “Artikel 65: Vrij verkeer van personen” (*Treaty*, Part III, Title III, Chapter I, Section 2: “Free movement of persons and services”); “Artikel 66: “Transport” (*Treaty*, Part III, Title III, Chapter III, Section 7: “Transport”); “Article 67: Agriculture and Fishing” (*Treaty*, Part III, Title III, Chapter III, Section 4: “Agriculture and fisheries”); “Article 68: Environmental Policy” (*Treaty*, Part III, Title III, Chapter III, Section 5: “Environment”); “Article 71: Migration” (*Treaty*, Part III, Title III, Chapter 4, Section 2: “Policies on Border checks, asylum and immigration”); “Artikel 73: Godsdienstvrijheid” (*Treaty*, Part II, Title II, Article II-70: “Freedom of thought, conscience and religion”); “Artikel 74: Veiligheid” [“Security”] (*Treaty*, Part II, Title II, Article II-66: “Right to liberty and security”; Article II-94: “Social security and social assistance” (*Treaty*, Part III, Title III, Chapter IV: “Area of Freedom, Security and Justice,” Part III, Title V, Chapter II: “Common Foreign and Security Policy,” Part III, Title V, Chapter II, Section II: “The Common Security and Defence Policy”); and “Article 75: Humanitarian Aid” (*Treaty*, Part III, Title V, Chapter IV: “Cooperation with Third Countries and Humanitarian Aid”). However, some of the articles in *The European Constitution in Verse* do not correspond with any of the articles in the *Treaty*, for example, “Article 70bis: Geostrateška himna Evropi” [“Geostrategic Hymn to Europe”], “Article 70ter ΟΔΙΚΟΣ ΧΑΡΤΗΣ” [“Street Map”], “Article 72: Exile,” and “Artikel 76: “Het falen van Europa” [“The Failure of Europe”]. Overall, one can say that *The European Constitution in Verse* draws topical inspiration from the *Treaty*'s articles and, furthermore, that it gains artistic surplus by deliberately and creatively transcending legal expectations. The poems also stage colourful and sometimes dark pictures of individual speakers' experiences and visions, for example, by confronting the European idea of a ‘free market’ with observations such as this:

> een zuid-frans pleintje
> schilferende uien
> de tenen mand van
> een tandeloz boerin
> neurieënd (EGV, 121)[42]
>
> [a little square in the south of France
> peeling onions
> the wicker basket

41 E.g.: “Representation of citizens shall be degressively proportional” (CE, 19).
42 The poem is by David van Reybrouck and Peter Vermeersch.

of a toothless farmer's wife
humming] (ECV, 71)[43]

The following poem appears to be particularly refined:

Artikel 61: Besluitvormingssonnet
Onder een gekwalificeerde meerderheid
van stemmen wordt verstaan :
ten minste 55% van de leden
van de Raad die lidstaten vertegenwoordigen

waarvan de bevolking ten minste 65% uitmaakt
van de bevolking van de deelnemende lidstaten.
Een blokkerende minderheid moet ten minste uit
het minimumaantal van die leden van de Raad bestaan

die meer dan 35% van de bevolking
van de deelnemende lidstaten vertegenwoordigen,
plus één lid;

in het andere geval wordt de meerderheid
geacht te zijn verkregen.
Of twijfelt men. (EGV, 119–121)[44]

[**Article 61: Decision-Making Sonnet**
A qualified majority
shall be defined as:
at least 55% of the other members
of the Council, representing Member States

comprising at least 65% of the population
of the participating Member States.
A blocking minority must include at least
the minimum number of these other Council members

representing more than 35% of the population
of the participating Member States,
plus one member,

failing which the qualified majority
shall be deemed attained.
Or one shall hesitate.] (ECV, 70–71)[45]

---

43 The translation is by Kate Ashton.
44 The author of the "Besluitvormingssonnet" is Peter Vermeersch.
45 The poem was translated by Kate Ashton.

The sophisticated wit of this poem results from its transposition of the mathematical parliamentary majority formula applied by the European Council and the Council[46] onto the aesthetical scheme of the number game played within a sonnet's verses (4 – 4 – 3 – 3). This section of *The European Constitution in Verse* finishes with:

> **Article 77: The Statute of Poetry**
> Les poètes sont des feux follets : ils n'éclairent rien mais rappellent que la lumière existe.
> Poeten sind der Husten und das Stottern, das Murmeln und Schweigen der Welt.
> Poets are the Echoes of Tomorrow. (EGV, 152)[47]

> [**Article 77: The Statute of Poetry**
> Poets are will-o'-the-wisps: they illuminate nothing but recall that light exists.
> Poets are the cough and the stutter, the murmur and the silence of the world.
> Poets are the Echoes of Tomorrow.] (ECV, 87)

This is a self-assured gesture from the perspective of poetry that deliberately claims the legal notion of a statute[48] in order to put the reality created by poetry on an equal if not superior footing with that created by law. Again, the reference to a legal form highlights the poetical claim to validity.

---

46 Cf. Article I-25 of the *Treaty*, Part I, Title IV: The Union's Institutions and Bodies, Chapter I (CE, 21):

> **Definition of qualified majority within the European Council and the Council**
> 1. A qualified majority shall be defined as at least 55% of the members of the Council, comprising at least fifteen of them and representing Member States comprising at least 65% of the population of the Union.
>   A blocking minority must include at least four Council members, failing which the qualified majority shall be deemed attained.
> 2. By way of derogation from paragraph 1, when the Council does not act on a proposal from the Commission or from the Union Minister for Foreign Affairs, the qualified majority shall be defined as at least 72% of the members of the Council, representing Member States comprising at least 65% of the population of the Union.
> 3. Paragraphs 1 and 2 shall apply to the European Council when it is acting by a qualified majority.
> 4. Within the European Council, its President and the President of the Commission shall not take part in the vote.

47 The verses are authored by Francis Dannemark, Franzobel, and Péter Kántor.

48 According to *Black's Law Dictionary* a 'statute' is "[a] formal written enactment of a legislative body [. . .]. An act of the legislature declaring, commanding, or prohibiting something; a particular law enacted and established by the will of the legislative department of government; the written will of the legislature solemnly expressed according to the forms necessary to constitute it the law of the state. Such may be public or private, declaratory, mandatory, directory or enabling, in nature." Henry C. Black, *Black's Law Dictionary*, 6th ed. (St. Paul: West Publishing, 1990), 1410, <https://archive.org/details/blackslawdiction00henr/page/1410/mode/2up?q=Statute> (acc. February 12, 2022).

4 The Idea of Europe in *The European Constitution in Verse*

The idea of Europe that is conveyed by *The European Constitution in Verse* is particularly clearly expressed in Part V where the European hymn receives new words. In 1972, the Council of Europe declared Beethoven's "Ode to Joy" its anthem. In 1985, the song was then adopted by the EU heads of state and government as the official anthem of the European Union. The melody of the EU anthem is from Ludwig van Beethoven's Ninth Symphony. The accompanying lyrics of the "Ode to Joy" were then written by Friedrich Schiller in 1785. However, the EU anthem does not use these words, but only the language of the music to express the European values of freedom, peace, and solidarity.[49] Naturally, the new European hymn, suggested by *The European Constitution in Verse* and 'composed' by David Van Reybrouck, does have words. It substitutes Schiller's wording, which sings high praises for brotherhood,[50] with the more down-to-earth word 'bread' in seventy-six "major world languages and several non-European minority languages" (ECV, 91; cf. EGV, 156). By singing about bread in such a way, the new hymn replaces Schiller's idealism with a more sensual and material reference that is probably closer to people's needs. Bread is a basic food, but also a delicacy. Using so many different languages is also important for the idea of Europe proclaimed by the *Constitution in Verse.* It conveys the vision that Europe should be multi-voiced and form a large choir in which the individual voices add up to a widely audible chant that renders every single voice heard. The multi-lingual concept of *The European Constitution in Verse* is far more than a fancy aesthetic idea. It stages a vision of European togetherness that should be as non-hierarchical and non-dominant as possible. Listening closely to each other and seeking to translate carefully what others have said into the range of possible meanings in one's own language could be a model for European communication and a starting point for a more sensible European community. That is probably why "Article 31" and "Article 32" proclaim "The Right to Language" and "The Right to Translation" as fundamental rights:

---

49 European Union, "Die Europäische Hymne," (n.d.), *Grundsätze, Länder, Geschichte: Symbole* <https://european-union.europa.eu/principles-countries-history/symbols/european-anthem_de> (acc. February 12, 2022), n. pag.

50 Friedrich Schiller, "Ode an die Freude," *Schillers Werke: Nationalausgabe*, Vol. 1: *Gedichte in der Reihenfolge ihres Erscheinens 1776–1779*, ed. Julius Petersen and Friedrich Beißner (Weimar: Böhlau, 1992), 169–172.

Article 31: The Right to Language
Proef alle talen op je tongen, Europa,
Gehikt, gehoest, vermaledijd, gezongen,
Toon trots je woordenschatten. (EGV, 68)[51]

[**Article 31: The Right to Language**
Taste every language on your tongue,
Hiccupped, coughed, cursed, sung,
Show your vocabularies with pride.] (ECV, 45)[52]

Article 32: The Right to Translation
Oh versos amics que us van traduint
d'una en l'altra llengua i formeu cent rius
a través d'Europa que es torna un desert,
¿quan remuntareu el curs traduït
tornant a l'origen i molt més enllà:
tornant a ser pluja, al núvol, al cel
que us va veure néixer? (EGV, 70)[53]

[**Article 32: The Right to Translation**
Oh poems, my friends they keep translating you
from one tongue to another you form a hundred rivers
across Europe which is becoming a desert,
when will you swim against the translated current
returning to the source and far beyond:
again becoming rain, clouds, the sky
that witnessed your birth?] (ECV, 46)[54]

The fact that *The European Constitution in Verse* has been performed throughout Europe by different performers and changing performance groups highlights that Europe must be performed and lived every day and that it must go and meet the people in their different locations in and throughout Europe. It is the performance itself that brings the people together – poets, performers, and audience – and thus creates living European communities.

The European Constitution in Verse is certainly an idealistic project that relies on the validity and force of literature. Its creators, however, are not naïve. Therefore, there is a "Final Provision" in Spanish, which reads as follows:

51 Article 31 is a multi-lingual poem written by Hedina Tahirović Sijerčić (Romani), Saila Susiluoto (Finnish), Geert van Istendael (Dutch), Aleš Šteger (Slovene), and Jean-Pierre Verheggen (French).
52 The Dutch lines were translated by Gregory Ball.
53 The poem was written by Carles Torner (Catalaans).
54 It was translated into English by Robin Vogelzang.

Fui ciego como piedra de cripta hasta que un día vi en el mundo las manos verdaderas.
No eran las manos sino aquella forma de estar unidas sin tocarse como las hojas en el bosque.

Ahora sé que el único canto, el único digno de los cantos antiguos, la única poesía,
es la que dice su amor a este mundo, a esta soledad que enloquece y despoja.

Yo me callo, yo espero hasta que mi dolor y mi esperanza sean como que anda por calle,
hasta que pueda ser yo mismo en el cuerpo de todos los seres humanos
hasta que pueda ver con los ojos cerrados el dolor que ya veo con los ojos abiertos. (EGV, 160)[55]

[I was blind as a tombstone until one day I saw in the world true hands.
Not hands but a way of uniting without touching like leaves in the forest.

Now I know that the only song, the only dignity of old songs, the only poetry is
what speaks its love to this world, to this loneliness that maddens and forsakes.

I keep quiet, I wait until my sorrow and my hope are like what walks in the street,
until I myself can be in the body of all humans
until it's possible to see with closed eyes the sorrow I already see with eyes open.] (ECV, 94)[56]

There are also several "provisions" in the *Treaty Establishing a Constitution for Europe*: "Common Provisions," "Specific Provisions," "General Provisions," and "Final Provisions" (cf. CE, 26, 29, 53, 55, 73, 84–86, 113, 131, 133, 141, 150, 170, 173, 178, 282, 186). A 'provision' in the legal sense

> is a stipulation within a legal document or in a specific law. This can also be known as a clause or contract clause [. . .]. Legal provisions are usually included in a contract or other type of legal agreement to protect the interests of the parties involved. [. . .] Provisions generally require action by one or all of the parties involved within a defined timeframe or before a particular date.[57]

Against the background of this definition, it might be considered significant that *The European Constitution in Verse* concludes with an individual reflective voice that combines pathos and scepticism. It refers to time as a factor that can turn visions into reality. Thus, if it is true that provisions "protect the interests of the parties involved" and "generally require actions," then the "Final Provision" of *The Constitution in Verse* very clearly addresses us, the readers of and listeners to its articles, motivating us to take action – for a united and diverse Europe.[58]

---

55 Antonio Gamoneda composed the "Final Provision."

56 The translation is by Frank Bergon and Holly St John Bergson.

57 Law District, "Provision," (n.d.), *Legal Dictionary*, n. pag., <https://www.lawdistrict.com/legal-dictionary/provision> (acc. February 13, 2022).

58 I thank Julie Davies and Jason Fisher for language editing.

Sidia Fiorato

Leavis Carroll's *Alice in Brexitland* (2017): Children's Literature's Juridical Perspective on Brexit and the Young Adult Citizen in the Narrative of the Law

The law is a grand narrative, a framework through which we make sense of our social world; it fosters specific and socially acknowledged worldviews, which are shaped to affect character development as well as national identity. The law relies on "stories, explanations, performances, linguistic exchanges – as narratives and rhetoric,"[1] and, through these features, it fosters an "awareness of the particular human lives that are the subjects or objects of the law, even when that particularity is subordinated to the generalizing impulses of legal regulation."[2] This narrative paradigm is shared by law and literature: as Robert Cover asserts, "[n]o set of legal institutions or prescriptions exists apart from the narratives that locate it and give it meaning. [. . .] Once understood in the context of the narratives that give it meaning, law becomes not merely a system of rules to be observed, but a world in which we live."[3] Literary works engage our collective and individual legal imagination, as their narratives give expression to the concrete experience of individuals and communities within a specific juridical context. In particular, they show the effects of the rule of law on the life of the individual and their sense of identity, as well as the effects of social and political development and its cultural implications.

Children's literature focusses in particular on the process of identity formation of its young readers as the future constituent members of society, and, for this reason, it has often portrayed acknowledged models of social and political behaviour. With regard to this, Jaqueline Rose has suggested the impossibility of children's fiction,[4] underlining how it becomes a privileged site for the projections of adults' ideas and idealisations of childhood, in the implicit conviction of their underlying values, and, we may add, in the attempt to impose a normative kind of identity

1 Paul Gewirtz, "Narrative and Rhetoric in the Law" in *Law's Stories: Narrative and Rhetoric in the Law*, ed. Peter Brooks and Paul Gewirtz (New Haven: Yale UP, 1996), 2–13, 2.

2 Gewirtz, "Narrative and Rhetoric in the Law," 3.

3 Robert Cover, "Nomos and Narrative," *Harvard Law Review* 97 (1983): 4–68, 5.

4 See Jacqueline Rose, *The Case of Peter Pan: Or The Impossibility of Children's Fiction* (London: Macmillan, 1992).

https://doi.org/10.1515/9783111075693-007

according to the arbitrary values of the different periods. However, there are also instances of resistance to accepted worldviews through the representation of unconventional characters which diverge from stereotypical representations of children, or processes of *Bildung* whereby the protagonists acquire a critical perspective on the issues at the centre of the narrative. As Grzegorczyk observes, since the 1990s, children's literature has been characterised by an attention to identity in relation to history and geography:

> Recent critical attention to such concepts as exile, migration and diaspora, together with a shifting understanding of personal and national identity, have created a demand for new narrative forms that would reflect changing social attitudes to the make-up of contemporary ethnic identities.[5]

In the same way, since the beginning of the twenty-first century, the imaginary of Europe has been put under discussion due to politcal trends that culminated in Brexit in 2016; issues such as the cultural implication of transnational mobility, open-borders policies, nationalistic issues and globalisation have entered the narrations and created the demand for new narrative forms capable of reflecting the new emerging Brexit identities. And "[t]hese new forms are by no means monolithic."[6]

As Eaglestone, quoting Anderson, observes, a nation is an imagined community, "produced in the imagination by concepts, narratives, memories and traditions: that is, through the work of culture."[7] At a troubled time such as the post-Brexit one, literary texts address the feelings that accompanied this legal and cultural transition, and foster a reflection on possible new understandings of Europe, "a revised and properly cosmopolitan definition of what Europe was and what its values would need to be in the future."[8] Imagined communities relie on the process of storytelling and the sharing of grounding myths and narratives for the creation of the symbolic space of the nation. As Shaw asserts, literature "must set itself the task of imagining new narratives [. . .] representative of the sociocultural changes such historical events inspire."[9]

Children's literature has contributed over time to the development of a national identity and can even anticipate and contribute to shape it. As a matter of

5 Blanka Grzegorczyk, *Discourses of Postcolonialism in Contemporary British Children's Literature* (London: Routledge, 2014), 1.

6 Grzegorczyk, *Discourses of Postcolonialism*, 1.

7 Robert Eaglestone, *Brexit and Literature: Critical and Cultural Responses* (London: Routledge, 2018), 1. See also Benedict Anderson, *Imagined Communities: Reflections on the Origins and Spread of Nationalism* [1983] (London: Verso, 2016).

8 Eaglestone, *Brexit and Literature*, 15.

9 Kristian Shaw, *Cosmopolitanism in Twenty-First Century Fiction* (London: Macmillan, 2017), 90.

fact, it contributed to a specific image of Britishness over time and to the spread of a common British culture. As Knuth observes:

> children's literature has become a tradition in itself – drawing on folk traditions as rich and fully developed as traditional lore but also replacing them. In effect, English children's authors have forged a new storytelling tradition, a nouveau folklore of an evolving people that has fostered cultural consensus and a common and constantly morphing national consciousness and identity.[10]

However, literature also represents the space to reflect upon those changes and try to understand their implications; as a matter of fact, Brexlit addresses the sociocultural, economic and political consequences of Britain's withdrawal from the EU, but mostly reflects upon identity crisis and relationship with the "other."

Alice in Brexitland engages with Brexit-emergent political reality. Published in 2017 by Leavis Carroll, *nom de plume* of Lucien Young, it closely followed the 2016 referendum and the process of cultural and political change that it has triggered. It is a pro-remain text which, however, broadens the perspective and the reflection on both positions – a result probably unintended by its author, but in line with the effect of Lewis Carroll's text. Like its model text, it relies on a comic use of neologisms, portmanteau words and blending to describe a new worldview which disrupts the stereotypical traits of the conventional one. Lewis Carroll's *Alice in Wonderland* (1865) engages with a world underground which "is radically indeterminate, a world from which most of the 'frames' that guide perception of the meaning of events, 'frames' usually unreflectively assumed by Victorian children (or adults, for that matter), have been removed."[11] Through the features of the fantastic, Lewis Carroll shows the Todorovian hesitation experienced by a person who is familiar with a specific worldview confronting an opposite one, which disrupts all its grounding tenets. This kind of fantastic persists as long as the issues under consideration remain inexplicable, and the possibilities verge towards the marvellous or the uncanny. The latter seems to prevail in *Alice in Brexitland*, which challenges the underlying tenets of the Brexit position, in particular its anti-immigration populist rhetoric. As Martha Nussbaum underlines, it is only by "looking at ourselves through the lens of the other, [that] we come to see what in our practices is local and nonessential, what is more broadly or deeply shared."[12] So the text, through the characters of a renewed

---

10 Rebecca Knuth, *Children's Literature and British Identity* (Lanham: The Scarecrow P, 2012), 12.

11 Daniel Bivona, "Alice the Child-Imperialist and the Games of Wonderland," *Nineteenth-Century Literature* 41.2 (1986): 143–171, 150.

12 Martha Nussbaum, "Patriotism and Cosmopolitanism" in *Twentieth Century Political Theory: A Reader*, ed. Stephen Eric Bronner (London: Routledge, 2010), 159–167, 163.

Wonderland, continues to act as a cautionary tale in its own sense, by presenting opposite world views for our consideration.[13] As previously observed:

> Law and legal systems are cultural products [. . .]. They form a structure of meaning that guides and organizes individuals and groups in everyday interactions and conflict situations. This structure is passed on through socially transmitted norms of conduct and rules of decisions that influence the construction of intentional systems, including cognitive processes and individual dispositions. The latter manifest themselves as attitudes, values, beliefs, and expectations.[14]

In Lewis Carroll's text the characters refuse to be pinned down through Alice's interpretative categories, and Alice herself has no access to the rules of the new realm but tries to infer them, which affects her conception of her own self in the process. Due to these specific features, the text has proved remarkably able to "absorb [and critically illustrate] new contexts,"[15] and it continues "to intellectually and imaginatively challenge readers."[16]

At the centre of both texts is Alice's quest for identity, as underlined by the question of the caterpillar – "Who are you?" – which is repeated in a sort of conversational loop during their encounter. Alice admits that she cannot answer, as she is not the same person she was that same morning; this is a possible allusion to the morning of June 23, 2016, when the results of the referendum sparked discussion of a common cultural identity; by finally showing the slight predominance of "leave," they started a process of exposing "rifts and challenges"[17] in the cultural texture. Lewis Carroll's text exerts its ongoing relevance precisely through its ability to challenge preconceived notions about identity and the world. Instead of questioning

13 Lewis Carroll's text has been instrumentalised for a range of commentaries about specific political leaders and policies expressed through criticism and parody, for example, Peggy Wireman's *Alice in Bushland: Fact and Fantasy in the Bush Administration* (2006), Joe Sansone's *Obama in Wonderland: Inside Insane Hussein's Looking Glass: A Silly Book for a Serious Time* (2010) or Hector Hugh Munro (Saki)'s *The Westminster Alice: A Political Parody Based on Lewis Carroll's Wonderland* (2017).

14 Gunter Bierbrauer, "Towards an Understanding of Legal Culture," *Law & Society Review* 28.2 (1994): 243–264, 243, qtd. in James L. Gibson and Gregory A. Caldeira, "The Legal Cultures of Europe," *Law & Society Review* 30.1 (1996): 55–86, 57.

15 See Gillian Beer, *Alice in Space: The Sideways Victorian World of Lewis Carroll* (Chicago: U of Chicago P, 2016), 1.

16 Carolyn Siegler, "Lewis Carroll, *Alice's Adventures in Wonderland* (1865)" in *Handbook of the English Novel, 1830–1900*, ed. Monika Pietrzak and Martin Middeke (Berlin: De Gruyter, 2020), 351–365, 362.

17 See Daniela Keller and Ina Habermann, "Introduction: In The Shallows of National Identity" in *Brexit and Beyond: Nation and Identity*, ed. Keller and Habermann (Tübingen: Narr, 2021), 9–19, 11.

Victorian political and social history, Leavis Carroll's text presents the counterposition between the cosmopolitan and nationalistic stances, exacerbated by the outcome of the Brexit referendum. As Müller underlines:

> The imaginary of Europe [. . .] is essentially transnational, that is it proffers a conscious notion of belonging to a community that transcends national borders, that affirms cultural exchange and that is essentially dynamic because its codes of inclusion and exclusion have not yet been agreed on unanimously – neither as far as its geographical borders are concerned nor as far as its values are concerned.[18]

Therefore, how is the imaginary of Europe being modified following Brexit, in particular in children's literature and in a peculiar kind of children's book such as the one represented by *Alice in Wonderland* and its rewritings? Brexit did not begin at the moment of the referendum, but the referendum's outcome gave rise to a series of political, social and cultural negotiations. As many critics observed, "Brexit has always been less about the economy than about (national) identity and culture."[19]

The book develops by embedding new elements of the contemporary plot into the structure (situations, sentences and passages) of the original, thus destabilising the reader's perspective and calling for an active engagement with the text. For example, in the opening scene of Alice getting bored while sitting on the river bank because of the absence of pictures or conversations in her sister's book, we learn that the book's title (in the new plot) is "THE DEBATE SURROUNDING MEMBERSHIP OF THE EUROPEAN UNION" (capitals in the original). It is curious that a book devoted to debate, the animating element of political dialogue, should be devoid of conversations. Alice suddenly sees a white rabbit, David Camerarabbit, who laments being late for the referendum of June 23, and follows him down the Brexit hole. As she is falling through a "hurricane of ballot papers,"[20] defying the laws of political gravity, she hears "nonsensical bubbling which spoke of 'bemoaners' and 'Bregret'" (AB, 5). Significantly, her chaotic fall is broken by a paper pile of EU regulations which thus prove advantageous for her health and safety.

Alice finds herself in the hall of doors and sees a journal, *The Daily Murdoch*, a parody of *The Sun*, upon the table with the exhortation "READ ME." As she reads the invectives against "the Eurocrat" to warn "the British bloke," Alice

---

18 Anja Müller, "Canons and Canonicity" in *The Edinburgh Companion to Children's Literature*, ed. Clémentine Beauvais and Maria Nikolajeva (Edinburgh: Edinburgh UP, 2017), 153–166, 162.

19 See Eaglestone, *Brexit and Literature*, 1.

20 Leavis Carroll, *Alice in Brexitland* (London: Ebury P, 2017), 5. Further references in the text, abbreviated as "AB."

becomes "furiouser and furiouser" and grows in stature until she occupies all the space available (AB, 11–12). She wonders how the EU can be so bad. She then returns to her normal size by reading *The Gordian* (that is, *The Guardian*), although, as Witen underlines, this newspaper is criticised for its "tiny" print and "smug" tone[21] and reports a more reassuring depiction of the EU. She then reflects that the EU could correspond to either depiction "depending on who was looking at it" (AB, 12), thus underlining the relativism of judgement as she realises that her own identity as well might be affected by the perspective of others. The relationality of identity, the fact that I define myself as an "I" in relation to a "you," is reversed and seems to have to take into consideration the "you" before possibly asserting the "I." When the sense of her identity is threatened in the original text, she tries to stabilise it by expressing it in relational terms: "sense of identity is, typical of most children, primarily external, defined by her relations to others rather than a strong internal sense of who she is."[22] The "others" here are the supporters of the two political positions on the EU, which initially affect the representation of her own identity, even before she understands the terms of the definitions themselves.

The stories of the law that find expression in literature give space to all the parties involved in a specific issue, and the reader, like a judge, witnesses competing versions of reality. Alice acts as the reader's *alter ego* in her search for juridical meaning. Her adventures tackle the issues related to the Brexit campaign, in particular Britain's diminished role on the European scene and the weakening of national sovereignity, working-class alienation and fears surrounding immigration, which represent "contributing factor[s] in the growing defamiliarization of the national imaginary."[23] With regard to this, the caucus race scene becomes a spirited debate about Brexit, under trees whose leaves have written upon them "in" or "out." This aligns with the origins of the term, imported from the United States at Lewis Carroll's time; as Bivona observes, it "carries the implication of a meeting to iron out differences in order to present a united front for exerting political pressure, a local game of political accommodation within a larger adversarial context rather than a contest with winners and losers."[24] In this case, the counterposition is between Britain and the EU. The debate takes place among a group of animals (fox, hedgehog, duck) that have been observed to be specifically

21 Michelle Witen, "The Story of Brexit: Nostalgia in Parody Children's BrexLit" in *Brexit and Beyond*, 147–166, 149.

22 Colleen Lorraine Harvan, *Voices from the Void: Lewis Carroll, Samuel Beckett, and Language* (PhD Dissertation: Drew University, 2013), 42.

23 Shaw, *Brexlit*, 144.

24 Bivona, "Alice the Child-Imperialist," 147.

English ones.[25] As they are talking about foreign bureucrats, immigration and GDP, Alice is confused. As she tries to explain that she is new and cannot understand the cause of the quarrell of the assembly, she is accused of being an illegal immigrant and expunged from the community. Sensing that "the popular mood had turned against her" (AB, 18), she retreats into the forest, where she meets the Corbyn-pillar (a parody of the then leader of the Labour Party Jeremy Corbyn).

The illustrations in Leavis Carroll's text show anthropomorphic animals that are mostly caricatures of the political figures that were active participants in the Brexit debate. They illustrate what is happening in the text in images that echo Tenniel's ones, as in the case of the Corbyn-pillar with Alice looking from an inferior position up towards the caterpillar, and the Cheshire Twat, with the iconic image of the cat on the tree branch and Alice looking up towards him. The feature of recognisable politicians destabilises the attention of the reader, but reproduces the same dynamic nesting of the intermedial original text.

Alice confesses: "Ever since I went down the Brexit-hole, I have had this tremendous pain in my head, and facts and figures, truth and lies, they all seem jumbled up. I've even started to forget things" (AB, 20). The key question of Wonderland shifts here to the conception of the EU itself: "E who?" (AB, 24), as the Corbyn-pillar asks. Although Alice seems to recognise that "[i]t is hardly an unreasonable question" (AB, 24), she then denounces the lack of straight answers on his part (AB, 25). The advice of the caterpillar seems to be related to the two sides of the mushroom that either would transform her into a representative of pro or against Brexit positions, maintaining the ambiguity of the original scene due to its circular shape and the impossibility of determining a right and a left side. This episode reinterprets Lewis Carroll's disruption of the Victorian ideal in permanent self-identity by suggesting the wavering connected with stances pro and against Brexit; it also points to the lack of political value in connection with the Leave position. The episode concludes with Alice chased as an enemy of the Corbyn-pillar party and taking refuge in the forest. There she meets the Cheshire Twat (a parody of Farage), drinking an English beer upon the branch of a tree with the symbol of the English pound upon its trunk. The cat articulates the famous depiction of Wonder-Brexit-land, contextualising it in the contemporary moment of Leavis Carroll's text: "We're all mad here. I've gone mad, you've gone mad, political correctness has gone mad . . . " (AB, 30); and he creates a strong opposition by defining himself as "the EU's greatest enemy" (AB, 31). As in Lewis Carroll's text, the cat is the only one among the creatures that Alice encounters that gives her an explanation of Wonderland and includes her in it: when Alice objects, "I don't want to go among mad people," the cat replies, "Oh, you can't help that [. . .].

25 See Witen, "The Story of Brexit," 150.

We're all mad here. I'm mad. You're mad."[26] To Alice's question – "How do you know I'm mad?" – the cat answers: "You must be [. . .] or you wouldn't have come here."[27] Alice had stated her purpose in Brexitland, that is, "I need to make up my mind regarding the EU" (AB, 30–31), but we can imagine her ending up remarking, like Lewis Carroll's Alice, that "[i]t's really dreadful, [. . .] the way all the creatures argue. It's enough to drive one crazy!"[28] The original Wonderland represented the disruption of the Victorian ordered world; Brexitland represents the disruption of the order of things as we have known them up to this moment. Rackin asserted that Alice "refuses to accept chaos completely for what it is," and Leavis Carroll's Alice refuses to entertain the possibility of political uncertainty and lack of clarity of vision. "[T]he adult reader [instead] almost invariably responds with the only defense left open to him in the face of unquestionable chaos – he laughs,"[29] like Leavis Carroll himself. After the encounter with the cat, Leavis Carroll's Alice concludes by observing that "this cat did not like the world, and so preferred to live in one that never really existed" (AB, 34). Interestingly, this is the same choice she seems to make at the end of the book, but she will not be allowed to pursue it by the presence of the cat himself, repeating once more, "we've all gone mad" (AB, 100).

The Cheshire Cat takes Alice to the Mad Tea Party in the USA, which parodies Brexit by invoking the initiative for the first Brexit, defined "Brempexit," when the Americans declared their independence from the British Empire; this creates a *myse en abime* of claims for political identities backwards and forwards in time, as the episode might evoke Scotland's and Wales's contemporary claims for independence as well. The Party disparages the most British tradition, that is, tea, and includes food such as hot dogs and beers. The issue of immigration is embodied in a parody of the then U.S. president Donald Trump as Humpty Trumpty, who is portrayed as seated on a piece of wall, which, being incomplete, can be easily circumvented. Alice finds this character unsatisfactory, as she manages to contradict his assertions with her matter-of-fact logic; moreover, she does not receive any useful answer to her enquiry about the EU referendum, and finds herself in an even stranger situation than Brexitland.

Once back in the UK, she participates in a pro-Leave debate with Tweedleboz (a parody of Johnson) and Tweedlegove (a parody of Gove), underlining the financial opportunities which would derive from Brexit; to her question, "what, specifically, are the economic advantages of Brexit?" (AB, 63), they answer quoting the "British values of decency, transparency and fairness" (AB, 63), an answer unrelated to the

26 Lewis Carroll, *Alice's Adventures in Wonderland* [1865] (New York: Bantam Books, 1988), 47.

27 Carroll, *Alice in Wonderland* 47.

28 Carroll, *Alice in Wonderland*, 42.

29 Philip Rackin, "Alice's Journey to the End of Night," *PMLA* 81.5 (1966): 313–326, 313.

question. It is in this context that the outcome of the referendum is communicated and the prevalence of Leave seems to catch everyone by surprise, revealing all their discourses as architecture of words. Tweedlegove kills Tweedleboz and becomes Prime Minister, while the Cheshire Cat disappears leaving behind only its grin: "As far as I am concerned, it's the people who *don't* want this who should have to sort it out" (AB, 70; emphasis in the original),[30] overturning, with this last remark, the relationship between a political position and its aims. Due to her connaturated faith in a principle of order, Alice believes that Brexit will produce an understandable framework for reality, which could adjust every aspect of social life, on the national and international level, and which is the object of her quest. Its absence reveals instead "the hollow form of [political] things."[31]

Alice subsequently meets the Queen of Heartlessness (a parody of Theresa May), who came into power without being wanted and who declares, "I shall deliver a Brexit that works for everyone" (AB, 76). Eventually, Alice, hoping to understand better, asks for details; when the queen answers, "[w]e shall strike a new trade deal with the EU that puts our country first" (AB, 76), she tries to apply political common sense and objects: "but why would they agree to that? Surely they have every reason to make an example of us" (AB, 76), provoking the fury of the monarch. The Queen is on her way to Westminster to trigger Article 50, the one that will allow the UK to leave the EU, and quarrels with three justices who remind her that she cannot do that without the consent of Parliament. Alice also discovers that the Queen had voted for Remain but is determined to bring to completion the process of Brexit, following her commitment to leadership. Alice protests that it is "madness! [. . .] A decision that barely anyone understood is being carried out by a bunch of people who don't think it should happen!" (AB, 78). As a consequence, Alice is accused of "*talking Britain down*" (AB, 79; emphasis in the original) and brought to trial to Westminster, "the pulsating heart of Brexitland" (AB, 83). Like the trial in Lewis Carroll's text, the trial in Leavis Carroll's text is carried out with the utmost confusion, until Alice gives her evidence: "ARE YOU ALL MAD?" (AB, 89; capitals in the original), and delivers her final harangue to all the people convened: "when we abandon the idea that there are basic facts that unite us all, we lose the ability to connect with anyone" (AB, 91). She seems to be pointing here to the absence of underlying narratives that could support the change of the political system. According to Cover, our "normative world" is "constituted by a system of tension between reality and vision."[32] This world, the

30 Rackin, "Alice's Journey to the End of Night," 316.
31 Rackin, "Alice's Journey to the End of Night," 324.
32 Cover, "Nomos and Narrative," 6, 9.

nomos, is constantly created and maintained through shared values and aspirations which are expressed through narratives, that is, "the codes that relate our normative system to our social construction of reality and to our vision of what the world might be."[33] Law has to be located in a discourse, supplied with "history and destiny, beginning and end, explanation and purpose."[34] The absence of such narrative provokes a nonsense loop typical of Lewis Carroll's Wonderland. Leavis Carroll's Alice ascribes the main responsibility to politicians who lie but shows understanding, as she observes that "we live in an incredibly complex world and there can be good reasons to lie" (AB, 90); however, she objects, "when we throw away the truth, we create a vacuum, a vacuum that is soon filled by the worst aspects of humanity: our fears; our superstitions; our darkest and most primal instincts" (AB, 91). Therefore, we can assert that the object of Leavis Carroll's Alice on her quest in Wonderland/Brexitland is the awareness of the lack of such underlying narratives to her contemporary world and she expresses her legal imagination by advocating for them.

Kokovec has observed how "the legal profession, scholarship as well as practitioners, fails if it is unable to explain how to use EU law as agency for human betterment rather than detriment and unable to portray an accurate analytical picture of society and consequences of legal change."[35] As Shaw underlines, "the EU referendum mobilized fears and prejudices as opposed to hopes and visions for a restructured and independent Britain,"[36] seemingly allowing the prevalence of simplistic binary categories of thought instead of an ethic of social responsibility. During the Brexit campaign, the word 'Europe' was associated with the UK's (in particular, England's) "other."[37] Shaw observs that "Brexit did not create a new national narrative: it symbolized a retreat to comforting fantasies out of step with the cosmopolitical realities of the twenty-first century."[38] He asserts the necessity of constitutional and economic change in order to allow the UK to come to terms with issues of identity in its body politic. At the same time, the EU will probably also change in order to establish relationships with the new political reality of the UK and a changing geopolitical landscape.

33 Cover, "Nomos and Narrative," 10.

34 Cover, "Nomos and Narrative," 5.

35 Damja Kukovec, "The Legal Profession's Responsibility for Brexit" in *On Brexit: Law, Justices and Injustices*, ed. Tawida Ahmed and Elaine Fahey (Cheltenham: Elgar, 2019), 39–54, 45.

36 Shaw, *Brexlit: British Literature and the European Project* (London: Bloomsbury, 2021), 218.

37 See Arno Van Der Zwet et al., "Brexit, Europe and Othering: Contemporary Social Science," *Contemporary Social Science* 15.5 (2020): 517–532.

38 Shaw, *Brexlit*, 218.

Seeing that her words do not produce the hoped-for effect, Alice gets furious and grows in size until she occupies the whole space of Westminster palace, called the House of Cards in the chapter title. Alice continues to grow over the body politics of Brexitland, composed by people who would have to suffer their leaders' madness. However, "while Brexitland had its flaws – all too many, in fact – she could not help but be fond of the place" (AB, 93), thus ending the episode on a note of hope.

Alice awakens on the riverbank and discovers that "[a]ll was as it had been: pleasant, green, and tranquil" (AB, 97), hinting by this image at the idealisation of a pastoral past of England that characterises Brexit. Actually, everything is not as it was; it looks more like a utopian setting as she learns from her sister that the outcome of the referendum was Remain with 99%, and that the U.S. President is Hillary Clinton, who is soon to host a peace conference. Alice reflects that "she had been wrong to wish away facts and figures, for one should never make a decision solely with one's gut. That road led to Brexitland, and, while it was certainly an interesting place to visit, to live there permanently would be a nightmare" (AB, 99). She even asks her sister for her book because she says "I should like to understand the subject" (AB, 99). However, it seems that reality will not be characterised by such apparent political stability, because the Cheshire Cat is revealed to be sitting upon a tree; he smiles down on Alice by saying "you, me and political correctness have all gone mad" (AB, 100). Lewis Carroll's disruption of a logical and coherent approach to the world has been transformed here into a denunciation of a lack of coherence in political thinking and a lack of a distinguishable pattern in political action. Alice's reaction leads to the open ending of the book, which directly addresses the reader: "'How can this be?' cried Alice. 'Was I dreaming then or am I dreaming now? Am I in a sane world dreaming of madness, or a mad world dreaming of sanity?' Which do you think it was?" (AB, 100). This is the evidence Alice, and with her the reader, is called to give.

As Shaw observes:

> Britain now exists in a liminal cosmopolitical zone, stagnating in political stasis and suffering from a form of national post-traumatic stress, with each passing month providing a parodic replay of the cyclical Brexit psychodrama. Waiting for Brexit has been a Beckettian experience – a constitutional drama with no evident final act.[39]

The trial scene was also the key scene of Lewis Carroll's book, where the law itself was on trial. Alice relied on what she had read in books in order to interpret Wonderland, convinced of the necessity of the existence of an underlying principle; and in Leavis Carroll's text she appeals likewise to a book (her sister's book),

39 Shaw, *Brexlit*, 215.

a repository of the correct interpretation of the EU and all its related issues, about which she also asks the creatures of Brexitland. However, as Rackin observed, "the 'principle' of Wonderland [is] that it operates on no principle whatsoever."[40] It can be considered a journey into the national political unconscious, a dream, which unlike the dream of Lewis Carroll's Alice, finally appears to invade the so-called reality, affecting it through its visionary qualities of uncertainty. "In Lewis Carroll, there is a clear line drawn between the fictional Wonderland and the adult world; however, Leavis Carroll represents this madness and Alice's helplessness as a Leaving reality that is disorienting for adult and child alike."[41] Wonderland was the world of nonsense, intended to reflect frustration at the common expectations of sense; this aspect is now transferred into the contemporary political context, underlying the apparent contradictions and ambiguities of the Brexit campaign. As Lewis Carroll's Alice brought with her the certainty of her world's conventions (doomed to failure), Leavis Carroll's Alice sees the same uncertainty of her world in the world under ground. Therefore, even though the text is a pro-remain one, it challenges both sides of the political situation after the referendum – like the original, which presented an analysis of Victorian reality through the lens of a fantastic world. What is missing is a dialogue that does not suppress difference: Brexitland ostracises it.

This literary text examines the norms and values of Brexit society in the light of the heated arguments that accompanied the trajectory towards the 2016 referendum and the impact its outcome would have. "The EU is an extremely complex legal construction, viewed both in terms of 'law in books' and 'law in action.' [. . .] It is managed by a complex structure of institutions and individuals, managed by a particular type of consciousness."[42] Moreover, with Brexit, "the UK is facing one of the biggest and most complex legal challenges in the country's history."[43] Apart from the pro-remain stance which satirises the Leave party, the choice of Leavis Carroll's text is indicative of the importance of the young generations to acquire a juridical conscience: "The humour of [the story] has a double function, since it offers both a satirical stance, and an emotional coping mechanism in the aftermath of a Brexit decision that has turned out to be extremely disruptive and divisive."[44]

A young girl is called to make sense of the recent political happenings. Lewis Carroll's text, in the Victorian context of Golden Age literature for children, represented a turning point, as it embodied a break with the moralising and instructional

40 Rackin, "Alice's Journey to the End of Night," 316.
41 Witen, "The Story of Brexit," 151.
42 Kukovec, "The Legal Profession's Responsibility for Brexit," 46.
43 Kukovec, "The Legal Profession's Responsibility for Brexit," 46.
44 Keller and Habermann, "Introduction," 11.

literature for children. Alice is a very unconventional Victorian child character, as she observes and questions the adults' world, becoming more assertive as she proceeds along her journey.[45] She expresses her intellectual curiosity and, as Beer asserts, "'wonder' [. . .] is not an unfocussed state but an active response. It demands an exploration of challenging phenomena; it is never passive."[46] This intellectual activity is in relation to the articulation of her identity; as a matter of fact, she has to adapt constantly to changes and proves her resourcefulness. As Gubar observes, the authors of Golden Age Children's literature like Lewis Carroll present their child characters as "fully socialized subjects [. . .] fully conversant with the values, conventions, and cultural artifacts of the civilized world."[47] This led to the realisation of the mind-shaping value of narratives in children's literature and, in particular, of new ones which showed how children can interrogate or even "rewrite the scripts handed to them by adults, taking a hand in the production of stories and their own self-fashioning"[48] in the active drafting of their own life stories. They are capable to enter into a relationship with their own social context and shape their identity in response to others' expectations and demands. Lewis Carroll aimed at actively engaging his young readers and at creating an interactive reading experience. They do not identify passively with the models proposed but question them, thus "allowing for the possibility that children – immersed from birth in a sea of discourse – can nevertheless navigate through this arena of competing currents in diverse and unexpected ways."[49] Alice is characterised by her attempts at making sense of her culture's discourses of power,[50] and Leavis Carroll's Alice by attempts at making sense of political definitions both of country and individual in the context of a confounding society characterised by "the arbitrary nature of [. . .] its authority structures and social norms."[51] The EU referendum seems to have underlined the nation's "unequal and disunited kingdom";[52] Shaw entrusts literature with the task of creating new narratives which mirror the contemporary aspirations, underlining how a cosmopolitan stance on ways of integrating with the EU could or should at the same time acknowledge national traditions and identities. With regard to this, he quotes Winterson who has asserted the need for "a narrative that unites us,

45 See Siegler, "Lewis Carroll, *Alice's Adventures in Wonderland* (1865)," 351.

46 Beer, *Alice in Space*, 182.

47 Marah Gubar, *Artful Dodgers: Reconceiving the Golden Age of Children's Literature* (Oxford: Oxford UP, 2009), 6.

48 Gubar, *Artful Dodgers*, 7.

49 Gubar, *Artful Dodgers,* 32–33.

50 See Jan Susina, *The Place of Lewis Carroll in Children's Literature* (London: Routledge, 2013), 33.

51 Knuth, *Children's Literature and British Identity*, 12.

52 Shaw, *Brexlit*, 217.

not one that divides us" and remarked on how every "political movement begins as a counter-narrative to an existing narrative."[53]

As Nussbaum observes, citizenship is both experienced and imagined,[54] and we can assert the primacy of the imaginative stance in this sense: that is, as the metanarrative function of law to shape a social vision, a narrative universe.

53 Jeanette Winterson, "We Need to Build a New Left: Labour Means Nothing Today," (June 24, 2016), *The Guardian* <https://www.theguardian.com/politics/2016/jun/24/we-need-to-build-a-new-left-labour-means-nothing-jeanette-winterson> (acc. April 21, 2022), n. pag.

54 See Martha Nussbaum, *Cultivating Humanity: A Classical Defence of Reform in Liberal Education* (Harvard UP, 1997), 10–11.

Contrasting Europe

The section “Contrasting Europe” questions the simplified notion of a clear separation between European and non-European spaces and societies, for questions of Europe’s collective identity have been and still are often negotiated through a consensus on the continent’s traditions that is predetermined in terms of an “elsewhere” or in differentiation from Europe. In order to do justice to more complex identity constructions within and beyond Europe, this section offers various historical perspectives in order to facilitate conclusions about the development of internal and external conceptions of Europe as well as European identities.

Silvia Reuvekamp examines “Strength as Recognition of One’s Weakness: Identity Constructions in Early Europe,” thereby offering insight into Europe in the Middle Ages. This demonstration is based on a literary example that highlights the strength of one’s own culture as the “ability to be aware of its own weaknesses and to create countervailing forces aimed at political, legal, and cultural integration.”[1] Eminent medieval texts, according to Reuvekamp’s argument, portray ancient culture as well as the Orient as being incontestably superior not only in power but also in wealth and artistry. But for that very reason they are taken to be susceptible to self-destructive forces.

In contrast, Norbert Oberauer’s contribution offers a perspective on Europe and on the construction of identity and meaning in the Muslim world as an example of an external perspective on Europe. In this vein, he traces the role of Europe using the development of modern Islamic legal discourse, such as appropriation, the fusion of “different traditions to new forms and patterns” as well as the view of Muslim intellectuals on Europe and the Muslim world. While Europe was used to advocate a democratization of the Muslim world, according to Oberauer, there was, however, also an unwillingness to renounce identification with their own cultural heritage, including Islam, and the need to defend this heritage against “the contemptuous judgement that was so typical of contemporary European thought.”[2]

Ultimately, cultural “Othering” is central in both historical contexts, yet comes to function in very distinct terms: in the medieval crusade novel discussed by Reuvekamp, the Muslim world is depicted as a superior society that is contrasted with Christian or European deficits; according to Oberauer, Muslim intellectuals “refused to accept the negative mirror image of European virtues that was projected on their culture in the process of othering.”[3] What is clear in both is that Europe as well as its respective *Other* act as a combined frame of reference for cultural identification and differentiation.

1 Silvia Reuvekamp, this volume, 93.
2 Norbert Oberauer, this volume, 106, 98.
3 Nobert Oberauer, this volume, 98.

https://doi.org/10.1515/9783111075693-008

Silvia Reuvekamp

Strength as Recognition of One's Weakness: Identity Constructions in Early Europe

In the search for the roots of a common European cultural identity, attention has repeatedly turned to the Middle Ages. In processes of transfer of power and education (*translatio imperii* and *translatio studii*), a dominion of power and culture has emerged from the ancient heritage – preceding the differentiation of nation-states – which, with the rapid spread of a common religion, also offered the best conditions for the emergence of a supra-regional community of values. Charlemagne, whose reign encompassed large parts of Europe and who promoted cultural, economic and legal integration in early Europe through Christianisation and a comprehensive educational reform, is still considered one of the most important pioneers of the European idea. This has been recognised not least by the renowned international *Karlspreis*, which honours public figures deemed to have rendered outstanding services to the unity of Europe.

However, research in cultural history and cultural theory over the past decades has made us sceptical about such grand narratives and, in particular, about concepts of unity among cultures. It has since been proven that medieval Europe was much less homogeneous in its identitary and cultural self-designs than had long been assumed. And yet the question of how a culture that essentially sees itself as the result of a successful translation of power and knowledge from antiquity could develop a sense of cultural superiority continues to be answered almost exclusively in terms of the history of religion. In my opinion, this falls short. Instead, I would like to draw attention in the following to a paradox in the cultural self-designs of the Christian Occident that has yet to be systematically considered and that can be observed equally, in both the diachronic identitary confrontation with antiquity and the synchronic confrontation with the identity of the Orient.[4] In each case, the superiority of the cultural Other is often taken for granted, while the deficits of one's own culture are glaringly exposed. It is not only the wealth, education, art, architecture or handicrafts of antiquity and the Orient that are admired by medieval authors. In their juxtaposition with other cultures, they also repeatedly profile the weakness of the Christian social bond.

4 The term "Orient" is used here in a decidedly historical perspective and refers to the totality of all Arab-Islamic dominions.

https://doi.org/10.1515/9783111075693-009

Such cultural self-diagnoses of the Christian West attain enormous validity in European literatures from the early twelfth century onward, at the latest. This will be highlighted in the following, through the use of two prominent examples.

In Wolfram von Eschenbach's crusade novel *Willehalm* (c. 1217),[5] the story of the victory of the Provençal margrave Willehalm of Orange, who wins an important victory against the Arab conquerors of Spain during the reign of Louis the Pious, is told neither as a heroic triumph of the true faith against evil infidels nor as a defence against a power-hungry invasion. On the contrary, it focuses on the manifold weaknesses of the Christian warriors. A prominent role is played by the fragmentation – even disintegration – of Christian society, which makes social and military action almost impossible; conversely, Oriental society is portrayed as a better functioning network of kin loyalties that are ultimately grounded in family structures. During the struggle, on the Oriental side, loving husbands, sons and fathers, who empathise with the suffering of others as their own, are confronted with Christian protagonists who, in order to protect their own interests, are prepared to accept the killing of their own brother or the severe physical abuse of their own sister in public. This asociality on the Christian side, which threatens its very existence, can be tied back to the marginalisation of the biological family, which is deeply anchored in the Christian religion. Contrary to its narrative precursors, the conflict in Wolfram's version is not motivated by the invasion of the Arab army, but by a Christian family drama. Because Willehalm's father disinherits his own children in favour of his godchild, thus placing spiritual kinship above biological kinship, his son is forced to earn his living in battle. In the process, Willehalm falls into Arab captivity, where he becomes infatuated with the young queen Arabell, who consequently leaves her husband Tibalt and elopes with Willehalm, going on to marry him, and converts to Christianity. Willehalm occupies part of Tibalt's domain and establishes his own earldom. Because Arabell's male relatives are not prepared to accept their loss, an alliance of father, husband and son goes to war against Willehalm. When Willehalm is crushingly defeated in the first battle, he in turn asks for the help of his family, but is rebuffed with the utmost harshness. Once again, family structures do not seem to function on the Christian side.

The aim of the narrative seems to be to lead the recipients deep into the aporia of their own religion and the culture around it. And yet the Christians defeat the overpowering Saracen army in a second great battle. What is more, they win not in spite of, but precisely because of the painful experience of self-inflicted

5 Wolfram von Eschenbach, *Willehalm* [c. 1217], ed. Joachim Heinzle (Frankfurt a.M.: Deutscher Klassiker Verlag, 1991).

losses, isolation and despair. The bitterly acquired knowledge of their own deficiencies forces them to form coping strategies that then enable social stability and future success in battle. Thus, after fierce and even violent conflicts with his family, Willehalm ultimately finds a basis of understanding which, although it does not solve his profound personal conflicts, at least allows for a united and ultimately successful struggle against the enemy. Even in victory, however, Christian society remains fragmented, and the morally and legally problematic justification for the war campaign corresponds to the fact that their triumph seems more than ambivalent to the Christians themselves.

It is not merely the plot of *Willehalm* that exposes the deficits of Christian society. The pagans' view of their Christian opponents, as sketched out in the text, also hones in on their weaknesses. When trying to persuade his daughter to return to her family and her old faith, the Saracen king Terramer, for example, is deeply irritated to have lost Arabell not only to a count without any property of his own, but also to a God who has not been willing or able to protect his own son from humiliation, torture and crucifixion. The rejection of the cross by Islam, whose image of God cannot be reconciled with the Christian idea of the incarnation and the crucifixion of Christ, is staged here in literature. The Qur'an tells us, as a correction to the Bible's concept of salvation, that Jesus escaped the death penalty and that someone else was crucified in his place (Sura 4, 157–158). In various plot contexts, Terramer bases the claim to the superiority of his own religion and his own personal association upon the weakness of the Christian God, which he finds unbearable. He is uncomprehending when his daughter attempts to explain to him the power that emanates from the incarnation of the Christian God. Instead, he starts with the family structures that seem dysfunctional to him: in his role as a father, he elevates himself above the Christian God who sacrificed his own son. However, his claim to superiority blinds him to his own weakness – as both father and army commander. Terramer cannot win back his daughter, and precisely because the clan bond is so strong on the Saracen side, there are no personal, social or religious mechanisms to deal with her breach of allegiance Regardless of his unwavering love for Arabell, Terramer finds himself compelled, not least by legal obligations, to destroy his daughter. Contrary to how it first appears, the strong ties of loyalty among the Saracens do not ultimately generate social stability and military superiority. Accordingly, it is not surprising that the Christians claim victory in the end, mainly because Terramer's own son, who believes himself abandoned by his father after a kidnapping, turns against him and his army.

In contrast to what one would expect from a narrative with a crusader theme, *Willehalm* does not paint a picture of a Christian culture that is superior across the board. Quite the opposite, two deficient societies meet and engage each other, with the weaknesses of the Christian side being even more pronounced. A closer look, however, reveals that it is precisely this confrontation with a culture's own deficits that ultimately secures it's continued existence. Thus, the literary text becomes a space for reflection for a culture that sees its strength in the ability to acknowledge the weaknesses inherent in the human condition and attempt to accommodate them. Art, and literature in particular, appears in this context to be an instrument of such integration.

Very similar observations can be made about the literary confrontation of the Middle Ages with antiquity. For example, the fall of Troy, an advanced civilisation that could never be replicated in the medieval mind, was seen to be justified by its own grand claim to perfection. In Konrad von Würzburg's *Trojanerkrieg* (before 1287),[6] for instance, a courtly festival that is supposed to represent the ideal of a flawless society forms the nucleus of all subsequent conflicts that ultimately lead to destruction. To live up to this claim, Jupiter excludes the goddess of discord, Discordia, from the festive party. Discordia takes revenge by stirring up strife in the festive company with an apple for the most beautiful woman. In what is staged as a legal dispute, Jupiter refuses to choose a victor among the goddesses present, on the one hand because his acting as judge would call into question the society's claimed perfection, and on the other hand because he is worried about fuelling the discord with a judgement that would compel him to take sides. Only because Jupiter seeks to exclude and cover up the deficiencies of a society threatened by internal rivalry does disaster take its course, culminating with the final destruction of Troy. Right at the beginning of the plot, the image of an elitist society emerges that lacks the social, political and especially the legal mechanisms to integrate its deficits. Throughout the rest of the plot, new conflicts repeatedly break out over attempts to keep the peace and conceal various rivalries which contribute to the eventual doom. In such a vein, for example, the first destruction of Troy only occurs because the Trojan king rudely expels the Argonauts, who have landed with peaceful intentions, out of fear of possible aggression, without even having come into contact with them.

What is special about Konrad's version of the Troy narrative is that he also reflects metapoetically on the role that art can play as a space for reflection on social weaknesses and thus as a medium for the cultural integration of the deficient. The novel's account of the Trojan War is interspersed with detailed descriptions of exceptional artefacts. Remarkably, what all these artefacts have in common is that, in their exuberant beauty, they distract the gaze of the text's protagonists from the

6 Konrad von Würzburg, *Trojanerkrieg* [before 1287], ed. Heinz Thoelen and Bianca Häberlein (Wiesbaden: Dr. Ludwig Reichert Verlag, 2015).

actual, usually problematic, conditions of their existence. This is particularly impressive in the case of the city of Troy, rebuilt after its first destruction; an artistic and architectural achievement of immense splendour, yet also an artificial and dysfunctional city in every respect. Everything in it serves not only to ward off enemies and ensure lasting peace, but also to exclude everything ugly and inferior. This goes so far that only the most respected nobles are even given the right to live within the city walls of metre-thick shiny white marble. The cosmopolitan mixture of social milieus that is characteristic of cities is systematically rejected. The beauty of the city and its elite status ultimately serve to foster a sense of self-assurance in Trojan society, which seeks to overcome the trauma of its initial devastation. At the centre of the new Troy is a gathering place of enormous proportions, completely overshadowed by an artificial tree. The roots and trunk of this tree are wrought of silver, the branches of gold and the leaves of rubies and emeralds. Within, there are artificial birds made of precious stones in every colour imaginable. A spell liberates the tree and the birds from the seasonal cycle, so that the place is filled at all times with birdsong, lifting the spirits of all who hear it and making them forget all suffering. However, all this magnificence merely attempts to conceal the trauma of Troy's first destruction, rather than seeking to overcome it. On the contrary, the self-conception of the city deliberately circumvents any confrontation with the suffering experienced and its root causes. In the further course of the plot, this leads to the final destruction. The Trojans plan to steal Helen under the very same tree that makes them forget past suffering. The rapture they experience in listening to the enchanting birdsong causes them to misjudge the dangers of the enterprise and thus becomes the vehicle for their doom.

Art, which serves to cover up the deep-seated weaknesses of society in favour of elitist self-assurance, unveils an enormously destructive potential here and in many other parts of the novel. The literary narrative in the *Trojanerkrieg* itself stands in opposition to this. Konrad's work systematically highlights all the factors that have contributed to the downfall of an advanced civilisation that initially seemed invincible. The medieval text thus paints a picture of an ancient culture that appears unassailably superior in power, wealth and artistry, but for that very reason proves susceptible to self-destructive forces. As in the discussion of Oriental society in *Willehalm*, the strength of a culture is viewed here in its ability to be aware of its own weaknesses and to create countervailing forces aimed at political, legal and cultural integration.

The basis for the described self-stylisation of Western culture in early Europe is formed by central aspects of the Christian image of God and Christian anthropology. The belief in a God who, in his incarnation, lovingly accepts the inescapable weakness of all humanity, forms the enabling framework for a corresponding self-image. However, the validity of this cultural model is far from being bound to purely religious contexts. Unlike the *Willehalm*, the *Trojanerkrieg* is a thoroughly secular text that shows how deeply the idea of a superiority grounded in the self-awareness of weakness is anchored in the laic society of the European Middle Ages. Against this background, it would be worthwhile to consider what significance they have for the emergence of structures of the collective imagination in Europe that reach beyond the Middle Ages.

Norbert Oberauer

Some Notes on the Role of Europe in the Development of Modern Islamic Legal Discourse

1 The Colonial Impact

Prior to the eighteenth century, Europe at best occupied a peripheral position in the consciousness of Muslim intellectuals. It is true that there were considerable trading activities between Europe and the Muslim world, and also some military confrontations, such as the crusades or the so called "Reconquista," but these circumstances had no significant impact on Muslim intellectual traditions.[1] Premodern legal, theological, or literary texts rarely contain references to the "Franks" (as Europeans were usually referred to by premodern Muslims).

This situation changed dramatically in the nineteenth century. The increasingly apparent military and economic inferiority of the Muslim world vis-à-vis European powers prompted the notion among Muslim elites that for Muslim political entities to prevail on the stage of global politics, what was required was an adoption of European ideas and cultural techniques.[2] From the middle of the nineteenth century onward, the rulers in Istanbul, Cairo, and other power centers of the Muslim world pursued a policy of explicit Europeanization that went along

1 As for the crusades, for example, Hilllenbrand points out that premodern Muslims "showed little interest" in these conflicts "as a discrete entity" or "as a phenomenon of world history." A specific Arabic term for the crusades (*viz.*, *al-ḥurūb aṣ-ṣalībiyya*) emerged only in the nineteenth century, and it was a calque from European languages; see Carole Hillenbrand, *The Crusades: Islamic Perspectives* (Edinburgh: Edinburgh UP, 1999), 591. Note, however, that the crusades, and especially the Reconquista, intensified the debate among legal scholars about whether it was obligatory for Muslims to emigrate from territory under non-Muslim rule; see Mathias Rohe, *Das islamische Recht: Geschichte und Gegenwart* (Munich: Beck, 2009), 159, with further references. For details on this legal debate, see Jocelyn N. Hendrickson, *The Islamic Obligation to Emigrate: Al-Wansharīsī's Asnā al-matājir Reconsidered* (PhD Dissertation: Emory University, 2009).

2 The idea to build an army based on European models dates back to the 1730s, when special schools were founded in which military recruits could study translations of French books; see Albert Hourani, *Arabic Thought in the Liberal Age (1798–1939)* (Oxford: Oxford UP, 1962), 41–42. Sultan Selim III (reg. 1798–1807) and his successor Mahmud II (reg. 1808–1839) intensified the efforts to reform the military along European lines (see Hourani, *Arabic Thought*, 41–42). It became common for Ottoman and Egyptian rulers from the end of the eighteenth century to send diplomats and student missions to Europe in order for them to acquire knowledge of modern ideas and techniques (Hourani, *Arabic Thought*, 43–44, 51).

https://doi.org/10.1515/9783111075693-010

with the somewhat naïve vision that the blessings of European "progress" and "civilization" would shortly be realized in their own dominions as well. The aspiration was that the Muslim world would soon be on par with the European powers, would indeed become "a part of Europe," to quote a speech prepared by the designated Egyptian prime minister Nūbār Pāshā for his ruler, the Khedive Ismāʿīl (reg. 1863–1879).[3]

This "euphoria of progress"[4] was soon to be tainted by two factors. First, it became more and more obvious that the opening of the Muslim world for European ideas and cultural techniques went along with asymmetrical power structures that resulted in subjection and exploitation. Many Muslim intellectuals had initially regarded the European powers as teachers and allies in a struggle for reform. However, events such as the French occupation of Tunisia in 1881 and the British occupation of Egypt in the following year made it very clear that Europe posed a threat to the political sovereignty of Muslim territories.[5]

Second, a far-reaching adoption of European ideas bore the risk of undermining the cultural identity of the Muslim world. This problem was exacerbated by the circumstance that European discourse involved the Muslim world, and indeed the entire "Orient," in a process of "othering": to construct and sharpen a "Western" identity, European intellectuals used "the East" as a mirror image to which they ascribed the opposite of those characteristics they considered "Western." Whereas Europe stood for progress, activity, and rationality, Eastern "civilization" was pictured as fatalist and religiously fanatic.[6]

---

3 See Alexander Schölch, "Der arabische Osten im neunzehnten Jahrhundert 1800–1914" in *Geschichte der arabischen Welt,* ed. Ulrich Haarman et al. (Munich: Beck, 1987), 365–431, 391.

4 Schölch, "Der arabische Osten, " 387.

5 See Hourani, *Arabic Thought,* 103.

6 On the European use of the Orient as an image of the Other, see Birgit Schäbler, "Der Islam und Europa: Eine Geschichte von Verflechtung und Verstrickung" in *Europa als Weltreligion: Zentrum, Modell oder Provinz?,* ed. Thomas Ertl, Andrea Komlosy, and Hans-Jürgen Puhle (Vienna: New Academic P, 2014), 166–177, 167; Aziz Al-Azmeh, *Islams and Modernities* (London: Verso, 1993), 130–133; Edward Said, *Orientalism* (London: Penguin, 1978), 1. Said provides an illustrative example of such Othering, *viz.*, a quote from the book *Modern Orient* by Lord Cromer, British Agent and Consul-General in Egypt from 1883 to 1907 (see Said, *Orientalism,* 38).

2 The Othering of the Orient and Counter-Hegemonial Responses

A paradigmatic example of European othering of Islam is the dispute between the French Orientalist Ernest Renan (1823–1892) and two influential Muslim reformers of his day, to wit, Jamāl al-Dīn al-Afghānī (1838/39–1897) and Namık Kemal (1840–1888). As Schäbler points out, Renan's thinking reflects many of the tensions in nineteenth-century French discourse, in which the relationship between religion and science was a key issue.[7] Originally a Catholic, Renan had broken with the church, owing to his conviction that Catholicism and science were incompatible. He was striving for a philosophical framework that accommodated science and religion, reconciling one with the other, and he considered German cultural Protestantism as a successful attempt at such reconciliation.[8] It was probably this intellectual struggle with European ideas and traditions that framed his perspective on Islam. In 1883, he gave a lecture at the Sorbonne entitled "Islam and Science," in which he depicted Islam in the most obscurantist colors. According to Renan, any true Muslim believer had a "kind of iron ring around his head, making it absolutely closed to science, incapable of learning anything or of opening itself up to any new idea."[9] Islam, Renan claimed, had "always harassed science and philosophy" and had eventually stifled them.[10]

Arguably, this harsh judgement was a projection of Renan's anti-Catholic sentiments rather than the result of historical analysis.[11] Al-Afghānī, who happened to stay in Paris at that time, wrote a reply to Renan that was published together with the original lecture in the *Journal des Débats*.[12] He conceded that Islam was debilitating rational sciences, but argued that Muslim civilization was no less

7 Birgit Schäbler, "Religion, Rasse und Wissenschaft: Ernest Renan im Disput mit Jamal al-Din al-Afghani," *Themenportal Europäische Geschichte* (2007), <www.europa.clio-online.de/essay/id/fdae-1447> (acc. June 7, 2022), 2.

8 See Schäbler, "Religion, Rasse und Wissenschaft," 2.

9 See the English translation of Renan's lecture by Sally P. Ragep: Ernest Renan, "Islam and Science: A Lecture Presented at La Sorbonne 29 March 1883," [1883] 2nd ed., trans. Sally P. Ragep (2011), <https://www.mcgill.ca/islamicstudies/files/islamicstudies/renan_islamism_cversion.pdf> (acc. June 7, 2022), 2.

10 Renan, "Islam and Science," 8.

11 It is interesting to note that in the early eighteenth century, some European intellectuals emphasized the rationality of Islam, contrasting it with what they considered an excessive mysticism in Christianity (see Schäbler, "Der Islam und Europa," 173; Al-Azmeh, *Islam and Modernities*, 129). Here, too, Europeans instrumentalized Islam as the Other, albeit with a different outcome and for the purpose of criticizing specific strands of their own religious tradition.

12 Schäbler, "Religion, Rasse und Wissenschaft," 3–4.

capable of breaking free from the yoke of religion than Christian civilization had proved to be. After all, Islam was much younger than Christianity, and considering that religions typically evolve from religious intolerance to free and progressive thought, Muslim civilization too would eventually develop this way.[13]

Another Muslim intellectual who wrote a critical response to Renan's lecture was Namık Kemal, an important representative of the "Young Ottoman" reform movement. Unlike al-Afghānī, he challenged Renan's proposition that Islam obstructed scientific thought. He objected that Renan's notion of Islam was distorted and based on selective evidence that only served to support European biases. In actual fact, Kemal argued, Islam encouraged scientific thinking rather than stifling it, and Muslim societies past and present had always supported scientific scholarship and education.[14]

The debate between Renan, al-Afghānī, and Kemal illustrates not only the othering undertaken by European thinkers, but also the way in which many Muslim intellectuals responded: They did not principally reject Western ideas, including the notion of Western cultural ascendancy. On the contrary, al-Afghānī and Kemal were nationalists and advocated for a democratization of the Muslim world. But they were unwilling to renounce identification with their own cultural heritage, including Islam, and they defended this heritage against the contemptuous judgement that was so typical of contemporary European thought. In other words, they refused to accept the negative mirror image of European virtues that was projected on their culture in the process of othering. It is important to note, however, that this attempt at self-assertion has a quality that Samuli Schielke[15] described as "counter-hegemonial": al-Afghānī and Kemal contested some specific propositions advanced by their adversaries regarding Muslim civilization, but they did not challenge the fundamental premises on which these propositions were based. For example, they did not question the pivotal role of rationality and progress, but merely insisted that Islam did not obstruct these virtues.

This counter-hegemonial style of thought also characterizes many of the Islamic reform movements that formed from the late nineteenth century onward and are often summarized under the catch-all term of "Islamism." A key paradigm of such movements is the notion that rationality and progress are in fact essential elements of Islam, provided that the latter is interpreted properly and

---

13 Schäbler, "Religion, Rasse und Wissenschaft," 5–6.

14 See York A. Norman, "Disputing the 'Iron Circle': Renan, Afghani and Kemal on Religion, Science and Modernity," *Journal of World History* 22.4 (2011): 693–714, 703–706.

15 Samuli Schielke, "Hegemonic Encounters: Criticism of Saints-Day Festivals and the Formation of Modern Islam in Late 19th and Early 20th-Century Egypt," *Welt des Islams* 27.3–4 (2007): 319–355, 338.

authentically. The backwardness of contemporary Muslim societies, the reasoning goes, results from centuries of religious misinterpretation and would soon be overcome if Muslims returned to the pristine roots of Islam.

3 Appropriation and "Multiple Modernities"

It is clear, at this point, that Islamist movements cannot simply be described as a rejection of modernity. Rather, such movements result from what anthropologists describe as "appropriation." Appropriation denotes a process of intercultural exchange where external influences and ideas are neither fully rejected nor simply adopted. Instead, they are adapted to local circumstances – a process that frequently involves a fusion with traditional ideas and practices and often results in entirely new patterns, unprecedented in both the local tradition and the tradition from which the appropriation has taken place.[16] For example, Islamist movements typically insist on certain traditional Islamic legal norms that discriminate against women or non-Muslims and therefore collide with modern values. They have no objections, however, to an implementation of these norms by way of state legislation and a centralized judicial system headed by a supreme court – all features distinctly modern and unprecedented in Islamic law. There are other aspects of Islamist movements that are distinctly modern: Their modes of propaganda, which include ample use of digital forms of communication, their totalitarianism, and, most importantly, their understanding of religion as a program for the advance and progress of the nation (or, alternatively, the *umma*, i.e., the Islamic community).[17] This understanding of religion is a novelty in the Islamic tradition, and some scholars have pointed out that it presents a striking parallel with Protestant reform movements of earlier centuries in Europe.[18] At the same time, Islamist movements show features of modern ideologies and mass movements such as

---

16 On appropriation as a theoretical concept, see Shmuel N. Eisenstadt, "Multiple Modernities," *Daedalus* 129.1 (2000): 1–29, 14–16; Hans Peter Hahn, "Diffusionism, Appropriation and Globalization: Some Remarks on Current Debates in Anthropology," *Anthropos* 103.1 (2002): 191–202.

17 On the modernizing aspects of Islamic reform movements, see Bjørn Olav Utvik, "The Modernizing Force of Islam" in *Modernizing Islam: Religion and the Public Sphere in the Middle East and Europe*, ed. François Burgat and John Esposito (London: Hurst and Piscataway, 2003), 43–67; Eisenstadt, "Multiple Modernities," 19–20. The complex and ambivalent relation between Islamist movements and modernity is also emphasized by Nilüfer Göle, "Snapshots of Islamic Modernities," *Deadalus* 129.1 (2000): 91–117, 92–93.

18 Utvik, "The Modernizing Force," 50–53; see also Roman Loimeier, "Is There Something Like Protestant Islam?," *Die Welt des Islams* 45.2 (2005): 216–54, 247–49.

communism or fascism. All in all, they can thus be said to constitute a combination of multiple elements, both traditional and modern, that are fused into an entirely new phenomenon.

Islamism is by no means isolated as an example of appropriation. Western ideas and practices were (and are) appropriated in practically all fields of life, ranging from style of dress to forms of literature and film or political and legal institutions. This appropriation of modernity (as opposed to its unmodified adoption) has resulted in a global diversity of distinct modern societies that has prompted the sociologist Shmuel Eisenstadt to speak of "multiple modernities."[19] In this essay, I present two examples taken from the field of law, one from Egypt and the other from Israel, to illustrate the phenomenon.

4 Examples from the Field of Law

4.1 Islamic Constitutional Jurisdiction: The Supreme Constitutional Court of Egypt

In 1996, an Egyptian father and ex-husband filed a suit in the country's Supreme Constitutional Court (SCC) claiming that the Egyptian Family Law of 1985 was unconstitutional.[20] The law had been passed *inter alia* to change certain earlier regulations that had caused hardship to divorced mothers and their children. According to these regulations, which were based on the traditional Islamic law of the Ḥanafī school, child support could not be claimed retroactively. Traditional Ḥanafī jurists argue that while a wife is entitled to maintenance on the basis of a contractual agreement with her husband (*viz.*, the marriage contract), no such contract exists between a father and his child. A father's duty to pay child support results solely from his duty to prevent damage to the child. Since damage cannot be prevented retroactively, a claim for retroactive child support has no legal basis.

This doctrine – which is specific to the Ḥanafī school of law – presented a loophole for Egyptian fathers who sought to escape their financial obligations toward their children. All they needed to do was to deny paternity. Any ensuing

19 Eisenstadt, "Multiple Modernities." For a discussion of the concept, see also Thomas Schwinn, "Multiple Modernities: Konkurrierende Thesen und offene Fragen," *Zeitschrift für Soziologie* 38.6 (2009): 454–476.

20 My presentation of the case relies on Baber Johansen, "The Constitution and the Principles of Islamic Normativity against the Rules of Fiqh: A Judgement of the Supreme Constitutional Court of Egypt" in *Dispensing Justice in Islam: Qadis and their Judgments*, ed. M. Kh. Masud, R. Peters, and D.S. Powers (Leiden: Brill, 2006), 169–193.

paternity dispute was likely to last many years – time in which the child's claim for support continually lapsed. In using this and other strategies, the plaintiff in the case under discussion had succeeded to pass 21 years without paying a penny (or *qirsh*) to support his child.

The Family Law of 1985 closed this loophole. The statute prescribed that child support must be treated as a debt and may therefore be claimed retroactively. However, the plaintiff claimed that the new regulation violated Art. 2 of the Egyptian Constitution, which states that "the principles of Islamic law are the primary source of Egyptian legislation" (*mabādiʾ al-sharīʿa al-islāmiyya al-maṣdar al-raʾīsī lil-tashrīʿ*):[21] since the new regulation ignored traditional Ḥanafī doctrine, the plaintiff argued, it disagreed with the principles of Islamic law, and was therefore unconstitutional.

The court dismissed the case, arguing that Art. 2 did not prevent the legislator from implementing an interpretation of Islamic law that differed from the doctrine of an established school of law.

The decision is relevant in several respects, as it touches upon the much-debated question to which extent a law characterized as "Islamic" may depart from the doctrines of the traditional Islamic schools of law. A particularly interesting aspect of the case, however, is the extraordinary institutional constellation reflected in the court's decision. Although the court dismissed the case, it clearly deemed itself authorized to check the parliament's legislation for compatibility with Islamic principles – a task that obviously involves a great deal of Islamic legal interpretation. In other words, a constitutional court assumes the right to check national legislation for compatibility with an uncodified system of religious norms. This scenario is hardly conceivable in a European country. Nor is it conceivable within the framework of traditional Islamic law, which knows only rudimentary forms of judicial review, let alone a constitutional court. The practice of the Supreme Constitutional Court of Egypt presents a new institutional configuration resulting from a fusion of European and Islamic concepts. A similar configuration exists in Pakistan, whose Federal Shariat Court also enjoys the competence

21 On this Article of the Egyptian Constitution, see Johansen, "The Constitution and the Principles," 177; Mathias Rohe, "Das neue ägyptische Familienrecht: Auf dem Weg zu einem zeitgemäßen islamischen Recht," *Das Standesamt/StAZ* (2001): 193–207, 198–199; Andrea Büchler, Amira Latif, and Firdavs Kuliev, "Supreme Constitutional Court of Egypt: A Commented Translation of Egypt's Supreme Constitutional Decision in Case No. 125 of Judicial Year 27 on Child Custody," *GAIR-Mitteilungen* 2 (2010): 79–92, 83.

to "examine and decide" whether a law passed by the legislator is "repugnant to the Injunctions of Islam."[22]

A fusion of Western and traditional elements can be observed not only at the institutional level of the law but also in the field of textual and literary production. The abovementioned judgement of the Egyptian Supreme Constitutional Court is a case in point. It is part of the Court's ongoing discussion, documented in a series of decisions, of the extent to which Islamic legal norms should be applied more flexibly within the framework of Egyptian law.[23] In this discussion, the Court has made extensive reference to Islamic legal hermeneutics, and therefore, the decisions draw on the textual tradition of Islamic law. At the same time, of course, they are texts produced by a modern constitutional jurisdiction and share many features with judgements passed by courts in Europe.

My second example further illustrates the literary dimension involved in the process of appropriating legal concepts and institutions of European origin.

4.2 "Hybrid" Legal Genres: The "Circulars" of Qāḍī Nāṭūr in Israel

In the 1990s, the President of the Appellate Sharīʿa Court of Israel, Qāḍī Aḥmad Nāṭūr, issued a number of so called "legal circulars" (*marāsīm qaḍāʾiyya*, Sg. *marsūm qaḍāʾī*) in which he promulgated a number of reforms in the field of Islamic family law as applied in Israel.[24] Such "circulars" were unprecedented as a genre in Islamic law. It is true that in colonial Sudan, the Grand Qāḍī (*qāḍī l-quḍāt*)[25]

22 See Art. 203D (1) of the Constitution of the Islamic Republic of Pakistan. On the court's jurisdiction, see Martin Lau, "The Re-Islamization of Legal Systems" in *The Ashgate Research Companion to Islamic Law*, ed. Rudolph Peters and Peri Bearman (Farnham: Ashgate, 2014), 235–246, 237–238.

23 See Rohe, "Das neue ägyptische Familienrecht," 201–202; Büchler, Latif, and Kuliev, "Supreme Constitutional Court of Egypt," 88.

24 See Ido Shahar, "Legal Reform, Interpretative Communities, and the Quest for Legitimacy: A Contextual Analysis of a Legal Circular" in *Law, Custom and Statute in the Muslim World. Studies in Honor of Aharon Layish*, ed. Ron Shaham (Leiden: Brill, 2006), 199–227; Aharon Layish, "Adaptation of a Jurist's Law to Modern Times in an Alien Environment: The Case of the Sharīʿa in Israel," *Die Welt des Islams* 46.2 (2006): 168–225, 184–190; Moussa Abou Ramadan, "Judicial Activism of the Sharīʿa Appeals Court in Israel (1994–2001): Rise and Crisis," *Fordham International Law Journal* 27.1 (2003): 254–298, 284–288.

25 A qāḍī is an Islamic judge. The "Grand Qāḍī" (*qāḍī l-quḍāt*) is an official whose function has varied in the course of Muslim history, but who typically occupies a central position within the judicial administration.

also issued legal circulars, which served a similar reformatory purpose.[26] However, the Sudanese circulars were ratified by the British colonial administration and thus did not essentially differ from other colonial legislation of that period. By contrast, the circulars issued by Qāḍī Nāṭūr were not ratified by any official body of Israeli legislation and therefore may be characterized as informal and unofficial – a "pseudo-legislation," in the words of Benhalim.[27] However, they were signed by all qāḍīs acting in Israeli courts at that time, who also seem to have implemented them with considerable diligence.[28] Despite their ambiguous institutional character, the circulars proved rather effective as a means of reforming judicial practice. Layish reported in 2006 that "[c]ircles closely related to the Sharīʿa Court of Appeal estimate that the *marsūms* have become an integral part of the binding law applicable in the sharīʿa courts."[29]

Why did the President of the Sharīʿa Court of Appeal choose legal circulars as a means to reform judicial practice, even though this instrument was both unconventional and constitutionally problematic? To understand this choice, we must consider the extraordinary institutional context of Islamic jurisdiction in Israel. Technically speaking, the sharīʿa courts in Israel are a remnant of the late Ottoman period, in which the various religious communities enjoyed autonomous jurisdiction in matters of personal status law. The Mandatory and Israeli administrations left this autonomy largely untouched, with the result that until 2001, the sharīʿa courts enjoyed a "virtual judicial-religious monopoly over the definition of the personal status of Israeli Muslim citizens."[30] However, neither the courts nor any other Muslim institution in Israel enjoys powers of legislation, and the country's official legislator, the Knesset, has been careful to limit its interference in Islamic legal matters.[31] As a result, the qāḍīs still apply legal codes dating from the last decades of Ottoman rule.[32] In short, one of the most important tools used in the Muslim world to adapt Islamic law to changing circumstances, i.e., reform-oriented legislation, is made little use of in Israel. In

26 See Layish, "Adaptation," 184–185.

27 Rabea Benhalim, "Religious Courts in Secular Jurisdictions: How Jewish and Islamic Courts Adapt to Societal and Legal Norms," *Brooklyn Law Review* 84 (2019): 745–800, 797. On the uncertain legality of the *marāsīm*, see also Abou Ramadan, "Judicial Activism," 287.

28 See Shahar, "Legal Reform," 209.

29 Layish, "Adaptation," 190.

30 Shahar, "Legal Reform," 205. On the historical development of the sharīʿa courts in the region, see Shahar, "Legal Reform," 205; Abou Ramadan, "Judicial Activism," 256–257; Layish, "Adaptation," 174–175.

31 See Layish, "Adaptation," 178–179.

32 See Abou Ramadan, "Judicial Activism," 293; Shahar, "Legal Reform," 206.

addition, such legislation lacks legitimacy in the eyes of many Muslims as it comes from a non-Muslim institution.[33]

In part, then, the legal circulars used by Qāḍī Nāṭūr may be interpreted as a kind of surrogate for proper legislation, as the latter was not viable owing to a mix of institutional limitations and political considerations. One might argue, however, that the qāḍī could have used less problematic means to instigate legal reforms, most notably the instrument of appellate jurisdiction, which – unlike quasi-legislative circulars – falls within his constitutional competence. Shahar has argued that the choice of circulars was motivated by some additional political factors.

For one thing, the sharīʿa courts faced criticism at the time from feminist activists who claimed that the courts systematically discriminated against women, particularly by awarding very low maintenance payments. Some feminist organizations waged a campaign demanding that the sharīʿa courts' jurisdiction in matters of personal status should be conferred to civil family courts. According to Shahar, the first circular – which introduced some reforms to maintenance law – was designed to thwart these attacks on the sharīʿa court system by proving the judiciary's reform-mindedness and sensitivity to feminist issues. This purpose demanded public attention, which could rather be achieved by circulars than by the slow and inconspicuous work of appellate jurisdiction.[34] Moreover, by choosing the circular as a tool for reform, the Qāḍī made it clear that Muslim functionaries were willing and able to shape Islamic law without the assistance of the Knesset. In other words, the use of circulars may be interpreted as an implicit claim for autonomous Muslim legislation.[35] In that case, the constitutional dubiousness of the circulars might have even added to the motivation to choose this particular instrument.

Clearly the *marāsīm* of Qāḍī Nāṭūr were written in a complicated institutional and political context, and this is also reflected in the text of the circulars – their language, their rhetorical style, and their references to various discourses. Shahar, who analyzed the abovementioned circular regarding maintenance, argues that the text was written to address very diverse audiences: The qāḍī demonstrates conversance with local feminist discourses, but also with the demands and expectations of the Islamic movement and, last but not least, with the technicalities of

33 See Shahar, "Legal Reform," 200, n. 4. According to Layish, it was suggested to Qāḍī Nāṭūr that a new bill of family law could be drafted by a committee of religious functionaries and Islamic legal experts and then be passed by the Knesset in full, i.e., without interference in its substance. However, he turned down the suggestion, arguing that statutory legislation of Islamic norms was appropriate only for independent Muslim countries (see Layish, "Adaptation," 214).

34 For this interpretation, see Shahar, "Legal Reform," 201–202.

35 See Shahar, "Legal Reform," 202, 209.

Israeli and Islamic law.[36] Even the choice of the circular as text genre seems to be born of the special institutional and political situation. As noted, *marāsīm* are not an established genre of Islamic or Israeli law. Shahar characterizes them as "a bricolage of different genres" that combines elements of *fatwa*,[37] of modern legal treatise, and of administrative circular to "a new textual form."[38]

5 Conclusion

The *marāsīm* are of course a very specific phenomenon, reflecting the rather unique situation of Islamic jurisdiction in Israel. Moreover, they seem to be a transitory phenomenon. Only three such circulars were issued between 1994 and 1996, and to my knowledge, the practice has not been continued. Nonetheless, they illustrate a more general phenomenon that is virtually ubiquitous in the legal systems of the Muslim world: the appropriation of European (or Western) concepts, institutions, cultural techniques, and text genres and the resulting emergence of new patterns and forms that may be characterized as "hybrid" (with the caveat that this term is sometimes understood as derogatory, which would be utterly inappropriate in this context).

The numerous examples of such "hybrid" genres include modern textbooks of Islamic law used for educational purposes; modern style encyclopedic works such as the *Mawsūʿa Fiqhiyya* edited by the Ministry of Endowments and Religious Affairs of Kuwait;[39] the numerous codifications of Islamic family law passed by national legislators, together with the commentaries written on these codes; the "resolutions" (*qarārāt*) published by international expert committees such as the Fiqh Academy or the Accounting and Auditing Organization for Islamic Financial Institutions (AAOIFI); but also new forms and styles of *fatwā*s that have emerged owing to the rise of new media and changing hierarchies of knowledge. These

36 Shahar, "Legal Reform," 209.

37 A *fatwā* is a response given by an expert to the enquiry of a layperson regarding a legal or theological problem. *Fatwās* are a traditional genre of Islamic law that continues into the present, although modern media and changing structures of authority in the Islamic religious discourse have much altered and diversified the genre. For an overview, see the editors' introduction in *Islamic Legal Interpretation: Muftis and their Fatwas*, ed. Muhammad Khalid Masud, Brinkley Messick, and David S. Powers (Cambridge: Harvard UP, 1996), 3–32; Jakob Skovgaard-Petersen, "A Typology of Fatwās," *Die Welt des Islams* 55 (2015): 278–285.

38 Shahar, "Legal Reform," 203–204.

39 *Al-Mawsūʿa al-fiqhiyya*, 45 vols. (Kuwait: Wizārat al-Awqāf wal-Shuʾūn al-Islāmiyya, 1983ff.).

various genres – which have only recently attracted systematic scholarly attention – reflect the profound impact of the globalization of European modernity on the legal systems of the Muslim world, but also the perseverance of the Islamic legal tradition as a frame of reference for cultural identification and the creativity of Muslim societies to fuse different traditions to new forms and patterns.

Defending Europe

The fourth and final section of Part I is dedicated to the European spirit, and potential threats and challenges to European values from both a historical and a contemporary perspective. Whereas Europe's diversity has resulted in coexistence of people with different values and cultural imprints, language biographies and life experiences, Europe is – to many – first and foremost also a community of values, constituted and defined by a set of central, common principles. Yet, at the same time, Europe is also founded on the negotiation and balance of divergent value systems, and from such a perspective, Europe is precisely the space in which these can and must be negotiated. In this context, the question of changing European values and norms and the future of Europe constituted a core part of the debate on the so-called "refugee crisis" in 2015.

From a historical point of view, Alberto Scerbo renders the explosion of nationalism as an immediate cause of the cultural poisoning of Europe, a fact substantiated by a range of European, and particularly German, authors and intellectuals. He explores the view of various European literati, such as Thomas Mann, Paul Valéry, and Stefan Zweig, in the period between the two World Wars and in response to the various political developments and ideological forces at stake at the time. This European spirit embodied by the respective authors becomes tangible, for instance, when Scerbo characterizes Zweig as a pacifist who upheld pro-European ideals or presents Mann's "heartfelt public appeal to collectively maintain a high, spiritual, and political idea of Europe, in the face of systemic manipulation by Hitler's regime."[1]

For a more contemporary perspective, Nicola Kramp-Seidel offers the micro-view of a Jewish Orthodox Rabbi, an important figure in European Jewry. Her contribution broaches a range of juridical and legal issues, challenges, and difficulties in the context of Europe, e.g., multicultural matters or the acceptance of diverse and different religious lives. Rabbi Goldschmidt's views thereby touch on and deal with various juridical matters and issues concerning European law as well as law in European countries, thereby underscoring the need to defend freedom of religion as a human right and ultimately a core European value – a freedom that is potentially threatened by the banning of minarets and burqas or laws against ritual slaughtering and circumcision. In Goldschmidt's view, intolerance towards divergent ways of life and a multicultural society ultimately target European values.

Europe, as well as European values – as is brought to light by both contributions – is not a matter of course, but must be actively maintained, repeatedly renegotiated, and sometimes passionately defended if Europe is to be sustained as a community of values.

1 Alberto Scerbo, this volume, 117.

https://doi.org/10.1515/9783111075693-011

Alberto Scerbo

The "Spirit" of Europe in Literature between the Two World Wars

1 Traces of a European Identity

The notion of the twentieth century as a short century,[2] whose salient events took place in the period between the two world wars, is clearly conveyed by literature, particularly if we think of the destiny forged by history through that time. In fact, in the decades between the two wars, after the vertiginous ascent to the summit, the most ruinous fall into the abyss was the collapse of the European spirit. The inter-war years thus represent Europe's apotheosis from a cultural and a social point of view. Writers and poets, as participants and interpreters, were fully aware of the "spiritual" idea of Europe, which would herald the "political" one, yet to come.

Whoever confronts this problem is sure to express similar feelings, capable of being instilled in a unified and idealized expression, which might have been vague and multifarious, had Paul Valéry not felt the need to attempt his own conceptual clarification. European identity is, in fact, shaped by the combination of three different influences, not concurrent, but converging into a single model. It is about the contribution of Roman civilization, which promotes legal unity effective political and military administration, and religious tolerance; it is also about the contribution of Christianity, which promotes moral unification and encourages knowledge of the inner life; and the legacy of Greek culture, in its discipline of spirit and development of science. Valéry writes: "These, it seems to me, are the three essential conditions that define a true European, a man in whom the European mind can come to its full [. . .]. Every race and land that has been successively Romanized, Christianized, and, as regards the mind, disciplined by the Greeks, is absolutely European."[3]

Therefore, the convergence of these intuitions during the passage from the nineteenth century to the decadence of the early twentieth century is not surprising. Idealistic fervor stimulated an ever-growing confidence in scientific rationalism and trumpeted the optimistic message of unstoppable progress, both in terms of technology and morality. Valéry believes that the philosophical implication of

2 Eric J. Hobsbawm, *Il secolo breve: 1914–1991* [1994], trans. Brunello Lotti (Milan: Rizzoli, 1995).
3 Paul Valéry, "The European" [1919] in *The Collected Works of Paul Valéry*, Vol. 10, ed. Jackson Mathews, trans. Denise Folliot (Princeton: Princeton UP, 1962), 307–323, 322.

https://doi.org/10.1515/9783111075693-012

this is the advance of an authentically liberal conception, which promotes the recognition and protection of individual rights and cultivates the desire to extend the sphere of different forms of democratic power. In this way, the boost given by liberalism, with echoes of socialist claims, is combined with the most heartfelt social claims, with the effect of intervening, through targeted economic policies, to reduce poverty and to implement a justice system inspired by claims for humanity. "The golden age of safety" is also characterized by the illusion of a political reality centered on peaceful coexistence between countries, motivated by uniformity of regimes, and by undermining religious radicalism.

Indeed, the "indefinite" opportunities of science and the sense of freedom without borders arguably pave the way for Europe's eventual collapse, since the variety and heterogeneity of notions and values prevent the formation of a common center of reference, and involuntarily lay the conditions, instead, for a new era of opposition and conflict. Modernity seems to have turned at some point into exasperated modernism, in which the logical-deductive subject has debased the problem of experience and the growth of relativism has moved away from the search for a thing "in itself." Valéry bitterly notes that in 1914's Europe,

> [e]very mind of any scope was a crossroads for all shades of opinion; every thinker was an international exposition of thought. There were the works of the mind in which the wealth of contrasts and contradictory tendencies was like the insane displays of light in the capitals of those days: eyes were fatigued, scorched.[4]

The European conscience, which seemed to evolve unwaveringly despite each nation's national pride, and which seemed to lead to a situation of general pacification, supported by a widespread principle of union and solidarity, is gradually turning into its very opposite. When the forces of technological development feed the will to dominate, and rationality morphs into unreasonable instinct, prosperity galvanizes the greed of men, and state institutions are no longer satisfied with internal consolidation, but yearn instead for external expansionism.

In general, the most discerning writers perceive the danger of this progressive intoxication, and claim the supremacy of Europe as an idea of common aims to overcome national differences and diverging visions. For example, Stefan Zweig regrets the disintegration of the common heritage infused by the European faith, which remains latent and cannot be dissolved, but nevertheless needs to be recomposed, by virtue of a vital impulse, in which "each one of us [. . .] increased his individual confidence out of the collective confidence."[5]

4 Valéry, "The Crisis of the Mind" in *The Collected Works of Paul Valéry*, 23–36, 28.

5 Stefan Zweig, *The World of Yesterday: An Autobiography* [1941], trans. Benjamin W. Huebsch and Helmut Ripperger (New York: Viking P, 1943), 143.

This process of degradation, far from ending, is later consolidated. Zweig himself does not hesitate to declare the demise of a Europe which torments itself “with murder spree” in another fratricidal war. The immediate cause of this European cultural poisoning is the explosion of nationalism, as pointed out by the German literati. The achievements of European culture are completely distorted and manipulated into a jumble of “barbaric and insulting vulgarity,” Mann writes. The principles of freedom and justice, the intensity of spiritual being, and the foundation of humanism, of European formation, are also denied by an irrational misunderstanding, which contrasts with the dictates of the corrective philosophical currents of idealistic teaching. Psychic traditions are revived with new and mysterious elements, and are complemented by pseudo-spiritual ingredients, which elevate primitive forces rooted in ethno racial instincts. Thomas Mann vehemently denounces Germany’s new form of nationalism as “fanaticism, coarse insanity, wild denial of reason, human dignity, spirituality,”[6] which disperse the legacy of European thought and barbarize the forms of a civilization hitherto only partially achieved.

2 The End of an Era

The idea of Europe as a spirit is therefore used as a manifesto coinciding with the dramatic events of the war, testifying to the end of one kind of world, the beginning of horror and death, and the forecast of an undecipherable unknown. The mind must be preserved and cultivated, so as not to get lost in the infinite void.

From the works of the most percipient writers, however, there emerges a fine thread of continuity. A key insight into Europe’s recent past is offered by the recollections of Stefan Zweig, who writes *Die Welt von gestern: Erinnerungen eines Europäers* in the midst of National Socialism, but evokes the events, and above all the atmosphere, of thirty years earlier. He describes the beauty of Italian art, the fervor of Vienna, the glitz and glitter of Paris, and the foggy gloom of London. He shows us how the light-heartedness of the *belle époque*, strengthened by scientific innovations, by the discovery of leisure time and an independent lifestyle comparatively free from formal conventions, has strengthened the reliance on reason and removed suspicion and anxiety from the social fabric – most obviously in the halls of political power. There is, in his writing, the certainty that the warning signs coming from disparate events would yet be nullified by the spiritual and moral strength of Europe. Thus, the nationalistic echoes, the imperialist dreams, the ethnic grievances,

6 Thomas Mann, *Un appello alla ragione* [1930], in *Moniti all’Europa*, ed. and trans. Lavinia Mazzucchetti (Milan: Mondadori, 2017), 73; my translation.

and the historical-geographical claims silently mounting, and occasionally suddenly breaking out, may yet be halted by the reality of a shared Europe, and the belief in a Europeanism founded on the promise of a future yet more radiant.

As a result, the intellectual circles do not perceive the danger, but display passivity and indifference, allowing for the regeneration and growth of minority-held views. Political ambitions and military targets end up allying themselves, as people realize that the only bulwark to fascism is the scream of art, fully committed to defending freedom of thought and, consequently, freedom of expression and a system of coexistence marked by inclusiveness, designed as a multicolored and multiverse kaleidoscope. Zweig's pacifist and pro-European ideals intersect with the ideals of other literary personalities, among whom the figure of Romain Rolland stands out. His works receive credit for having taken all European countries into account, forging feelings of closeness and unity between them. In a Parisian meeting, Rolland explains how the novelist in that historical moment is not called to serve art, but to fight the impending evil; and how, through his work, he intends to rally the intellectual world to watch and admonish, "each in his own position, in his own country, in his own language," in order to guide people back to the path of peace and justice, doing their utmost to implement and maintain "European unity."[7]

Having experienced firsthand the brutality of the Hitler regime, Zweig is able to starkly contrast the differences between Europe of the present and Europe of the past. The result is a literary voice full of nostalgia, motivated by a belief in the value and persistence of culture, which is completely annihilated on the threshold of the Second World War. The contempt for knowledge, the homologation of thought and institutional lying had not yet prevailed, so that critical interventions and polemical writings were able, for a brief period, to see the light, to provoke debates and start thinking anew. "The moral conscience" had not yet been stifled and the indignation about human rights violations, about the torture and violence of the war, continued to be shouted through verse, essays, stories, and novels, later to be extrapolated into universal principles of humanity intended to challenge and defeat the feelings of aversion, willful ignorance, and self-interest among the people, to make them feel part of the common house of Europe. Zweig admits to having published an article, "An die Freunde im Fremdland," with the sole purpose of clearly and visibly highlighting the need for mutually supportive brotherhood. He calls "to all friends in foreign countries that, although relations were now impossible, I would remain loyal to them so that, at the very first opportunity, *we might again collaborate in the reconstruction of European culture*."[8]

7 Zweig, *The World of Yesterday*, 147.
8 Zweig, *The World of Yesterday*, 169; my emphasis.

Zweig is sorry for the miscalculations marking the end of the First World War and those made during the post-war period. In particular, he focusses on his Austrian homeland and on the collapse of its empire. The ideals of peace should have supported the serious "Austrian ideality" beyond the mere literary field, to create a movement opposed to militarist ambitions and German annexation politics. In fact, the basis of the European cause was gradually breaking down, together with the foundation of the empire and the reasons for the existence of the monarchy. The consequences of this will become clear later, when the illusion of peace and the dreams of reconstruction crash against the sad reality of a new, contrasting European geopolitical order, as different in structure but similar as far as the system of values are concerned and, therefore, at last capable of constituting a kingdom of justice and solidarity. Instead, however, he remembers a flourishing and magnificent Austrian empire, the essential center of the European spirit, since dissolved in the insanity of the war and replaced by a small republic afflicted by misery and at the mercy of the victors, left now to search for an identity which is invested solely in past glories never to return. With gloomy resignation, Zweig admits that the post-war political reorganization was needed in order to forget the idea of that kind of Europe, to reconstitute it in a new form, so that the European "spiritual" essence could be turned into a broader "political" project, through the creation of a superordinate unity of all states.

The nefarious consequences of the choices made, and also of those not made, would last for years to come. Moreover, the anguished cries of the mid-1930s sound, in hindsight, like a warning to the present: young people indoctrinated by lies of propaganda, by street riots and gratuitous violence, by weapons and uniforms that augur a devastating future for Europe, which is now but a shadow of the "cradle and temple of Western civilization." Facing the prospect of death, which cruelly stalks the Jewish community in the madness of war, Zweig re-establishes the good Jewish bourgeoisie to a central role in order to transmit the main values of Viennese culture. The emancipation from religious orthodoxy, and the sharing of principles of liberalism and progressive ideas, allows for active participation in political life and economic development. This cultural contribution also promoted the creation of a cosmopolitan environment: Judaism, in arts and science, was able to promote the revival of the European spirit, transforming its own culture into a synthesis of all Western cultures.[9]

In 1942, Zweig decides to abandon earthly life; we do not know how much the Nazi experience affected him; surely such a convinced pacifist and pro-European cannot have watched with indifference at the destruction and disintegration of

9 Zweig, *The World of Yesterday*, 28.

his civilization; cannot have countenanced the contempt of thought and the annihilation of all forms of humanity, and above all, the total darkening of law, the main and universal bedrock of European consciousness.

3 Against Fascist Regimes

In the same year of 1942, on September 27, in a radio message addressed to the German people, Thomas Mann urges his compatriots to rediscover the meaning of their humanity in the face of the horrors being perpetrated against the Jews. This was not limited to persecution or torture but extended to the "maniacal decision to totally eradicate the Jewish people from Europe."[10] This project speaks not only to those in power, clearly endowed with "rotten brains," but also to the reason and heart of the entire community, which is called upon to exorcize feelings of inner hatred, to renounce the practices of violence and cruelty, not to close their eyes in the face of atrocities and injustices, and to rediscover the equilibrium of social coexistence. It is not just a matter of resisting the present poisoning of society, but of getting rid of "morally stolid and abnormal killers"[11] for the training of future generations.

These notes represent the conclusion of the German writer's journey that starts from afar and continues uninterrupted. He makes an effort to pinpoint both the causes of historical events within a broader European perspective, and also the interpretative tools of the National Socialist movement.

The journey begins with a speech in Berlin in 1922 dedicated to the German Republic, in which he seems to abandon the conservative, militarist, and antidemocratic thesis of a few years earlier. The opposition between *Kultur* and *Zivilisation*, expressed by the "unpolitical," aims to enhance the figure of the artist and free him of political backsliding, and reveals a conceptual apparatus that contrasts with democratic, pacifist, and internationalist ideology.[12] Mann recognizes within the German cultural heritage some European traits. Regardless of the critical interpretations provided on either the continuity or the rupture of Mann's ideas, or on a substantial conservatism he never renounced, it should be clarified that his change of perspective essentially depends on his need to immerse himself

10 Mann, *Ascoltatori tedeschi* [1942], in *Moniti all'Europa*, 241; my translation.

11 Mann, *Ascoltatori tedeschi*, 242; my translation.

12 Thomas Mann, *Considerazioni di un impolitico* [1918], ed. and trans. Marianello Marianelli and Marlis Ingenmey (Milan: Adelphi, 1997).

in the field of politics for the triumph and wellbeing of *Humanität*.[13] The literary oscillations that compare Novalis to Whitman, the rhetorical miscalculations that deny pacifism and oppose war, and the cultural acrobatics that equate romanticism with political enlightenment, all serve to direct Mann's attention to the recovery of a superior European spirit, possibly a prelude to Kantian cosmopolitan unity. However, despite the reality of irreversible barbarism, the shared responsibility of Europe, which first annihilated and then shattered its own vocation, cannot be ignored. In the initial post-war period, Europe ignored the promises made to the German people and implemented a policy of degradation and oppression, threatening ruin and despair. Thereafter, European values and the "collective European will" were betrayed and sacrificed on behalf of economic and political interests of lower material value. Previously robust democracies, overshadowed by the fear of socialism, were thus overwhelmed by the obfuscations of fascist demagogues so that Germans were suddenly forced to admit that actually there was no "Europe behind [them], in which [they] had either put [their] faith or which [they] believed – because this Europe wished 'not at all' the National Socialist dictatorship to fall."[14]

Mann's gloomy comments delivered throughout the 1930s did not prevent him from making a heartfelt public appeal to collectively maintain a high, spiritual, and political idea of Europe, in the face of systemic manipulation by Hitler's regime. In fact, the irrational ideological apparatus of the Nazis instilled in people a great sense of supremacy, justifying the belittling of freedom as a principle and dissolving the notion of humanity in law. Political categories became mangled, clouding minds, through programs of distorted personal power. Thus, a wild desire for oppression prevailed to quash any voices for peace and turned the idea of Europe into a monopolistic national projection, "an accessory of monopolistic Germany, an empty, emasculated, miserable accessory, scarcely inhabited by exploited slave races, a German 'protectorate' in the most dishonorable sense of the word."[15]

During the Nazi period, Mann pursued humanism. By doing so the main principles of liberalism were restored to the collective memory, the true spirit of conservatism was displayed, and the innovative and revolutionary character of the socialist currents was highlighted. On the other hand, this just underlined the rejection of the Nazi period and the direction of a new European political reconstitution.

---

13 See Paolo Ridola, "La Costituzione della Repubblica di Weimar come 'esperienza' e come 'paradigma,'" *Rivista AIC* 2 (2014): 1–27; Alessandra Di Martino, "L'identità dell'Europa tra le due guerre mondiali e la resistenza," *Nomos* 3 (2018): 1–42.

14 Mann, *L'altezza dell'ora* [1938], in *Moniti all'Europa*, 48; my translation.

15 Mann, *Ascoltatori tedeschi*, 238; my translation.

Germany seemed stained with the sin of omnipotence, deceiving itself into existing "without humanity" and rising to become absolute. The main goal was the subjugation of people, in order to enslave all of Europe. At this point, we must remember Mann's warning, stemming from the progressive side of the spectrum, of the risks of fascism and of the annihilation of European humanism leading inevitably to war, that is, the main hallmark of fascism on the right.

For Mann, it was crucial that the tragedy of this experiment must also serve as a warning for the future, helping the German people to exorcize the ghosts of the present and pursue the goal of cultural integration in Europe, according to the model of free and democratic governments. At the same time, it must act as a reminder to Europe to avoid the mistakes of the past and to achieve the restoration of supranational unity, in order to guarantee peace and safety.

4 The European Spirit as Root of Hope

Mann's invitation to practice militant humanism advances the view that politics will, in the future, be led by culture and will find the resources to renew the European spirit. Paul Valéry voices an articulate and profound criticism of this idea, which traces the course of history in the first half of the twentieth century. It focuses in particular on the "crisis of the spirit," an expression found in the title of his 1919 publication, describing a spiritual disorder.

The French writer highlights the clear gap between the results of scientific evolution and the dominant moral and social conceptions, creating a huge chasm between the "true scientific" and the "real political," with the effect of rendering a different representation of the world, due to a different conception of man and spirit. The fact that the world of law and politics, far from viewing things objectively, is often linked to mythical factors and offers imaginary solutions, causes the higher spiritual values of society to be contorted. This occurs as a result of greater insensitivity, an increase of mental confusion and superstition, and the relentless suppression of individuals. The illusions of historical-philosophical memory and the deceptions of politicians are thus, in practice, unable to stem the flow, while, on the contrary, they keep relations among men in a kind of retarded empiricism, stimulating their worst material instincts.[16] The situation described in the immediate post-war period remains unchanged in the decades that follow, until it reaches the delirium of Europe in its

16 These topics are developed in particular in Valéry, "Politics of the Mind" [1932] in *The Collected Works of Paul Valéry*, 89–113.

death spiral, having decided to collect "the ruins of a civilization surrendering to the barbarians and one fool."[17] We must bitterly concede that

> since 1914, in Europe, we have been the witnesses and victims of colossal phenomena of social, political and economic geology, whose shakes will probably dig an abyss of subjugation and credulous ignorance, right there where the mountains full of gods and divinities rose, of which our works were nothing but the oracles, or the praises.[18]

For Valéry, this process of decay was irreversible and the crisis of the spirit irremediable. Nevertheless, at the beginning of the 1930s he took refuge in the virtues of the spirit, "our common good," and issued a hopeful warning to preserve "the will to lucid understanding and precision of mind, a sense of greatness and risk."[19] But he spoke of the European spirit, where curiosity, caused by anxiety, the will to learn, the meeting of peoples and cultures, had shaped the most important material and spiritual achievements of humanity. Recognizing the miracles thus far accomplished must surely be the justification for endorsing the European spirit, with its prerogatives, as the main tool for overcoming impending disasters, recovering harmony and balance, and restoring civilization as it was conceived in ancient times, with the contributions of culture, science, and art. Man can only reaffirm the essence of his being if Europe remains "what it seems – that is: the elect portion of the terrestrial globe, the pearl of the sphere, the brain of a vast body."[20]

17 Paul Valéry, "'L'Europa vuole perire': Lettere di Paul Valéry a Victoria Ocampo (1939–1945)" [1945] in *In morte di una civiltà*, ed. and trans. Massimo Carloni (Turin: Aragno, 2018), 157–179, 162; my translation.
18 Valéry, "'L'Europa vuole perire,'" 164; my translation.
19 Valéry, "Politics of the Mind," 113; my translation.
20 Valéry, "The Crisis of the Mind," 31.

Nicola Kramp-Seidel

Rabbi Pinchas Goldschmidt's View on Europe

1 Introduction

Since 2011, Rabbi Pinchas Goldschmidt has been the president of the Conference of European Rabbis (CER), the "primary Orthodox rabbinical alliance in Europe,"[1] which was founded in 1956 by the chief rabbis of the Netherlands, Great Britain, and France.[2] On its website, the Conference of European Rabbis describes one of its main goals as "to defend the religious rights of Jews in Europe."[3] In addition to being a voice highlighting the importance of religious rights, in relation to circumcision or ritual slaughter, for example, it provides Jewish legal decision-making or certification of "conversions or kashrut operations"[4] with its legal court (Bet Din) and its committees.

In his role as president of this organization, Pinchas Goldschmidt has often given statements on his view of or on Europe, either in articles published in newspapers like *The New York Times* or on the occasion of ceremonies like the presentation of the *Harav Lord Jakobovits Prize of European Jewry*. Some of his articles and speeches in which considerations about Europe are the main issue are collected in his book *Communitati et Orbi: To the Community and to the World*, which was first published in 2017 and later translated into German and Russian. In the present contribution, I would like to illustrate Goldschmidt's perspective on Europe and the dangers and difficulties for Europe in general, or rather for Jews in Europe as presented in these articles and speeches. In the process, I also intend to highlight some measures taken by the CER, as outlined by Pinchas Goldschmidt in his book, to combat anti-Semitism, any form of terrorism, and to fight for a broad remembrance of the history of injustice, persecution, and mass killings of Jews, especially in countries and regions in which there is a trend towards a reactionary glorification and/or manipulation of the past.

1 See Conference of European Rabbis, "Our History," (n.d.), *Who We Are* <https://rabbiscer.org/who-we-are/our-history/> (acc. April 4, 2022), n. pag.

2 See Pinchas Goldschmidt, *Communitati et Orbi: To the Community and to the World* (Tel Aviv: May Editions/Mantanel Foundation, 2017), 15.

3 See Conference of European Rabbis, "Our History," n. pag.

4 See Conference of European Rabbis, "Our History," n. pag.

https://doi.org/10.1515/9783111075693-013

Goldschmidt's view on Europe is worth mentioning and highlighting because he is acknowledged as an important voice in European Jewry.[5] His statements on Europe thus have an impact on the ongoing dialogue in Europe concerning religious issues such as religious freedom. In addition, European politicians like Frans Timmermans recognize Goldschmidt's "tireless work in building Europe's future – a future when we can all live together with mutual respect, in freedom and in peace."[6] He is therefore seen as an advocate for an important vision of Europe.

2 Goldschmidt's Vision of Europe and the Reality

In his speeches and his articles, Goldschmidt emphasizes the values and goals Europe should have and should fight for, especially after World War II. In his view, Europe should stand for pluralism and freedom, including freedom of religion. Although Europe stands for these principles on paper, they do not seem fulfilled in reality. He demands that Europe shall defend these values, e.g., by way of welcoming strangers and accepting different ways of life.[7] In his ideal view of Europe, there should be room and acceptance for people who want to live a secular life, but also for pious people who intend to live their lives according to their spiritual values. Goldschmidt calls for "an atmosphere of tolerance and mutual respect between the secular modern state and the current religious movements,"[8] and he stresses the importance of a dialogue among and between different people with diverse opinions and backgrounds. Otherwise, his reasoning goes, the idea of the European Union would be at risk.[9]

It is not only on behalf of Jews that Pinchas Goldschmidt demands religious freedom, but he does so also on behalf of Muslims. His criticism of the lack of acceptance of different ways of life often entails a deep concern about the treatment of Muslim

---

5 See, for example, Goldschmidt's depiction in Peter Münch, "Profil: Pinchas Goldschimdt," (June 9, 2022), *Süddeutsche Zeitung* <https://www.sueddeutsche.de/meinung/russland-moskau-oberrabbiner-pinchas-goldschmidt-israel-exil-1.5600341> (acc. June 27, 2022), n. pag.; see also a press release of the Bavarian State Parliament: Bayerischer Landtag, "'Der Dialog zwischen Juden, Christen und Muslimen ist mir wichtig': Pinchas Goldschmidt, Präsident der Europäischen Rabbinerkonferenz (CER), zu Gast im Landtag," (July 11, 2019), *Aktuelles* <https://www.bayern.landtag.de/aktuelles/veranstaltungen/gaeste-und-begegnungen/gub-2019/11072019-pinchas-goldschmidt-im-bayerischen-landtag/> (acc. June 27, 2022), n. pag.

6 Frans Timmermans, "Foreword" in Goldschmidt, *Communitati*, 11–14, 14.

7 Goldschmidt, *Communitati*, 140.

8 Goldschmidt, *Communitati*, 235.

9 Goldschmidt, *Communitati*, 238.

citizens. He recognizes a growing social rejection of different lifestyles or of an open-mindedness toward people who live and act differently, which he primarily traces back to relatively high migration rates from Muslim countries, among other reasons. In addition, most of the official goals of minimizing dangers emanating from radicalized Muslims or of answering fears caused by immigration seem to threaten the visibility of Islam (or Judaism).[10]

After the ban on minarets in Switzerland and the ban on burqas and niqabs in France, Goldschmidt wrote about his concerns in an op-ed for *The New York Times*,[11] in which he clearly lays out his criticism concerning these bans.[12] He sees them in connection with common fears, spread throughout the continent, about losing a national identity. However, he is convinced that these bans only reduce freedom, security, and prosperity in Europe. By attacking minorities and their beliefs, Europe uses tools like intolerance against minorities, which he refers to as "Middle Eastern practices."[13] In addition, it seems incomprehensible how these measures should help fight extremism and forms of hatred practiced only by a minority of migrants or Muslims. Goldschmidt elaborates that the ban on minarets does not have an influence on the existence of mosques and what is preached inside them. Similarly, to him, a ban on burqas and niqabs will not change ways of thinking and belief systems. Instead of such regulations, he claims, there are more important ways of fighting different forms of religious extremism and intolerance and of achieving successful integration of migrants. According to Goldschmidt, it is crucial to integrate people into the public school system or universities.[14] Furthermore, "Europe should take the lead in demonstrating tolerance of religious pluralism."[15] The rabbi is thus a strong advocate for religious freedom, not only for Jews, but for all who are in danger of not being able to live their lives according to their spiritual values.

Of course, he recognizes the threat posed by "radicalized migrants from the Middle East,"[16] mentions attacks on Jewish citizens and buildings, and stresses anti-Semitism as embodied by Muslim extremists.[17] He highlights the attacks against Jewish citizens performed by Islamists, such as the attack in a Jewish school in Toulouse or in a Jewish museum in Brussels. Nevertheless, this danger accordingly poses only

10 Goldschmidt, *Communitati*, 139.

11 See Goldschmidt, *Communitati*, 138–141.

12 Further examples of Goldschmidt's criticism on these bans include their mention in a holiday greeting and in his speech on the presentation of the *Harav Lord Jakobovits Prize of European Jewry* 2014/15, also published in his book; see 149, 215.

13 Goldschmidt, *Communitati*, 237.

14 Goldschmidt, *Communitati*, 140–141.

15 Goldschmidt, *Communitati*, 141.

16 Goldschmidt, *Communitati*, 214.

17 Goldschmidt, *Communitati*, 215, 226.

one of two threats for Jews living in Europe. In addition to this first threat, Goldschmidt recognizes a danger emanating from secular members of European societies and communities who pretend to combat "Muslim radicalism" or who use anti-Semitic expressions that are disguised as seemingly politically correct statements. Even though most of these strategies purportedly directed against Muslim radicalism primarily threaten Muslim citizens, Jewish citizens often seem to be "collateral damage."[18] Certain laws and objectives in different countries are recognized by Goldschmidt as a threat to living an observant Jewish life in Europe, just as some debates and speeches seem to show "the new face of politically correct anti-Semitism."[19] In particular, the debates on circumcision and ritual slaughter are presented as central problems. The rabbi firmly criticizes the elaborations concerning circumcision as found in Resolution 1952 (2013), "Children's Right to Physical Integrity," formulated by the Parliamentary Assembly of the Council of Europe (PACE).[20] He elaborates how this recommendation attacks and threatens Jewish faith and life in Europe: Thus in Section 7.7, the Assembly advises the Member States to

> raise awareness about the need to ensure the participation of children in decisions concerning their physical integrity wherever appropriate and possible, and to adopt specific legal provisions to ensure that certain operations and practices will not be carried out before a child is old enough to be consulted.[21]

Since circumcision, according to Jewish law, is primarily (with some exceptions) done on the eighth day after the child is born,[22] this advice threatens a core element of Jewish ritual. Goldschmidt therefore describes this resolution as a recommendation for banning "male circumcision altogether"; he is afraid that this advice could be implemented as binding law throughout Europe and localizes a generally unwelcoming atmosphere for Jews.[23] Due to the widespread tradition of circumcision among the various Jewish denominations, this alarm seems reasonable. In addition to this criticism and fear, Goldschmidt highlights that a "demonization" of Jewish ritual is occurring. He quotes Marlene Rupprecht, Member of the German Parliament and member of the Social Democratic Party, who refers

---

18 Goldschmidt, *Communitati*, 175.

19 Goldschmidt, *Communitati*, 176.

20 Parliamentary Assembly of the Council of Europe, "Resolution 1952 (2013) Final Version: Children's Right to Physical Integrity," (October 1, 2013), *Files* <http://assembly.coe.int/nw/xml/XRef/Xref-XML2HTML-en.asp?fileid=20174> (acc. April 21, 2022), n. pag.

21 Parliamentary Assembly, "Resolution 1952 (2013)," n. pag.

22 See, for example, Moses Maimonides, Mischne Torah, Hilkhot Mila, 1:8 und 1:9.

23 Goldschmidt, *Communitati*, 176.

to circumcision – according to Goldschmidt – as the "dark side" of religion and traditions.[24] Goldschmidt sees anti-Semitic tendencies that occur via demonization of and attacks on ritual slaughter obscured and disguised as the fight for animal rights.

However, in addition to the more obvious slurs against ritual slaughter, oftentimes coming with a seemingly progressive emphasis on the well-being of animals, the rabbi also mentions far-right anti-Semitism and sees an even more disquieting lack of reaction and indifference by mainstream politicians or the media:[25] Thus in a Parliamentary Question entitled "Child Deaths Caused by Halal Meat" Andreas Mölzer, politician from the Freedom Party of Austria, asks if the high death rate of children in France caused by bacterial infections due to contaminated meat is connected to the higher consumption of halal or kosher meat.[26] Not without reason does Goldschmidt connect this Parliamentary Question to the issue of blood libel. Since the Middle Ages, Jews have been recurrently and falsely accused of killing children especially in Europe, at times even resulting in trials against them, as in Trent in 1475.[27] Blood libel as anti-Semitic imagery has often been observed as well.[28] Similar to these conspiracy narratives, Mölzer – by posing this question – blames Jews (and, in this case, Muslims as well) for children's deaths. Although Goldschmidt is shocked by this Parliamentary Question, he is even more concerned about the lack of response by large parts of the media and other politicians.[29] By writing about this incident, Rabbi Pinchas Goldschmidt intends to raise his voice against the tendencies from the far right, especially in times in which the latter is becoming more and more influential in several countries across Europe.

---

24 Goldschmidt, *Communitati*, 176–177.

25 Goldschmidt, *Communitati*, 158.

26 Andreas Mölzer, "Parliamentary question-E-003880/2012: Child Deaths Caused by Halal Meat," (April 13, 2012), *European Parliament: Documents* <https://www.europarl.europa.eu/doceo/document/E-7-2012-003880_EN.html> (acc. April 21, 2022), n. pag.

27 See Magda Teter, *Blood Libel: On the Trail of an Antisemitic Myth* (Cambridge: Harvard UP, 2019), 15.

28 Ute Caumanns and Andreas Önnerfors, "'Ritualmord' – konspiratorische Konstante antisemitischer Bildcodes vom Mittelalter bis zur Gegenwart," *Antisemitismus als Code: Forschung – Prävention – Intervention*, special issue of *Juden in Mitteleuropa* (2021): 12–18.

29 Goldschmidt, *Communitati*, 157–159.

3 Activities of the CER for Combating Anti-Semitism and Remembering Pogroms

In 2006, the CER, in cooperation with the Claims Conference (Conference of Jewish Material Claims Against Germany), founded the organization *Lo Tishkach* (Do not forget) with the goal of remembering Jewish history consisting of pogroms, repressions, or killings, and of recording Jewish mass graves or cemeteries, especially in regions where no Jewish citizens live today. In addition to this main directive, the organization intends to protect and preserve Jewish cemeteries and mass graves across Europe. The collected data is presented online in a database accessible to everyone.[30] In one of his op-eds, Rabbi Pinchas Goldschmidt highlights the importance of the organization: firstly, because many mass graves, especially in the Eastern part of Europe (Belarus, Ukraine, Russia, and the Baltics), have not been identified yet; secondly, the argument goes, due to the fact that many European leaders aim to rewrite history from a nationalist viewpoint or opt to be silent about persecution or killings, it remains central to remember the Shoah.[31] Goldschmidt mentions several examples of how political leaders or countries engage in reactionary historical agendas, such as in Lithuania: In order to obscure the fact that anti-Semitic militia carried out killings of Jews prior to the Nazi occupation, the country highlights the rescue of Jews by a small number of Lithuanians "while consistently refusing to bring to justice any of its own war criminals, including those extradited to them from the United States."[32]

The Conference of European Rabbis has repeatedly demanded that European governments support the provision of security for Jewish synagogues or institutions. For example, in 2012, Rabbi Pinchas Goldschmidt said the following in celebration of the *Harav Lord Jakobovits Prize of European Jewry*:

> The Conference of European Rabbis is turning to the European Parliament and to the European Commission to ask the governments of Europe to provide heightened security at institutions and places of worship of those minorities in Europe who have been targeted by extremists. Local faith communities, especially in Eastern Europe, do not have the means or the know-how to provide for their own security without the support of state security organizations.[33]

30 Lo Tishkach/European Jewish Cemeteries Initiative, "About Us," (n.d.), *About Lo Tishkach* <http://www.lo-tishkach.org/about-us> (acc. April 25, 2022), n. pag.

31 Goldschmidt, *Communitati*, 134–137.

32 Goldschmidt, *Communitati*, 137.

33 Goldschmidt, *Communitati*, 152–153.

In 2017, the Conference of European Rabbis attended the Munich Security Conference and appealed to all European governments to maintain security for Jewish institutions based on the fact that governments have the duty to provide security for every citizen. With this appeal, the Conference of European Rabbis highlighted the widespread reality in which the communities alone are responsible for the security of Jewish institutions.[34]

In addition to these activities, the Conference of European Rabbis speaks up against any form of extremism. After the attacks on Charlie Hebdo and a Hyper Cacher market in Paris in particular, enforced actions against religious extremism in its totality were seen as a necessity. Therefore, in consultation and cooperation with Jewish, Muslim, and Christian leaders, the Conference of European Rabbis wrote a "Manifesto for Combating Religious Extremism" and sent it to all European ministers of the interior. In this manifesto, they demand that religious communities establish a formalized training of spiritual leaders. This training, according to the manifesto, should be carried out in Europe and mention the dangers of extremism as well. However, as it might not be possible to hold every training unit in Europe, a certification for schools outside of Europe is suggested. In order to combat extremism, a second important point is mentioned in the manifesto: It proposes that the payment for religious leaders should come from "internal European sources."[35] Funds of over 5,000 Euros should be made public in order to identify their origin. Furthermore, it demands a review of funds originating from non-European sources and the appointment of an Extremism Prevention Officer who would write regular reports listing concerns with regards to extremism. Last but not least, the registration of all religious congregations in a national register is recommended.[36]

As we can see, Rabbi Pinchas Goldschmidt considers the Conference of European Rabbis, a central alliance for Orthodox rabbis, primarily to be a representative and an advocate for Jewish religious issues in Europe. In his view, it stands up for religious freedom so that Jews in Europe can live their lives without oppression and restrictions. However, in addition to his advocacy for the acceptance of Jewish principles, he demands religious freedom for every group, especially Muslims, as well. Rabbi Pinchas Goldschmidt therefore sees the Conference of European Rabbis and himself as a voice in Europe for European principles based on the fact that freedom of religion is one of the core elements of a free and multicultural society. According to Goldschmidt's elaborations, demands for religious freedom are situated in this framework of a free and pluralistic Europe.

34 Goldschmidt, *Communitati*, 226.
35 Goldschmidt, *Communitati*, 206.
36 Goldschmidt, *Communitati*, 204–209.

Part II: **Commitments**

Rule of Law

The first section of the second part of this volume, dedicated to European "Commitments," addresses the rule of law as one of the core principles or values of Europe. This is exemplified by the fact that the rule of law is enshrined in the Treaty on European Union and thereby constitutes one of the fundamental values of the EU. It is also essential for the protection of all other fundamental values of the Union, most notably fundamental rights and the principle of democracy. Respect for the rule of law is crucial for the functioning of the EU, e.g., the effective application of EU law; to maintain the rule of law, effective legal enforcement is necessary which can only be guaranteed by an independent, high-quality, and efficient judiciary.

Both contributions in this section address the significance of the rule of law as well as respective challenges to or a deplorable lack of enforceability of the rule of law. Even as Dominik Brodowski mentions multiple challenges in the area of European criminal justice – concerns in relation to questionable human rights protections, e.g., in Hungary or Poland, an overly heavy reliance on national criminal justice, or the possibility that other member states could become "blind aiders" in the execution of excessive criminal norms – he ultimately highlights the values of a "European" approach to criminal justice. As Brodowski demonstrates, relying on human rights serves both as a shield and as a sword in criminal justice. Since criminal justice is built on the foundation of human rights and the rule of law, if either principle is violated, European values are violated in equal part, according to Brodowski.[1] Tetyana Dagovych's contribution contrasts the aspirations for the principle of the rule of law with the deplorable absence of law and subsequent lawlessness in Belarus as negotiated in Belarusian poetry, a situation that results in abuse, harassment, violence, torture, and a constant state of fear. The specific perspective of the Belarusian poets – both inside and from outside of Europe – conceptualizes the European territory as an ideal of the rule of law, which also serves as a figurative and imaginative realm for the projection of various aspirations of a better future. While there is a stark contrast between the rule of law as depicted by Brodowski and the lawlessness in Belarus as demonstrated in the Belarusian poems examined by Dagovych, both contributions share a common vision of Europe as a place founded on and protective of human rights as well as the rule of law – both an aspiration and an ideal that is not only acknowledged and addressed in European criminal legislation, but in Belarusian poetry as well.

1 Dominik Brodowski, this volume, 141–142.

https://doi.org/10.1515/9783111075693-014

Dominik Brodowski

European Criminal Justice

While some consider criminal justice to be a *domaine réservé* for nation-states, criminal justice systems in Europe become ever more intertwined, the legal codes ever more harmonized, and transnational cooperation ever more common. On a supranational level, the investigation and prosecution of some crimes has been transferred by 22 EU Member States to the European Public Prosecutor's Office in 2021. In this essay, I will provide a short overview of the genesis and *status quo* of what commonly is referred to as European Criminal Justice or European Criminal Law. Particular focus will be put on the activities of the Council of Europe and the European Union (1). On this basis, I will sketch out three current challenges of European Criminal Justice, namely, rule of law concerns regarding some European states, the continuing focus on nation-states, and a Europe with multiple speeds of integration (2). Finally, I will provide an outlook on the future path European Criminal Justice may take (3).

1 Genesis and *Status Quo* of European Criminal Justice

When Europe awoke from the ruins of World War II, one of the central goals was to protect Europe against war, genocide, and heinous violations of human rights ever happening again within its boundaries and beyond. One cornerstone of this attempt was the foundation of the Council of Europe (CoE)[2] and the creation, within its framework, of the Convention for the Protection of Human Rights and Fundamental Freedoms, commonly called the "European Convention on Human Rights" (ECHR).[3] Its fundamental guarantees, such as the right to a fair trial (Art. 6

2 Cf. in the preamble of the Statute of the Council of Europe (European Treaties Series [ETS] No. 001), the reference to the conviction "that the pursuit of peace based upon justice and international co-operation is vital for the preservation of human society and civilization," and the statement in Article 3 that "[e]very member of the Council of Europe must accept the principles of the rule of law and of the enjoyment by all persons within its jurisdiction of human rights and fundamental freedoms."

3 ETS No. 002, as amended by Protocols 11 (ETS No. 155), 14 (ETS No. 194) and 15 (ETS No. 213); supplemental – and optional – are Protocols 1 (ETS No. 009), 4 (ETS No. 046), 6 (ETS No. 114), 7 (ETS No. 117), 12 (ETS No. 177), 13 (ETS No. 187) and 16 (ETS No. 214).

https://doi.org/10.1515/9783111075693-015

ECHR) and the right to life (Art. 2 ECHR), in combination with the jurisprudence of the European Court of Human Rights (ECtHR) which interprets the Convention dynamically as "a living instrument,"[4] create a normative structure of the highest importance also in the domain of criminal justice.[5] As famously coined by Christine Van den Wyngaert, human rights serve both as a shield and as a sword in criminal justice:[6] on the one hand, such provisions shield individuals against excessive provisions of criminal law, excessive sanctions, and misuse of the criminal process, for example, for political persecution. On the other hand, human rights also oblige states to protect individuals, including by means of criminal investigations against those individuals who infringe upon the rights of others. Still, there remains much "margin of appreciation"[7] for the formerly 47, since Russia's suspension and subsequent withdrawal 46 nation-states that are bound by the ECHR – from Ukraine to Portugal, from the United Kingdom to Turkey and Georgia, from Norway to Malta.

Within the framework of the CoE, a multitude of further treaties under international law were tabled and then signed and ratified by fluctuating groups of European and sometimes non-European states. In relation to criminal justice,[8] their focus was, at first, to strengthen the transnational cooperation, such as when criminals flee across borders (European Convention on Extradition[9]) or when evidence required for a criminal trial is located abroad (European Convention on Mutual Assistance in Criminal Matters[10]). Later on, the focus shifted to topical treaties, such as the landmark Convention on Cybercrime,[11] which contains minimum standards states have to implement with regard to (a) criminal law provisions against cybercrime, (b) criminal procedural rules to investigate cybercrime, and (c) international cooperation in the investigation and prosecution of cybercrime.

4 See Robert Esser, *Europäisches und Internationales Strafrecht*, 2nd ed. (Munich: C.H. Beck, 2018), § 9 mn. 129; Helmut Satzger, *International and European Criminal Law*, 2nd ed. (Munich: C.H. Beck, 2018), § 9 mn. 20.

5 For an overview, see Kai Ambos, *Internationales Strafrecht. Strafanwendungsrecht, Völkerstrafrecht, Europäisches Strafrecht, Rechtshilfe*, 5th ed. (Munich: C.H. Beck, 2018), § 10 mn. 11–141; Esser, *Europäisches Strafrecht*, § 9; Satzger, *European Criminal Law*, § 9; Edward Schramm, *Internationales Strafrecht: Strafanwendungsrecht, Völkerstrafrecht, Europäisches Strafrecht*, 2nd ed. (Munich: C.H. Beck, 2018), 93–128.

6 Cf. Françoise Tulkens, "The Paradoxical Relationship between Criminal Law and Human Rights," *Journal of International Criminal Justice* 9 (2011): 577–595, 578.

7 See Satzger, *European Criminal Law*, § 9 mn. 20.

8 For an overview, see Ambos, *Internationales Strafrecht*, § 11 mn. 2–4, § 12 mn. 10.

9 ETS No. 024, with additional protocols in ETS No. 086, 098, 209, 212.

10 ETS No. 030, with additional protocols in ETS No. 099, 182.

11 ETS No. 185, with additional protocols in ETS No. 189, 224.

In contrast to the fragmented and nation-state-oriented approach within the CoE, the European Union (EU) with its currently 27 Member States strives for an "ever closer union among the peoples of Europe" (Art. 1 Treaty on European Union [TEU]). According to its normative basis, it is

> founded on the values of respect for human dignity, freedom, democracy, equality, the rule of law and respect for human rights, including the rights of persons belonging to minorities. These values are common to the Member States in a society in which pluralism, non-discrimination, tolerance, justice, solidarity and equality between women and men prevail. (Art. 2 TEU)[12]

A strong interplay with criminal law began in 1989, when, to put it simply, the European Court of Justice (ECJ) called upon Greece to utilize criminal law against subsidies fraud – to the detriment of the financial interests of the (then) European Communities – in the same way Greece utilized criminal law to protect its own financial interests.[13]

While the protection of the EU budget in particular and of the EU financial interests in general remains a core topic of EU criminal justice,[14] the thematic extension from a (more) economy-oriented community to "an ever closer union" has also left its footprints on criminal justice:[15] Although the EU, as of today, has enacted neither provisions of criminal law nor a code of criminal procedure on its own, it strives to establish an "Area of Freedom, Security and Justice" (AFSJ) "with appropriate measures with respect to [. . .] the prevention and combating of crime" (Art. 3 [2] TEU).[16] Broadly speaking, the EU utilizes, in furtherance of this goal, the following modes of integration in the field of criminal justice.[17]

12 On the fundamental importance of this provision, see recently ECJ [Full Court], judgment of February 16, 2022 – C-156/21 = ECLI:EU:C:2022:97.

13 ECJ, judgment of September 21, 1989 – 68/88 = ECLI:EU:C:1989:339.

14 In relation to substantive criminal law, see Directive (EU) 2017/1371 of the European Parliament and of the Council of July 5, 2017, on the fight against fraud to the Union's financial interests by means of criminal law.

15 I will exclude measures of quasi-criminal law – such as cartel law enforcement by the European Commission, or a hybrid model of sanctioning violations of the General Data Protection Regulation (GDPR) – in this contribution. On such matters, see recently Vanessa Franssen and Christopher Harding, eds., *Criminal and Quasi-criminal Enforcement Mechanisms in Europe* (Oxford: Hart, 2022).

16 For a recent overview, see Sergio Carrera, Deirdre Curtin, and Andrew Geddes, eds., *20 Year Anniversary of the Tampere Programme: Europeanisation Dynamics of the EU Area of Freedom, Security and Justice* (San Domenico di Fiesole: European University Institute, 2020).

17 For more detail, cf. André Klip, *European Criminal Law: An Integrative Approach*, 4th ed. (Cambridge: Intersentia, 2021); Satzger, *European Criminal Law*, §§ 5–8; Schramm, *Internationales Strafrecht*, 129–212.

The EU has enacted minimum standards in relation to various areas of substantive criminal law – such as racism and xenophobia,[18] money laundering,[19] and trafficking in human beings[20] (cf. Art. 83 TFEU) –, and more recently in relation to aspects of procedural rights of victims *and* the accused (cf. Art. 82 [2] TFEU), for instance in relation to their right to interpretation and translation.[21] These minimum standards, if enacted as Directives (and not as mere so-called "soft law"), are binding upon Member States, which then have to bring their national laws in alignment with the requirements of Union law; therefore, this mode of integration is best described as "harmonization."

Such "harmonization" of substantive and procedural norms also helps to build "mutual trust" between the various criminal justice systems within the EU, and therefore to bolster transnational cooperation. That cooperation aims to balance the need to enforce criminal justice with increased and easier travel across borders within the EU and is founded on a "principle of mutual recognition of judgments and judicial decisions" (Art. 82 [1] TFEU). This means that, generally speaking, judgments and decisions such as arrest warrants should be recognized and executed consistently, regardless of whether they are issued in the same or in another EU Member State. The legal instruments implementing this principle, such as the European Arrest Warrant[22] and the European Evidence Order,[23] indeed require other Member States to execute such warrants and orders unless they can refer to a specific ground for refusal contained in Union law.[24] Similarly increased cooperation can also be seen in police matters (see Art. 87 TFEU), for instance in relation to information exchange between police agencies across the EU. Going beyond cooperation

---

18 Council Framework Decision 2008/913/JHA of November 28, 2008, on combating certain forms and expressions of racism and xenophobia by means of criminal law. Notably, present EU primary law does not allow amending this Framework Decision. However, a proposal to modify EU primary law to include hate crimes in the list of "Eurocrimes" has recently been launched by the European Commission; see COM (2021) 777 final of December 9, 2021.

19 Directive (EU) 2018/1673 of the European Parliament and of the Council of October 23, 2018, on combating money laundering by criminal law.

20 Directive 2011/36/EU of the European Parliament and of the Council of April 5, 2011, on preventing and combating trafficking in human beings and protecting its victims, and replacing Council Framework Decision 2002/629/JHA.

21 Directive 2010/64/EU of the European Parliament and of the Council of October 20, 2010, on the right to interpretation and translation in criminal proceedings.

22 Council Framework Decision of June 13, 2002, on the European arrest warrant and the surrender procedures between Member States.

23 Directive 2014/41/EU of the European Parliament and of the Council of April 3, 2014, regarding the European Investigation Order in criminal matters.

24 Setting aside views taken, in particular, by national constitutional courts that a national constitutional "identity" may provide for additional grounds for refusal.

between institutions of the Member States, the European institutions of Eurojust (Art. 85 TFEU) and Europol (Art. 88 TFEU) aid in the coordination of criminal investigations and prosecutions, yet do not (broadly speaking) exert state powers themselves directly.

This aspect has changed with a new institution launched by 22 of the 27 EU Member States in June 2021 on the basis of Art. 86 TFEU. The European Public Prosecutor's Office (EPPO) investigates and prosecutes criminal offenses and brings them to justice before national criminal courts.[25] Although its scope has been thus far limited to offenses protecting the financial interests of the EU (such as subsidies fraud and corruption), first political steps have been taken to expand that scope to other types of crime, in particular transnational terrorism.[26]

While the normative framework and influences by the CoE and the EU encompass the core of what commonly is called European Criminal Justice, there is an increasing awareness that national criminal law must be interpreted *with* Europe, that is, with European values and with the idea of Europe in mind. For instance, it is a violation of German criminal law if one fails to render assistance in case of an accident or emergency (§ 323c [1] German Penal Code). But does this also relate to accidents and emergencies which happen across the border? If one takes European integration into account, the answer is a clear "yes" – at least within the European Union.[27]

2 Current Challenges in European Criminal Justice

Even if we focus on the EU as the forum of closest integration, a number of challenges are evident in current European Criminal Justice.

First and foremost, the very foundations of the EU are shaken by continuing challenges to the values enshrined in Art. 2 TEU, in particular relating to the protection of human rights, the rule of law, and specifically judicial independence, notably

25 Council Regulation (EU) 2017/1939 of October 12, 2017, implementing enhanced cooperation on the establishment of the European Public Prosecutor's Office ('the EPPO').

26 COM (2018) 641 final of September 12, 2018.

27 See Dorothea Magnus, "Unterlassene Hilfeleistung gegenüber Covid-19-Patienten über die Landesgrenze hinaus?," *Zeitschrift für Internationale Strafrechtswissenschaft* 1.1 (2022): 106–112; Dominik Brodowski, "Strafrechtliche Verhaltenspflichten in Zeiten der Covid-19-Pandemie: Europäisch-transnationale Perspektive statt (Re-)Nationalisierung des strafrechtlichen Lebensschutzes" in *Pandemisches Virus – nationales Handeln: Covid-19 und die europäische Idee*, ed. Brodowski, Jonas Nesselhauf, and Florian Weber (Wiesbaden: Springer VS, 2023), 251–270.

in Hungary and Poland.[28] Yet a well-functioning national judiciary, independent of other branches of government, is essential for the current model of European Criminal Law, which makes significant use of harmonization, cooperation, coordination, and supranationalization while still relying to a large extent on national criminal justice systems.[29] Unlike in (former or present) CoE members as Russia[30] and Turkey,[31] a misuse of criminal prosecution for political persecution is not (yet?) apparent in EU Member States. Nonetheless, this deterioration threatens to undermine a sufficient level of "mutual trust" between the Member States and their respective criminal justice systems – and therefore the basis for the close cooperation under the model of mutual recognition.

The reliance on the principle of mutual recognition[32] is also criticized, as its focus is on nation-states and not on the whole EU,[33] and because it places too much trust in the criminal justice system which issues requests for evidence-gathering and arrests, and their "blind" execution throughout the EU.[34] Indeed, a system of mutual recognition comes with the risk that other Member States become "blind" aiders and abettors in the execution of excessive criminal norms enacted in one Member State. Therefore, as I have already pointed out elsewhere, judicial checks in the state executing arrest warrants or evidence orders "should not only be seen as a hindrance to 'combat' crime, but as a strength of an area of freedom, security and justice," in particular when we consider "which forum can best assess the situation, and [as] sometimes two checks might be better than only one."[35] Moreover, more coordination may be required to "set out clear, non-ambiguous standards to citizens on what freedoms they enjoy [across the Union], what conduct is prohibited, and what punishment in what Member State they will face" for a given violation.[36]

A third challenge worth pointing out is that European integration in the field of criminal justice occurs at different speeds. As already noted above, there is a high degree of fragmentation with respect to the CoE, as its various conventions only

28 See recently ECJ [Full Court], judgment of February 16, 2022 – C-156/21 = ECLI:EU:C:2022:97.
29 Ulrich Sieber, "Die Zukunft des Europäischen Strafrechts," *Zeitschrift für die gesamte Strafrechtswissenschaft* 121.1 (2009): 1–67, 16–63; Brodowski, "European Criminal Justice – from Mutual Recognition to Coherence" in *20 Year Anniversary of the Tampere Programme*, 225–238, 229.
30 See ECtHR, judgment of October 17, 2017 – No. 101/15 (Navalnyye v. Russia).
31 See ECtHR, judgment of January 25, 2022 – No. 27684/17 (Yücel v. Turkey).
32 See recently Christoph Burchard, *Die Konstitutionalisierung der gegenseitigen Anerkennung* (Frankfurt a.M.: Klostermann, 2019).
33 Cf. Klip, *European Criminal Law*, 634–635.
34 Cf. Klip, *European Criminal Law*, 638–639.
35 Brodowski, "European Criminal Justice," 232.
36 Brodowski, "European Criminal Justice," 232.

bind those specific states which have signed each respective treaty. But within the EU there is incoherence as well: Denmark has opted-out of the AFSJ altogether; Ireland selects the measures it wants to participate in ("opt-in"); three further Member States have, so far, declined to participate in the spearhead of European Criminal Justice, the EPPO; and the level of Member States' compliance with binding EU rules is differing. While progressing at different speeds in European integration has clear advantages, in particular if it follows concentric circles, it comes at the risk of incoherence, imbalance, and cherry-picking.

3 Outlook: Protecting 'Europe' by – and within – Criminal Justice

Despite such challenges, we should not tire of reminding ourselves of the values of a "European" approach to criminal justice – values which are intertwined, yet resemble the "shield and sword" metaphor coined by Christine Van den Wyngaert.

On one side, European Criminal Justice serves as a "sword" to defend "Europe." This is most evident in the protection of the financial interests of the EU, where harmonized provisions of substantive criminal law are enforced by a supranational prosecutorial institution, the EPPO. In relation to specific, finance-related interference and misuse, criminal justice serves to defend the EU and its institutions, financial resources, and decision-making processes. In other areas, the protection of Europe as an institution – for example, against corruption – and European values (as enshrined in Art. 2 TEU) – for example, against racism and xenophobia – is executed on the national level, but in a Europeanized setting and with close transnational cooperation. It seems important to strengthen European Criminal Justice in particular in such areas where "Europe," European institutes, European values, and the European idea are at stake – up to and including acts endangering or violating peace in Europe.[37]

On the other side, European Criminal Justice also serves as a "shield" to defend "Europe" within criminal justice: European Criminal Justice is built upon the foundations of human rights – including the right to a fair trial (Art. 6 ECHR), the right to liberty and security (Art. 5 ECHR), and the proportionality principle[38] – and the

---

37 So far, EU activities focus on assisting either the International Criminal Court (e.g., on the basis of an Agreement between the International Criminal Court and the European Union on cooperation and assistance) or national judicial systems in prosecuting crimes under international criminal law.

38 See recently ECJ, Judgment of October 6, 2021 – C-35/20 = ECLI:EU:C:2021:813.

rule of law. Whenever these principles and guarantees are violated in Europe – also in seemingly purely national situations by national criminal justice systems – European values and thereby Europe itself are violated. It is therefore the task of *all* institutions of European Criminal Justice – ranging from the courts to the legislators – to protect and preserve these European values in criminal justice, and to also make national criminal justice all over Europe ever more European.

Tetyana Dagovych

The Inaccessible Rule-of-Law Paradise: Europe and Law in Modern Belarusian Poetry

Belarus, although historically and geographically intertwined with Central Europe, was once a terra incognita, an overlooked and forgotten country for most Western Europeans. However, the mass protests triggered by the manipulated presidential election in summer 2020 forced Europeans to suddenly take notice of the country, where the self-proclaimed president Lukashenko, often referred to as "Europe's last dictator," has been in power for almost three decades. Furthermore, the man-made refugee crisis at the border between Belarus and the EU drew global attention to the nation. In this context, the following questions naturally arise: How do Belarusians identify themselves? What image(s) of Europe do they harbor?

This essay seeks to establish some answers to these questions through the lens of modern Belarusian poetry. Poetry in Belarus is not merely a marginal art enjoyed by a select group of intellectuals; published during and after the protests on non-governmental websites, poems were, and still are, widely read and shared on social networks. In a seemingly unwinnable situation, such literature inspires Belarusians to maintain hope. It reflects experiences of detention, fear, violence, torture, the death of friends – but also faith, solidarity, love, and hope. This paper will therefore engage with a poetry collection which emerged on the Belarusian website *wir.by* in 2020, in five parts: "Summer at the Shore of Freedom" [Лета на беразе Волі], "Voices of June" [Галасы жніўня], "The Call of Belarus" [Званок Беларусі], "The Choir of my People" [Хор майго народа], and "100 and 1 Days of Fighting" [100 і 1 дзень барацьбы],[1] as well as "My European Poem" by Julia Cimafiejeva, published in this volume.[2] As this poem has been intended to be read by Europeans, it has not been translated, but written in English.

The oblivion and the lack of distinction from Russia is reflected by Ihar Kulikoŭ [Ігар Кулікоў] in his poem "Belarus."[3] The speakers of the poem, represented

1 Translations of the titles are mine. The whole collection is available on the following website: <https://wir.by/be/collection/vierszy2020>. Unfortunately, the domain is instable, but the content can still be retrieved from the Web Archive, <https://web.archive.org/>. Most poems are written in Belarusian, although some are in Russian.

2 Julia Cimafiejeva, "My European Poem," this volume, 389–391.

3 Ігар Кулікоў, "Беларусь," (n.d.), *Званок Беларусі* <https://wir.by/be/article/kaniec-leta2020/> (acc. March 10, 2022), n. pag.; my translation.

https://doi.org/10.1515/9783111075693-016

by the pronoun *we*, have been citizens of the Republic of Belarus (and therefore live in the geographical heart of Europe) for nearly thirty years. Nevertheless, in spite of this legal status, they are repeatedly asked when they are abroad – and here the poet switches to broken English –, "You from Russia?" The speakers initially try to deny this allegation, but doing so appears increasingly futile, and they accept the false denotation as "From Russia." Afterwards, they attempt to dispel their own doubts about their identity by holding on to their passport, *propiska* (residence record), Chernobyl, and the history of their land. However, as a result of the new and painful experience of the protests, they are now aware that not only are they from Belarus, but that Belarus is in their very souls. It is in such a vein that the 'lyrical *we*,' which the reader encounters in numerous poems in the collection, emerges: this is the *we* of the newly born civil society.

The aforementioned poem highlights – as does a poem by Artur Kamaroŭski [Артур Камароўскі] which this paper subsequently discusses[4] – the fact that Belarus is geographically located in the center of Europe. However, in other poems, Europe is portrayed, in personified fashion, as a happy, powerful, and mysterious *Other*, with whom one frenetically seeks contact – both abroad and sometimes at home – and who remains mostly out of reach. This ambivalence is crucial for understanding the tragic worldview of modern Belarusian poetry, as well as for understanding the migration crisis on the EU border in 2021. Even Belarus at first seemed extremely attractive for migrants as an ostensible part of an imagined Europe, before they would painfully learn what Belarusians have long known: that geographical location alone is not the determining factor in terms of belonging to what is considered the 'real' Europe. Generally speaking, Europe tends to be associated not just with prosperity – many Arabic states, China, and other countries are at least as rich as European states – but also with the promise of offering protection through robust human rights and the rule of law.

This ambivalence of Belarus towards Europe is subtly on display in "My European Poem." To fit in at European literary festivals, the poet has to pretend that she belongs to this 'true' Europe:

4 Артур Камароўскі, "твая самая чаканая цяжарнасць," (n.d.), *Галасы жніўня* <https://wir.by/be/article/halasy08/> (acc. March 10, 2022), n. pag.

> As if I am another person,
> As if I am like all those European poets and writers[5]

This refers to people who, being intellectuals, do not have to permanently fear for their lives or that of their friends and relatives, who have the freedom to think about other things; beautiful, fascinating, or curious things – who may freely engage with tragic themes in history or in the poetry of other countries without having to fear being threatened themselves. It is worth examining this additional notion of 'Europe' as a territory governed by justice and the rule of law in Belarusian poetry in order to find the conceptual border that separates the country from its European siblings. In any case, one thing is clear: contrary to appearance, this dividing line is not the EU border alone, as Switzerland is often perceived as 'more European' than, for instance, Hungary.

One vital theme in the poems is the law, or, more precisely, the lawlessness of modern Belarus; a situation overseen in large part by those officially obligated to protect the law within the state, namely, civil servants and the police. Special forces from "OMON" break the limits of "human law and of non-[human law],"[6] writes Kaciaryna Hłuchoŭskaja [Кацярына Глухоўская], and the broken doors in her poem become a symbol for mistreated human bodies. In the poem "The Call of Belarus,"[7] Daša Bialkievič [Даша Бялькевіч] broaches the subjects of harassment, abuse, and violence by the authorities, and the fear which one feels when phoning someone, and there is still no reply after the fifth beep. She asserts the absence of conscience and law, which she describes as a fall to rock bottom. Additionally, Julia Cimafiejeva posits:

> Shall I take it calmly that I
> Could be beaten and ultimately
> Found guilty for that
> Because (They would say)
> I cried antistate slogans like "Freedom!"
> Or "Release all political prisoners!"
> Though I would not need to cry them out at all
> (Like my Facebook friends and thousands of
> Someone else's friends)
> In order to be arrested or beaten.[8]

---

5 Julia Cimafiejeva, "My European Poem," this volume, 390.

6 Кацярына Глухоўская, "Выламаныя дзверы," (n.d.), *Лета на беразе Волі* <https://wir.by/be/article/leta2020/> (acc. March 10, 2022), n. pag.; my translation.

7 Даша Бялькевіч, "Званок Беларусі," (n.d.), *Званок Беларусі* <https://wir.by/be/article/kaniec-leta2020/> (acc. March 10, 2022), n. pag.; my translation.

8 Julia Cimafiejeva, "My European Poem," this volume, 389.

The answer to Cimafiejeva's question can be found in a poem by Taćciana Svietašova [Таццяна Светашова].[9] Her lyrical subject knows that, born in Belarus, he is guilty by default. He has many skills: he knows the regulations, he knows how to behave when being arrested, how to hide his phone number or messages. But at least – and here Svietašova uses legal language – he is provided with the record of interrogation and he does not accept it. Although he is guilty by default, he eventually chooses not to plead guilty.

In this poem, one can detect the same protest against statelessness as in the poem by Kulikoŭ. In his poem, the nation state is missing and ultimately created by its citizens, whilst Svietašova's misses the constitutional state with its inherent lawfulness, with its option to plead not guilty if one has not broken the law.

The lawlessness itself is terrifying, potentially even more so than unjust laws. A citizen cannot predict what will happen to them at any given moment, and whether any regulation, or limit to state power, will protect them. Even without shouting any slogans, one can still be arrested und beaten. Unlike countries such as Saudi Arabia, which have laws that actually constitute human rights violations and do not pretend to be democratic, Belarus is ostensibly still a Republic and the arbitrariness of the law there leads to the legally inconsistent and chaotic creation of new regulations against the principle of *nulla poena sine lege praevia*, or to detentions and tortures without any degree of control or accountability. On account of these unstable conditions, fear of such an arbitrary system, and the surmounting of it, are prominent issues in many poems. Vol´ha Hronskaja [Вольга Гронская] speaks about the country "where we are afraid to live, but where we want to live."[10]

In such a vein, fear caused by the capriciousness of violence becomes the boundary between 'Europe' and 'non-Europe' (some EU citizens also had to experience this fear in Belarus, as the Ryanair Flight 4978 was suddenly diverted, and they neither knew what would happen to them nor had they any recall to legal advice). For this reason, Cimafiejeva has found she could only speak about her fear and hope in 'European' languages, not in Russian, not in Ukrainian, not in Belarusian. It is in Europe that she has the right to be afraid or to be hopeful.

Europe is, for Cimafiejeva and for many other Belarusians, a place where people have clearly defined rights; hence it is understood as the land of human rights, the land of the rule of law, and the land of freedom, considered not as anarchy, but as a fair distribution of opportunities and limitations. In this sense, Europe is not

9 Таццяна Светашова, "Я нарадзіўся тут," (n.d.), *Лета на беразе Волі* <https://wir.by/be/article/leta2020/> (acc. March 10, 2022), n. pag.

10 Вольга Гронская, "Тут, дзе адвечную песню пяе Белавежа," (n.d.), *Хор майго народа* <https://wir.by/be/article/chor/> (acc. March 10, 2022), n. pag.; my translation.

merely the EU, as Norwegian, for example, is not an EU language. Conversely, the languages of the Baltic states *are* EU languages, but the poet is not convinced about their belonging to 'true' European languages: the native speakers of them have had too many past negative experiences of fear and lawlessness to ascribe such languages to the alleged ideal of 'Europeanness.'

For Andrej Chadanovič [Андрэй Хадановіч], Europe is also the symbolic territory of lawfulness. In his poem "The Letter for the Past,"[11] he deplores the lawlessness of Belarus under Lukashenko, but is convinced that in the future, Europe will share lawfulness and freedom with the new Belarus.

In contrast, Artur Kamaroŭski[12] is merely worried about the acceptance of his country by Europe(ans). His poem is very metaphoric: in the middle of Europe lies a woman in labor; the speakers, again represented by the plural pronoun *we*, are surrounding her, being her older children. The birth is very painful and dangerous. The woman is Belarus, the speakers are the Belarusian people, and the expected baby is the future of the country. The speakers are worried about the child's future: if it is too frail, will it be accepted in kindergarten and school, along with the other European children? Or will the little girl[13] be doomed to repeat the unfortunate destiny of her mother and marry a violent abuser, such as 'the Father?'[14] The jury is out.

In a lawless dictatorship, the normative order could only be constituted by prohibitions, and never by rights, and the poet picks a prohibition as a central theme for another poem, "I Am the Forbidden Flag."[15] The poem begins with the line "I am the forbidden flag in the land of allowed violence." The speaker describes himself once as a rainbow flag of the LGBT community, and once as a white-red-white flag of the Belarusian opposition. Those who are loyal to the regime persecute both incarnations of the "forbidden flag" with the same ferocity. The prohibition of the symbols of human rights and the simultaneous allowing of physical violence both embody the opposite of the European legal model.

The absurdity of such 'normative orders' is highlighted by the Belarusian-Russian writer Saša Filipenko [Саша Филипенко] in this poetry collection. His

11 Андрэй Хадановіч, "Ліст да былога," (n.d.), *Лета на беразе Волі* <https://wir.by/be/article/leta2020/> (acc. March 10, 2022), n. pag.; my translation.

12 Камароўскі, "твая самая чаканая цяжарнасць."

13 In Belarusian, the term for future – "будучыня" – is grammatically feminine; that is why the baby must be female in the allegory.

14 "Бацька" – the Belarusian word for "Father" – has long been used as an ironical denomination of Lukashenko.

15 Артур Камароўскі, "я і ёсць забаронены сцяг," (n.d.), *100 і 1 дзень барацьбы* <https://wir.by/be/article/viershy-listapad/> (acc. March 10, 2022), n. pag.; my translation.

short prosaic text “Tourist Guide to Minsk”[16] ironically explains to foreign visitors the rules to be respected. While one may run in sweatpants with a gun (like an undercover police agent), it is illegal to walk in a dress with flowers in hand. It is acceptable to destroy monuments, but prohibited to paint graffiti. If one is bothered by an aggressive man, one should not argue with him, because that person is a policeman. The speaker offers advice about clothes: one should take a down jacket to Belarus. The reason is not to protect oneself from the cold, but simply that a down jacket is more comfortable when one has to sleep in prison. The poem concludes by the address, “Welcome to Belarus, it is possible that you will not be detained, because all prisons are full.”[17] Sometimes the sheer arbitrariness of the system can give a person the chance they need.

For many young Belarusians, Belarus is – according to its geographic location – Europe, and they want to live in European Belarus, in ‘true’ Europe, enjoying human rights and a life without permanent fear. Nevertheless, the lyrical speakers in Hanna Sieviaryniec’s [Ганна Севярынец] poem[18] – one more time rendered as *we,* thereby expressing the solidarity of the people – know that the European sanctions against the dictatorship will place a heavy burden on *their* shoulders. The realistic picture, which the poet describes, is tragic and unfair: a boy picks up a grenade, thrown by a policeman, because he wants to save his friends from the explosion. It explodes at that very moment, and the authorities assign blame to him, as the grenade was in his hands. This is also the victim-blaming logic of the Belarusian government. If there were no protests, the EU would not impose new sanctions; therefore the protesters themselves are responsible and have to suffer accordingly. As the government widely controls the distribution of wealth, it is not difficult to punish those who are deemed “culpable.”

In this situation, Europe does not have many opportunities to intervene. Moreover, not all Belarusians hold this positive, even idealized image of Europe, and surely not the parents of Cimafiejeva. For them, Europe has been an enemy, perhaps since World War II.

The poem “The Council of Europe” by Dmitrij Strocev [Дмитрий Строцев][19] is a parody, imitating a conversation between “Berlin” and “Warsaw,” which was broadcast on official Belarusian TV. The European politicians portrayed in the

16 Саша Филипенко, “Путеводитель по Минску,” (n.d.), *100 і 1 дзень барацьбы* <https://wir.by/be/article/viershy-listapad/> (acc. March 10, 2022), n. pag.; my translation.

17 Филипенко, “Путеводитель по Минску,” n. pag.

18 Ганна Севярынец, “І тады хлопчык хапае рукамі гранату,” (n.d.), *Лета на беразе Волі* <https://wir.by/be/article/leta2020/> (acc. March 10, 2022), n. pag.

19 Дмитрий Строцев, “Совет Европы,” (n.d.), *Званок Беларусі* <https://wir.by/be/article/kaniec-leta2020/> (acc. March 10, 2022), n. pag.; my translation.

poem speak like the clowns Bim and Bom, a famous Russian comedy duo from the twentieth century. While the poet makes a point of satirizing the poor quality of this reproduction, it is not without palpable bitterness towards European politics.

The question is then whether Europe seriously seeks to protect global human rights or whether it just purports to do so, just as clowns purport to hold everyday conversations. European politicians permanently evince their concern at international human rights violations; nevertheless, their concerns and cautious, often belated sanctions, rarely change the situation. Moreover, migrants at the EU border would suffer not only because of the manipulations and lies of the Belarusian authority, but also because the indifference of the European authorities has persisted for too long.

In the case of Belarus, the problem goes beyond the dictatorship of Lukashenko – were he a lone actor, the EU would probably find leverage. But crucially, he is supported and protected by the Russian President Putin, also known for his antidemocratic politics. Consequently, the little bird of hope in the poem by Cimafiejeva should not sing in Russian, although, after decades of linguicide, Russian is the native language for most Belarusians. The EU, in spite of the human rights violations in Russia and the war in Donbas, not to mention the bombed hospitals in Syria, continues in its desire to cooperate with Russia, as seen in the Nord Stream 2 case.[20]

International relations are a sophisticated issue; it is crucial even for the well-being of the detainees that the EU seeks to continue the dialogue with dictators. However, one only has to look at a former German Chancellor and a former French Prime Minister, both of whom working in Russian governmental companies, to wonder whether it is really the interest of Europeans or the interests of European *politicians* that are at stake here. And yet it would be too easy to assume that the whole responsibility lies with politicians; even the interests of the 'average' citizen are often protected by unethical deals. Many jobs, not to mention the energy supply of many households, depend on good relations with dictators around the world, far beyond Europe's borders. It seems that the problem could only be resolved by rethinking the fundamental way of life enjoyed by consumer societies in European democratic states. The central question is: are Europeans willing to lower their incomes and living standards if it will help to spread justice in the world?

20 The essay was written in December 2021 and refers to the situation at that time.

Postscript: War in Ukraine

I submitted this essay in December 2021. On February 24, 2022, the Russian Federation attacked my native country Ukraine. While I am writing this postscript, on March 29, 2022, people in Ukraine are dying under Russian rockets. An important condition for the war is the support that Russia receives from China, a state with which Europe entertains very active and close cooperation. Ultimately, when it comes to doing business and not simply giving lip service, Europe turns a blind eye to the human rights violations there. However, the key condition for starting the war rests on Russia's collaboration with the Belarusian dictator Lukashenko. This collaboration is only possible because the Belarusian protesters' cries for help were hardly heard in the EU. We have read the poems, but we have done nothing. The Belarusians are saying today: "Our country is already occupied by Russia; some are in prison, others in emigration, and those who stay have no rights. We cannot do anything against the war now." The question posed at the end of my essay has thus become a question of survival for democratic Europe. Are we ready to lower our quality of life if it is necessary for democracy? In recent times, the EU and other European countries have begun to impose sanctions on Russia, which also causes people in Western and Central European countries to suffer. If we had paid this price for Belarus, there would probably not be war in Ukraine now. But the price for Ukraine is unfortunately much higher, and the sanctions are not enough to stop Putin. Once again, Europe is slow and undetermined; it helps the victims, but it does not provide enough help to those who fight for democracy. The editing of a book is a long process and I do not know how the situation will be when this essay comes to be published. Though I cannot but wonder whether the price for democracy in Germany might someday become unaffordable if we choose to sacrifice Ukraine today.

Legal Actors

In order for the rule of law to be sustained in Europe and beyond, viable legal actors and institutions are needed to secure its operations and render it enforceable. Lawyers not only play a critical role in promoting the rule of law and social order, but they are also crucial in administering or implementing the law in a manner that meets the fundamental requirements of justice, to produce just results through fair procedures and adjudication. Both contributions in this section are therefore dedicated to legal actors, the legal principles that govern their profession. More specifically, in their respective discussions, the contributions look at individual legal professionals who do not work in a principled manner and specific misrepresentations of the legal profession in general, both of which function as exemplary representations of the significance of legal actors in European law and literature.

Massimo La Torre's contribution on "Citizenship and Advocacy: The Jurist as Parrhesiast" presents the lawyer as someone who performs *parrhesia*, a fundamental component of the democracy of classical Athens. As a form of free speech, the concept demands justification, frankness, courage, and independence, all qualities crucial for the combative ethical profession of the lawyer. It is through the advocacy of the lawyer that the citizen can participate in the trial process, the lawyer acting as representative of his client and as a citizen "whose role involves special responsibility for the quality of the administration of justice."[1]

Alfred Sproede elaborates on La Torre's theoretical framework and applies it in the context of Ukrainian fiction, namely, Ivan Franko's *Fateful Crossroads* and Vynnychenko's *Notes of a Pug-Nosed Mephistopheles*. Sproede recognizes the concept of *parrhesia* in both depictions of lawyers – in fact, Franko's central character in *Fateful Crossroads* "is a more competent and multifarious agent of justice, since his professional duties lead him to become a social reformer as well."[2] Compared to Franko's novel, *Notes of a Pug-Nosed Mephistopheles* is more ambivalent; the novel's main character is a failure as a lawyer who erodes any hope of an honest, truthful treatment of court cases, but "Vynnychenko legitimizes his protagonist with the doctrine of 'honesty with oneself,'" according to Sproede.[3] Ultimately, both contributions render the legal profession crucial for the rule of law and just procedures, and individual lawyers as "capable of *parrhesia*" as well as of legal and "politically efficient truth-telling."[4]

1 Massimo La Torre, this volume, 168.

2 Alfred Sproede, this volume, 187.

3 Alfred Sproede, this volume, 205.

4 Alfred Sproede, this volume, 205.

https://doi.org/10.1515/9783111075693-017

Massimo La Torre

Citizenship and Advocacy: The Jurist as Parrhesiast

1 Ancient Greek Roots

As both an institution and living reality, citizenship has its origins in the political culture of classical Greece; especially in the history of Athens, a democratic city. There was much debate in Ancient Greek over this notion – one that is reflected in the entire cultural production of classical Greece, especially in its most revered literary expression, tragedy. Whoever wishes to study citizenship and its theory cannot avoid reading Plato and Aristotle. The *Politics* of the Stagirite, more specifically his third book, is really a treatise on citizenship. Its term in Greek, *politeia*, denotes both the constitution and the public politics of the city.[5] In that cultural context, I believe we can also sustain that citizenship makes it possible for one of antiquity's fundamental virtues, continence, *enkràteia*, ἐγκράτεια, to be turned from a private into a public virtue.

As is well known, *enkràteia* is the provision that Plato, more than once (for example in his *Republic*, 560d, or *Apology*, 412a), suggests is a central or structural virtue of good human life; and this is so because it then ensures the possibility, standing and enactment of the remaining three virtues. Continence, *enkràteia*, is, as indicated by the etymology of the Greek word, the ability to control oneself, i.e., self-control. It is, in this meaning, the opposite of unrestraint, and of *akrasía*, denoting a lack of will, letting oneself go. It is only by controlling oneself, if a person is *enkratès*, that one is validated and can then be courageous, prudent and just. Self-control, in a public capacity, becomes the faculty of self-governance; that is to say, citizenship is the ability or obligation to behave legally. Just as *continence* is the fundamental virtue of private life, likewise *citizenship* will become the fundamental virtue of political life. As Aristotle then adds, the unrestrained person is like a city setting itself good laws but not applying them (*Nicomachean Ethics*, VII, 1152 a, 20–23).

But how can we define citizenship more specifically? Aristotle answers that question in a number of his works; first and foremost in the *Constitution of the*

5 Cf. Édouard Will, *Le monde grec et l'Orient*, Vol. 1 (Paris: Presses universitaires de France, 1972), 419; Cornelius Castoriadis, *La cité et les lois: Ce qui fait la Grèce*, Vol. 2, ed. Enrique Escobar, Myrto Gondias, and Pascal Vernay (Paris: Seuil, 2008), 90.

https://doi.org/10.1515/9783111075693-018

Athenians (XXVI, 3), which declares that citizenship means "participating in the city [*metéchein tês póleos*]." The citizen "takes part" in the *res publica*. This formula ("participate," *metéchein)* recalls the relationship attributed to a thing with respect to its "essence" or "form," both in Aristotelian metaphysics (see, for example, *Metaphysics*, VII, 1037b, 18–19, and *De anima*, II, 415a, 25–415b, 7), and above all in Plato (for example in *Laches*, 197d, and in *Phaedo*, 101c, but largely in *Parmenides*, 130e–131a).[6] It also appears at an important point in the oration *Against Neera* (28) by Demosthenes, where Athenian citizens are qualified as owners of *parrhesia* as they "participate in citizenship [*metechóntas tês póleos*]."[7]

The formula therefore has a special significance. It does not simply declare that the citizen is a "part" or "member" of the city, but, above all, that the city *becomes real* in the citizen; that citizenship is the practice or element in which the "form" of the city materialises. Just consider the famous statement, "man is by nature a political animal [ζῷον πολιτικόν]" (Aristotle, *Politics*, I, 1253a). Endless discussions have revolved around this phrase,[8] where the characteristic "political" has often been translated as "social," hence: man is an animal "who lives in society." However, another more plausible translation could be the following: man is an animal "who lives in the city," or "who is a citizen," or possibly even more accurately, "is capable of citizenship."[9] Here it is instantly apparent that the civic dimension, citizenship itself, is raised to being an Archimedean property, actually qualifying the very nature of the human being.

The *city* in this world is the same as *citizenship*. For Aristotle it is the "community of citizens" (*Politics*, III, 1276b, 1–4). Thucydides shares this view (*Stories*, VII, 77, 7) in a famous statement: men are the city, *ándres gàr polis*,[10] not the walls, or empty ships.[11] Aristotle then illustrates how the citizen *takes part* in the life of the city, and he does so especially extensively in *Politics*. The *participation*

6 In this vein, cf. Francesco Fronterotta, *ΜΕΘΕΧΙΣ: La teoria platonica delle idee e la partecipazione delle cose empiriche: Dai dialoghi giovanili al Parmenide* (Pisa: Scuola Normale Superiore, 2001); Veronika Roth and Christian Schäfer, "Teilhabe/Partizipation (metochê, methexis)" in *Platon-Lexikon: Begriffswörterbuch zu Platon und der platonischen Tradition*, ed. Christian Schäfer (Darmstadt: Wissenschaftliche Buchgesellschaft, 2007), 277–282. But also see Francesco Adorno, *Introduzione a Platone* (Rome: Laterza, 2008), 153–159.

7 Cf. Giuseppe Scarpat, *Parrhesia greca, parrhesia Cristiana*, rev. ed. (Brescia: Paideia, 2001), 42–43.

8 Cf. Otfried Höffe, "zôon politikon" in *Aristoteles-Lexikon*, ed. Höffe (Stuttgart: Kröner, 2005), 620–621.

9 Cf. Humphrey Davy Findley Kitto, *The Greeks* (London: Penguin, 1991), 11.

10 Cf. Victor Ehrenberg, *The Greek State* (Oxford: Blackwell, 1960), 88–89; Castoriadis, *La cité et les lois*, 54.

11 "La *polis* non era un luogo, benché occupasse un territorio definito: era una popolazione operante di comune accordo." Moses I. Finley, *Gli Antichi Greci*, trans. Fausto Codino (Turin: Einaudi, 1965), 50.

in question is specified thus: "Citizen in an absolute sense is not defined by anything but participation in the function as judge and in offices" (*Politics*, III, 1275a, 22–25; my translation). This is with reference to: *metéchein kríseos kai archês*, of participation in judgement and power. "Who the citizen is clearly emerges from these considerations: those who have the right to take part in the office of counsellor and judge we say is without doubt citizen of the state in which he holds that right" (*Politics*, III, 1275b, 17–21; my translation).

Therefore, the core of citizenship is the right to access legislative and judicial power.[12] From this perspective, the genealogical criterion, mere family or historical "belonging" to the community, becomes less important. In fact, Aristotle expresses a certain irony regarding this point:

> They define citizen as someone who descends from parents who are both citizens and not from just one, for example from the father or the mother. And there are those who take this requisite a step further, that is, to the second and third and further still. But given that popular, coarse definition, some ask themselves: "How would that ancestor from three or four generations ago have become a citizen?" (*Politics*, III, 1275b, 23–27; my translation)

This passage is especially important, and indeed surprising in certain ways, when we recall that the basic myth of the Athenian city is one of "native" citizens: i.e., subjects born in the same land as where the city is located.[13] Such a citizenship, therefore, consists of an indissoluble mixture of blood and soil. But Aristotle goes on to question and even ridicule this myth, introducing a concept of civic participation that is no longer just based on heredity and ethnicity.

2 Citizenship as Free Speech

We can safely say that *parrhesia* (παρρησία), both as a concept and a practice, typified the political culture of Athens and of classical Greece in general.[14] There

12 In Athens, Finley writes, "il popolo non solo aveva il diritto di essere eletto a ricoprire cariche pubbliche e di eleggere a sua volta i funzionari, ma anche quello di decidere su ogni argomento di pubblico interesse e di giudicare, costituendosi in tribunale, su tutti i casi importanti, civili e penali, pubblici e privati." Finley, *La democrazia degli antichi e dei moderni*, trans. Gianni di Benedetto and Francesco de Martino (Milan: Mondadori, 1982), 25.

13 Cf. Nicole Loraux, *L'invention d'Athènes: Histoire de l'oraison funèbre dans la cité classique* (Paris: Mouton, 1981); Loraux, *Les enfants d'Athéna: Idées athéniennes sur la citoyenneté et la division des sexes* (Paris: Maspero, 1981); Loraux, *Né de la Terre: Mythe et politique à Athènes* (Paris: Seuil, 1996).

14 Foucault's examination of this concept is essential, and is alluded to again below. Two excellent studies, originally in Italian, give a useful overview: Giuseppe Scarpat, *Parrhesia greca*; Luigi Spina, *Il Cittadino alla Tribuna: Diritto e Libertà di Parola nell'Atene Democratica* (Naples:

is no record of this term before the fifth century B.C. It first appears with Euripides, is found more widely in the writings of Plato and Aristotle and is then often used by Hellenistic philosophers and writers. Finally, it features regularly in the Greek New Testament. The concept changed during this process, or rather the term underwent a shift in meaning.[15] This happened to many terms in classical Greek that later entered the language of the *Gospels* and the *Acts of the Apostles* and assumed a different sense and usage from those of the original Attic Greek.

But it is *parrhesia* in its ancient sense that defines its semantic field and establishes its historical and cultural importance in an understanding of classical Greek culture. Indeed, no other concept or term more fittingly describes the particular "spiritual moment" that occurred in that culture. In this sense, Foucault is right to describe it as a "notion-araignée"[16] or "spider-concept," as it really does create a web, containing and interconnecting the fundamental concepts behind Greek political and civic culture; and it also reflects that culture's view of the good life and the exemplary man, with a focus on free speech and liberty. And yet, in all the huge body of work about classical Greece, very little has been written about *parrhesia*.

In more than one exploration of classical Greek thought, the word and idea of *parrhesia* is not even mentioned. In fact, it has only recently become a focus of research, with many studies dedicated to this theme. This is largely due to the interest shown in the subject by Michel Foucault, during the last courses he conducted at the Collège de France, and during a series of conferences and lectures that focused specifically on *parrhesia*.[17] And so, when one examines this theme, it

---

Liguori, 1986). It is also worth consulting Arnaldo Momigliano's classic study, "La libertà di parola nel mondo antico" in *Sesto contributo alla storia degli studi classici e del mondo antico*, Vol. II, ed. Arnaldo Momigliano (Rome: Edizioni di Storia e Letteratura, 1980), 403–436; and an old, but still relevant essay by Max Radin, "Freedom of Speech in Ancient Athens," *The American Journal of Philology*, 48 (1927): 215–230. For more recent studies, see Arlene W. Saxonhouse, *Free Speech and Democracy in Ancient Athens* (Cambridge: Cambridge UP, 2006); Sara S. Monoson, *Plato's Democratic Entanglements: Athenian Politics and the Practice of Philosophy* (Princeton: Princeton UP, 2000), especially ch. 6. An important collection of essays on this theme can be found in Ineke Sluiter and Ralph M. Rosen, eds., *Free Speech in Classical Antiquity* (Leiden: Brill, 2004).

15 "Dislocation des sens," Michel Foucault calls it. Michel Foucault, *Le courage de la verité: Le gouvernement de soi et des autres II: Cours au Collège de France 1984*, ed. Frédéric Gros (Paris: Seuil/Gallimard, 2009), 177.

16 Foucault, *Le gouvernement de soi et des autres: Cours au Collège de France 1982–1983*, ed. Frédéric Gros (Paris: Seuil/Gallimard, 2008), 45.

17 The two courses that focus particularly on *parrhesia* are quoted in the preceding two footnotes. For other specific lectures about *parrhesia* delivered at Berkeley University, cf. Foucault, *Fearless Speech*, ed. Joseph Pearsons (Los Angeles: Semiotext(e), 2001). The Berkeley lectures, together with another lecture given in Switzerland, are published in the original French in Foucault, *Discours et*

is fitting to use those courses and lectures as a starting point, reviewing some of their content while also appreciating their lively, intelligent approach.

There are two main, original references to the term *parrhesia* that also deserve a mention. They occur in a fragment by the fifth-century philosopher Democritus. Unfortunately, very little of his work has survived to this day. We know that Plato never mentions him in his work, an omission that is clearly biased and suspicious. For the theoretical views held by Democritus were the mirror image of those advocated by Plato. Democritus is a materialist, but he is also and above all a democrat, as opposed to an Athenian idealist and oligarch. In fragment 226 of his writings, we find the line, "*Oikéion eleutheríes parresíe,*" which translates as "*parrhesia* is the property of freedom." This fragment is evocative and inspiring, because it indicates that the challenge of free speech should be regarded as a quintessential element of individual freedom. Freedom manifests itself in a person's ability and capacity to say what he or she wants.

But there is another fragment that is equally, or perhaps even more, significant. We only have a few remaining fragments of Euripides' tragedy *Temenides*, one of which tells us the following: "*kalon g'alethès k'athenès parresía*" (fragment 737). This could be translated as: "True and tenacious *parrhesia* is a wonderful thing." But the adjective *athenès* could also be interpreted as: excessive, intense, radical or – better still – confrontational. It would appear from this that confrontation and challenge, rather than tenacity, reflect the true character of free speech. So the following translation seems to me to offer a plausible alternative: "The challenge of free speech that itself produces freedom and tension is a wonderful thing." The fact that in this version freedom is associated with conflict and confrontation seems to me to describe the essence of parrhesiastic behaviour very well. My interpretation seems to find support in the work of Euripides, where the theme of *parrhesia* is treated and referred to quite explicitly.

The term *parrhesia* is first used in his tragedy *Ion*. Ion is a young man who is ignorant of his parentage. In particular, he is unaware that his mother is Creusa, a young Athenian woman once seduced by Apollo but now married to Xuthus. Creusa bears a son by Apollo and abandons him on the Acropolis. However, the child Ion is rescued by Hermes and then brought to the oracle of Delphi. Creusa and Xuthus come to consult the oracle about their childless marriage, and there they encounter Ion. Ion does know who his mother is, and so he says the following to Xuthus: "If it is right to pray for it, my mother would be an Athenian, so that I might have freedom

vérité, précédé de La parrêsia, ed. Henri-Paul Fruchaud and Daniele Lorenzini (Paris: Vrin, 2016). Some notes on the same theme can also be found in Foucault, *L'herméneutique du sujet: Cours au Collège de France 1981–1982*, ed. Frédéric Gros (Paris: Seuil/Gallimard, 2001).

from her to speak my mind [*parrhesia*]" (671–672).[18] In the following, he goes on to say: "If a stranger arrives in a city of unmixed race, even if he is called an inhabitant of that city [*astós*], he must restrain his tongue."[19] "And he has no freedom of speech [*kouk échei parresían*; my translation]." In this passage, the writer distinguishes between the city as a place of residence – a collection of houses and walls – and the city as a political community and group of citizens. In classical Greek, the difference is shown in the use of *ásty*, ἄστυ, for the first, and *pólis*, πόλις, for the second.[20] This difference is accentuated by the reference to an inhabitant of the city (ἀστός, *astós*) who is not a full citizen,[21] such as a woman. For unlike a citizen in the strictest sense (πολίτης, *polítes*), she has no right to freedom of speech (*parrhesia*). *Parrhesia* and citizenship form a whole; the capacity for one derives from the condition of the other.

Euripides addresses the theme again in his tragedy *The Phoenician Women*. The play is about the siege of Thebes by Polynices, deprived of his right to govern the city by his brother Eteocles. Polynices manages to sneak into the city and meet his mother Jocasta. She asks him about his status as an exile, because once he was driven from his homeland: "Well then, first I ask you what I long to have answered. What is it like to be deprived of one's country?" (387–388).[22] "Is it a great misfortune [*kakón méga*]?"[23] to which Polynices replies: "Very great [*mégiston*]; and harder to bear [*meîzon*] than tell" (389).[24] But Jocasta wants to know more: "And what is it like? What most torments the exile [*phygásin*]?" (390),[25] and Polynices replies to this further question by recalling the painful lack of freedom of speech for the exile, in what seems to me a real celebration of *parrhesia* as an essential feature of citizenship. "One thing most of all [*hèn mèn mégiston*]: he cannot speak his mind [*ouk échei parresían*]" (391); Jocasta then points out how this deprivation of freedom of expression reduces someone to a condition of servitude: "This is a slave's lot you speak of [*doúlou tód'eípas*], not to say what one thinks [*mè légein há tis phroneî*]" (392).[26]

This theme is repeated in the work of both Plato and Aristotle. But here we also see a shift in meaning that is not present in the tragedies of Euripides, nor in

18 I use the translation by Maria Serena Mirto, *Ione* (Milan: Rizzoli, 2016), 151.
19 Mirto, *Ione*, 151, slightly modified by my translation.
20 Cf. Kitto, *The Greeks*, 70–71; Castoriadis, *La cité et le lois*, 53ff.
21 On the difference between *astós* and *polítes*, cf. Claude Mossé, *Le citoyen dans la Grèce antique* (Paris: Nathan, 1993), 40.
22 I use the translation by Enrico Medda, *Euripide* (Milan: Fenicie, Rizzoli, 2018), 161.
23 Medda, *Euripide*, 161, slightly modified by my translation.
24 Medda, *Euripide*, 161, slightly modified by my translation.
25 Medda, *Euripide*, 161, slightly modified by my translation.
26 Medda, *Euripide*, 161, slightly modified by my translation.

the fragment of work by Democritus, quoted above. For both Euripides and Democritus, *parrhesia* seems to refer to a power, a capacity – or what is traditionally called a *right* – associated with citizenship or the full freedom of the individual. Plato later uses and indeed emphasises this same meaning in his work, but he also gives the term an additional significance. *Parrhesia* is seen as not just a "right" but also a *virtue*. A similar approach can be found in the work of Aristotle, who followed Plato's thinking rather closely. In the *Gorgias*, Socrates famously disagrees with Càllicles,[27] who nevertheless recognises one's ability to act as a "parrhesiast," seen here as someone who tends the soul of a third party. The passage reads as follows: "For I believe that if you wish to test a soul as to the rectitude or otherwise of his life, you require three attributes, all of which you possess: knowledge, goodwill and frankness [*epistémen te kai eunoían kai parresían*]" (487).[28] Here *parrhesia* is counted among the qualities required for someone to be a teacher, and to serve as a critical reflection on a human life. We find the same idea in the *Laches*, the dialogue about courage. Laches addresses Nicias in the following way:

> Now of Socrates' words I have no experience, but previously, I believe, I have witnessed his deeds; and there I found him living up to any fine words however freely spoken [*kai páses parresías*]. So if he has that gift as well, his wish is mine, and I should be very glad to be cross-examined by such a man, and should not baulk at learning. So if he has that gift as well, his wish is mine, and I should be very glad to be cross-examined by such a man, and should not chafe at learning. (188e–189a)[29]

Here, too, *parrhesia* is regarded as a virtue, and specifically the type of virtue possessed by one who teaches by examining the learner. The teacher here is epitomised in the figure of Socrates, whose care for himself (*epimeleia tou eautou*) – an integral part of the self-control that is recommended for the virtuous man – is sustained by his care for the other. In fact, such care presupposes *parrhesia*, the ability to tell the other frankly what he is and what he deserves: behaviour that is diametrically opposed to adulation, flattery or complacency.

Plato, however, also uses *parrhesia* in his work to describe a political situation, or a citizen's "right" or power.[30] At one point in the *Gorgias*, Socrates is addressing Polus and claims that in Athens "there is more freedom of speech than anywhere

27 On this mysterious sophist figure, cf. William Keith Chambers Guthrie, *The Sophists* (Cambridge: Cambridge UP, 1971), 101–107.

28 I use the translation by Adorno, Platone, *Gorgia* (Rome: Laterza, 1997), 99.

29 I use the translation by Giovanni Reale, Platone, *Lachete* (Milan: Bompiani, 2015), 161.

30 Aristophanes also uses the term in the sense of a public licence or political "right" in *Women at the Thesmophoria* (540).

in Greece [*Elládos pleíste estìn exousía toû légein*]" (461e; my translation).[31] The term *parrhesia* does not appear in this passage, but instead the expression *exousía toû légein*. This is essentially a synonym, or rather a definition of *parrhesia*: i.e., the license, the power or as we would say, the "right" (*exousía*) to speak (*toû légein*). If we are to understand the meaning of *parrhesia*, and above all its original and intrinsic connection with the idea and practice of democracy, the following passage from the *Republic* seems to me of particular importance in this context. It is part of the dialogue between Socrates and Glaucon, where the democratic regime is first criticised in an oblique and ironic way and then more overtly and explicitly. Here then is Socrates' description of democracy: "To begin with, are they not free? And is not the city chock-full of liberty and freedom of speech [*eleutherías he pólis mestè kai parresías gígnetai*]? And has not every man licence to do as he pleases [*kai exousía en autêi poieîn hóti ti boúletai*]?" (557b, 4–6).[32] "But where there is such licence [*Hopou dé ge exousía*], it is obvious that everyone will arrange to lead his own life in the way he chooses" (557b, 8–9; my translation). The *exousia*, the licence or right to autonomy associated with democratic citizenship, makes democracy a very unstable form of government, open to many different interpretations and constitutions: "Thanks to this licence [*dià ten exousían*], it includes all kinds of constitutions [*pánta géne politeiôn échei*]" (557d, 2; my translation).

Plato is ironic about these multiple possible constitutions, but the underlying significance of his words reveals the true character of the open, liberal society of classical Greek democracy that he is seeking to mock. Socrates states the following:

> "And maybe," I said, "this is the most attractive of the constitutions [*kallíste aúte tôn politeiôn*], like a multicoloured cloak embroidered with every shade, so that it too appears beautiful, embellished as it is with every type of character [*pepoikilméne*]. And perhaps," I said, "many would consider it beautiful, like children and women when they see coloured things." (557c, 4–9; *my translation*)

Yet, the reality is that this is not a matter for women and children, and Socrates is indicating that democratic pluralism leads inexorably to "anarchy." So, the "multicoloured" or "colourful" (*poikíle*) constitution itself becomes "anarchic" (*ánarchos*) (558c, 2–3).[33] Plato rejects the idea of free speech as a constitutional "right"

---

31 Cf. Jennifer Tolbert Roberts, *Athens on Trial: The Antidemocratic Tradition in Western Thought* (Princeton: Princeton UP, 1994), 72.

32 I use the translation by Mario Vegetti, Platone, *Repubblica* (Milan: Rizzoli 2010), 971, slightly modified by my translation.

33 On this passage by Plato, cf. Thomas A. Sinclair, *Il pensiero politico classico* (Rome: Laterza, 1961), 219–220.

or *exousia*, although he accepts it can be a virtue, while also distorting it to some extent and reducing its political importance.

And we find almost the same reasoning in the ethical and political theory of his disciple, Aristotle. For him, the virtuous man par excellence is also magnanimous, *magalópsychos*, μεγᾰλόψῡχος. He suggests in the *Nicomachean Ethics* (1124b, 28–30) that *parrhesia* is one of the most important qualities for the magnanimous man: "He should care more about truth than opinion (or good reputation), and speak and act openly [*légein kai práttein phanerôs*]"; and he adds: "He is a parrhesiast [*parresiastés*]."[34]

The theme of *parrhesia* as a specific virtue in the context of Hellenistic culture is treated in the work of Plutarch, and in particular in his essay, "How to Tell a Flatterer from a Friend" (*Moralia*, I, 261–395). Here, *parrhesia* is seen as an effective antidote to *philautia* – self-love or self-centredness – which would only be encouraged by praise or flattery. A true friend is frank in revealing his companion's faults and limitations, and so creates an impediment to self-satisfaction and a failure to universalise from one's own standards. *Parrhesia*, in the form of open and sincere criticism, provides an external viewpoint, holding up a mirror in front of a person and furnishing clear evidence of any meanness in his soul. This is the form of behaviour recommended for the teacher or philosopher, and to which the philosopher can lay a special claim. Epicurus does so, for example, when he states proudly: "I have made a study of nature in order to reveal to all men what is useful to them by means of *parrhesia* [*parresiai*]" (fragment 29; my translation). The accepted meaning of the term now seems to be "speaking openly" or "speaking frankly."

This is the meaning we find throughout the New Testament, and in Saint John's Gospel in particular. In *John* 16. 25, Jesus says that he will no longer speak in proverbs, and then he adds (in the King James Version): "but I shall shew you plainly of the Father." Here, in the original Greek, "plainly" corresponds to "with *parrhesia*" (*parresiai*). When Jesus reveals that Lazarus is dead, he again states this "plainly" (King James Version), or in the original Greek, "with *parrhesia*" (*John* 11. 14). Then there is a passage where Jesus echoes the words of Epicurus, quoted above: "I spake openly to the world [*Egò parresíai leláleka tôi kósmoi*]" (*John* 18. 20). This last passage also appears significant for another reason. "To the world" (*tôi kósmoi*) could also be translated here as "to the universe," and so could apply to everyone, or *universally*. This speaking "to the world" or "to everyone" takes on the further significance of speaking "for everyone," a more pointed and challenging meaning of *parrhesia*. The idea of "saying everything," or speaking frankly, has come to mean "speaking for everyone," and so the term has

34 I use the translation by Carlo Natali, *Etica Nicomachea* (Rome: Laterza, 1999), 149.

taken on a universal application, implying a degree of challenge to the established order and to authority. The original libertarian meaning of "free speech" seems to survive the moral and mystical gloss that appears in the context of both Hellenistic and New Testament culture.[35]

And it is in the context of Hellenistic culture that we find a reference to *parrhesia* that seems to me particularly important. It concerns a passage from the Greek Old Testament, or Septuagint. Here in *Leviticus* 26. 13, we read the following (King James Version): "I am the LORD your God, which brought you forth out of the land of Egypt, that ye should not be their bondmen; and I have broken the bands of your yoke, and made you go upright." In the Latin Vulgate Bible the passage is rendered as: "Ego Dominus Deus vester, qui eduxi vos de terra Egyptiorum, ne serviretis eis, et qui confregi vectes iugi vestri, ut incideretes erecti." The Greek version in the Septuagint reads as follows: "ἐγώ εἰμι κύριος ὁ θεὸς ὑμῶν ὁ ἐξαγαγὼν ὑμᾶς ἐκ γῆς Αἰγύπτου ὄντων ὑμῶν δούλων καὶ συνέτριψα τὸν δεσμὸν τοῦ ζυγοῦ ὑμῶν καὶ ἤγαγον ὑμᾶς μετὰ παρρησίας." Now the Greek "metà parresías" is translated as "erecti" in Latin, as "a capo erto" in Diodati's Italian version, as "la tête levee" in Calvin's French Bible, as "el rostro alto" in the *Biblia del Oso*, as "aufrecht" by Luther, as "upright" in the King James Bible and finally as "erguidos" in the Portuguese version by Ferreira de Almeida. But what is the original Hebrew? It is "qôm'mijjût": a participle meaning "upright."[36]

The idea or parable behind *parrhesia* has evolved in the following manner: essentially, it has become a way to overturn the relationship between the governor and the governed. Aristotle maintains (in *Politics*, book 3) that the citizen is someone who alternately directs and is directed, governs and is governed. But the condition of the subject who directs and is directed, governs and is governed, are apparently not discussed in this context. Now, *parrhesia* provides a way to change these alternative scenarios. The relationship between authority and the subject is in some ways overturned, introducing a sort of right to "subversion": not so much subversion of the community, but rather of the relationships within in the community. The task of authority is to govern, but it should also accept challenging words from subordinates. This changes the relationship with the authority itself, making it no longer a matter of a single sovereign power, but opening it to participation and conflict with the other. Accordingly, the subject is emancipated, becoming a real citizen. *Parrhesia* in this sense remains the central meaning of the term,

---

35 Cf. Heinrich Schlier, "παρρησία, παρρησιάζομαι" in *Theologisches Wörterbuch zum Neuen Testament*, ed. Gerhard Kittel and Gerhard Friedrich, Vol. 5 (Stuttgart: Kohlhammer, 1954), 869–884. Also see Erik Peterson, "Zur Bedeutungsgeschichte von Παρρησία" in *Zur Theorie des Christentums: Festschrift für R. Seeberg*, Vol. 1, ed. Wilhelm Koepp (Leipzig: Deichert, 1929), 283–297.

36 Cf. Scarpat, *Parrhesia greca*, 92.

despite all the various shifts that have taken place. It denotes the power, capacity and "right" that is an essential part of being free and, better still, of being a citizen.

As a result, *parrhesia*, or frank speaking, is classed as a special virtue, and also as a sort of "stochastic" art (one dependent on circumstances), similar to navigation or medicine. There are at least three possible variations. The first refers to a gift and technique for teaching and spiritual guidance (already suggested in Plato's *Gorgias* or *Lachetes*, and then officially recognised by Philodemus). For Plato, *parrhesia* is an epistemic virtue, which principally helps to promote knowledge. For Philodemus, who devotes a treatise entitled *Perí Parrhesías* to this theme, it is an existential virtue or art, beneficial for the care and salvation of the soul, and important for maintaining its tranquillity. This is illustrated in the particular art of the Prince's adviser, who uses it as a way to counteract the tyrant's propensity for *philautia*, or self-love.[37] *Parrhesia* also refers to a specific style of speech in the art of oratory, the *free speech* as described by Quintilian (*Institutio Oratoria*, IX. 2. 27):[38] the art of speaking frankly, without too many embellishments or similes, as Jesus himself speaks in Saint John's Gospel. *Parrhesia* becomes the opposite of a seductive way of speaking and takes on the more general meaning of rhetoric itself. It is forthright speech, which does not seek to persuade, but rather to shock and convince. This is a technique deployed by the teacher to educate his disciple, encouraging him to know and take care of himself.[39] Finally, it is a device used within a hierarchical relationship, a paternalistic way of managing one's inferiors. Here, it is no longer a way for an inferior to resist or defy his superior, giving him equal dignity and rights – as was essentially the political practice in democratic Attica.

In short, the parable behind the idea starts with its original significance, the meaning found in Euripides' tragedies. Here, *parrhesia* is a citizen's "right," making him truly free; it is a form of public licence, which is basically used in the public sphere, involving the figure of authority and the subject who confronts him or her. But it is not just the right to free speech. This is already enshrined in the culture of classical Athens in the idea of ισηγορία (*isegory*), meaning the equal right to deliberate in the assembly – as the etymology of the word itself suggests.[40] *Parrhesia* means something more than *isegory*, and indeed references

37 Cf. Foucault, "La parrêsia" in *Discours et vérité*, 33–35.

38 Cf. Foucault, "La parrêsia," 33.

39 Cf. Foucault, *L'hermeneutique du sujet: Cours au Collège de France 1981–1982*, 350–351, 356ff.

40 Cf. Guido Fassò, *La Democrazia in Grecia* (Milan: Giuffrè, 1999), 26ff. But see also the following description by Arnaldo Momigliano: "*Isegoria* was not necessarily a democratic virtue: it meant equality of rights in relation to freedom of speech and could easily be applied to a limited number of aristocrats." Momigliano, "Freedom of Speech in Antiquity" in *Dictionary of the History of Ideas*, ed. Philip P. Wiener (New York: Charles Scribner's Sons, 1980), 427.

to the term seem to occur later than those to *isegory*. Moreover, *parrhesia* has a more *forceful* meaning. It is not only formal freedom of speech, but is also the capacity and licence to use brazen and cutting discourse, which is free to challenge authority without fear or reservations. *Isegory* only becomes truly democratic thanks to *parrhesia*, and so these two powers or "rights" can be considered "les deux traits fondamentaux du citoyen"[41] in Athenian democracy.

Meanwhile, *parrhesia* is a licence and indeed a "constitutional right," and central to the business of self-understanding in Athenian democracy.[42] Consequently, the equal right to speak, the egalitarian intention of *isegory*, is given effective power by *parrhesia*, or actual freedom of speech. The latter was not limited to equal licence to participate in discourse and deliberation, but rather endowed this licence with particular, targeted force, aimed at subverting the hierarchy which traditionally formed the background to discourse and deliberation. In the case of classical Athens, for example, it was still evident in the way the city was divided into classes according to the census,[43] or how those with expertise in governing would be appointed to a particular office or magistracy or the fact that superior status was always associated with a better education or a richer and more noble family.

3 The Dual Dimension of Lawyering

Advocacy is a problematic activity when it comes to institutions and norms. It reflects the dual character of law, which moves between a real dimension, that of facts and efficacy, and an ideal dimension, that of accepted norms or standards – or, if you like, of justice.[44] The law aims to be effective in regulating the behaviour

---

41 Castoriadis, "La 'polis' grecque et la création de la démocratie" in *Domaines de l'homme: Les carrefours du labyrinthe*, ed. Castoriadis (Paris: Seuil, 1999), 368.

42 It is interesting to note in this context that there was a trireme called "Parrhesia" in the Athenian battle fleet. On the one hand, there is no evidence of a vessel being called "Isonomia" or "Isegoria"; cf. Mogens Herman Hansen, *Die Athenische Demokratie im Zeitalter des Demosthens: Struktur, Prinzipien und Selbstverständnis* (Berlin: Akademie Verlag, 1995), 84. On the other hand, in a text by Aeschines (*Ctesiphon*, 6) the judicial procedure against an attempt to change the constitution (the *graphaì paranómon*) is linked to protecting the basic right to *parrhesia*; cf. Sinclair, *A History of Greek Political Thought* [1967] (New York: Routledge, 2012), 220. See also Castoriadis, "La 'polis' grecque," 373–374.

43 As known, the four classes were *pentakosiomedimnoi*, *hippeis*, *zeugitai* and *thetes*. Cf. Hansen, *Die Athenische Demokratie*, 108ff.

44 Cf. Massimo La Torre, *Il giudice, l'avvocato e il concetto di diritto* (Soveria Mannelli: Rubbettino, 2012), especially ch. 2.

of members of society, and it must therefore have a considerable basis in facts. A rule that was frequently either not applicable or violated could hardly be classed as part of a workable system of law. Law has a judicial dimension, which cannot be explained without reference to material facts. On the other hand, law refers to what "should be" as opposed to what "is," and aims to transform the latter to comply with a set of values and principles. The gap between that which "should be" according to the law and that which "is" in actual human behaviour is the basis for the very existence of law. If what "is" always corresponded to what "should be" according to the law, then the law itself would be superfluous. The law operates within the fissures of this relationship between "is" and "should be," so between the real and ideal dimensions. Conversely, a system in which all the rules of conduct were disobeyed, but still inexorably followed by punishment, could hardly be described as a functioning juridical order.

Here we should note a rather unusual fact in relation to the theory and history of law. Philosophy and legal theory have not made much mention of the lawyer, at least in the modern legal context. When legal theory does turn its attention to experts operating in the legal field, it generally only focuses on three specific roles: those of the legislator, the judge and the doctor of law, i.e., the professor. The lawyer's role is not considered. His role is not discussed in analytical jurisprudence, or in Savigny's legal dogmatics or indeed in the contemporary legal positivism of Herbert Hart and Hans Kelsen. "Legal realism" mainly centres on the role of the judge, and the lawyer is generally depicted as a purely strategic player predicting the moves of the judge: the true ruler over the law. The reason for this silence, or scant attention to the role of the lawyer by modern philosophers (and also those writing in antiquity), probably originates in the idea of a law that is first set out and then subjected to critical analysis. It is generally a concept that focuses on the function of decision-making and to a lesser extent that of describing. This dualistic approach is supported by a restricted philosophy of language, which admits only two basic functions: the descriptive function and the prescriptive function.

The prescriptive nature of such a legal philosophy does not therefore do adequate justice to the figure of the lawyer. Such a theoretical system, operating within the emergence of a modern state with a powerful sovereign legislature at its core, and with a contemporary and codified body of laws that are intended to cover the entire system of regulations, ensures that the practice of law is generally depicted as a rather barren option. Either it deals with the decision-making aspect of the law (prescription) or it records decisions that have already been taken and enshrined within the legal code. Either you make decisions, like the legislator, and – depending on your particular theory, also like the judge (as Kelsen and Hart believe) – or you "describe," i.e., you "know" the law, and therefore you know the "science" of the law.

Therefore, the concept of the law falls within this second category and does not need any conceptual link with values, principles or virtues; that is to say, with morality. Clearly, the figure of the lawyer has no place within this dualism, since he neither decides nor describes the law. What he does, on the face of it, is argue, prepare for the jury's decision and suggest that the point of view that he maintains is correct. In such a vein, advocacy is seen as an ephemeral aspect of legal practice, an aspect about which there is nothing more to be said.

The dual character of the law is reflected in the way the lawyer's work is conceptualised. Although there are variations between different legal systems, the lawyer always remains caught in a dilemma. On the one hand, he is acting as a public figure, an "agent of justice," the holder of a public function within his jurisdiction. On the other hand, he is acting as an auxiliary to the plaintiff in the trial, a private representative for certain specific interests that he aims to guarantee and secure. This affects and determines in an important way the deontological structure of advocacy as well as its lasting ambiguity. The lawyer is tasked to defend the interests of a certain party, and to further his particular subjective rights, but he is also aligned with the public good, and with the implementation of general principles of justice. He is at the same time an "individual" actor and a "community" representative. This duality of the lawyer's role is addressed in more than one code of ethics, and it seems to me to be accurately depicted in the Preamble to the *Model Rules of Professional Conduct*, the code of ethics for the *American Bar Association*. This preamble lists the main functions of the lawyer, but in so doing only emphasises the tension between them: "A lawyer, as a member of the legal profession, is a representative of a client, an office of the legal system and a public citizen having special responsibility for the quality of justice."[45]

Therefore, a lawyer acts as the representative of his client – and thus as a defender of the interests of a private subject, an official of the legal system – but also as a citizen whose role involves special responsibility for the quality of the administration of justice. A similar description is given in the Preamble to the *Code of Conduct for European Lawyers*, underscoring the fact that this model of the legal profession involves ethical duties that may initially appear to contradict each other: "A lawyer's function therefore lays on him or her a variety of legal and moral obligations (*sometimes appearing to be in conflict with each other*) towards: the client; the courts and other authorities before whom the lawyer pleads the client's cause or acts on the client's behalf; the legal profession in general and

45 American Bar Association, *Model Rules of Professional Conduct* [1983] (Chicago: ABA 2020), Preamble [1] <https://www.americanbar.org/groups/professional_responsibility/publications/model_rules_of_professional_conduct/> (acc. July 5, 2022), n. pag.

each fellow member of it in particular; the public [. . .]."[46] And the Prologue (*Vorspruch*) of the German *Grundsätze des anwaltlichen Standesrechts* opens with the following statement of principle: "The lawyer is an independent body in the administration of justice. His role is to act as a counsellor and representative in all types of legal affair. He exercises a free profession. His work is not a business [*Der Rechtsanwalt ist ein unabhängiges Organ der Rechtspflege. Er ist der berufene unabhängige Berater und Vertreter in allen Rechtsangelegenheiten. Er übt einen freien Beruf aus. Seine Tätigkeit ist kein Gewerbe*]."[47] Therefore, within the German legal system, the lawyer is also portrayed as both a representative of justice for the community, and an actor representing private interests.

The duality of the lawyer's role obviously reflects on its ethical position, but more generally on the image that is perpetuated in history and culture. We could say that there are two dominant perceptions of the lawyer: the negative view depicts him as cynical and immoral, while the positive image is edifying and mildly moralistic. The first type is widely found in literature, notably in the novels of Charles Dickens, which are filled with negative depictions of lawyers, such as Sampson Brass in *The Old Curiosity Shop* (1841) or the greedy Mr. Vholes and the cold Mr. Tulkinghorn in *Bleak House* (1853). Another Victorian novelist, Anthony Trollope, develops a whole storyline around a question of legal ethics. This is the case in his *Orley Farm* (1861), a novel which also features infamous lawyers such as Samuel Dockwrath, the cunning shyster who sets the story in motion. Advocacy is mercilessly depicted as a profession that deals in lies ("lawyers are all liars"[48]). Things are not much better among philosophers, who also express a recurring suspicion of the legal profession.

The lawyer is therefore faced with the difficult task of reconciling his disparate and apparently conflicting duties, finding a way to practise his craft that is perceived as consistently inspired by principles of morality and justice.[49] However, this is not always regarded as possible or feasible. As a result, two opposing views of advocacy appear in the cultural tradition of our legal systems and permeate distinct and broad sectors of our society. Firstly, there is the pessimistic view of the lawyer. Pascal represents this attitude very well, and it is indeed fairly widespread. He says in his *Pensées*: "L'affection ou la haine changent la justice de face et combien un avocat bien payé par avance trouve-t-il plus juste la cause

46 Conseil des Barreaux Européens – Council of Bars and Law Societies of Europe, *Code of Conduct for European Lawyers* (Brussels: CCBE 2006), Preamble 1.1.

47 Bundesrechtsanwaltskammer, *Grundsätze des anwaltlichen Standesrechts* (Bonn: BRAK 1982), I.

48 Anthony Trollope, *Orley Farm* [1861], ed. David Skilton (Oxford: Oxford UP, 2008), 22.

49 Cf. Deborah L. Rhodes, "Lawyers as Citizens," *William & Mary Law Review* 50.4 (2008–2009): 1323–1334, 1323ff.

qu'il plaide?" (fragment 41). The lawyer is compared to a mercenary, who argues for the rightness of one or the other cause or claim, depending on who hires him. Truth for him has a price, and so is put up for auction by the highest bidder. Such a situation has no sincere claim to justice. It simply reflects the selfish interests of a single party; the public good is never really considered. Plato also states something similar in the *Laws* (937e–938a). Kant, although implying that his method in the *Critique of Pure Reason* will follow the course of a judicial process with himself acting as a lawyer, still maintains a dim view of the profession. This is summed up in two pages of his essay, "Towards Perpetual Peace," where the lawyer is mainly accused of exchanging legality for justice and morality, and so of raising the status of "what is" to a positive norm, while in fact the "must be" would be the correct principle and reflects the values of the ideal constitution. Kant adds the remark that this is what makes it possible for the lawyer to always sit straight in either saddle. Moreover, he ironically points out that between the scales and the sword – both symbols the lawyer uses to justify his occupation – it is generally the sword that prevails when the scales fail to tilt in the desired direction. Ultimately, it is the sword that is slammed down on one of the plates of the scales, and thus determines the result.[50]

The lawyer is depicted as a servant of the powerful, or as someone who only protects the interests (whatever they may be) of the party who pays him – or even those of his own. This image of the lawyer as someone who exploits the weakness of those seeking remedy and protection is frequently evoked in Western culture and literature – and not only here. The biased attitude of the lawyer impels him not to clarify the law, but to complicate it and distort its meaning by interpreting it in subtle and cunning ways, using all the clever moves and tricks of a consummate swindler without any mercy for his victims. "Puss in Boots," the tale of a cunning cat who turns his poor ragged master into a prince, can be seen as a subtle critique of the figure of the lawyer. For he, like the cat, can outwit his interlocutors, especially other parties and clients in the legal profession.[51] Another character that reiterates this negative portrayal of the lawyer is Dr. Azzeccagarbugli in Alessandro Manzoni's *The Betrothed* (1827), although he is hardly a model of *parrhesia*.

This dim view of the lawyer's persona contrasts with some much more positive descriptions. One such example can be found in the Code of Justinian, the

---

50 See Immanuel Kant, "Zum ewigen Frieden" [1795] in *Werkausgabe*, Vol. 11, ed. Wilhelm Weischedel (Frankfurt a.M.: Suhrkamp, 1977), 191–251, 235, 227–228.

51 Cf. Stefano Bolla, *L'avvocato con gli stivali: L'immagine popolare dell'avvocato e la fiaba di Charles Perrault* (Bellinzona: Casagrande, 2008). "Puss in Boots" can be traced back to "Il gatto con gli stivali," a 1697 Italian-French fairy tale that later spread throughout the rest of Europe and is recorded in various international adaptations.

Corpus Juris Civilis (Body of Civil Law), where the lawyer is treated with great reverence. We are told there that lawyers resolve the ambiguity inherent in a case, giving powerful support to shaky aspects of public and private affairs. Ultimately, they are like a special type of soldier, also fighting to defend the sovereign order. The lawyer is compared to a soldier who takes up arms to defend the public good and the Empire: "Nec enim solo nostro imperio militare credimus illos qui gladiis, clyperis, et thoracibus nituntur, sed etiam Advocatos" (L. 14 Cod., De Adv. Div. Jud.). A positive view is also offered by St. Thomas Aquinas, who in his *Summa Theologiae* (II–II, q. 71) has no objection to the fact that the lawyer sells his (rightful) patronage and the jurist his (true) opinion, and therefore are in the pay of the client.

In literature, this positive image is reflected in the work of Balzac, who writes at some length about the legal profession. In the work of this great French novelist, the lawyer is not generally depicted with the shady and even perverse qualities that Dickens attributes to him. In such a vein, in the novel *Colonel Chabert* (1832), where we are told that "tout se plaide"[52] – i.e., anything can be the subject of a lawsuit – lawyers are described as follows: "Les avoués ne sont-ils pas en quelque sorte des hommes d'Etat chargés des affaires privés?"[53] However, Balzac does not try to gloss over the dual pathway that is open to the legal profession, i.e., the fact that it can either consist of work that is simply in defence of private interests, or it can serve a highly public function and be directed towards a sense of justice. In "La Maison Nucingen" (1837), a short story in the collection *La Comédie humaine* (1829–48), Balzac tells us that there are generally two types of lawyers: "L'avoué n'a que deux nuances: il y a l'avoué honnête homme qui demeure dans les termes de la loi [. . .]. Puis il y a l'avoué famélique à qui tout est bon pourvu que les frais soient assurés."[54]

In a short story by Balzac, "Un homme d'affaires" (1845), we find the lawyer compared to an ambassador. "Quelle différence y a-t-il entre un ambassadeur et un avoué? Uniquement celle qui sépare une nation d'un individu. Les ambassadeurs sont les avoués des peuples!"[55] So it follows that if ambassadors are advocates of the people, i.e., of the citizenship as a whole, then advocates are ambassadors of individuals, of particular citizens, as subjects of the legal order. For Balzac, therefore, the lawyer is (or can be) a kind of "statesman" or "politician," or better still, a

52 Honoré de Balzac, *Le Colonel Chabert* [1832], ed. Patrick Berthier (Paris: Gallimard, 1999), 103.

53 Balzac, *Le Colonel Chabert*, 111.

54 Balzac, "La Maison Nucingen" [1837] in *La Maison Nucingen: Melmoth réconcilié*, ed. Anne-Marie Meininger (Paris: Gallimard, 1989), 162.

55 Balzac, "Un homme d'affaires" [1845] in *Un debut dans la vie: Un homme d'affaires: Un prince de la bohème*, ed. Samuel de Sacy (Paris: Le livre de Poche, 1969), 209.

representative of the citizens, who is responsible not for public but for private affairs. But in what sense can it be said that the lawyer is a public actor, or that he fulfils a public function? The main question here is whether the reference to the public role of the lawyer makes any sense, given its close association with defending private interests.

The way to resolve this tension between the public function and the defence of private interests seems to lie in establishing a possible connection between advocacy and citizenship. It seems that such a connection can be found where defending the interests of a private subject is regarded by the lawyer as his public duty and mission, and so can be seen more generally as defending the *rights of the citizen*. But in what sense can the lawyer really be described as a public actor? I believe the lawyer is a public actor in a special sense, in that he helps the citizen enjoy one of his basic prerogatives, that of the right to access the power of jurisdiction, by allowing him to exercise his citizenship through the essential right to free speech, without either fear or favour. This is the type of speech that demands an account, i.e., a reason and justification, and that is prepared to confront authority boldly and brazenly; this in a word is *parrhesia*. For the legal profession, freedom of speech and the ability and right to seek reason and justification from the opposing party, the prosecution, as well as from the judge, seem to me essential to its very character and raison d'être. Ultimately, it is by these means that the lawyer can create controversy or explain the conflict between rights and claims to justice.

The lawyer helps to make citizenship – in its basic sense of participating in the creation of general and individual rules, legislation and jurisdiction – into a full, effective and active right. And this is done so by assisting and empowering an essential faculty for the citizen, his free speech: his ability to challenge those who seek to take away or restrict his rights. The lawyer adds his powerful, official voice to the weaker, subjective voice of the citizen, making it stronger, intelligible to the public and clearly audible to the authorities. Therefore, it is with the help of the lawyer that the free speech of the citizen is made clearer and more formalised, as he argues before the powers of the state and within their parameters.

4 Asking for Reasons

In conclusion, when we take into account its accepted meanings, it seems to me that *parrhesia* could be described as an attitude and practice that typifies the moral virtues of the lawyer, as these are traditionally regarded. Indeed, it mainly involves knowing how to speak, knowing how to ask the right questions and not remaining silent or at a loss for words. It is therefore tantamount to the professionalism, wisdom and diligence of the lawyer who offers his knowledge and expertise to the client, demonstrating these skills when he is required to speak, and in arguments with the opposing party. In situations of legal argument, professionalism can even turn to zeal, as the lawyer becomes attached or even devoted to the cause for which he has assumed responsibility. In addition, *parrhesia* typically presupposes courage, and an ability to challenge and not to be intimidated. In the case of the lawyer, it involves being willing to take risks in defence of the client. Metaphorically speaking, it could be seen as holding one's head up high, not lowering one's gaze in front of the other party, the prosecution or the judge.

It is also about asserting the dignity of the party that he represents, the client, allowing him to stand up straight with his head held high. *Parrhesia* implies the independence of the speaker. The "parrhesiast" uses his own words, which are not dictated to him by a third party; this is in contrast to the classical Greek figure of the herald, who is the direct opposite of a parrhesiast.[56] The herald repeats the words of others, while the parrhesiast speaks his own words. The herald depends on the authority of another, who tells him what he must say; the parrhesiast, on the other hand, is completely independent, at least in terms of speech. This is how the lawyer should also be, independent of the power of others, and especially of political authority.

Even though – like the judge – the lawyer is bound by the law, he can also challenge it to some extent, consulting it on various occasions and reinterpreting its meaning. Plato recommended that every law be given a "preface" or prologue (for example in the *Laws*, IV, 722b–723d), a public statement of the end (or good) the law is designed to achieve. The prologue is then followed by the provisions of the law. Now, it could be said that, while the judge is not so attentive to the prologue but is very careful to apply the law, the lawyer studies the prologue, construes its meaning and proposes the result to the judge, thus offering him a specific interpretation of the law. We cannot ask the judge – as Ronald Dworkin[57] does – to undertake the Herculean task of absorbing in a single glance all the many complex interests at stake in the case, and of arranging all the principles of law involved in a coherent system, without glorifying the monochrome nature of the judge's decision-making in a quite implausible and uncritical way, and without also running the risk of

56 This contrast is particularly evident in the work of Euripides. It can be found in *The Trojan Women*, 424ff., where the herald is pitted against Cassandra, also a good example of a parrhesiast; or again in *The Suppliants*, 426. More especially, it is evident in *Orestes*, 895–897, where the herald is generally criticised as someone always ready to jump on the chariot of the fortunate man, and a friend to the powerful ruler who governs the city (ἐπὶ τὸν εὐτυχῆ πηδῶσ' ἀεὶ κήρυκες: ὅδε δ' αὐτοῖς φίλος, ὃς ἂν δύνηται πόλεος ἔν τ' ἀρχαῖσιν ᾖ).
57 See Ronald Dworkin, "Hard Cases," *Harvard Law Review* 88.6 (1975): 1057–1109.

deviating from the rule of law. Judge Hercules can only fulfil his role if much of his strength is provided by the arguments and speeches of the lawyer. On the other hand, this is the sort of speech that "challenges" and "produces conflict," and its existence and use prevent a rather saccharine and conciliatory type of legal argument and trial process – a situation that can occur with a theory of speech whose only purpose is to facilitate "understanding," without the element of "contesting."[58] Monocracy and decision-making merge in the clash or agreement of debate.

As we have seen, *parrhesia* – as a right to speak – implies participation in the trial process and legal judgement. This is why both Plato and Aristotle describe it as a right of citizenship. *Parrhesia* allows the plaintiff (and the lawyer acting on his behalf) to constitute himself as an agency of justice and the administration of the law, as a *constitutional power of the state.* But *parrhesia* also counteracts the "philautia," egocentrism and complacency, which always threatens the claim to justice by the plaintiff, the lawyer's client. By the use of free speech, the lawyer can act as a sort of *speculum rei,* or mirror for the plaintiff, reminding him that his interests in the court must be discernible as "rights": legitimate interests and standpoints that are not egocentric, but legally valid and applicable as well as acceptable and sustainable in ethical terms. In this way, the lawyer makes use of his independence, and demonstrates its importance, maintaining a distance between his own beliefs and the interests and feelings of his client.

In conclusion, *parrhesia* in the form of free speech, the demand for justification, frankness, together with courage and independence, offers the lawyer a constructive and convincing way to pursue his unique and combative ethical profession. This is achieved by his crossing that bridge between advocacy and citizenship that is constructed by the sort of frank speaking that produces both freedom and conflict and is an essential way to exercise citizenship. Citizenship is allied with *parrhesia,* and is sustained by it, and *parrhesia* in turn is both practised and guaranteed in the professional work of the lawyer.[59]

---

58 This is the major criticism of legal theory as a discursive legal practice proposed by Jürgen Habermas, which cannot avoid a conciliatory and reconciliatory tone in the complex interplay of powers and demands that lead to a judicial decision. See Jürgen Habermas, *Faktizität und Geltung: Beiträge zur Diskurstheorie des Rechts und des demokratischen Rechtsstaates* (Frankfurt a.M.: Suhrkamp, 1992), especially 135ff., 272ff.

59 In such a vein, cf. La Torre, *Il giudice*, especially ch. 2.

Alfred Sproede

Driven by Ressentiment and Sophistry or – Indeed, *Parrhesia*? The Protagonist as Lawyer in Ukrainian Fiction

1 The Protagonist as Lawyer: A Failure of the Word?

In one of the key contributions to law and literature scholarship, Richard Weisberg has drawn an unflattering portrait of the literary role of jurists, especially lawyers. He confronts the reader with representatives of advocacy from three national literatures: after three Russian (Dostoevskii's *Notes from the Underground, Crime and Punishment, The Brothers Karamazov*) and four French novels (Flaubert's *Salammbô* and *L'éducation sentimentale*; Camus' *L'étranger* and *La chute*), he addresses one American example (Melville's *Billy Budd*). The central dimension that interests Weisberg in these novels is "the relationship of aesthetics to ethics"; his interpretations reveal a wealth "of language systems bereft of ethical referents":[1]

> The entire thrust of the legal procedure, and the task for which "artistic legality" is eminently suited, is to recreate verbally, and thus to devalue, the existence of the spontaneous, vital individual who stands accused. Like the modern novelist, the lawyer employs his verbal gift to produce ironic or negative portraits of positive heroes. The personal problems of the examining and prosecuting lawyers (which in many cases fall under the category of ressentiment) become institutionalized in the *seemingly* rational procedures of criminal law.[2]

The vices that, according to Weisberg's investigation, burden the action of *lawyers as protagonists* are ressentiment and sophistry; the conclusion of the book estimates that they often culminate in a denial of justice:

> Verbalizers all, these figures exhibit the deep ambivalence of the novelists who have created them. It is astounding how violent their passive medium becomes, and how small the tangible benefits to the community from their [. . .] eloquence. [. . .] Time after time in these texts, narrative acts lead to passivity in the face of clear injustice or, worse still, to the creation of injustice itself.[3]

1 Richard Weisberg, *The Failure of the Word: The Protagonist as Lawyer in Modern Fiction* (New Haven: Yale UP, 1984), 179.
2 Weisberg, *The Failure,* 59; emphasis in the original.
3 Weisberg, *The Failure,* 178.

https://doi.org/10.1515/9783111075693-019

Now, Weisberg's definition of a "lawyer" applies, as a rule, to the body of officers acting in a criminal court; his critique concerns specifically the examining magistrate ("prosecution attorney") or the public prosecutor (*juge d'instruction, procureur; sudebnyi sledovatel', prokurator*), illustrated by the court officers in Camus' *The Stranger* or by Porfirii Petrovich in Dostoevskii's *Crime and Punishment*. These are the representatives of advocacy that, according to Weisberg's argument, are acting as sophists or under the influence of ressentiment.[4]

Curiously, the lawyer as *defense attorney* is taken into account only by exception (cf. Clamence in Camus' *La chute*) or not at all. This ommission has irritating consequences at least for the interpretation of Dostoevskii's *The Brothers Karamazov*. Defense attorney Fetiukovich is a decisive figure of the court procedure concluding the novel (Book 12: "A Judicial Error"); Weisberg's book nowhere mentions the only significant antagonist of the public prosecution and the erroneous sentence the latter stands for. This is all the more troubling as Fetiukovich is not at all driven by ressentiment – unlike Dostoevskii himself, who, from the very beginning, discredits this character transparently modelled on Polish-born lawyer Vladimir Spasovich (Włodzimierz Spasowicz), Dostoevskii's notorious *bête noire*.[5]

For an intelligent defense of and, compared to Weisberg, more equitable approach to the defense lawyer, we can turn to Massimo La Torre, who deplores the almost complete absence of the lawyer from modern legal theory:

> If one had to pick three characters who figure prominently in the string of legal positivist theories [. . .], they would have to be the judge, the legislator, and the law professor [. . .]. Scarcely a word is devoted to the lawyer: neither Savigny nor Jhering, nor Jellinek, nor Kelsen, nor Hart – just to mention a few of the great luminaries of the legal positivist tradition – have had much to say about the lawyer, except by way [of] a few passing remarks. [. . .] It is the decision-making moment that obsesses legal positivists. [. . .] Now, lawyers, despite

---

4 Weisberg, *The Failure*, 45–50, 55–57, 115, 117–119. In his next book on law and literature – *Poethics and Other Strategies of Law and Literature* (New York: Columbia UP, 1992), ch. 2 "Let's Not Kill *All* the Lawyers [. . .]" – Weisberg seems to adopt a more benign position on literary lawyers. However, the attempt to explain the unexpected picture of "sympathetic" or even "nice" lawyers with the difference between continental and Anglo-American fiction or between nineteenth- and twentieth-century attitudes to the law (*Poethics and Other Strategies*, 51–53, 67) does not really support his point.

5 The 'talking' name given to the lawyer is a term of abuse: literally, Fetiukovich is the "son of an impotent." For Dostoevskii's stance on Spasovich, which is not exempt of xenophobia, cf. the entries "Fetyukovich" and "Spasovich" in the index to Gary Rosenshield's *Western Law, Russian Justice: Dostoevsky, the Jury Trial, and the Law* (Madison: U of Wisconsin P, 2005).

> themselves, do not decide anything, when it comes to the making of the law; hence the perception of them as not much relevant, if at all.[6]

La Torre substantiates his claim by pointing to the contrast between, on the one hand, the irrelevance of the lawyer in legal positivism and, on the other hand, the rich modern history of reflection about the role of lawyers in the administration of justice. Among the many varieties of the status of lawyers in European countries, as shown in one of La Torre's earlier publications, the crucial divide concerns the distinction between an officer acting as an *employee of a court of law* ("un avvocato tendenzialmente 'collaboratore' [del] guidice-funzionario") and the *representative of a liberal profession* acting as the counsel of a defendant or (in civil proceedings) a petitioner ("l'avvocato [come] soggetto centrale dell'emergente società civile").[7]

It is the last definition, with the lawyer as a "central subject of an emergent civil society," on which La Torre elaborates in a more recent statement. Looking for "a concept of civic participation that is no longer just based on heredity and ethnicity,"[8] he now identifies the lawyer's action as an instance of "*parrhesia*" (free speech, truth-telling) as discussed by Michel Foucault:

> In the Greek conception of *parrhesia* [. . .] there does not seem to be a problem about the acquisition of the truth since such truth-having is guaranteed by the possession of certain moral qualities: when someone has certain moral qualities, then that is the proof that he has access to truth.[9]

The moral qualities required for the exercise of *parrhesia* are an acute sense of duty and resilience in the face of danger as, for instance, in the confrontation of the philosopher with tyranny – "since the tyrant may become angry, may punish him, may exile him, may kill him."[10] While resisting the temptation of self-interest and moral apathy, the *parrhesiastes* also promotes the civic virtues on which the practices of democratic institutions rest:

> As it appears in Euripides' plays and also in the texts of the Fourth Century BC, *parrhesia* is an essential characteristic of Athenian democracy. [. . .] we can say quite generally that

6 Massimo La Torre, "Lawyers, Advocacy and the Concept of Law," *Rechtstheorie*, 43.1 (2012): 1–25, 1–2.

7 Massimo La Torre, *Il giudice, l'avvocato e il concetto di diritto* (Soveria Mennelli: Rubbettino, 2002), 53–155 (ch. 2 "L'imparziale parzialità. Avvocatura e concetto di diritto"), especially 80–86.

8 Massimo La Torre, this volume, 155–174, 157.

9 Michel Foucault, *Discourse and Truth: The Problematization of Parrhesia (Six Lectures Given by Michel Foucault at Berkeley, October–November 1983)*, 3. This course offers the most extensive version of Foucault's numerous statements on "*parrhesia*" (franc-parler, dire-vrai); a partially reworked edition of the lectures is available at <foucault.info/downloads/discourseandtruth.doc> (acc. April 2022).

10 Foucault, *Discourse and Truth*, 4.

> *parrhesia* was a guideline for democracy as well as an ethical and personal attitude characteristic of the good citizen. [. . .] *Parrhesia*, which is a requisite for public speech, takes place between citizens as individuals, and also between citizens construed as an assembly. [. . .] the agora is the place where *parrhesia* appears.[11]

With this working definition of the term, let us return to Massimo La Torre. By asserting *parrhesia* as a regulative idea for the lawyer's action, he provides a double clue to our subject matter: his conception counters Weisberg's gloomy assessment, and it introduces productive tension into the analytical framework for 'reading' Eastern European literary images of the lawyer.

From older literary (esp. dramatic) conventions up to the era of realism, Ukrainian representations of the lawyer mostly follow the tradition of *law court satire* (harking back to Aristophanes' *The Wasps* and Racine's *Les Plaideurs*); the most telling examples are the dark comedies *Outwitted!* (*Peremudriv*; 1884) and *Ruin* (*Zhuba*; 1896) written by Panas Myrnyi (1849–1920). The departure from the plot convention based on the derision of lawyers as *pettifoggers or crooks* is to be credited to West Ukrainian writer and poet Ivan Franko (1856–1916).

2 The Lawyer as Public Intellectual and Social Reformer: Ivan Franko's *Fateful Crossroads* (1900)

With *Fateful Crossroads* (*Perekhresni stezhky*), Ivan Franko completed a series of novels intended as a Galician 'panorama' of social criticism.[12] The earlier titles of this series were *Boryslav is Laughing* (*Boryslav smiiet'sia*; 1881/82), *For the Home*

11 Foucault, *Discourse and Truth*, 7.

12 *Fateful Crossroads* (*Perekhresni stezhky*) first appeared in the journal *Literaturno-naukovyi visnyk*, 1900, T. IX, № 1 – T. XII, № 12, and was reprinted the same year as a one-volume edition in L'viv [Lemberg]. For quotations from the novel, I draw on the English translation *Fateful Crossroads: A Novel* (*Turbulent Times*, Vol. III), trans. Roma Franko (Saskatoon: Language Lanterns Publications, 2006); in the interest of a faithful rendering of the Ukrainian original, I submit occasional modifications. Quotations in Ukrainian are drawn from Franko's *Zibrannia tvoriv u 50-i tomakh* [*Collected Works in 50 Vols.*], red. Ivan I. Bass et al., T. 20 (Kyiv: Naukova dumka, 1979), 173–459. Both references – firstly to the 2006 English edition and secondly (after the slash /) to the Ukrainian *Collected Works in 50 Vols.* – are included in the body of the main text. In order to facilitate identification of the excerpts in other editions, I also indicate the corresponding chapter of the novel (I–LX).

Hearth (*Dlia domashn'oho ohnishcha*; 1892/97), and *Pillars of Society* (*Osnovy suspil'nosti*; 1894/95; unfinished). Just like the preceding novels in the series, *Fateful Crossroads* is based on events drawn from the criminal chronicle. However, it does not follow the model of the detective novel; the entertaining drive and the suspense of the narration are created by devices of retrospection and changing point of view. As a variant of the novel of society, *Fateful Crossroads* takes part in literary naturalism; recent Slavic scholarship has pointed to the privileged connection of this literary current with the presentation of crime subjects.[13]

As the following discussion will show, *Fateful Crossroads* links naturalism and the theme of "degeneracy" with a reformist program close to the conceptions of German social democracy; Franko establishes a link between modernized justice and social reform at large. The novel stages the lawyer as a central representative of this modernized justice. *Fateful Crossroads* features the legal order established – or, rather precariously reigning – in a multi-ethnic region of the Habsburg Empire. As the intended audience of the novel is a Galician middle class, *Crossroads* can be considered a statement on justice that is significant not only for Ukrainian culture, but also for the intellectual history of Central Europe. Franko's contribution to crime literature deserves attention for revealing the deficits of legal consciousness and institutional justice in Central Europe, but, at the same time, for suggesting a genuine program of 'legal enlightenment.'

2.1 The Plot

Franko depicts the chronicle of a small Galician town under *k.u.k.* administration 'hijacked' by local networks of deliquency; as a corrolary, the author delves into the conflict between a hegemonic Polish minority and the disinherited Ukrainian population. The counterpart of these plot lines is the struggle of a lawyer to defend the victims of the local oligarchs and their mafia agents.

After successfully defending his doctoral dissertation, young jurist Ievgenii Rafalovych leaves L'viv/Lemberg for another (unnamed) Western Ukrainian town in order to establish a lawyer's practice there. The description of the environment and of the river landscape surrounding the town suggests references to Stanislau (today's Ivano-Frankivs'k), but the town can actually only be a place invented in analogy to it (Chapter IV; 29/186). Soon after his arrival, Rafalovych is able to gain

13 Cf. Riccardo Nicolosi, *Degeneration erzählen: Literatur und Psychiatrie im Russland der 1880er und 1890er Jahre* [*Narratives of Degeneracy: Literature and Psychiatry in Russia during the 1880s and 1890s*] (Paderborn: Wilhelm Fink, 2018); Tamara Hundorova, *Franko ne kameniar: Franko i kameniar* [*Franko is no Quarrier: Franko and the Quarrier*] (Kyiv: Vyd. Krytyka, 2006), 36–95.

much attention by successfully defending regional peasants against overdrawn or downright fabricated judicial charges (I). Rafalovych is praised and courted by Valerian Stalski (Stal's'kyi)[14] (II–IV), an employee of the local Court of Justice and, in Rafalovych's youth at a L'viv secondary school, a school tutor whom Rafalovych remembers as a tormentor of animals and a sadistic educator. Stalski lives up to his former image with anti-feminist tirades and even awkward talk about his wife (VII–X).

Shortly after establishing his office in town, Rafalovych encounters a mysterious woman clothed in black (IV); he does not immediately recognize Regina Twardowska, his love from his years in L'viv as a law student. Ten years prior, just when Rafalovych had begun to get closer to her (XIII–XVI), Regina had surrendered to "aunt Susi" or Zuzanna (*ciocia Zuzia*), a highly persuasive marriage broker, and had married a local officer named Valerian Stalski. She had then followed her husband to his professional destination in the province (XVII) and, since that time, had been leading a toxic marital life there (IX–X, XX–XXIII, LII). Rafalovych is taken aback when meeting her in her home; an invitation by Stalski brings him into direct contact with the target of his infatuation from his student days, who after a short period of time had disappeared from L'viv without leaving a trace (XX–XXIII).

When Rafalovych is introduced to the town administration and to the notables' houses (V–VI), he discovers how narrow-minded the local elites are and how irretrievably the *k.u.k.* authorities, the Polish nobility, and the Jews are at odds with one another. He becomes an object of the town gossip after the ruling circles learn that he fights in favor of the national aspirations of the Ukrainian population (the "Rusyny" or "Ruthenians", as *k.u.k.* terminology has it). In fact, this ethnic majority is an object of constant discrimination:

> Dr. Rafalovych established himself at once as an innovator, persistent and unyielding: from the outset he introduced the Rusyn language into his office and laid down the rule that not "a single scrap of paper" was to go out of it in any other language. This was a genuine revolution. [. . .] A few times his petitions were refused, but he defended his rights. He was not swayed by any persuasions or grievances, but rather, in his usual manner, turned them into jokes, disarmed his critics with laughter and good-natured banter, behind which, like an

14 Where the names reveal the ethnic identity of a character (especially for Polish names), my paper tries to mark this in the transliteration: cf. Regina Twardowska, Rafalovych's love from his university years. Marriage broker aunt Susi (цьоця Зюзя) (VIII) is transliterated as "ciocia Zuzia"; the Marshal of the Polish Nobility Брикальський (VI) as "Brykalski."

> armed regiment, stood his invincible legal arguments. And, after some time, his determination began to win the upper hand. (XI; 66)[15]

Rafalovych gains more and more insight into the conflicts amongst the Polish magnates and into the role of the Jewish pawnbrokers, especially into the hostility towards Brykalski, the Marshall of the Polish Nobility, by the rich Jew Vagman (XII). Vagman's only son had been drawn into the army due to a Polish intrigue and perished in one of the battles (XXXI). Since that event, his father has brooded over the possibility of vengeance against Brykalski, the person mainly responsible for the intrigue. Vagman plans to buy all the credit bills and promissory papers issued by Brykalski to different debtors and then to claim the whole debt at once in order to ruin the intriguer.

In the meantime, lawyer Rafalovych, suspected of a subversive socio-political commitment, gets drawn into the line of fire of the local conservatives. He had provided legal support for the peasants' General Assembly (*viče*, XXXVIII), convocated to avert an unlawful reform of their collective credit and insurance funds for retirement and cases of professional accidents. In fact, the nobility is being pushed by Brykalski to fuse the well-endowed funds of the peasants' cooperative bank with the notoriously poor bank reserve of the nobility (XXXIX). Rafalovych also initiates criminal proceedings against two local crooks, Schwarz and Shnadel's'kyi, the latter a lawyer who has been excluded from the Lawyers' professional association. The duo had not only frightened the peasants by circulating rumors about an impending war; they had also collected considerable amounts of cash, promising in exchange to use fake high-reaching connections to help the solvent 'investors' "avert military conscription."[16] Shnadel's'kyi had promised that

15 "д-р Рафалович виступив відразу новатором, консеквентним і впертим: він відразу зробив свою канцелярію руською і поклав собі правило, що ні один „кавалок" із неї не сміє вийти на іншій мові, як тільки на руській. Се була правдива революція. [. . .] Кілька разів йому відкидувано подання, але він достоював свойого права, не подавався ні на які підмови ані жалі, але, навпаки, своїм звичайним способом зводив їх на жарти, обезсилював сміхом, добродушністю, за котрою, мов оружні полки, стояли непереможні юридичні аргументи. І його впертість по якімсь часі почала одержувати побіду" (XI; 215–216).

16 The counterpart to these crooked deals is the aid to the poor provided by the Jewish merchant Vagman, which is one of the reasons for rejecting the accusation of Franko as an *anti-Semite*, an issue compellingly discussed in recent papers by Tamara Hundorova, Jaroslav Hrycak, and George Grabowicz in *Ivan Franko und die jüdische Frage in Galizien: Interkulturelle Begegnungen und Dynamiken im Schaffen des ukrainischen Schriftstellers* [*Ivan Franko and the Jewish Question in Galicia: Intercultural Encounters and Dynamics in the Ukrainian Writer's Work*], ed. Alois Woldan and Olaf Terpitz (Göttingen: Vandenhoeck & Ruprecht, 2016).

the 'loan' he received from his 'clients' would repay considerably, as he boasted of "direct access to the Kaiser in Vienna" (XXXII, XXXVI).

Rafalovych is a witness to many other scandals caused by the regional administration. He is called upon to be an assessor to a village judge of the neighboring region, who – debilitated and mentally ill – is unable to conduct the process (XXXIII). Rafalovych also brings to trial a dubious village doctor who had tried to cover up his professional errors that had led to child disease and to numerous deaths in several villages (XXXIII).

In the second part of the novel, the conflicts advance in the form of a number of parallel sub-plots: (a) The head of the provincial government wants to forbid the assembly of the peasants and denounces Rafalovych as a troublemaker heading for sedition (XLIX, LI). (b) Stalski is increasingly eager to humiliate his wife Regina, causing her to ultimately turn to Rafalovych for help. In response, Stalski instructs Baran, the caretaker in Rafalovych's house, to spy on the lawyer and especially to eavesdrop on Regina's visits (XXVIII). (c) Baran, who many years prior had killed his wife and who, after this crime, was able to return to normal life only through Vagman's clemency and help, is threatened by growing mental illness. He fantasizes about the impending arrival of the Last Times and, influenced by the whisperings of a local Jesuit father, identifies Rafalovych as the servant and herald of the Antichrist (XXVII–XXVIII). (d) Vagman, having acquired the totality of Brykalski's credit bills and promissory notes, is about to ask for the wholesale payment, thus pushing the intriguing magnate to bankruptcy (L, LV).

2.2 Scandal, Delinquency, and Catastrophe: Opportunities and Pitfalls of Franko's Plot

Having thus cleared the main paths towards a dramatic dénouement, Franko sets the narrative mechanism in motion. On New Year's Day, *Fateful Crossroads* turns into a whirlpool of events reminiscent of Dostoevskii's *The Possessed* (*Besy*; 1872/73) with its atmosphere of chaos and social disruption. The swindlers Shnadel's'kyi and Schwarz steal from Baran's house a letter containing Vagman's receipt for a huge sum that the merchant had gained by reselling Brykalski's promissory notes; the receipt allows the swindlers to presume that Vagman holds a significant amount of money in his house (LVI). Stalski has once again humiliated his wife in the presence of witnesses; Regina finally decides to leave him for good. Since her husband presumes that she would search refuge and help at Rafalovych's home, Stalski and several accomplices break into the lawyer's house (LIV–LV). Regina actually is there as she wanted to wish Rafalovych good luck for the peasant assembly; she narrowly escapes through the back door. However, when she returns late at night to her own home, her drunken husband again treats her harshly (LVII). She knocks Stalski dead with a hammer and flees to the suburbs covered in snow. Once there, she has a sudden encounter with Baran, who is roaming around in an apocalyptic delirium; the caretaker attacks Regina and pushes her from a bridge into the freezing river before continuing his crazy – and ultimately suicidal – path into the snowstorm (LVIII; 347, 371 / 439, 458).

In the meantime, Shnadel's'kyi und Schwarz have killed Vagman and plundered his safe (LVI; 329–331 / 426–427). Before setting out to Przemyśl and Berlin for their planned escape to America, they try to mislead the criminal investigation by placing clues pointing to suicide by their victim (LX). But the strategy fails: Shnadel's'kyi, who was already suffering from incipient pneumonia before fleeing, is arrested by the Berlin police in a critical state of health; he confesses to the murder and burglary at Vagman's house and, incarcerated, hangs himself in his cell (LX; 372 / 458). The enigma surrounding the other missing or murdered people is not solved until springtime: after the onset of thaw, the river and the snow release the corpses of Regina and Baran (LX; 371 / 458). The novel concludes with the complaint of the head of the provincial government over the ruin of his career: now that the gloomy events are in plain view, he must abandon all hope on earning a decoration for outstanding administrative performance.

The novel's conclusion, thus turned into sarcasm, and the success that Rafalovych gains with the peasant assembly (cf. the background action, LIX–LX), do not allow the reader to forget the atmosphere of scandal, nay, of a world's end. The apocalyptic finale of *Fateful Crossroads* reminds us of sensational *fin de siècle* novels like Stanisław Przybyszewski's *Satan's Children* (*Dzieci Szatana*; 1899; in German 1897); we have already mentioned another 'godfather' of scandalous provincial chronicle – Dostoevskii and his novel *The Possessed*. But unlike Dostoevskii, who celebrated religiously inspired people and the "fools in Christ" (*iurodivye*), Franko promotes a politically committed jurist to the role of his positive hero.

The politically aware jurist thus eclipses the scenery of corruption and political intrigue. Franko does not exploit this theme to its full extent, however, as he idealizes the lawyer's work beyond all recognition. In a dialogue with Regina, Rafalovych's fight for justice and national dignity is so enthusiastically blown up to a goal in life (*meta zhyttia*) that the dialogue slips into the realm of kitsch: Rafalovych's combative spirit and altruism ostensibly result from the fact that he has – without being conscious of that choice – taken his love for Regina as his "guiding star" (*providna zvizda*, XXVI; 141 / 275). But he must not sacrifice his profession and his therapeutic power on his environment to the beauty of private life, let alone to conjugal felicity (XXIX; 159–160 / 290); this would lead to an immoral enrichment or would be, in Regina's words, nothing but "stolen happiness" (*kradene shchastia*, XXVI; 144 / 277).

At this point, Franko's writing is running off the rails and ends up as a mix of *Jugendstil* and a trashy dime novel.

Franko himself would have conceded that *Fateful Crossroads* resembles popular novels published in newspaper installments. However, despite its flirtation with a social utopia, the novel is not taken over by primitive social didactics and ideological indoctrination. This judgement is confirmed by the comparison with a truly tendentious novel – Maksim Gor'kii's *The Mother* (*Mat'*; 1909), which presents some parallels to *Fateful Crossroads*. But it is easy to distinguish between Franko and his colleague (his junior by twelwe years): Gor'kii stages a crew of conspirative party soldiers that, except for their working-class accomplices, must avoid all publicity, while Franko lets his hero fight in public for politics of the law and through the law. The vanishing point of Gor'kii's novel is a fanatic onslaught against tsarism and the Russian bourgeoisie; Franko, for his part, embarks on a *struggle for law*.

2.3 Advocacy and Franko's Views on the Politics of Law

The mission of Franko's lawyer is to push Western Ukraine towards a modern order of society and administration. *Fateful Crossroads* pursues literary anticipation in a Ukrainian political public sphere; it does so in a spirit of critical solidarity with and fundamental acceptance of the rule of law established by the Austrian Double Monarchy.[17] Franko's commitment to the rule of law is a remarkable phenomenon in the cultural history of his people; one of the few Ukrainian intellectuals fighting for comparable ideas is (Eastern) Ukrainian jurist Bogdan Kistiakovskii (Bohdan Kistiakivs'kyi; 1868–1920), who, nine years after Franko's novel, published the article "In the Defense of Law (The Intelligentsiia and Legal Consciousness) in Moscow."[18]

17 After the confiscation of Franko's work for Marxist-Leninist purposes, the post-Soviet generation of Ukrainian legal scholars is trying to reclaim his writings, especially his interest in legal matters, formerly a blind spot in scholarship; cf. Oksana Bunchuk, *Pytannia prava u naukovii spadshchyny Ivan Franka* [*Legal Issues in Ivan Franko's Scholarly Legacy*] (Chernivtsi, PhD in History and Theory of State and Law, 2009); Nadiia M. Pavlusiv, "Obrazy sudu ta sudochynstva u tvorakh pys'mennykiv zakhidnoï Ukraïny kintsia XIX – pochatku XX st. iak ob"iekt filosofs'ko-pravovoho analizu" [Images of Justice and Jurisdiction in the Work of Western Ukrainian Writers from the End of the Nineteenth to the Beginning of the Twentieth Century: The Perspective of Legal Philosophy], *Derzhava i pravo: Zbirnyk naukovych prats'* 45 (2009): 49–53; Nadiia M. Pavlusiv, *Filosofs'ko-pravovi pohliady zakhidnoukraïns'kykh pys'mennykiv kintsia XIX – pochatku XX st.* [*Philosophy of Law in the Thought of Western Ukrainian Writers from the End of the Nineteenth to the Beginning of the Twentieth Century*] (Kyiv: Natsional'na Akademija Vnutrishnikh Sprav, PhD in Philosophy, 2010).

18 Bogdan Kistiakovskii, "V zashchitu prava (Intelligentsiia i pravosoznanie)" [In the Defense of Law (The Intelligentsiia and Legal Consciousness)] in *Vekhi. Sbornik statei o russkoi intelligentsii,*

Franko devotes long passages to the trials conducted in provincial courthouses (XXXIII–XXXV); Rafalovych's aim is to fight against the oppression of the Galician peasantry and to help this discriminated social group attain political emancipation:

> The peasants, who initially had asked him to write their petitions in Polish because anything written in Rusyn created problems for them with administrative bodies, became more confident about their rights and began demanding [. . .] respect for their nationality [. . .]. And among the city elite, whose putrid tranquility was disturbed by these innovations, a second snap judgement was made about the true character of Dr. Rafalovych: "The man's a *Moskal*!" [. . .] A Rusyn who did not bow down under the Polish yoke, who did not belong to the Polish eparchy, had to be either a demagogue and socialist, or a Moskal. Tertium non datur. (XI; 67)[19]

Franko confronts the narrow-minded elites of the region with the prototype of an idealistic lawyer. The jurist featured in *Fateful Crossroads* is a far cry from the dubious hedge lawyers that dominated the stage in Eastern Ukrainian literary realism, for example, in the plays of Panas Myrnyi, Franko's elder contemporary (cf. ch. I above). Unlike these strange creatures, Franko's protagonist is a conscientious and loyal professional:

> His [sc. Rafalovych's] reputation as one of the best lawyers quickly spread through the district. Peasants gravitated towards him with their grievances and concerns [. . .]. He established a primary rule for himself: to always tell everyone the unvarnished truth, to never mislead anyone by raising false hopes. At first this approach did not appeal to the peasants who, with their run-of-the-mill lawyers [. . .] had learned to expect that at first they would invariably be promised a speedy and easy victory, then they would be milked dry of their funds, and finally, they would be ruined financially or, in the best-case scenario, simply sent away with nothing to show for the money they had spent. It was obvious that Dr. Rafalovych was not anxious to gain an overly quick and easy popularity, that he [. . .] defended only solid

---

2-e izd. (Moscow: n.p., 1909), 125–155; reprinted Frankfurt a.M. 1967. On this significant statement, see Andrzej Walicki, *Legal Philosophers of Russian Liberalism* (Notre Dame: Notre Dame UP, 1992), ch. VI; Alfred Sproede, "Rechtsbewußtsein (pravosoznanie) als Argument und Problem russischer Theorie und Philosophie des Rechts" [Legal Consciousness as Argument and Problem of Russian Legal Theory and Philosophy] (§ II) in *Gewohnheitsrecht – Rechtsprinzipien – Rechtsbewußtsein: Transformationen der Rechtskultur in West- und Osteuropa*, ed. Werner Krawietz and Sproede (Berlin: Duncker & Humblot, 2006), 151–220.

19 "Самі селяни, що зразу не раз просили його, щоб писав їм подання по-польськи, бо з руськими мають клопіт в урядах, почали впевнятися в своїм праві і [. . .] почали домагатися пошанування для своєї народності [. . .]. А серед міських головачів, котрих гнилий супокій був збентежений сими новаторствами, зараз знайшлася друга готова формула на означення властивого характеру д-ра Рафаловича: *се москаль*! [. . .] Русин, що не клониться під польське ярмо, не лижеться до польської єрархії, – се або демагог і соціаліст, або москаль. Tertium non datur" (XI; 216; emphasis in the original).

> cases, those that he thought had a possibility of being won. The city elite, who from the first moment had summed up their impressions of him in a single sentence – "*this one will be a demagogue*" – were soon forced to take back their hasty judgement. (XI; 65–66)[20]

Unlike the majority of the Russian writers, whose interest is focused on noisy *causes célèbres* and on the problem of state-administered punishment, Ivan Franko approaches the domain of the law and justice under the auspices of civil society. The conclusion of his novel – rather than focusing on the circumstances and penal consequences of crime – probes into the capacity of advocacy for educating law-abiding citizens and developing an emphatic idea of the lawyer's work as a kind of 'primer charge' of political reform.

Rafalovych's program of political action is densely interwoven with his duties as a lawyer; his reflections on issues of "local" or "national work" (misceva pracia, narodna pracia, XI; 68 / 217; LIV; 314 / 413) hark back to the theories of "organic work" ("praca u podstaw," "praca organiczna") as promoted by Polish "positivists" like writers Aleksander Świętochowski, Bolesław Prus, and others:[21]

> he never missed an opportunity to impress upon all and sundry the need for local leaders to work for the economic betterment of the people. "Our peasant is a beggar – a slave of a lord, of a Jew, of whomever you want. What good is it to talk about politics? What politics can you engage in with peasants? [. . .] Try to organize the people for an economic struggle, establish stores and credit unions in your communities, granaries for wheat; train people to administer, to trade, to think about tomorrow [. . .]. You will see that we will attain our

20 "Слава його [sc. Рафаловича] як одного з найліпших адвокатів швидко облетіла всі повіти. Селяни горнулися до нього зі своїми кривдами і жалями [. . .]. Він поклав собі головним правилом говорити кождому щиру правду, не дурити нікого марними надіями, і се зразу не сподобалося многим селянам, що звичайними [. . .] адвокатами були привчені до того, що спочатку їм у всякім разі обіцювано скоре і легке виграння справи, потім видоєно їх добре, а вкінці доводжено до руїни або в найліпшім разі відправлювано з канцелярії ні з чим. Д-р Рафалович, очевидячки, не рвався до надто швидко і дешево популярності, але спокійно і витривало тяг свою лінію спокійно і витривало тяг свою лінію, заступав тільки реальні справи, де бачив можність виграння; міські головачі, що вже від першої хвилі зложили були про нього формулу: «*се буде демагог*» – швидко були змушені взяти її назад" (XI; 215; emphasis in the original).

21 Cf. "Warsaw Positivism and the Idea of Organic Work" (Pozytywizm warszawski i idea pracy organicznej), ch. VII, 5 in Jan Skoczyński and Jan Woleński, *Historia filozofii polskiej* [*A History of Polish Philosophy*] (Kraków: Wyd. WAM, 2010), 311–317. Franko encountered Polish positivism during his student semesters in L'viv, especially in the lectures of Polish philosopher Julian Ochorowicz (1850–1917) (Skoczyński and Woleński, *Historia*, 319–322); about this phase in Franko's political maturation, cf. the rich study by Iaroslav Hrytsak, *Prorok u svoïi vitchyzni: Franko ta ioho spil'nota (1856–1886)* [*A Prophet in His Country: Franko and the Community (1856–1886)*] (Kyiv: Krytyka, 2006), 156–157.

national rights and garner respect for our nationality in proportion to the strength or our economic growth." (68)[22]

The fact that *Fateful Crossroads*, as is evident here, puts a lawyer in the role formerly reserved for detectives or examining magistrates (that is, the stock protagonists of canonical detective literature) follows a perfectly plausible logic. In comparison with the above-mentioned concurrents, Franko's central character is a more competent and multifarious agent of justice since his professional duties lead him to become a social reformer as well.

2.4 Literature and "The Struggle for Law"

The literary appraisal of advocacy in *Fateful Crossroads* takes place in a quite significant moment in the history of ideas. As an ethnic Ukrainian citizen of the Habsburg Empire, Franko was socialized in an environment that held one of the highest ranks of European progress, especially in the legal domain. The 1867 Austro-Hungarian Constitution proclaimed a catalogue of fundamental rights that the Galician radicals could take as a serious basis for further legal and democratic development. This situation also had a decisive impact on Franko's novel. By staging Rafalovych's action on behalf of the rule of law, Franko's plot transparently alludes to the title and substance of a lecture that Rudolf von Jhering (1818–1892), law professor at Vienna University since 1868, presented in March 1872 to an audience of the "Wiener Juristische Gesellschaft" and which he (shortly before leaving Vienna for a professorship at the University of Göttingen) published in an extended booklet version: *The Struggle for Law*.[23]

22 "він не переставав товкти про конечність місцевої праці над економічним піднесенням народу. «Наш селянин – жебрак, слуга панський, жидівський, чий хочете. Що тут балакати про політику? Яку політику ви можете зробити з жебраками? [. . .] Пробуйте організувати його до економічної боротьби, закладайте по громадах каси позичкові, зсипи збіжжя, крамниці, привчайте людей адміністрували, купчити, дбати про завтра [. . .]. Будете видіти, що в міру того, як буде рости наша економічна сила, ми будемо здобувати собі й національні права, і повагу для своєї народності»." (XI, 217).

23 Rudolf von Jhering, *Der Kampf um's Recht* (Vienna: n.p., 1872); Franko read German and must have known one of the editions available between the first and the tenth printing published in 1891, that is, in the decade preceding *Fateful Crossroads*. Among the translations that may have been *known or available* to Franko's Ukrainian readers unfamiliar with German, I can mention two Russian (*Bor'ba za parvo*; Moscow 1874; Petersburg 1895) and two Polish editions (*Walka o prawo*; Lviv 1875; Petersburg 1894). For my summary, I refer to the English translation *The Struggle for Law*, 5th ed., trans. John J. Lalor (Chicago: Callaghan & Co, 1915), first printed in 1879. Concise presentations of Jhering are available in Thomas Gil, "Jhering, Rudolf von (1818–1892)" in

In this 'manifesto' on the politics of law, composed in an interim between two of Jhering's central treatises, *The Spirit of Roman Law* (*Der Geist des römischen Rechts*; 1852–1865) and *Finality in Law* (*Der Zweck im Recht*; 1877), Jhering formulates his program of "productive jurisprudence" as an alternative to the idea of a legal order understood as a systematic construction of concepts. Rather than being established without regard to 'fluid' social realities and conflicts, a singular law, but also the legal system as a whole, relies for its validity on the combativeness of its beneficiaries. It is the effort of the latter to enforce their subjective rights as a protection of legitimate interest which ultimately confers life and authority to the legal order. In this sense, the struggle for a subjective right must be considered an ethical service to the community and to the legal order as a whole. Instead of an unshakable 'will to order,' it is the compatibility of divergent interests wrought by the creative endeavor of a judge that makes the law.

The literary echo of Jhering's booklet is not limited to Franko's novel: in 1882, the German-speaking Galician Jewish writer Karl Emil Franzos took inspiration from Jhering's text for his novel *Der Kampf um's Recht* (*The Struggle for Law*).[24] The novel is set in South-Eastern Galicia near Kolomyia, on the edge of the Carpathian Mountains. The Ruthenian peasant son Taras Barabola from the Podolian plains marries into a well-off family of the Hutsul highlanders and is soon elected village judge. A conflict between the village community and the corrupt estate manager of the local Polish lord is decided to the disavantage of the Hutsuls. Barabola's legal recourse repeatedly suffers defeat, resulting in him being discredited in his village, where long-standing Hutsul customs of revenge and of armed conflict curb the effect of modernized Habsburgian law. After constant denial of justice before the local and regional judges, Barabola consults a lawyer in Kolomyia and finally travels to Vienna to win the Emperor over to his case.

When this lamentably fails as well, he assembles a band of *haydamaks* (brigands) and, over many months, takes revenge for peasants from the entire district that were exploited or illegally penalized by their Polish overlords. The spectacular raids gain wide acclaim, since Barabola, instead of engaging in *haydamak* traditions of killing and plundering, takes punitive measures only after a detailed examination of the case, including the hearing of witnesses. Extorted money found in

---

The Philosophy of Law: An Encyclopedia, ed. Christopher Berry Gray (New York: Garland Publishing, 1999), 448–449; Guido Fassò, *Storia della filosofia del diritto*, Vol. III: *Ottocento e Novecento* (Roma: Editori Laterza, 2001), ch. XI ("Teorie giuridiche antiformalistiche").

24 I use the second edition of the novel: Karl Emil Franzos, *Ein Kampf um's Recht*, I–II (Breslau: Verlag S. Schottlaender, 1882).

the Polish aristocratic houses is not looted, but instead returned to the communities affected by aristocratic abuse. The popular avenger abides by a struggle for law that leaves the authorities divided over the course of action to take.

Barabola's final defeat comes from within the *haydamak* forces; after the false deposition of a witness manipulated with the intent of personal retaliation, Barabola pronounces a wrongful death sentence. This event shakes his conviction that he is waging a just war against the Polish lords and the Austrian judicial authorities; he surrenders and is executed by a firing squad. In the meantime, however, the stolen land has been restituted to his village community; the aristocratic wrongdoers must step back or flee abroad.

Taras Barabola is a kind of 'legalistic revision' of Heinrich von Kleist's *Michael Kohlhaas* (1810). Unlike the conflict in the German story, the Western Ukrainian rebellion does not arise from a personal conflict of the protagonist, but from his mandate as the guarantor and protector of his village's rights. Franzos depicts two regional mentalities (the Ruthenian and the Hutsul community) confronted by the Austro-Hungarian legal order, which had been established by the strong Emperors Joseph II (ruling from 1765 to 1790) and Franz I (1804–1835), but had then gone into decline under the weak regime of Emperor Ferdinand I "the Kindhearted" ("der Gütige," 1835–1848).[25] Taras Barabola is a remarkably loyal follower of the constitutional order; the admonitions to his fellow *haydamaks* often read like praise of the Habsburgian legal ideal. As a motto for his novel, Franzos quotes two long excerpts from Jhering's booklet – the famous praise of the struggle for law as "the poetry of character" and as a "tempest [producing] a purification of the moral atmosphere."[26]

We have thus followed the journey from Franko's novel *Fateful Crossroads* (1900) back to von Jhering's popular legal manifesto *Der Kampf um's Recht* (1872) and then forward to Karl Emil Franzos's novel *Der Kampf um's Recht* (1882) as an

25 Franzos, *Ein Kampf um's Recht*, I: 161 ("Ja, wenn der gute, große Kaiser Joseph noch lebte!" [Yes, if the good, great King Joseph was still alive!]); I: 174 ("Aber um Rechtssachen kann er sich ja nicht bekümmern, dem armen, kranken Manne ist ja die Regierung ohnehin zur Last. [. . .] Ja, wenn er so wäre wie sein Onkel Joseph oder wenigstens wie sein Vater Franz." [But he cannot take care of legal affairs, this poor, illness-stricken man toils anyway under the burden of government. [. . .] If only he were like his uncle Joseph or at least like his father Franz.]); I: 272 (on Ferdinand I as a distracted, senile weakling); I: 275 ("Da der Kaiser nicht seine Pflicht gegen mich erfüllt, so bin ich meiner Pflicht gegen ihn entbunden." [Since the Emperor does not do his duty to me, I am absolved from my duties to him.]).

26 Cf. von Jhering, *The Struggle for Law*, 59–60 ("This ideal conception of the law is not a privilege → the struggle for law, in the battle for one's legal rights, is the poetry of character."); 81–82 ("Every man who sees the law violated → that moral force, which like a tempest [. . .] produces a purification of the moral atmosphere enjoyed both by the individual and by all.").

intermediate juncture on the path of reception. Franko's documented legacy shows no comment on Franzos's novel, but there is good reason to assume that he knew this work. Franko is familiar with even highly specialized publications of the Jewish-German writer and repeatedly quotes from his literary criticism.[27] Hence, for their legal subtext, Franko's and Franzos's novels possibly stem from a common 'pre-text'; a thorough comparative reading of Franzos's *Der Kampf um's Recht* and Franko's *Fateful Crossroads* (which we must postpone to another occasion) could be expected to be a plausible and enlightening venture. While Franzos included attorney Eugen Starkowski in his novel as a reasonable and law-abiding, albeit weak, support for the rebellious central figure, Franko's protagonist Rafalovych is a lawyer himself, and he attains his aims without previously challenging the legal order by open insurgency. His own overview of Habsburgian justice and legal order in *Fateful Crossroads* marks an alternative literary reworking of Jhering's *Struggle for Law*. At any rate, the study of the intellectual triangle Jhering–Franzos–Franko seems to be a worthwhile task for the future.

3 The Lawyer as Disenchanted Revolutionary and Womanizer: Volodymyr Vynnychenko's *Notes of a Pug-Nosed Mephistopheles* (1917)

The next step of our discussion leading to a novel published seventeen years after *Fateful Crossroads* will give further credit to our assumption that the density of legal discourse in Ukrainian literature is anything but negligible.

27 The register to Franko's *Zibrannia tvoriv u 50-i tomakh* [*Collected Works in 50 Vols.*], *Dovidkovyj tom*: T. 51 (Kyiv: Naukova dumka, 1989), 284, carries no mention of Franzos's *Der Kampf ums Recht*, except for the editor's statement that a Ukrainian translation of the novel – *Bor'ba za pravo* – appeared in 1913. However, Franko repeatedly quotes the work of Franzos as a literary critic (on Ukrainian poetry and Christmas carols; on Swiss writer Conrad Ferdinand Meyer; on Ukrainian literary history and folklore): *Zibrannia tvoriv u 50-i tomakh*, T. 28: 9–10, 21; T. 31: 408–410, 427–429, 453; T. 41: 21, 33. It is improbable that Franzos's novel should have escaped Franko's attention.

3.1 Habsburgian Ukraine (Galicia) vs. Russian-Administered (Eastern) Ukraine

Before the 'integration' of East and West forced on Ukraine by Stalin's Red Army, the Ukrainian people lived divided between two empires; roughly 80% resided in the South-Western periphery of Russia (i.e. 'Little Russia'), and the rest in the Eastern extremity of the Habsburg Empire (Galicia).[28] Despite this division, there existed intellectual and literary exchange between both parts of the country. This is the backdrop against which we now proceed to a comparison between Franko's and Vynnychenko's portrait of a lawyer. However, before juxtaposing these portraits, we should briefly recall their respective historical and legal contexts.

Towards the end of the nineteenth century, the Austro-Hungarian Empire could boast of sailing at the peak of European progress thanks to a large effort towards legal reform and to the modern constitution of 1867. By comparison, the Russian Empire did not envisage a constitution before the short-lived "Fundamental Laws of the State" (Основные государственные законы) promulgated in April/May 1906 and derided by Max Weber as a symptom of "pseudo-constitutionalism"; the legislative committee had even been urged to avoid the term "constitution" so as not to revive the memory of the Decembrist conspiracy and its rallying cry.[29] The 1864 reform of procedural law in Russian-administered Ukraine has been described as the introduction into the autocratic system of an institution defined by criteria of uninhibited public speech (*glasnost'*); the contradictory jurisdiction and the jury were actually perceived as the injection of an anti-systemic, 'disfunctional' institution into a precarious political framework.[30] The reform gave rise to a profession that was new for Russian-administered Ukraine: the professional lawyer.

At least in the mirror of literature, this figure is not always a paragon of juridical wit, let alone of integrity. In Panas Myrnyi's dramatic satire *Outwitted!*

---

28 See Orest Subtelny, *Ukraine: A History*, 2nd ed. (Toronto: U. of Toronto P, 1994), 201 and part IV ("Ukraine Under Imperial Rule").

29 Max Weber, "Rußlands Übergang zum Scheinkonstitutionalismus" [Russia's Transition to Pseudo-Constitutionalism] *Archiv für Sozialwissenschaft und Sozialpolitik*, Vol. XXIII, Neue Folge, 5.1, Beilage (1906): 165–401. For the conflict over the label "Fundamental Laws of the State" or "Constitution," cf. Valentin Gitermann, *Geschichte Russlands* [*History of Russia*], Vol. III (Frankfurt a.M. 1965), 420.

30 Cf. Friedhelm Berthold Kaiser, *Die russische Justizreform von 1864: Zur Geschichte der russischen Justiz von Katharina II. bis 1917* [*The Russian Reform of Justice: On the History of Russian Justice from Catherine II to 1917*] (Leiden: Brill, 1972); Jörg Baberowski, *Autokratie und Justiz: Zum Verhältnis von Rechtsstaatlichkeit und Rückständigkeit im ausgehenden Zarenreich 1864–1914* [*Autocracy and Justice: On the Relationship Between the Rule of Law and Backwardness in the Last Years of the Tsarist Empire 1864–1914*] (Frankfurt a.M.: Vittorio Klostermann, 1996).

mentioned above, the shady lawyer Khrapko presses for a fraudulent proceeding on the basis of advance payment, then gets in touch with the adverse party and encourages their people to engage as well in a costly process against the opponents. In order to hide his illegal role as the representative of both the accusation and the defense, he hires a straw person – the juridically incompetent schoolteacher Pecharycia, whose central motif is to profitably marry Khrapko's daughter. By secretly pulling the strings for both sides, Khrapko is able to manipulate the legal process and to grab considerable sums from both sides. Beside these financial advantages, Khrapko's victory has another significance; the legal victory is supposed to promise him success for his candidature as Judge of the Peace and to grant him access to the town's notabilities. Myrnyi's comedy *Ruin* follows a similar plot.

When compared to such antecedents, Franko's lawyer Rafalovych seems like an alien; Ukrainian intellectuals living under Russian rule must have perceived the Galician champion of multi-cultural democracy and of the rule of law more as an envoy from cloud cuckoo land than as an instance of real socio-political and legal progress. In one word, *Fateful Crossroads* was scarcely appreciated at its full value, or was even misunderstood – and all the more so in times of consecutive wars; the dramatic defeat the Russian troops suffered in 1905 was just nine years in the past when the First World War broke out.

Vynnychenko wrote his *Notes of a Pug-Nosed Mephistopheles* (*Zapysky kyrpatoho Mefistofelia*) in 1916 and published it the following year.[31] The novel sacrifices to the trend of 'diabolic literature' fashionable in the last decades of the Russian Empire: *Notes of a Pug-Nosed Mephistopheles* appeared between Fedor Sologub's novel *A Shabby Demon* (*Melkij bes*; 1905) and the satirical narrative *Satan's Diary* (*Dnevnik Satany*; 1921), a posthumous publication by Leonid Andreev (1878–1919). Scholarship dedicated to *Notes of a Pug-Nosed Mephistopheles* emphasizes Vynnychenko's contribution

31 Volodymyr Vynnychenko, "Zapysky kyrpatoho Mefistofelia: Roman" in *Literaturno-naukovyi visnyk*, 1917, T. LXVII, No. 1; No. 2–3; T. LXVIII, No. 4; No. 5–6; for quotations in Ukrainian, I use the recent edition, Volodymyr Vynnychenko, *Zapysky kyrpatoho Mefistofelia. Roman, povist', opovidannia, p'iesa* (Kharkiv: Folio, 2006), 3–203; the page number referring to this edition is given in the main text – preceded by the pagination [Engl. page (or the lack of it —) / Ukr. page] of the English translation, Volodymyr Vynnychenko, *Notes of a Pug-Nosed Mephistopheles: A Novel*, trans. Theodore S. Prokopov (Godeffroy: Guymard P, 2001). As this English translation presents a host of inadequacies, errors, and even arbitrarily deleted passages – cf. the much too conciliatory review by Marta Tarnawsky in *Journal of Ukrainian Studies*, 28.1 (2003): 141 – I have modified the English quotations here and there (or supplied my own translation) in the interest of an adequate rendering of the Ukrainian original. Among the few editions in non-Slavic languages, the German translation (affected by occasional flaws, but complete) deserves mention: Wolodymyr Wynnytschenko, *Der schiefnäsige Mephisto: Ein Beziehungsroman*, trans. Rolf Göbner (Berlin: Rütten & Loening, 1994).

to the international 'Diavoliada' trend of later years (Stanisław Przybyszewski, Mikhail Bulgakov, Thomas Mann *et al.*).[32]

Nowhere, however, can we find an analysis or even mention of the fact that Iakiv Mykhailiuk acts as a lawyer (*advokat*) or attorney-at-law (*prysiazhnyi povirenyi*, 16, 80 / 18, 89). No academic readers so far have taken notice of the fact that it is only this profession that could have provided him with deep insights into the private lives of the couples heading for divorce. The 'devilish' nature of Vynnychenko's protagonist delegitimizes his legal action. *Notes of a Pug-Nosed Mephistopheles* does not leave even a bit of Franko's depiction of a lawyer intact; the author from Eastern Ukraine literally 'wipes out' his predecessor. In 1900, when *Fateful Crossroads* came out in print, Vynnychenko (1880–1951) had just registered as a law student at Kiev University. His stay, however, did not last beyond three semesters since he was dismissed for leftist agitation and arrested. His novel forcefully vetoes Franko's role model of the enlightened, reasonable attorney at law. Whether Vynnychenko intended to refute his colleague's novel (which we can safely assume he knew) is a matter of future scholarship; but at any rate, he demolishes Franko's idea of a lawyer working in the loyal service of the legal order.

3.2 Mykhailiuk: Divorce Lawyer, Shabby Demon, Man in Love (Vynnychenko's Plot)

Notes of a Pug-Nosed Mephistopheles is the first-person report of Kievan lawyer Iakiv Vasil'ovych Mykhailiuk on his city, his profession, and his love affairs. Professionally, Iakiv is confronted with the failed bonds of matrimony weighing on his friends' shoulders. Former womanizer Sosnytskyi, Iakiv's rival in that matter, is now married to Sonia, one of Iakiv's intimate relationships of former times. Sonia herself does not know whether Sosnyts'kyi or Iakiv is the father of her only son Andrii; together with Iakiv, she speculates over the resemblance of her son's face – until Sosnyts'kyi appears to her as the more plausible progenitor.

Iakiv faces a still more difficult case with the married couple Kryvulia; Varvara Fedorivna is unwilling to divorce, while her husband Panas Pavlovych has already left the apartment and joined his lover Oleksandra Mykhailivna. But Panas Pavlovych cannot enjoy this situation of de-facto divorce because Varvara Fedorivna is adamant about their child, Dima; the separation from his son hits

32 Valentina Kharkhun, *Poėtika romana Vladimira Vinnichenko «Zapiski konopatogo Mefistofelia»* [*The Poetics of Volodymyr Vynnychenko's Novel «Zapysky kyrpatoho Mefistofelia»*] (Kyiv, PhD in Philology/Avtoreferat dissertatsii, 2000), 10.

the father so desperately that Iakiv Mykhailiuk finally suggests abducting Dima – a crude betrayal of all lawyerly ethics:

> – In my opinion, Panas Pavlovich, – I say it as calmly and casually as possible (in order to soothe the bitter ring of the thought itself) – we must kidnap Dima from Varvara Khvedorovna . . .
>
> As I expected, they cast each other a terrified glance. I feel fine with this fear, which means that they find my suggestion very scary. Isn't it delightful to incite somebody to a frightful deed?
>
> – Yes, kidnap . . . This is the simplest way to solve the problem. By legal, or more exactly, by juridical means you will attain nothing. In such cases, the law keeps a neutral stance, like a bystander. [. . .] Obviously, there remains only the way I am suggesting. (29)[33]

His wife opposes divorce on principle and uses Dima against her unfaithful husband.

Vynnychenko tries to spice up this dilemma by the hint of devilishness he conferred to his protagonist. Mykhailiuk openly confesses his leaning towards the humiliation of other people:

> I like to lure somebody to a mountain peak and then to push him down into the precipice. The most beautiful moment is when his eyes, wide open with hope and rapture, suddenly light up in terror. It's pleasant when the attention declines, and you carefully, softly, turn him in the direction you need. And he smiles, thinking that he moves by his own will, "by himself"! Now that feeling is priceless: when you have him under control to a point where he does not even notice it. (2)[34]

As Tamara Hundorova has shown, Vynnychenko's 'sympathy for the devil' is an important step leading towards the "construction of the modernist discourse."

33 "– На мою гадку, Панасе Павловичу, – як-мога спокійніше та недбаліше (щоб цим загладити гострість самої думки) кажу я, – треба викрасти Діму в Варвари Хведорівни . . .

Як я й сподівався, скидуються очима обоє злякано. Мені цей ляк приємний, значить, їм дуже страшне те, що я пропоную. А хиба не приємно посунути когось на страшне? [. . .]

– Так, викрасти . . . Це найпростіший спосіб розвязати питання. Законним, чи, краще сказати, юридичним шляхом, ви нічого не можете осягти. Закон у таких випадках стоїть собі набоці. [. . .] Значить, лишається той спосіб, який я пропоную" (34–35).

34 "Мені приємно заманути чоловіка на саму гору й зіпхнути його вниз. І той момент, коли в очах, поширених надією й захватом, блискає жах – є найкращий. Приємно, коли увага застигає, й ти обережно, м'ягко повертаєш його в той бік, який тобі потрібний. А він усміхається й гадає, що сам іде, «сам іде»! От за це ще можна багато дати: коли ти так запанував над ним, що він уже й не помічає того" (3).

The modern hero has to confront the temptation of evil without recourse to the framework of traditional moral convictions.[35]

This is not the same as moral indifference. When Varvara Fedorivna tries to win back her husband, Iakiv follows these manœuvers with sympathy. He discovers in her a heart-breaking and likeable 'kindergarten teacher' and gives her support, at least in the beginning of Panas Pavlovych's divorce efforts (103–127 / 107–120). For a while, Oleksandra is tempted to renounce the relationship with Panas Pavlovych; she starts looking for a new partner but is not successful (134–135 / 137–138). Mykhailiuk has pity for her and tries to give her a sense of her attractiveness and of her chances of finding a lover. In these dialogues, Vynnychenko depicts the ambivalence of Mykhailiuk's feelings; while giving his former lover signs of support and friendship, he is constantly tempted by the sensuality of Oleksandra's presence. In the meantime, the marriage of the Kryvulias pursues its laborious course: the partners continue to see each other – and to battle passionately against each other. During one dispute, Panas Pavlovych shoots a bullet at the person who is still his wife; he then panics and runs to Iakiv's office as he fears he has killed her (— / 176–178). After this clash, Varvara Fedorivna consents to divorce and even to leave her son Dima to her husband; at last, Panas can return to his lover Oleksandra (— / 176–181).

After interminably wooing her, Iakiv finally gets acquainted with Hanna Pylypyvna Zaberezhna, who is preparing to be an opera singer (76, 85 / 81–82, 92). Mykhailiuk calls her "Little White Riding Hood" (Bila Shapochka) on account of the cap she wears. Bila Shapochka is the woman of his dreams. Shortly before this acquaintance, he had dated a divorced woman, Klavdiia Petrivna, whom he accompanied (jointly with her son Kostia) on a trip to Crimea. There, he begets a child with her without realizing it right away. When she informs him about her pregnancy, he offers her money for an abortion and then leaves her. It is only after he is in an even more serious relationship with Bila Shapochka that he gets a letter from Klavdiia Petrivna in which she informs him that she did not (or did not want to) have an abortion, with the result that Iakiv finds himself the father of baby Mika (Mykhailo). He experiences this turn of his previous relationship as a cruel surprise and, infuriated, demolishes his apartment's interior (— / 147–149).

This crisis and, surprisingly, the help of Bila Shapochka (141–142 / 149–151) provide the link to the last part of the novel. Iakiv sees his fatherhood as an obligation to start a stable relation with Klavdija; he tries hard to get rid of this

35 Tamara Hundorova, *ProIavlennia slova: Dyskursiia rann'oho ukraïns'koho modernyzmu* [*The Emerging Word: The Discourse of Early Ukrainian Modernism*], 2nd, rev. ed. (Kyiv: Krytyka, 2009), 271–333 (ch. "Konstruiuvannia modernists'koho dyskursu (Volodymyr Vynnychenko)").

irksome duty. In moments of fury, he even twice tries to kill the baby that Klavdija begged him to guard. In front of an open window, he fetches the child from the cradle and holds it out into the winter cold (150–151, 157–159 / 187–188, 194–196); here we return to Mykhailiuk's evil drive, his habit of playing with the terror of other beings: "I like to lure somebody to a mountain peak and then to push him down into the precipice" (2).[36] However, the helpless little being survives despite the grave mistreatment. At last, Iakiv accepts his obligation and puts an end to his affair with Bila Shapochka; his lover takes the initiative to leave Kyiv and – as Iakiv later learns – moves to Moscow, where she works as a singer and lives with an artist (203). Here is Iakiv's self-description after this turning point:

> And now I am no longer the lawyer-predator that feeds on the law's carrion and on the foolishness, helplessness, and greed of his victims. I am a modest attorney-at-law who defends credulous and desperate beasts of prey against the law. (16)[37]

Iakiv boasts of Sonia's commentary that praised him for his new "sense of responsibility": "They all are very much excited by my strong sense of responsibility" (Їх усіх особливо зворушує таке сильне почування морального обов'язку в мене; 169 / 203).

3.3 "Roman à thèse"? The Children of a Lost Revolution

The narrative in form of a confession, occasionnally alluding to Dostoevskii's *Notes from the Underground* (*Zapiski iz podpol'ia*; 1864), unfolds in episodes that alternate between the couples eager to separate from each other on the one hand, and Mykhailiuk's encounters with Klavdija Petrivna (the mother of their child) or Bila Shapochka on the other. A basic motif, especially in the first half of the novel, is the cynicism and anti-feminism of the first-person narrator.

Oleksandra Mykhailivna, Panas Pavlovych's lover, once inflicts on Mykhailiuk a discussion on justice, morality, and the law (104–109 / 109–115); here is an excerpt from this dispute:

---

36 "Мені приємно заманути чоловіка на саму гору й зіпхнути його вниз. І той момент, коли в очах, поширених надією й захватом, блискає жах – є найкращий" (3).

37 "І от я вже не хижак-адвокат, що годується стервом закона, дуростю, безпорадностю та жадностю своїх жертв. Я скромний повірений, що боронить проти закона й хижаків довірливих та безпорадних" (18).

– You ruin yourself by violating the laws of nature. As far as I know, you do this in the name of man's spirituality, in the name of moral imperatives and the like. But don't you see that you violate genuine morality?

Oleksandra Mykhailivna carefully shoves the saucers aside [. . .], then she sits down and says:

– But what does this genuine morality look like?

– It's a morality, Oleksandra Mykhailivna, which requires neither commandments nor human laws, neither prisons nor lawyers; a morality providing that a mother loves her children, a man is attracted to a woman, and *vice versa*; this morality makes us live as a community instead of in isolation, and it makes a revolutionary accept the death verdict pronounced on him . . . Would you imagine a commandment like "A mother must love her child"?! Or "It is forbidden to live alone"?! We do not need such a commandment, because there are higher commandments, the violation of which is much more severly punished by the supreme law of nature than the violations of man-made laws. Under the supreme law of nature there are no sentences "by leniency." Guilty – and that's that!

I feel that my words have an excessive smell of courtroom and I switch to another style.

– In other words, Oleksandra Mykhailivna, you alone make your life difficult, pale, monotonous and harmful to yourself. (105–106)[38]

On the next occasion, Iakiv's opponent is less easily silenced: Bila Shapochka aggressively confronts him with questions concerning his dubious barrister mandates (117–120 / 120–124):

– When I read in the newspapers a report about some lawsuit against an evident villain, I always wondered: what kind of lawyers are the people who defend him? [. . .]

---

38 "– Ви губите себе тим, що нарушуєте закони природи. Наскільки мені відомо, ви робите це в ім'я духової сторони людини, в ім'я заповідей моралі й ще чогось там. Але хиба ви не бачите, що нарушуєте дійсну мораль?

Олександра Михайлівна обережно відсуває набік тарілочки, [. . .] сідає на стілець і каже:

– Яка ж ця дійсна мораль?

– Така, Олександро Михайлівно, яка не потребує ні заповідей, ні людських законів, ні тюрем, ні панів адвокатів; така, на підставі якої мати любить своїх дітей, мужчину тягне до женщини, і навпаки; на підставі якої ми живемо громадою, а не поодиноко, на підставі якої революціонер іде на смертну кару . . . Хиба є заповідь: «Мати хай любить свою дитину»?! Або: «Забороняється жити поодиноко»?! В таких заповідях немає ніякої потреби, бо це є вищі заповіді, яких нарушення далеко краще, ніж у людських, передбачив вищий закон природи. Там немає присудів «по снисхожденію». Винен і край!

Я почуваю, що мої слова занадто тхнуть залею [*correction:* судовою залею], й я зміняю стиль.

– Иншими словами, Олександро Михайлівно, ви самі робите своє життя трудним, блідим, одноманітним і шкідливим для вас" (110–111).

– That is a complicated question, Hanna Pylypivna. First of all, you cannot always say that the person is a villain. [. . .] Even if this is clear, then the lawyer is not a judge; he does not pronounce a verdict on the defendant, but he pleads not guilty and alleviates the weight of the punishment; to the best of his ability he corrects the imperfection of our social relations. It is well known that punishment does not attain its aim and that everybody it better off if punishment is less severe. That is why one can defend even the worst villain.

– But is it allowed to plead for him in a way that makes him win his case to the detriment of the other party that is innocent? [. . .] You know, when I read about such lawsuits, I imagine the lawyers acting on behalf of these robbers as awfully cruel and obtuse monsters, – morally speaking, of course. [. . .] After all he, the lawyer, knows that if his client wins the case, then by the same token he robs the opposing party, an honest and righteous person. Right? He knows it, after all. But all the same he takes the defense and helps the thief. But when he helps the thief, then he can also steal himself as soon as a good occasion arises. It's true, isn't it? (117–118)[39]

After the dramatic crisis brought about by the information that Klavdiia Petrivna did not have an abortion, Iakiv sinks into a soliloquy on morality and the laws of nature:

What actually is morality? Morality is a pink cosmetic powder spread over the laws of nature. Shapochka thinks that pleading for Kubechka [a person indicted for blackmail, defended by Mykhailiuk] is immoral. But she considers it as normal and moral to defend the laws of the strong and those in power, because this stance is sanctioned by a millenium-old layer of pink powder, i.e. the dominant morality. She embraces and kisses her sister's husband, who works for a bank where different cases of fraud took place, clearly to the husband's profit and maybe even with his aid and abet. [. . .] the pink powdered people [. . .] defend this powder-morality: it helps them keep the simple-minded in their hands. Morality is a wall that these people erected between the fundamental laws of life and life's highest manifestation – reason. All of humanity's moral progress comes from the fact that the

39 "Коли я читала в ґазетах про якийнебудь судовий процес, у якому фіґурує очевидний мерзотник, то я за–вжди дивувалась: що то за адвокати, що боронять його? [. . .]

– Це питання складне, Ганно Пилипівно. Насамперед не завсіди можна сказати, що це мерзотник. [. . .] Коли навіть ясно, то адвокат – не суддя; він не судить, а боронить, полегчує силу кари; він у міру сил виправляє недоскональність наших соціяльних відносин. Відомо, що кара не досягає своєї мети, і що, коли та кара буде менша, краще буде для всіх. От через що можна боронити й найбільшого мерзотника.

– А чи можна боронити його так, щоб він виграв справу на шкоду другого, невинного? [. . .] Знаєте, коли я читала про такі процеси, то я в'являла собі адвокатів, що ведуть грабіжницькі справи, якимись бузувірами, – моральними, звичайно, – страшенно жорстокими й тупими. [. . .] Адже він, адвокат, знає, що коли його клієнт виграє справу, то цим він ограбує противника, чоловіка чесного і правого. Так? Знає ж! І все ж таки боронить, помагає грабувати. А коли він помагає грабувати, то й сам, як трапиться добрий випадок, може те саме зробити. Правда? Адже правда?" (122–123).

> humans try to destroy, stone after stone, the personal wall that encloses them. But the people fond of rosy powder, from their side, scrupulously protect that wall, an effort in which they are reliably helped by the fools whom they milk. (121)[40]

Vynnychenko does not indicate the time of the events. There is no explicit allusion to war or to the upcoming revolution, but the past revolution of 1905 and the disillusions of its supporters are felt throughout the text.[41] Vynnychenko's poetics is situated between, on the one hand, literary naturalism (cf. the scenes in the last part of the novel dealing with fatherhood and determination by the bonds of blood) and, on the other hand, the devices of contemporary psychological prose; in a conversation with Shapochka, Vynnychenko points to the deft narration in Maupassant's tales (164 / 199). Maupassant is a major presence in Vynnychenko's work, not only due to his narrative technique, but also because of the shocking exposal of the 'vices' that accompany modern life (extra-marital sex, prostitution etc.).

3.4 Popular Nietzscheanism

Vynnychenko's lawyer experiences the crisis of the notion of reason that is central for the Decadents and for Modernism. Unlike Franko's character, he is not fighting for the legal protection of peasants and workers, but instead working to legally separate failed couples and lead divorce procedures. While in the previous contexts, Iakiv was mainly a reasonable bystander observing other peoples's emotional strife, he loses all decency towards a friend who years ago as "comrade Anton" (*tovarysh Anton*) accompanied him in revolutionary actions (a transparent allusion to Mykhailiuk's pre-1905 militancy). Iakiv wants Nechyporenko to manipulate a witness for a shady legal procedure (— / 144). After the end of the

40 "Що ж таке моральність? Моральність це рожева пудра на законах природи. Шапочка вважає неморальним боронити Кубешку. Але боронити закони сильних і пануючих – річ нормальна й моральна, бо вона санкціонована тисячолітньою верствою пудри – пануючою мораллю. Чоловіка своєї сестри, який служить у банку, де робляться ріжні шахрайські операції, який годується з цих операцій і, мабуть, сам бере в них участь, – вона й обнімає, й цілує. [. . .] припудрені [. . .] боронять пудру, яка помагає їм тримати дурнів у руках. Моральність – це стіна, яку вивели припудрені між основними законами життя й вищим його проявом – розумом. Увесь моральний поступ людськости є в тому, що люде по камінчику стараються знищити цю свою власну стіну. Але припудрені, з свого боку, дбайливо бережуть її, при чому їм ретельно допомагають дурні, яких вони доять" (125).

41 This interpretation of the novel is persuasively developed by Oxana Pachlovska, *Civiltà letteraria ucraina* [*Ukrainian Literary Civilization*] (Rome: Carocci editori, 1998), 991–994, 993.

revolutionary adventure, the former comrade could not find a job like Iakiv's position at the bar, and Iakiv exploits his friend's situation:

> – for the time being we arrange the following work for you. [. . .] It's work of a diplomatic character, so to speak. Look, you must travel to a town and convince a man that there is no absolute truth on earth and that the world is nothing but our imagination. My dear, in court that poor man must depict in the most elementary words certain facts the way we imagine them. And you help him so that he may achieve this result more easily. This is still labor, – to lead one's imagination in a new direction. [. . .] You've been a good agitator, and you will easily manage to do this. What do you think about that?
>
> – That is, what do you mean?! [. . .]
>
> There is nothing more pathetic than the moment when honesty thus stands on its hind legs. (5)[42]

Hence, Mykhailiuk embarks on the forthcoming trial under the provision "that there is no absolute truth in this world, and that the world is nothing but our imagination" [що абсолютної істини на світі немає, і що світ є не що инше, як тільки наша уява] (5 / 7).

For this gross infringement of a lawyer's ethics, he justifies himself by pointing – although without mentioning the philosopher's name – to Friedrich Nietzsche's critique of the notions of truth and morality. The impact of Nietzsche's philosophy in Ukraine has been manifest since the middle of the 1890s. Initially under the spell of George Sand, Ol'ha Kobylians'ka creates the female version of Nietzsche's aristocratic *Übermensch* in her novel *The Princess* (Tsarina, 1896). The most important tribune of Ukrainian Nietzscheanism (in theory, art criticism, and literary practice) is the monthly journal *Ukraïns'ka khata* (*Ukrainian Home*; 1909–1914).[43]

Vynnychenko has left a Ukrainian translation of Nietzsche's *Thus Spake Zarathustra* (*Also sprach Zarathustra*), completed during one of his terms of imprisonment (the

42 "– роботу поки-що ми вам примудруємо таку. [. . .] Так би мовити, дипломатичного характеру. Треба, розумієте, поїхати в один город і вмовити одного чоловіка, що абсолютної істини на світі немає, і що світ є не що инше, як тільки наша уява. Простішими словами, дорогий мій, треба, щоб цей чоловічок змалював на суді деякі речі так, як ми їх уявляємо собі. А щоб це легче було зробити йому, ви поможете йому. Це все ж таки праця, – направляти свою уяву по иншому напрямі. [. . .] Аґітатор із вас добрий, і вам це легко буде зробити. Як ви на це, га?

– Себто, як же це?! [. . .]

Нема нічого більш зворушливого, як оця настовбурченість чесноти" (7).

43 On Nietzsche's presence in Ukrainian culture since the turn of the century, cf. Solomiia Pavlychko, *Dyskurs modernizmu v ukraïns'kii literaturi* [*The Discourse of Modernism in Ukrainian Literature*], 2nd, rev. ed. (Kyiv: Lybid', 1999), part I–II. Among the most important recent studies on Nietzsche and the development of *fin de siècle* Ukrainian literature, cf. Hundorova, *ProIavlennia slova*, cf. footnote 35.

unpublished manuscript is preserved in Kyiv archives).[44] Even before participating in *Ukraïns'ka khata*, Vynnychenko lets the attraction that the German philosopher's writings held for him permeate his own literary works. After occasional references in his plays and tales from roughly 1907 on, Nietzschean themes acquire a more and more systematic presence starting with the novel *Chesnist' s soboju* (*Honesty with Oneself*, 1911). The impact of Nietzscheanism on *Notes of a Pug-Nosed Mephistopheles* can easily be illustrated by the parallels with *Beyond Good and Evil* (1886) and *On the Genealogy of Morality* (1887).[45]

Mykhailiuk's instruction to his former revolutionary comrade resembles the aphorism from *Beyond Good and Evil*: "It is no more than a moral prejudice that the truth is worth more than appearance; in fact, it is the world's most poorly proven assumption" (BGE 35; No. 34). The disdain of bourgeois morality, as expressed in his dispute with Oleksandra Mykhailivna (*Zapysky*, 104–109 / 109–115; cf. above), are reminiscent of Nietzsche's endless tirades against "immediate certainties": "The belief in 'immediate certainties' is a moral naiveté that does credit to us philosophers: but – we should stop being 'merely moral,' for once! Aside from morality, the belief in immediate certainties is a stupidity that does us little credit!" (BGE 34; No. 34). Mykhailiuk's propensity to evil deeds (such as precipitating gullible fellow-travellers down from a mountain peak [*Zapysky*, 2 / 3], exposing a baby to the winter cold [*Zapysky*, 150–151, 157–159 / 187–188, 194–196, or others) can be explained as a way of assuming "the weight and duty of a hundred experiments and temptations of life: – [. . .] he plays *the* rough game . . ." (BGE 96; No. 205).

---

44 See ch. 4 on Vynnychenko and Nietzsche in Volodymyr Panchenko, *Tvorchist' Volodymyra Vynnychenka 1902–1920 rokiv u henetychnykh i typolohichnykh zv"iazkakh z ievropeiskymy literaturamy* [*V. Vynnychenko's Works of the Years 1902–1920 in Their Genetic and Typological Relations With European Literatures*] (Kyiv, PhD, 1998), available at <https://library.kr.ua/wp-content/elib/panchenko/panchenko.pdf>; (acc. April 2022); Mykola Soroka, *Faces of Displacement: The Writings of Volodymyr Vynnychenko* (Montreal: McGill-Queen's UP, 2012), 26–27. The journal *Ukraïns'ka khata* published early comments on Vynnychenko's encounter with Nietzsche: I. Koshits, "Volodymyr Vynnychenko (Eskiz)" [Volodymyr Vynnychenko (a Sketch)], *Ukraïns'ka khata* 3 (1910): 169–177; P. Khrystiuk, "V. Vynnychenko i F. Nitsshe" [V. Vynnychenko and F. Nietzsche], *Ukraïns'ka khata* 4/5 (1913): 275–299; for the second article, cf. <http://sites.utoronto.ca/elul/Vynnychenko/Khrystiuk-Nietsche.pdf> (acc. March 2022).

45 The quotations to come (followed by page numbers and section [№]) refer to the editons published by Cambridge UP; see Friedrich Nietzsche, *Beyond Good and Evil: Prelude to a Philosophy of the Future*, trans. Judith Norman (Cambridge: Cambridge UP, 2002); Nietzsche, *On the Genealogy of Morality*, trans. Carol Diethe (Cambridge: Cambridge UP, 2006); further references in the text, abbreviated as "BGE" and "GM," respectively. For the German originals (*Jenseits von Gut und Böse*; *Zur Genealogie der Moral*), cf. Friedrich Nietzsche, *Sämtliche Werke: Kritische Studienausgabe in 15 Bänden* [*Complete Works: Critical Student Edition in 15 Vols.*], ed. Giorgio Colli and Mazzino Montinari (Munich: dtv, 1999), Vol. 5.

Vynnychenko's protagonist despises his fellow humans for their "deadly hatred against suffering" and their "faith in the morality of *communal* pity"; he enjoys fighting "the almost feminine inability to sit watching, to *let* suffering happen" (BGE 91; No. 202). Accordingly, Nietzsche's *Genealogy of Morality* has a brilliant paragraph on *bad conscience*, which is defined as:

> a serious illness to which man was forced to succumb by the pressure of [. . .] that change whereby he finally found himself imprisoned within the confines of society and peace. It must have been no different for [. . .] the sea animals when they were forced to either become land animals or perish – at one go, all instincts were devalued and 'suspended.' Now they had to walk on their feet and 'carry themselves,' whereas they had been carried by the water up till then: a terrible heaviness bore down on them. They [. . .] did not have their familiar guide any more for this new, unknown world, those regulating impulses that unconsciously led them to safety [. . .]. The whole inner world, originally stretched thinly as though between two layers of skin, was expanded and extended itself and gained depth, breadth and height in proportion to the degree that the external discharge of man's instincts was *obstructed*. [. . .] all those instincts of the wild, free, roving man were turned backwards, *against man himself*. Animosity, cruelty, the pleasure of pursuing, raiding, changing and destroying – all this was pitted against the person who had such instincts: *that* is the origin of 'bad conscience.' (GM 56; Second Essay, No. 16)

Vynnychenko's onslaught on social conventions and taboos, on civility and 'bourgeois manners' certainly stands in the tradition of critical naturalism. But in his debunking of "the soul's wardrobe" (an expression of his Polish contemporary Karol Irzykowski[46]), Vynnychenko refers continually to Nietzsche's critical discourse. He dissects human relations with a strong dose of cynicism; as an example, one may recall the protagonist's first visit to Bila Shapochka which – in view of her reserved mood – Iakiv compares with a dentist appointment (79 / 85).

Notes of a Pug-Nosed Mephistopheles does not flatly 'illustrate' Nietzschean philososphy, however. The first-person narrative resembles the confession in Dostoevskii's *Notes from the Underground*, since Vynnychenko – very much like Dostoevskii – mixes the protagonist's cynicism with soaring declamations on justice, morality, and natural law. However, Vynnychenko eschews Russian legal nihilism, to which some of his prominent colleagues, with Lev Tolstoi as the leading figure, confessed in embarassing statements of the two pre-war decades. To explain Vynnychenko's prudence, taking a glimpse of his Ukrainian context is useful – foremost the apology of the law that Nikolaj Kostomarov developed in his famous article on "Two Nationalities of Rus'" (Dve russkie narodnosti)[47] by distinguishing between a

46 Cf. Irzykowski's novel *Pałuba* [*The Hag*; 1903] and its program of a desperate fight against inauthenticity.

47 Nikolaj Kostomarov, "Dve russkie narodnosti," *Osnova* 3 (1861): 33–80, available in a digital version at <http://litopys.org.ua/kostomar/kos38.htm> (acc. March 2022). An English translation

specifically Ukrainian – *civic* – notion of politics and the Russian doctrines of autocracy. We can surmise that on this point Vynnychenko was also influenced by his elder contemporary Bogdan Kistiakovskii, who condemned the "police state mentality" of the Russian intelligenciia (including its Marxist avant-garde) and tried to promote the notion of a "socialist rule-of-law state."[48]

3.5 The Lawyer as Narrator – What For?

As we mentioned above, Iakiv Mykhailiuk's work as a lawyer is not adequately discussed in the literary studies of Vynnychenko's work. In fact, Vynnychenko astutely moved the specificity of this role into the background of the novel so that the protagonist's profession exercizes its effect from the margins of the plot:

> I again see the lady in black with her boy [. . .]. Every day, leaving the courthouse, I meet them there. [я знову бачу даму в чорному з хлопчиком [. . .]. Щодня, виходячи з суду, я зустрічаю їх тут.] (24 / 29);
> I go home from the courthouse. [Вертаюся з суду.] (41 / 45);
> Coming home from court, [. . .] [Вернувшися з суду, [. . .]] (76 / 82);
> I feel now exactly the same way as I felt then, when the jury said "not guilty," in the case which I defended so poorly. [В мене зараз такий стан, який був тоді, коли присяжні винесли виправдуючий присуд у справі, яку я боронив невдало, погано.] (102 / 106);
> From the courthouse I go directly to Claudia Petrivna's house. [Просто з суду я йду до Клавдії Петрівни.] (— / 159);
> Today I do not need to work at the courthouse, but I go there all the same [. . .]. – Hello! I'm coming directly from the tribunal. [Мені в суд сьогодні не треба, але я все ж таки їду туди [. . .] – Добридень! Я просто з суду.] (152 / 189)

These background characteristics, however, provide the protagonist with a whole cluster of interesting narrative functions. Precisely as a lawyer among whose clients are couples seeking divorce, Vynnychenko's protagonist (1) has access to large portions of his clients' private lives. He is therefore able to compare his own excentric way of life with the situation of his friends and contemporaries. (2) As a professional jurist, Mykhailiuk has every opportunity to meditate on moral questions, the legal order, and the limits of the law. In this sense, he is a logical product of his

under the title "Two Rus' Nationalities" has been published in Serhiy Bilenky, ed., *Fashioning Modern Ukraine: Selected Writings of Mykola Kostomarov, Volodymyr Antonovych, and Mykhajlo Drahomanov* (Edmonton: U of Alberta P, 2013), 134–174, esp. 168–173.

48 Bogdan Kistiakovskii, "Gosudarstvo pravovoe i sotsialisticheskoe" [Rule of Law State and Socialist State], *Voprosy filosofii i psikhologii* 85 (1905/06): 469–507. For Kistiakovskii's indictment of the Russian "police state mentality," cf. Kistiakovskii, "V zashchitu prava," § iv–v; cf. footnote 18.

author, Vynnychenko; the point where the legal regulation of conflicts borders on the domain of ethical reasoning was of special interest for an author who had placed his numerous plays – and their basic tenet *épater le bourgeois* – under the banner of "honesty with oneself" (*chesnist' s soboiu*) and a radical critique of conventional morality. (3) Vynnychenko's lawyer is the most appropriate promotor of arduous moral controversies, as his rhetorical skills and deft use of language – having been, in the first place, nothing more than a device for the exercise of his profession – acquire new significance for the novel's dialogue and style.

(4) In many ways, Mykhailiuk is staged as *parrhesiastes* – not in spite, but exactly on account of his 'Mephistophelian' qualities. He enjoys the privileges of a Russian lawyer as proclaimed in 1864; the legal reform notably guaranteed the right of lawyers to free speech. (5) In Mykhailiuk's case – and here the lawyer's discourse mirrors Vynnychenko's program of a reckless "honesty with oneself" – freedom of speech has clearly cynical implications, if 'cynicism' is taken in the historical sense discussed by Foucault in the context of *parrhesia*. In the lectures mentioned above, Foucault comments on the basic devices of cynic *parrhesia*: (a) critical preaching; (b) scandalous behavior; and (c) 'provocative dialogue.' In these forms of communication, Mykhailiuk's 'Mephistophelian' leanings converge with the aggressive frankness of the cynics:

> There is [. . .] very little positive doctrine in Cynic preaching: no direct affirmation of the good or bad. [. . .] most of their preaching seems to have been directed against social institutions, the arbitrariness of rules of law, and any sort of life-style that was dependent upon such institutions or laws. In short, their preaching was against all social institutions insofar as such institutions hindered one's freedom and independence. Cynic *parrhesia* also had recourse to scandalous behavior or attitudes which called into question collective habits, opinions, standards of decency, institutional rules.[49]

The scandalous behavior of the cynics ultimately leads up to a "game" in which the central *parrhesiastic* device is played out – "provocative dialogue":

> The Cynic parrhesiastic game is, in some respects, not unlike the Socratic dialogue [. . .]. But [. . .] whereas Socrates plays with his interlocutor's ignorance, Diogenes wants to hurt Alexander's pride. [. . .] Diogenes [. . .] voluntarily angers Alexander, and then says, 'Well, you can kill me; but if you do so, nobody else will tell you the truth.' [. . .] the aggressive encounter between Alexander and Diogenes [is] a struggle occurring between two kinds of power: political power and the power of truth. In this struggle, [. . .] the main effect [. . .] is not to bring the interlocutor to a new truth [. . .]; it is to lead the interlocutor to internalize this parrhesiastic struggle – to fight within himself against his own faults, and to be with himself in the same way that Diogenes was with him.[50]

---

49 Foucault, *Discourse and Truth*, 46.

50 Foucault, *Discourse and Truth*, 49–50, 52.

In sum, by making his protagonist a lawyer, Vynnychenko aims to lend real-world plausibility to a character steeped in the methods of cynic questioning and capable of articulating unpleasant truths. The institutions of justice are presented as an unobtrusive backdrop; they function as the literary device that motivates the narrator's intrusion and grip on his clients' private lives.

4 A Tentative Conclusion

The two texts that we have compared here seem to add new qualities to the established class of legal novels. Franko's *Fateful Crossroads* stands in direct opposition to Richard Weisberg's pessimistic account of "protagonists as lawyers." In a novel placed half-way between literary naturalism and *Jugendstil*, the author unfolds a juridical utopia and invents a lawyer capable of *parrhesia* and of politically efficient *truth-telling*. To do so, the novel does not start 'from scratch'; besides the utopian moments, it is a matter-of-fact illustration of the 1867 Austro-Hungarian constitution. The struggle for law waged by the central character marks the integration of Eastern Galician politics into the pursuit of legal advancement in the Habsburg Empire.

Compared to Franko's novel, *Notes of a Pug-Nosed Mephistopheles* strikes a sensibly more ambivalent key. As a jurist, the central character of the novel is a failure. But is he also a complete refutation of his Western Ukrainian counterpart, for that matter? True, Mykhailiuk undermines all hope for an honest, truthful handling of court cases. But his 'cynical' attack on bourgeois morality is – even if it drowns all sense of cosiness – a welcome relief from painful conventions. Vynnychenko legitimizes his protagonist with the doctrine of "honesty with oneself" that he had expounded in numerous plays before featuring it as the title of a novel published in 1911. Although this doctrine lacked philosophical depth (much like the ideas in Jean-Paul Sartre's plays, close to journalism throughout), its literary promotion and courageous defense can well be called an example of *parrhesia*, despite the occasionnally satirical debunking of the law.

Our cursory, narrowly 'thematic' reading of the two Ukrainian novels should be extended, in the long run, into a more extensive study of Ukrainian Modernist fiction. But it seems that our paper, even with its inevitable lacunae, uncovers in the texts of both authors an interesting complexity of thought and a remarkable level of legal consciousness. One should hope that further investigations will lead to a more complete view on Ukrainian culture and go beyond the trivial notions associated with the pre-revolutionary 'ethnography' of imperial 'Little Russia.' A tableau of this 'enlargened' kind would be an ideal means for dissipating Western prejudice, and foremost the obdurate doubts about the "reality of a Ukrainian nation," as once expressed by a wisecracking German Chancellor and peddled up to the current day by historians and political scientists who are blatantly 'Ukraine-illiterate.'[51] It is the barbaric Russian onslaught on the country that has recommended Ukraine to a more sustained attention of the West. Both Europe and Ukraine are faced with tasks that require much staying power: for Ukraine, once the war is over, to break free from the entanglement with Russia, its criminal politicians and depraved church authorities; Western Europe, for its part, should discover Ukraine as it emerges from its 'Little Russian' past and develop a genuine understanding of its culture.

51 Helmut Schmidt, "'Putins Vorgehen ist verständlich': Helmut Schmidt über Russlands Recht auf die Krim, die Überreaktion des Westens und den Unsinn von Sanktionen" ["Putin's Course of Action is Comprehensible": Helmut Schmidt on Russia's Right to Crimea, the Overreaction of the West, and the Nonsense of Sanctions], *Die Zeit* 14 (March 27, 2014), 9; Jörg Baberowski, "Der Westen kapiert es nicht" [The West Doesn't Get it] *Die Zeit* 11 (March 12, 2015), 47; Christian Hacke, interview on the Russian invasion of Ukraine, *Deutschlandfunk: Informationen am Mittag* (June 8, 2022), <https://www.deutschlandfunk.de/hacke-merkel-entschuldigung-russlandpolitik-100.html> (acc. August 2022). In a penetrating recent paper, Timothy Snyder has explained this illiteracy as the corrolary of a colonial stance on Ukraine persisting in Germany; cf. Snyder, "Deutschlands Verantwortung: Die Ukraine ist im historischen Bewussstsein der Deutschen ein blinder Fleck – mit fatalen Folgen (Eine Replik auf Jürgen Habermas)" [Germany's Responsibility: Ukraine is a Blind Spot in the Germans' Historical Consciousness – with Disastrous Consequences (A Reply to Jürgen Habermas)], *Frankfurter Allgemeine Sonntagszeitung* (June 24, 2022), 7.

Justice

While the lawyer could be seen as the individual whom the rule of law presupposes and who in turn upholds it, institutions are also required to guarantee the enforceability of the law and to guarantee the fairness of both the process and procedure. Multiple institutions and actors such as courts, judges, prosecutors, and attorneys ensure the administration of the law, whether it be the impartial resolution of conflicting demands, the allocation of just rewards or punishments, or the adjudication or specification of rights in accordance with the rules of law or equity. The trial in particular features prominently in both contributions in this section, and both explore the literary portrayal of legal proceedings in view of Europe and European notions of justice.

Melanie Foik and Kathrin Löhr examine the European tradition of legal case collections consisting of *causes célèbres* by and in the tradition of François Gayot de Pitaval, whereas Irina Wutsdorff focuses on specific aspects of the fictional trial depicted in Dostoevsky's novel *The Brothers Karamazov* in terms of its implication for Dostoevsky's view of Europe.

In the first of these contributions, the analysis of the reception of Pitaval's *causes célèbres* and the historical development of the pitaval genre in Germany and Poland becomes indicative for various notions of justice and legal procedure in European countries such as Germany, France, and Poland, but also for contingencies in terms of contemporary legal features and the literary critique of legal institutions and processes in crime fiction.

In the second contribution, Wutsdorff focuses on the presentation of the prosecutor's speech and specifically on his portrayal of the brothers Karamazov in varying proximity to or distance from pro-European ideas. This inquiry is embedded in the context of Dostoevsky's anti-European view and the ongoing debate in nineteenth-century Russia against Westerners or Western views. As Wutsdorff observes, such "a messianic thinking" is based "on a radical rejection of all forms of secular and formal rule of law which are associated with Europe."[1] Whether critical or celebratory of the European conception of justice and its respective legal institutions, both contributions in this section allow interesting conclusions to be drawn about the historical development of different perceptions of law and justice, which emerge in especially prominent ways at the borders within and outside Europe.

1 Irina Wutsdorff, this volume, 230.

https://doi.org/10.1515/9783111075693-020

Melanie Foik and Kathrin Löhr

Pitaval's Journeys: On the European Tradition of Literary Legal Case Collections

In the eighteenth century, the French lawyer and writer François Gayot de Pitaval (1673–1743) published a collection of written legal cases entitled *Causes célèbres et intéressantes, avec les jugements qui les ont décidées*. From France, this extensive compilation quickly spread to many other European countries such as Germany, Britain, and the Netherlands, where it was soon translated and imitated, finally coming to establish a genre of its own. From the beginning, it was marketed and received not only as instructional material for lawyers, but also as popular literature for a wider audience. Over time, the name Pitaval came to be used in many countries as a generic name for similar case collections, usually attributed to certain regions or epochs. Even today, they are often referred to as "pitaval" (except in English and in his native France, where the term "causes célèbres" is more prevalent). Less known than the Western European line of the tradition are a number of continuations of the pitaval genre coming from Polish jurists and writers. Although few such publications existed in Poland prior to the twentieth century, there was a boom in pitaval books beginning in the mid-1950s. Certainly, the pitaval – also Polonised as "pitawal" – had achieved an astonishing popularity in Poland, too, and remains widespread today.

This essay centres on how the *Causes célèbres* made their way from France to Germany and from there on to Poland. It explores the development of the pitaval genre from a literary-historical perspective, focusing on the processes of transfer and appropriation within a European context. Using pertinent examples from German and Polish literature, this contribution to the subject seeks to demonstrate both the pitaval's ongoing connection to contemporary legal features as well as its references to crime fiction, thus illustrating the genre-specific oscillation between the two spheres of law and literature.

1 Gayot's *Causes Célèbres* and their Eighteenth-Century Editions and Translations

Between 1734 and 1743, the French lawyer and writer François Gayot de Pitaval published his collection of *Causes célèbres*. Not much information is available

https://doi.org/10.1515/9783111075693-021

about Gayot.[2] He was born in Lyon in 1673, and his father was also a jurist. He studied law and became a lawyer at the Parlement de Paris, at that time the highest court in France.[3] Gayot practiced his profession there, so he belonged to a legal elite of the time, but did not appear at any important trials. While he was not a famous lawyer, with his *Causes célèbres*, he quickly became a famous writer or compilator of stories of legal proceedings.

He compiled legal cases and their judgments from different French regions and times which ranged from past centuries to his own life span. As the title excerpt, *célèbres et intéressantes*, suggests, he chose cases which captured the public interest at the time they occurred. He not only collected cases of high crime or criminal law, but those of civil law as well.[4] His approach was to offer a wide range of interesting cases for both law students and the general public at the same time. On the one hand, he wanted students to use his collection to learn about the law and possible problems that could occur in legal proceedings; on the other hand, he aimed to appeal to a wide readership among non-legal professionals. Interested readers may refer to Gayot de Pitaval's preface, in which he explicitly addresses law students, the general public, and specifically women.[5]

Gayot intends simultaneously to both entertain and teach. The stories resemble each other in structure, because Gayot integrates the (legal) documents into the narrative to emphasize the authentic aspects of the stories and to offer law students (and the readership in general) the opportunity to see, read, and judge the documents for themselves. Gayot aids the reader's understanding through the use of short explanations and annotations. The first volume of

2 The use of the name "Gayot" refers to the historical person, while the term "pitaval"' denotes the literary genre.

3 There are only a few dictionary entries, which obviously go back to the same origin, such as: François Xavier de Feller, ed., *Dictionnaire historique, ou Histoire abrégée de tous les hommes qui se sont fait un nom par le génie, les talens, les vertus . . .: Depuis le commencement du monde jusqu'à nos jours*, 6 vols. (Paris: Gaume Frères, 1832–1833), 88. The only article about the person Gayot (which does not provide any new and proven information) is by Aldo Mazzacane, "Letteratura, processo e opinione pubblica: Le raccolte di cause celebri tra bel mondo, avvocati e rivoluzione" in *La costruzione della verità giudiziaria*, ed. Marcella Marmo and Luigi Musella (Naples: Clio P, 2003), 53–99.

4 For details, see Hans-Jürgen Lüsebrink, *Kriminalität und Literatur im Frankreich des 18. Jahrhunderts: Literarische Formen, soziale Funktionen und Wissenskonstituenten von Kriminalitätsdarstellung*, 2nd ed. (Munich: R. Oldenbourg, 1983), 112–116.

5 François Gayot de Pitaval, *Causes célèbres et intéressantes, avec les jugemens qui les ont décidées*, Vol. 1 (Paris: Poirion, 1739), XVI; François Gayot de Pitaval, *Causes célèbres et intéressantes, avec les jugemens qui les ont décidées*, Vol. 3 (Paris: Poirion, 1742), II–III.

his *Causes célèbres* was an immediate success, despite the many documents that made the text fairly demanding to read. Accordingly, the first volume was quickly followed by others, published simultaneously by different publishers in Paris. Altogether, Gayot compiled twenty volumes until his death in 1743.

Gayot's stories were soon translated into several languages. The translators had to contend with two problems: firstly, the specific legal vocabulary and secondly, with the fact that the legal systems differed from each other. Nevertheless, editors unanimously endorsed the two-pronged utility of the compilation to simultaneously entertain the readers and educate them about the legal system.[6] Some editors, however, came to lament that there were no such cases in their own language, rendering a translation necessary. Nonetheless, they recognized the common backdrop of Roman law and concluded that the civil law issues were similar in the legal systems of France and Germany.[7]

The first German edition appeared in 1747, published by Kiesewetter, a publishing house in Stockholm and Leipzig, by the title, *Gayott von Pitaval, Parlamentsadvocat zu Paris: Causes Célèbres oder Erzählung sonderbarer Rechtshändel, sammt deren gerichtlichen Entscheidung*. Over a period of twenty years, nine volumes with a selection of stories from Gayot's *Causes célèbres* were published. This edition remained very close to Gayot's original text, leaving the documents and most of Gayot's annotations in the text untouched. This was the first German edition, but it would ultimately transpire to be of little importance for the further circulation of the *Causes célèbres* in Germany.

In Poland, the *Causes célèbres* were read both in German translations (especially in the so-called Schiller edition[8]) as well as in the French original.[9] Ignacy Krasicki (1735–1801), a future bishop and one of the most famous writers of the Polish Enlightenment, was greatly interested in Gayot's collection.[10] In 1765, Krasicki, as president of the Crown Tribunal (the highest court of the Kingdom of Poland), attempted

6 François Gayot de Pitaval, *Causes célèbres oder Erzählung sonderbarer Rechtshändel samt deren gerichtlichen Entscheidung*, unknown trans., Vol. 1 (Leipzig: Kiesewetter, 1747), 3; Julius Eduard Hitzig and Wilhelm Häring [Willibald Alexis], *Der neue Pitaval: Eine Sammlung der interessantesten Criminalgeschichten aller Länder aus älterer und neuerer Zeit*, Vol. 1 (Leipzig: Brockhaus, 1842), 12.

7 Unknown trans., "Vorbericht des Uebersetzers" in Pitaval, *Causes célèbres oder Erzählung*, *3–*4.

8 Friedrich Schiller, *Merkwürdige Rechtsfälle als ein Beitrag zur Geschichte der Menschheit: Nach dem Französischen Werk des Pitaval durch mehrere Verfasser ausgearbeitet und mit einer Vorrede begleitet herausgegeben von Schiller*, 4 vols. (Jena: Cuno, 1792–1795).

9 Stanisław Milewski, "Zaczęło się od Pitavala," *Palestra* 7–8 (2011): 203–213, 203.

10 Stanisław Szenic, *Pitaval warszawski* (Warsaw: Czytelnik, 1955), 5–6.

to procure copies of the original *Causes* for the Lviv advocates, whereby he intended to leave "a kind of keepsake of [his] presidency."[11] In addition to this, he began to translate them into Polish, a project which, however, would remain unfinished.[12]

Thirty years after Gayot's death, another edition of his *Causes célèbres* was published in France, which had a huge impact on all subsequent editions in Germany and France. François Richer (1718–1790) was, like Gayot de Pitaval before him, a lawyer at the Parlement de Paris. As in Gayot's case, he was not a lawyer at any significant trials, but became famous via a compilation of sensational proceedings. But unlike Gayot, he neither invented this genre nor collected the cases himself, but edited and reworked Gayot's collection. Afterwards, he proudly proclaimed that he had transformed a poorly written collection with superfluous comments of a writer, who possessed neither taste nor philosophy, into a very well readable, truly original work.[13] This statement is highly debatable, though he did indeed remove all the documents and many of Gayot's notes and comments. He also added other comments, sometimes contributing his own perspective, which differed from Gayot's. Following his self-confident (and somewhat dubious) assertion that he should be considered the actual author, due to extensive edits, the edition was published by the title, *Causes célèbres et intéressantes, avec les jugemens qui les ont décidées: Rédigées de nouveau par M. Richer, ancien avocat au Parlement.*[14] In fact, by deleting the original documents, he made the collection practically worthless for law students, thereby redirecting the work to another audience entirely. While legal insights are still to be gleaned from the work, they take a definite back seat to entertainment. Obviously, Richer sought to reach readers who wished first and foremost to be entertained and to learn about the legal system only

11 "Ignacy Krasicki to Jacek Ogrodzki, May 8, 1765" in *Korespondencja Ignacego Krasickiego: Z papierów Ludwika Bernackiego*, Vol. 1: *1743–1780*, ed. Zbigniew Goliński, Mieczysław Klimowicz, and Roman Wołoszyński (Wrocław: Zakład Narodowy im. Ossolińskich, Wydawnictwo PAN), 102–103. [Translations here and below by M.F.]

12 Szenic, *Pitaval warszawski*, 5–6. On a side note: Krasicki, in turn, used his insights regarding the functioning of the Crown Tribunal – most of which he had probably gained already prior to his presidency – with satirical intent in his own literary works, particularly in the novel *Mikołaja Doświadczyńskiego przypadki* [*The Adventures of Mr. Nicholas Wisdom*] published in 1776. Cf. Piotr M. Pilarczyk, "Doświadczyński przed Trybunałem: Twórczość Ignacego Krasickiego w świetle historii prawa," *Pamiętnik Literacki* 108.3 (2017): 79–100.

13 François Richer, ed., *Causes célèbres et intéressantes, avec les jugemens qui les ont décidées, Redigées de nouveau par M. Richer, ancien Avocat au Parlement*, Vol. 1 (Amsterdam: Michel Rhey, 1772), IV–V.

14 François Richer, ed., *Causes célèbres et intéressantes, avec les jugemens qui les ont décidées, Redigées de nouveau par M. Richer, ancien Avocat au Parlement*, 18 vols. (Amsterdam: Michel Rhey, 1772–1781).

secondarily (if at all). Perhaps this is the reason why this edition was more successful in other countries than the original one and perhaps it was a matter of time, taste, and image (it is very doubtful that it matched the literary quality of Richer's adaptation). However, this collection was decisive for the further spread of the *Causes célèbres* in Germany. All further translations would thenceforth rely on different editions of Richer's *Causes célèbres*.

The first German edition of Richer's *Causes célèbres* is a translation by Carl Wilhelm Franz published by Cuno, Jena, and going by the title, *Gayot von Pitaval sonderbare und merkwürdige Rechtsfälle, umgearbeitet und vermehrt, von Herrn Richer, Parlamentsadvocat zu Paris, deutsch herausgegeben von Carl Wilhelm Franz, Regierungsadvocat zu Gera*. It is a selection of four volumes published between 1782 and 1792.[15]

Surprisingly, the best-known German edition appeared shortly thereafter, by the same publisher, in a new translation as *Merkwürdige Rechtsfälle als ein Beitrag zur Geschichte der Menschheit: Nach dem Französischen Werk des Pitaval durch mehrere Verfasser ausgearbeitet und mit einer Vorrede begleitet herausgegeben von Schiller*.[16] Schiller attributed the quick succession of new editions by the same publishing house to be the result of shifting requirements in the readership. The new edition was aimed at a non-legally educated or generally less educated audience and should offer insights into the human heart. He argued that it was precisely in court that the inner drives of people are revealed, and these cases could then serve to entertain and morally educate the readership.[17] Out of consideration for the changing readership, editing was necessary to shorten the legal explanations and details. However, it should be noted that this edition, probably translated by Friedrich Immanuel Niethammer, does not differ much from the one by Franz. Often labelled the "Schiller edition," it is the one that would subsequently be referred to the most. This was certainly due to Schiller's preface,[18] which made this type of literature accessible to a wide audience. On the one hand, he addressed a readership that was not particularly well-educated, but on the other hand, a book endorsed by Schiller was, and still is, worth reading – even for the more well-educated in society.

15 For details, see Rudolf Behrens and Carsten Zelle, "Französische und deutsche Causes célèbres im Vergleich" in *Die Causes célèbres des 19. Jahrhunderts in Frankreich und Deutschland: Narrative Formen und anthropologische Funktionen*, ed. Rudolf Behrens and Carsten Zelle (Wiesbaden: Harrassowitz, 2020), 207–325, 218–220.

16 Schiller, *Merkwürdige Rechtsfälle*.

17 Schiller, "Preface" in *Merkwürdige Rechtsfälle*, Vol. 1, n. pag.

18 Schiller, "Preface," n. pag.

2 The Genre's Further Adaptations in the Nineteenth and Early Twentieth Century

After Schiller's success, it took a while for another major edition to appear in Germany that referred to Gayot, but this time it would be a vast project. From 1842 onwards, *Der neue Pitaval* began to appear.[19] Its pages contained more than 550 stories of court cases in sixty volumes. The publisher Brockhaus had set out to compile a new collection of stories following the example of Gayot de Pitaval's *Causes célèbres*, whose German editions had already been a great success. He asked Julius Eduard Hitzig (1780–1849), a lawyer, publisher, and writer he knew for his opinion on the project. Hitzig commented that such an enterprise would require two types of people, an experienced lawyer and a writer. Hitzig agreed to publish the series together with Wilhelm Häring [Willibald Alexis, 1798–1871], a writer with a legal background.[20] As before, it was lawyers who were also experienced writers that edited these cases for a wider audience. They drew inspiration from Gayot's original, from Schiller's and Franz's editions, and from the German jurist Paul Johann Anselm von Feuerbach, who had published his own compilation of cases, collected during his time in the Bavarian judiciary.[21] Hitzig and Häring selected cases from each of these works and collected other cases in addition. Their stated objective was to produce a collection of criminal cases, encompassing all periodical and geographic contexts, that was supposed to entertain and educate at the same time. Like all editors before them, they worked on the stories to make them comprehensible to a wide audience without a legal background. However, they also used these issues to point out elements of the justice system that they believed were working well or those that needed to be improved. In this regard, they were united with all the previous editors, who had witnessed the judicial systems of their own respective times and countries. None of them fundamentally questioned the judiciary, but instead discussed problems that were topical for them, based on specific cases from different regions and times. The mere fact that sixty volumes of *Der neue Pitaval* appeared, is testimony to the huge success of, and demand for, this collection.

Unlike in Germany, no translations or adaptations of the *Causes célèbres* – apart from Krasicki's efforts – were published in Poland prior to the nineteenth

---

19 Hitzig and Häring, [continued by Anton Vollert from Vol. 31 onwards], *Der neue Pitaval: Eine Sammlung der interessantesten Criminalgeschichten aller Länder aus älterer und neuerer Zeit*, 60 vols. (Leipzig: Brockhaus, 1842–1890).

20 Anna Busch, *Hitzig und Berlin: Zur Organisation von Literatur (1800–1840)* (Hanover: Wehrhahn, 2014), 272–275.

21 Paul Johann Anselm Ritter von Feuerbach, *Merkwürdige Criminal-Rechtsfälle*, 2 vols. (Gießen: Tasché und Müller, 1808–1811).

century. In fact, it was only in the middle of the nineteenth century that the first – and for several decades the last – two pitaval collections appeared in Polish. The earliest of these collections, published by Zygmunt Schletter in Wrocław, was Felix Górski's 1848 *Czarna księga: Zbiór najciekawszych procesów kryminalnych dawniejszych i nowszych czasów* [*Black Book: A Collection of the Most Interesting Criminal Trials from Older and More Recent Times*]. "Felix Górski" was a pseudonym which the bookseller, journalist, and writer Henryk Emanuel Glücksberg (1802–1870) went by,[22] a brother-in-law of Schletter and a lawyer by training, who had previously demonstrated his interest in crime literature by translating Eugène Sue's *Les Mystères de Paris* into Polish. In his *Black Book*, he subsequently compiled fourteen court cases from the years 1560 ("The False Martin Guerre") to 1843 ("The Vow of the Three Thieves"), each of which are abridged versions of selected stories from the *New Pitaval* by Hitzig and Häring. Glücksberg translated them largely verbatim, but he removed them from their metanarrative and their broader legal historical commentary.

Only four years later, in 1852, the same Zygmunt Schletter published a six-volume case collection of the title, *Tajemnice społeczeństwa wykryte w sprawach kryminalnych krajowych i zagranicznych* [*Mysteries of Society, Revealed in Domestic and Foreign Trials*], and he singled out Ludwik Tassillon Tripplin (1814–1864), a court counsellor, censor, and journalist, as the sole author. Tripplin, about whom little is known, was the son of the Weimar-born classical scholar Friedrich Christian Ludwig Tripplin, who had consorted with Schiller and Goethe since his student years in Jena from 1793 to 1796.[23] Friedrich Tripplin was certainly also acquainted with Friedrich Immanuel Niethammer, who at that time, and in collaboration with Schiller, had published the *Remarkable Legal Cases*. It is unclear to what extent Schiller's invitation to "record important legal cases also by other writers and from other nations"[24] was an inspiration for Ludwik Tripplin, to write a Polish pitaval more than half a century later. However, it is possible that his father had passed the German pitaval on to him, either intellectually as an idea or physically as part of the considerable family library.

22 Maria Rotterowa, following Karol Estreicher, cites Emanuel August Glücksberg, the younger brother of Henryk Emanuel Glücksberg, as the author of the *Black Book*. Maria Rotterowa, *Księgarnia i wydawnictwo Zygmunta Schlettera we Wrocławiu 1833–1855* (Wrocław: Państwowe Wydawnictwo Naukowe, 1956), 54. Estreicher, in turn, has revised this information in a later edition of the *Polish Bibliography* and then identified Henryk Emanuel Glücksberg as the author. Karol Estreicher, *Bibliografia polska*. 2nd ed., Vol. 8. (Kraków: Nakład. Polskiej Akad. Umiejętności, 1975), 418.

23 Krzysztof Tomasz Witczak, "Śladami tomaszowskich filologów klasycznych: Fryderyk Chrystian Ludwik Tripplin (1774–1840)," *Meander* 62.3–4 (2007): 329–343.

24 Schiller, "Preface," n. pag.

Although Schletter only named Tripplin as the collection's author, the latter, in fact, wrote merely three of the six volumes published.[25] The other three once more contained Glückberg's 1848 *Black Book* which had earlier proved to be a shelf warmer. In order to prevent another disappointment, the publisher deliberately chose the title, *Tajemnice społeczeństwa* [*Mysteries of Society*], in reminiscence of Eugène Sue's serial novel *Les Mystères de Paris* which was incredibly popular in Poland at that time and would encourage the many fans of mystery among the readership to buy it. Nevertheless, the contemporary press soon got to know about this and accused Schletter of defrauding his clientele.[26]

Despite the scandal at the Wrocław book market, the three volumes that actually came from Tripplin's pen can be considered the first genuine Polish pitaval containing stories based around real Polish criminal cases. According to the preface in his *Mysteries*, Tripplin wanted to show, on the one hand, how individual people in different epochs violated the legal order by breaking written norms in an extraordinary way; on the other hand, he wished to reveal that many of these violations were ultimately rooted in a discrepancy between positive law and natural law as well as the legislators' disregard for the latter. The exploration of the individual, in addition to the systematic reasons for legal violations, was of central importance to Tripplin. Through his case stories, he wanted to offer his readers psychological insights and even lead them "into the mysterious workshop of crime."[27] At the same time, he aimed to provide insights into the Polish courtrooms from the sixteenth to the nineteenth century. He considered both historical inquisition trials and modern criminal procedures, thus also providing legal-historical knowledge and a sense of justice to his audience.[28]

Regarding the relationship between pitaval literature and crime fiction, it seems worth mentioning that Ludwik Tripplin also had a then-famous brother, Teodor Tripplin, a physician and writer. Teodor was, among other things, the author of adventure fiction with occasional crime plots, which may be considered a nineteenth-century precursor of the Polish crime novel.[29] It would certainly be interesting to study the ways in which Ludwik Tripplin's pitaval inspired the writing practices of his brother and other Polish crime writers of that, and later times.

25 Rotterowa, *Księgarnia*, 60–61.

26 Józef Bachórz, *Romantyzm a romanse: Studia i szkice o prozie polskiej w pierwszej połowie XIX wieku* (Gdańsk: Wydawnictwo Uniwersytetu Gdańskiego, 2005), 209–210.

27 Ludwik T. Tripplin, *Tajemnice społeczeństwa wykryte w sprawach kryminalnych krajowych i zagranicznych*, Vol. 1 (Wrocław: Zygmunt Schletter, 1852), IX–X.

28 Tripplin, *Tajemnice*, VII–XII.

29 Marta Ruszczyńska, *Polski kryminał i wiek XIX* (Zielona Góra: Oficyna Wydawnicza Uniwersytetu Zielonogórskiego, 2019), 48–53.

During the interwar period, only a small number of pitaval collections were published in either Poland or Germany. In the 1920s and 1930s, Poland underwent the upheaval of unification and the subsequent enforcement of a new legal order that had previously been split into several systems, and there was an enormous interest in court proceedings in Polish society. The press reported in great detail on the course of legal events and printed entire court speeches to be read by both legal professionals and the broader public. Astonishingly, only one pitaval-style publication is known from that time: Stanisław Wasylewski's 1922 collection of criminal cases from the era of the Polish Enlightenment entitled *Sprawy ponure* [*Gloomy Cases*]. Contrary to a common assumption, Wasylewski (1885–1953) was not the author, but rather compiled and edited the stories from other sources, such as Tripplin's *Mysteries of Society*. In Germany, a handful of pitaval collections appeared during this period, the best known surely being Egon Erwin Kisch's *Prager Pitaval* [*Prague Pitaval*].[30] The period of the two world wars marks a decline of pitaval stories, but they did not disappear completely and experienced a great revival after the Second World War, particularly in socialist countries.

3 The Revival of the Pitaval Genre in the GDR and in Socialist Poland

In the case of the German Democratic Republic (GDR), pitaval stories usually appeared as books, but they even made their way to the television screen. One of the most important and flamboyant lawyers of the GDR, Friedrich Karl Kaul, was responsible for the huge success of pitaval stories (and not only in the GDR).[31] Kaul was a well-known lawyer. He used television to educate the public about everyday legal issues, and he was himself one of the most important GDR lawyers. He was also the only lawyer from the GDR who was additionally licensed to practice law in the Federal Republic of Germany (FRG). In the Auschwitz trials, for example, he represented victims of the Nazi regime who had since settled in the GDR.[32] In the true tradition of pitaval stories, Kaul collected German legal cases

30 Egon Erwin Kirsch, *Prager Pitaval* (Berlin: Reiss, 1931).

31 One of Kaul's pitaval collections, the *Bonn Pitaval*, was also translated into Polish: Friedrich Karl Kaul, *Wytworni ludzie: Sensacyjne procesy w NRF i Berlinie Zachodnim* (Katowice: Wydawnictwo "Śląsk," 1970).

32 There is a study on Kaul's important role for the judiciary of the GDR and his legal and political work in the West and East: Annette Rosskopf, *Friedrich Karl Kaul: Anwalt im geteilten Deutschland (1906–1981)* (Berlin: Berlin Verlag, 2002). Only recently has there been a research

from various decades. He made several books out of this material and adapted some of the stories for television using the title, *Fernsehpitaval* [*TV Pitaval*]. These films, starring some famous actors were a major success and more than forty episodes were screened between 1958 and 1978. The episodes span the period between the German empire and the time period of the episodes themselves. There is no episode taking place in the GDR, leaving one to speculate over the possible compelling political reasons behind this omission. By contrast, Western Germany is the scene of some of these stories. The viewers in East Germany learned how German Nazi criminals, such as public prosecutors or doctors who had committed crimes in the medical field, were enabled to continue their professional career in West Germany's institutions. The only story that takes place outside of Germany is a double feature about the Watergate affair. The pitaval genre, comprising case stories in court, was thus kept alive not only in literature but also became familiar to an extensive television audience. In this way, it reached a much larger audience than Schiller was able to garner in his time.

Greater interest in pitaval literature also developed from the mid-1950s onwards in socialist Poland, starting with the Warsaw lawyer Stanisław Szenic (1904–1987). Inspired by Kisch's *Prague Pitaval,* Szenic set out to explore the Polish contribution to the European pitaval tradition. However, he realised that this contribution was relatively minor with only three collections of this kind, namely, those by Glücksberg alias Górski, Tripplin, and Wasylewski. Consequently, he decided to work on his own pitaval.[33] Szenic had been raised to be bilingual in German and Polish, had been a member of the Polish Military Mission in Berlin in the first years after the Second World War, and he was to become the head of the editorial department for German-language literature at the State Publishing Institute (Państwowy Instytut Wydawniczy). As a proven connoisseur of German literature and culture, Szenic was also familiar with Kaul's pitaval collections published in the GDR at that time, which might also have spurred him on to write a new Polish pitaval and to (re-)activate the tradition of the genre in his country.

Szenic eventually published his *Warsaw Pitaval* in 1955, the first edition of which contained thirteen case stories from the sixteenth to the eighteenth centuries, i.e., mainly from the period of the Polish-Lithuanian Commonwealth. A few years later, the author expanded his collection with fifteen more cases from the period of

project by Katharina Rauschenberger at the Fritz Bauer Institute on the life and work of Friedrich Karl Kaul; see Katharina Rauschenberger, "Friedrich Karl Kaul und die Rolle der DDR in westdeutschen NSG-Verfahren," (n.d.), *Fritz Bauer Institut: Geschichte und Wirkung des Holocaust* <https://www.fritz-bauer-institut.de/forschungsprojekte/friedrich-karl-kaul-und-die-rolle-der-ddr-in-westdeutschen-nsg-verfahren> (acc. June 27, 2022), n. pag.

33 Stanisław Szenic, *Garść wspomnień* (Poznań: Wydawnictwo Poznańskie, 1990), 163–169.

Poland's partition, bringing it up to 1914. A subsequent third volume, focusing on cases from the interwar period, could not be published due to political interventions. The stories collected in the *Warsaw Pitaval*, which are largely true to the sources, are based primarily on court records and other archival materials as well as various further types of publications.

As a lawyer passionate about literature, Szenic was not only interested in the legal intricacies of the cases and their potential to serve as material for his own stories, but also in their inherent literary qualities. A good example of this is the story centered around the 1891 trial of Aleksandr Bartenev, who stood accused of murdering the famous Polish actor, Maria Wisnowska. The key legal issue raised by this story was that, although the hussar officer Bartenev had confessed to the crime from the outset, the court had to decide on whether the killing was an ordinary murder or a failed double suicide. In the spirit of classic pitaval literature, Szenic devotes the bulk of the story to the court proceedings, basing its content largely on the case documentation published contemporarily by Marian Łodyga,[34] which includes the indictment, the witness reports, the final speeches, and the verdict. In his literary adaptation, Szenic preserves the chronology and style of the original documents for the most part, often even quoting them literally, but adds a smattering of information from other sources, such as press reports and the memoirs of an unheard witness written down several years after the trial.

Two aspects of the court procedure seem particularly important to Szenic: first, its theatricality and second, its rhetoric. He begins the story by delineating the arrangement of the courtroom, staged in a former ballroom of the representative Pac Palace, and continues by describing the participants directly involved in the trial, the traditional rituals and ceremonies practiced in legal culture, and the many spectators exclusively admitted after acquiring one of the sought-after tickets due to the overwhelming public interest. Furthermore, Szenic comments specifically on the pleadings, quoting verbatim what he considers to be the particularly auspicious ones. The speech of the Moscow advocate Fëdor Plevako, "recited from memory," for instance, he classifies as "almost a work of fine literature," and he goes on to quote it at great length.[35] Finally, Szenic explores the case's resonance in press and literature, citing above all the novel *The Case of Cornet Elagin* (1926, Дело корнета Елагина) by Ivan Bunin, who would later win the Nobel Prize.

Although the *Warsaw Pitaval* was Szenic's best-known collection of cases, it was not his only one. In 1960, he published the *Pitaval wielkopolski* [*Greater Poland*

---

34 Marian Łodyga, *Zabójstwo Maryi Wisnowskiej: Dokładne sprawozdanie sądowe* (Warsaw: n.p., 1891).

35 Szenic, *Pitaval warszawski*, 2nd ed., Vol. 2.1 (Warsaw: Czytelnik, 1958), 247.

Pitaval], a collection of stories largely based on press reports, but also drawing, for example, on Tripplin's *Mysteries* and Paul Wiegler's case collection *Schicksale und Verbrechen* [*Fates and Crimes*, 1935]. In 1965, as a part of the state-mandated anti-alcohol campaign, Szenic published a number of stories revolving around alcohol-linked crime cases from the 1940s through the 1960s, all of which involved the killing of at least one person. Szenic compiled this thematically unique collection – titled *Pitaval makabryczny czyli sprawy pijackie* [*The Macabre Pitaval or, Cases under Drunkenness*] – at the request of the Social Committee against Alcohol. Both the *Warsaw Pitaval* and the *Greater Poland Pitaval* were reissued in the 1970s with several cases added.

Szenic's first Pitaval of 1955 had been such a runaway bestseller that his publishing house, Czytelnik, immediately set about making a complete pitaval series ("pitavalova seria"). Szenic's case collection was followed by a reprint of the 1848 *Black Book* by Emanuel Glücksberg, alias Feliks Górski, which was interestingly accompanied by a foreword by the then-popular crime writer Andrzej Piwowarczyk. At the beginning of the 1960s, the *pitavalova seria* was joined by Olgierd Missuna's *Warszawski pitaval literacki* [*Warsaw Literary Pitaval*] which contains solely lawsuits that were related to literature in a broader sense, as well as by Kazimierz Larski's *Współczesny pitaval polski* [*The Contemporary Polish Pitaval*]. These publications shifted the genre away from its historical predecessors and more towards popular literature. Apart from the above-mentioned publisher, Czytelnik (the name incidentally translates as "reader"), the Literary Publishing House (Wydawnictwo Literackie) also began issuing literary case collections at that time, including a reprint of Stanisław Wasylewski's 1922 *Gloomy Cases*.

In socialist Poland, the interest of readers was enormous, and sales figures were also reliably high. For instance, the legal scholar Stanisław Waltoś (b. 1932), who was captivated by reading the *Warsaw Pitaval*, published the *Pitaval krakowski* [*Cracow Pitaval*] in 1962, together with his colleagues Stanisław Salmonowicz (1931–2022) and Janusz Szwaja (1934–2022). As Waltoś recalls, it was their only financially profitable book project in the communist era.[36] The city pitaval of these three Cracow lawyers, all of whom were later to become professors in their field, was reprinted several times in the Polish People's Republic. It was also reprinted after the political upheaval of 1989/90, when it included cases that had previously not been published for censorship reasons. Six editions have been printed to date, making it the most successful Polish pitaval of the twentieth century. The fact that it was alternately published by both legal and literary publishing houses once again underlines pitaval's oscillation between the spheres of law and literature.

36 Stanisław Waltoś, *Wędrowanie po wyspach pamięci* (Warsaw: Wolters Kluwer, 2019), 258–259.

The great success of pitaval collections in socialist Poland is part of a wider captivation for all kinds of crime literature during this period. In the Stalinist era, the literary depiction of crime was nearly impossible, and crime fiction had almost completely disappeared. It was not until the political thaw of the mid-1950s that the first crime novels would start to sprout again. In comparison to other national literatures, however, it is striking how very few courtroom novels and dramas there are in Poland in general, and in socialist Poland in particular. Yet the court is renowned for yielding a wealth of material for literature, and the parallels between the court and the theatre are obvious.[37] The reasons for this may be seen, firstly, in the continental European-style court procedure practiced in Poland, which tends to be less suitable for the stage than its Anglo-Saxon counterpart. Secondly, there was a considerable distance between the court and wider society, especially in the communist era, and only politically favorable information from the judicial sector reached the public sphere. Like court reports, pitaval collections functioned as substitutes for courtroom dramas and thrillers.[38]

However, pitaval collections were not only popular with a broad audience more interested in entertainment value than in legal details; they were also devoured by legal professionals. For example, the lawyer Andrzej Bąkowski (1927–2020) recalled that for him and many of his colleagues, this kind of literature had not only an "anecdotal character," but sometimes even "inspired them to improve their own skills."[39] In particular, the court speeches found in those books, which were often rhetorically sophisticated but no longer printed extensively in the press as they had been in the interwar period, certainly constituted instructive material for jurists practicing in court. For the militia's investigative work, however, pitavals also represented – at least ideally – some sort of a reference library. The contemporary crime writer Jerzy Edigey, a lawyer by training, even wove into one of his novels the story of an investigator who, while working on her current case, had not only "looked through all the books on criminology" but also "read the various pitavals."[40]

While compilations of historical court cases such as the *Warsaw Pitaval* and the *Cracow Pitaval* were still "securely embedded in history,"[41] many of the subsequent case collections moved increasingly closer to the present, which would lead

37 Ewa Łętowska, "Teatr i prawo," *Zeszyty Naukowe Akademii Sztuk Teatralnych w Krakowie* 9 (2018): 106–120.

38 Ewa Łętowska, "O prawie w literaturze kryminalno-sensacyjnej PRL" in *Prawo, literatura i film w Polsce Ludowej*, ed. Jarosław Kuisz and Marek Wąsowicz (Warsaw: Wydawnictwo Naukowe Scholar, 2021), 99–119, 108–111.

39 Andrzej Bąkowski, "Moje pitavale," *Palestra* 46.7–8 (2002): 105–108, 105.

40 Jerzy Edigey, *Mord nach Alphabet* [1981] (East Berlin: Das Neue Berlin, 1986), 51.

41 Łętowska, "O prawie w literaturze," 110.

to a further differentiation of the genre. Thus Kazimierz Larski's aforementioned 1962 *Współczesny pitaval polski* [*The Contemporary Polish Pitaval*] focused for the first time on criminal cases that had taken place after the Second World War. Larski, who was presumably a lawyer,[42] closely follows the underlying documents, which he would accumulate from both militia files and court records. The resulting documentary style includes precise dates, the exact names of the militia offices involved, and detailed quotations from offender and witness statements. In contrast to the earlier pitaval collections, it focuses on the investigations of the militia and the prosecution, whereas the court proceedings tend to play a subordinate role. In this way, Larski retraced the shift in the Polish judicial system after 1945, which had led to a weakening of the courts in favor of the prosecution, the militia, and the Security Service. This weakening had resulted, among other things, in the abolition of the institution of the examining magistrate at the end of the 1940s.

Via his *Contemporary Polish Pitaval,* Larski did not intend to simply entertain his readers, but rather to educate them in an entertaining way. In this sense, his case collection can be understood first and foremost as a form of teaching material pertaining to certain criminal acts as well as their corresponding police investigations. To this effect, the author considered his pitaval a key counterweight to popular crime fiction, from which most people at that time, as Larski wrote, drew their (usually poor) knowledge of the legal system. The only crime that tended to occur in most contemporary novels was murder, which was why the terms "crime" and "murder" were largely equated in everyday life.[43] Larski also noted that detective novels often depicted crimes, as well as their solving, in an extremely simplified way as compared to reality.[44] To remedy this situation somewhat, the *Contemporary Polish Pitaval* examines not only murder cases but also more minor crimes such as pickpocketing and marriage fraud and, in addition to the concrete case stories, it also provides information on various other types of crime and their legal ramifications in general.

During the 1960s and '70s, lawyers were no longer the sole authors of case collections. Journalists and writers increasingly wrote pitavals, too, placing them, through a strategic use of their title or other references, in the European tradition. In 1973, the journalist Bogdan Daleszak published a collection of criminal cases from the late 1940s through the early 1970s, subtitled *Pitaval dolnośląski* [*Lower Silesian Pitaval*]. However, Daleszak had drawn neither on court records nor press reports but solely on "hours of conversations and discussions" with

42 Despite thorough research, we have not been able to secure further information about Kazimierz Larski, which includes even the dates of his life and his profession.
43 Kazimierz Larski, *Współczesny pitaval polski* (Warsaw: Czytelnik, 1962), 47.
44 Larski, *Współczesny pitaval*, 92–93.

militia agents.[45] Accordingly, the author focuses on the crimes themselves as well as the investigations by the militia. The court trials, by contrast, play a subordinate role, which – as already mentioned above – corresponded to the realities of the contemporary justice system. With its detailed and embellished portrayal of militia work, this pitaval is strikingly reminiscent of the mass-produced socialist-style crime novels of that time, the so-called militia novels, which made it their task to polish up the tarnished image of the police authorities.[46]

In the 1970s and 1980s, original pitaval stories were again resurrected, this time in another area. Researchers in social and cultural history, the best-known being Michel de Certeau in France and Natalie Simon Davies in the United States, selected stories of the *Causes célèbres* as a starting point for their research. And following Natalie Zemon Davies, first French and later U.S. cinema rediscovered the story of Martin Guerre.[47] In today's Poland, numerous other literary legal case collections have since been published, albeit differing greatly in form and content. By now, the term "pitaval" covers not only historical trial stories but also contemporary court reports, case stories taken from police work, criminal chronicles, academic treatises, and at least one pitaval pastiche.[48] Furthermore, as in crime fiction, regionality still plays a prominent role since by now, almost every big city and region (and some smaller ones) can claim their very "own" pitaval. In Germany, too, the idea of the pitaval survives mainly in regional case collections, for example in two different books entitled *Dresdner Pitaval* [*Dresden Pitaval*] as well as in the *Thüringer Mord-Pitaval* [*Thuringian Murder Pitaval*].[49] While these compilations use the pitaval moniker to create a unique literary genre, there are many popular stories which are no longer explicitly termed pitaval stories but nevertheless follow the tradition (such as Ferdinand von Schirach's stories, which are true pitaval literature).

45 Bogdan Daleszak, *Strzały w Małpim Gaju: Pitaval dolnośląski* (Katowice: Wydawnictwo "Śląsk," 1973), 285.

46 On the so-called militia novel, see Wolfgang Brylla, "Verbrechen im Dienst des Sozialismus: Polnische Kriminalromane bis 1989" in *Investigation – Rekonstruktion – Narration: Geschichten und Geschichte im Krimi der Slavia*, ed. Nina Frieß and Angela Huber (Potsdam: Universitätsverlag Potsdam, 2019), 95–114; Dorota Skotarczak, *Otwierać, milicja! O powieści kryminalnej w PRL* (Warsaw: Instytut Pamięci Narodowej – Komisja Ścigania Zbrodni przeciwko Narodowi Polskiemu, 2019).

47 Michel de Certeau, *La possession de Loudun* (Paris: Julliard, 1970); Natalie Zemon Davis, *Le retour du Martin Guerre* (Paris: Éditions Robert Laffont, 1982).

48 Ludwika Woźnicka, *Najdziwniejsze i osobliwe zdarzenia czyli pitaval fantastyczny* (Warsaw: Iskry, 1980).

49 Willy Forner, *Dresdner Pitaval: Kriminalfälle aus vier Jahrhunderten* (Berlin: Militärverlag, 1979); Hansjoachim Paech, *Dresdner Pitaval: Ernstes und Heiteres aus Dresdner Gerichtssälen* (Leipzig: Schubert, 1994); Frank Esche, *Thüringer Mord-Pitaval*, 2 vols. (Arnstadt: Kirchschlager, 2016–2017).

Irina Wutsdorff

The Court Trial in Dostoevskii's *The Brothers Karamazov*, or, The Rejection of the Rule of Law and of European Principles

In Dostoevskii's novel *The Brothers Karamazov* (1878–80), which in some way resembles a crime novel, as the reader wishes to find out who of the brothers Karamazov has murdered the father, we find in the end a very detailed description of the trial against Dmitrii Karamazov. At some length, we are presented with the prosecutor's speech, who at the beginning gives a characterization not only of the accused Dmitrii, but also of the two other brothers, Ivan and Alesha:

> "The elder is one of those modern young men of brilliant education and vigorous intellect, who has lost all faith in everything. He has denied and rejected much already, like his father. [. . .] Another personage closely connected with the case died here by his own hand last night. I mean an afflicted idiot, formerly the servant, and possibly the illegitimate son, of Fyodor Pavlovitch, Smerdyakov. At the preliminary inquiry, he told me with hysterical tears how the young Ivan Karamazov had horrified him by his spiritual audacity. 'Everything in the world is lawful according to him, and nothing must be forbidden in the future – that is what he always taught me.' [. . .]
>
> Then the third son. Oh, he is a devout and modest youth, who does not share his elder brother's gloomy and destructive theory of life. He has sought to cling to the 'ideas of the people,' or to what goes by that name in some circles of our intellectual classes. He clung to the monastery, and was within an ace of becoming a monk. He seems to me to have betrayed unconsciously, and so early, that timid despair which leads so many in our unhappy society, who dread cynicism and its corrupting influences, and mistakenly attribute all the mischief to European enlightenment, to return to their 'native soil,' as they say, to the bosom, so to speak, of their mother earth, like frightened children, yearning to fall asleep on the withered bosom of their decrepit mother, and to sleep there for ever, only to escape the horrors that terrify them.
>
> For my part I wish the excellent and gifted young man every success; I trust that youthful idealism and impulse towards the ideas of the people may never degenerate, as often happens, on the moral side into gloomy mysticism, and on the political into blind chauvinism, two elements which are even a greater menace to Russia than the premature decay, due to misunderstanding and gratuitous adoption of European ideas, from which his elder brother is suffering."[1]

1 Fedor Dostoevskii [Fyodor Dostoyevsky], *The Brothers Karamazov* [Russian orig. 1878–80], trans. Constance Garnett (Michigan: Generic NL Freebook Publisher, 1998), 488–489; further references in the text, abbreviated as "BK."

https://doi.org/10.1515/9783111075693-022

One wonders how we have to understand that confrontation of the elder brother Ivan, who "has lost all faith in everything," having adopted European ideas, and the younger Alesha, who "has sought to cling to the 'ideas of the people.'"

The nineteenth century in Russia was marked by discussions in the intellectual realm on one's own cultural identity and sense of belonging. Europe in these discussions became a cipher for what Russia was not. For the so-called Westerners it was what Russia should become or at least become oriented towards. For the so-called Slavophiles it was the opposite of what Russia was by its very nature and something Russia never should become. The start of this debate that shaped the century is usually located in the publication of Petr Chaadaev's (French written) *First Philosophical Letter* from 1829–30.[2] The editor of the journal in which it had been published was banished to Siberia after that and Chaadaev himself was declared mad. In that letter, which had previously circulated in the noble salons, he had declared that Russia's contribution to the history of mankind was not, as Herder had proclaimed, yet to come, but could not take place under the given circumstances. Whereas the Western Church in its resistance to the state had made emancipation from state domination possible, Orthodox-missioned Russia was incapable of any progress. This caused the opponents of Chaadaev, the later Slavophiles, to stress the importance of Orthodoxy for Russia. For them the Orthodox belief, which according to its own principles is the only true Christian belief, stands at the core of Russia's self-understanding, has been defended by Russia, and preserved mainly within the Russian people, whereas the Russian *intelligenciia* (intelligence) similar to the West (or Europe) has been poisoned by the destructive spirit of rationalism. The height of this construction is reached in Ivan Kireevskii's article "O kharaktere prosveshcheniia Evropy i o ego otnoshenii k prosveshcheniiu Rossii" ["About the character of 'prosveshchenie' of Europe and its relationship to the 'prosveshchenie' of Russia"] (1852).[3] By the title already he contrasts the two worldviews he sees represented by Russia and Europe, respectively: 'prosveshchenie' literally means 'enlightenment,' and Russian enlightenment for Kireevskii means spiritual illumination, whereas enlightenment in Europe for him stands for a purely rationalistic and formalistic movement, which he sees negatively. In his stylized confrontation of European and Russian education and culture (all this he implies by the term 'enlightenment'), he finds rampant disintegration and degeneration in Europe, concerning the way of thinking, the sciences, the state, society, family life, ethical consciousness, and

2 Petr Jakovlevich Chaadaev [Petr Jakovlevič Čaadaev], *Lettres philosophiques adressées à une dame* [1829–30] (Paris: Librairie des Cinq Continents, 1970).

3 Ivan Kireevskii [Ivan Kireevsky], "On the Nature of European Culture and on Its Relationship to Russian Culture" [Russian orig. 1852], in *On Spiritual Unity: A Slavophile Reader*, trans. and ed. Boris Jakim and Robert Bird (New York: Lindisfarne Books, 1998), 187–231.

all forms of individual and collective life. In Russia, on the contrary, he sees wholeness everywhere, based on a deep Orthodox belief.

This background information might make it less surprising that the prosecutor in Dostoevskii's novel *The Brothers Karamazov* typifies the three brothers according to this scheme: on the one hand the Europeanized Ivan, whose doubts culminate in his repeated articulation that "if there is no immortality, then all things are lawful"; on the other hand the somehow naive Alesha, who with his deep belief, his admiration for the Starets Zosima, and his conviction that everyone is answerable to everyone else is close to the people's faith.

> "But to return to the eldest son," Ippolit Kirillovitch went on. "He is the prisoner before us. We have his life and his actions, too, before us; the fatal day has come and all has been brought to the surface. While his brothers seem to stand for 'Europeanism' and 'the principles of the people,' he seems to represent Russia as she is. Oh, not all Russia, not all! God preserve us, if it were! Yet, here we have her, our mother Russia, the very scent and sound of her." (BK, 489)

It is noteworthy that the prosecutor, who is convinced of Dmitrii's having committed the murder, is associating him with Russia. The prosecutor, for sure, does not represent the implicit standpoint of the author. The real author Dostoevskii, who very frankly laid out his worldview in his *A Writer's Diary*, published from 1873 onwards, was not much convinced of any earthly form of jurisdiction. What was more important for him was the belief in a divine judgment, and in the strength of a real Russian to reach salvation, not only for himself but prospectively for the whole world, by repentance.

In one of the first articles in *A Writer's Diary* Dostoevskii described a simple Russian, named Vlas, who for him was revealing characteristics typical of "the Russian people in their entirety":[4] on the one hand there is an overexaggerated "urge to go beyond the limit," an "urge for negation":

> this fateful maelstrom of violent and momentary negation and destruction of self that is so typical of the Russian national character at certain fateful moments in its existence. On the other hand, it is with the same force, the same impetuosity, the same urge for self-preservation and repentance that the Russian, like the Russian People as a whole, saves himself; he does this usually when he reaches the outermost limit, that is, when he has nowhere farther to go. (V, 161)

4 Dostoevskii [Dostoyevsky], "Vlas" [Russian orig. 1873], in *A Writer's Diary*, Vol. 1: *1873–1876*, trans. and ed. Kenneth Lantz (Evanston: Northwestern UP, 1994), 156–169, 160–161; further references in the text, abbreviated as "V."

The third of the brothers, Dmitrii, who is accused of having murdered his father, is presented exactly as such a figure: a "Russian wrongdoer[]," who is "first of all, a suffering person himself" (V, 162), who in the end – as Dostoevskii proceeds in his characterization of the typical Russian – will follow Christ's suffering and thus "save himself and us as well, for once more the light and the salvation will come radiating from below" (V, 168).

As the reader learns in the end, the actual murderer was not Dmitrii, but the illegitimate fourth son of Fedor Karamazov, Smerdiakov. Already the title of the chapter (Book XII), which depicts the trial at length, signals in that direction, declaring that Dmitrii's condemnation was "a judicial error." However, for Dostoevskii it was not just an error of earthly jurisprudence, but a categorical error: the institution of the judiciary itself is questioned by that case, as the guilt of all four brothers, who all in one way or another had at least wished their father to die, cannot be atoned by juridical ways of punishment. However, paradoxically, the juridical trial, by condemning Dmitrii to a Siberian penal camp, can potentially further his way towards salvation by making him suffer – very much along the lines of Dostoevskii's example of the simple Russian Vlas in his *Diary* article.

In his first novel, *Crime and Punishment* (1866), Dostoevskii presented a similar case. Here the literary example is Raskolnikov, in contrast to Dmitrii an actual murderer, who, having committed, rather by accident than by rational planning, a perfect crime, and thus being unable to be convicted by means of legal justice, finally pleads guilty not in court, but to the people in the streets, kneeling in front of them and kissing the Russian soil. In the subsequent court trial he is also condemned to a Siberian penal camp. There, with the help of the unconditionally faithful Sonia, he rediscovers his belief, and in the end, we find him facing "the dawn of a new future, of a full resurrection into a new life."[5] We learn that this is the starting point "of a new story – the story of the gradual renewal of a man, the story of his gradual regeneration, of his passing from one world into another, of his initiation into a new unknown life" and that "[h]e did not know that the new life would not be given him for nothing, that he would have to pay dearly for it, that it would cost him great striving, great suffering" (CP, 636). Here again we find the messianic thought figure of a "wrongdoer" who turns into a "suffering person" and thus is not only saved himself but becomes the savior of potentially the whole world.

This messianic thinking is based, not only in Dostoevskii's writings, on a radical rejection of all forms of secular and formal rule of law which are associated

5 Dostoevskii [Dostoyevsky], *Crime and Punishment* [Russian orig. 1866], trans. Constance Garnett (Minneapolis: Lerner Publishing Group, 2015), 634; further references in the text, abbreviated as "CP."

with Europe. Today, in the Russian aggression towards the independent state of Ukraine we see an overtly open negation of the rule of law, of human rights, of the basic principles of international law, and of the rules of war established in the Hague and Geneva Conventions. Unfortunately, this rejection of written principles of law and of undeniable rights has a long tradition in Russian thinking, as has been indicated by this brief glimpse into the treatment of questions of law in Dostoevskii's novels, where we find, instead of the principle of the rule of law, a plea for an all-embracing salvation based on a vague feeling of suffering.

As the historian Stephen Kotkin put it recently in an interview with *The New Yorker*, rejecting the wide-spread thesis that Russia's invasion was a reaction to NATO's extension:

> What we have today in Russia is not some kind of surprise. It's not some kind of deviation from a historical pattern. Way before *NATO* existed – in the nineteenth century – Russia looked like this: it had an autocrat. It had repression. It had militarism. It had suspicion of foreigners and the West. This is a Russia that we know, and it's not a Russia that arrived yesterday or in the nineteen-nineties. It's not a response to the actions of the West. There are internal processes in Russia that account for where we are today.[6]

6 Qtd. in David Remnick: "The Weakness of the Despot: An Expert on Stalin Discusses Putin, Russia, and the West," [Interview with Stephen Kotkin] (March 11, 2022), *The New Yorker* <https://www.newyorker.com/news/q-and-a/stephen-kotkin-putin-russia-ukraine-stalin> (acc. March 15, 2022), n. pag.

Borders

Both the European continent, and the EU in particular, is very perceptibly defined by its borders – in geographical as well as in political terms –, by its demarcation from the outside, and exclusion of those who are deemed to not belong. An intricate system of border security underpins what is sometimes denounced as "Fortress Europe" and the EU has so far devoted billions of euros to various efforts to deter migrants, whether on surveillance, border patrol, or more than one thousand kilometers of walls. In this regard, the Schengen Zone was created with a twofold purpose in mind; while it is aimed at opening internal borders, this alleged permeability comes at the price of reinforcing external borders. EU border policies operate on various levels, all of which intend to prevent, deter, incept, and return migrants and refugees from within European borders. While several of the contributions collected in this volume touch upon the borders and boundaries of Europe in geographical, political, or conceptual terms, the two essays in this section do so with special emphasis.

Paola Chiarella's essay "Like Stone Rafts in the Ocean: Reading José Saramago in Times of the Pandemic" addresses multiple moments of crisis and the insecurity of the future with recourse to a work of literature. Chiarella analyses *The Stone Raft* in the context of the Coronavirus and draws parallels between the fictional rendering of Saramago's novel and the pandemic. The fictional event that causes the moment of crisis in Saramago's novel is the geographical separation of Europe, when a piece of the European continent physically breaks away and floats freely in the ocean, thus constituting "the occurrence of an unpredictable, dystopian event, the fear of death, separation and isolation, the search for the causes as well as a solution" very similar to the pandemic. The non-fictional event of the Covid-19 outbreak, however, according to Chiarella, has led to "a strong sense of cooperation and collaboration" within the EU and therefore reinforced the unity of the Union.[1]

In contrast, Irina Wutsdorff focuses on border politics on a micro-level as she explores immigration policy and the ambivalent notions of home and belonging. In her reading of Saša Stanišić's *Origins*, she discusses the autobiographical, albeit fictionalized, experience of gain and loss in the process of immigration. The very act of border crossing presents various challenges in terms of identity and identification, as Wutsdorff illustrates; this act frequently leaves the immigrant with "neither a fixed point where you begin from, where you come from, nor a fixed point where you end at, where you belong to."[2] Both contributions ultimately

1 Paola Chiarella, this volume, 239, 240.
2 Irina Wutsdorff, this volume, 246.

https://doi.org/10.1515/9783111075693-023

share a common interest in the negotiation of borders and their meaning for society as well as for the individual, pointing out different instances of inclusion and exclusion, but also considering the border as necessary to enable its potentially productive crossing in the first place.

Paola Chiarella

Like Stone Rafts in the Ocean: Reading José Saramago in Times of the Pandemic

1 When the Unimaginable Happens: The Allegory of an Unexpected Crisis in Europe

The Stone Raft is an exciting and original "what if tale" by José Saramago with a political overtone about Europe, its unity and experience of community. In the first pages of the book, the old continent is presented as "a loving mother," saddened by the "misfortune of her lands on the extreme west."[3] The reason for the pain is the sudden fracturing of the Iberian Peninsula, transformed into an island cast adrift. The protagonists find themselves in an absurd situation in which the rational mind struggles to comprehend the enormity of events. Scientists go in search of the causes of events, without finding any explanation. Therefore, it seems an obvious expedient to seek clarification in the realm of magic and superstition: The sign of an elm stick on the ground, the strange and incessant barking of dogs, and the presence of flocks of animals during the protagonists' journey are all charged with prodigious meaning.

The Stone Raft is a novel about the rupture of European unity and the reconfiguration of stronger Iberian identities and new relationships. The main themes are the sense of insecurity, the change of territorial identity, the uncertainty of the future, social bonds, and human frailty in the face of nature: "Human strength could do nothing on behalf of a cordillera which was opening up like a pomegranate" (SR, 22) drifting away at a speed of 750 kilometers a day, splitting the earth and bringing down cables, and leaving familiar territory behind in the direction of an unknown future. Nobody knows if the raft will stop and under what conditions. What effects will it have on people? How much will the opening of new geographic distance affect European identity?

What once was solid and fixed is transformed into a floating, unstable, and fast entity, acting autonomously, guided by a force out of control. The fracture of the continent can be read as a metaphor for the colossal events of life that happen – for better or for worse – without being sought out, which present themselves suddenly in full force. People must now adapt to survive. They must rethink the

3 José Saramago, *The Stone Raft* [1986], trans. Giovanni Pontiero (London: The Harvill P, 2000), 22; further references in the text, abbreviated as "SR."

https://doi.org/10.1515/9783111075693-024

meaning of human connections, build new ones, learn new skills, and open up to strangers in order to reassert the primacy of human organization and intelligence over the forces of nature.

The emotions arising from this disaster generate a real sense of insecurity in each one of the protagonists and in the nations concerned; a feeling never experienced before with such intensity. We read that "the everlasting does not last forever as the modern age has clearly shown us" (SR, 22). Indeed, the terrestrial fracture is the perfect paradigm as a symbol of this uncertainty to which the continuous mobility of the island is added to aggravate the emergency. The inhabitants are, despite themselves, transformed into sailors without a rudder. By embarking on a journey in which seasickness is mostly psychological and the geographical location is constantly changing, the solidity of the earth is thus replaced by the liquidity of the ocean. In times of uncertainty, it is essential to keep abreast of events as they unfold. In the novel, the eyes of the characters remain glued to the TV screen in order to absorb as much information as possible from experts in both the geological and political fields. Nobody is able to save themselves individually, and specific knowledge must be shared for the common good of all.

The dismay is also felt keenly on the European landmass. Can Europe ever be the same after such a cataclysm?

Before the fracture, it had been protected from the Atlantic Ocean by the Iberian Peninsula, which acted as a kind of outpost. Now, however, the Mediterranean Sea is no longer enclosed by the protective arms of Gibraltar. The *Mare Nostrum* is now an open sea of uncertainty. In the Early Modern Age, Spain and Portugal forged the new maritime routes that launched Europe as the dominant power on the world stage and allowed for the globalization of history. Now, another globalization is at work: the globalization of risk and the fragility of formerly held beliefs. Last but not least to be challenged is the misguided conviction that has held Europe to be one of the safest continents in the world.

Europe itself remains vulnerable to the ocean's power and cannot be certain that another fracture will not occur within its territories: Will it be France's turn next? Who can exclude the possibility that in the future, the land, rather than detaching itself horizontally, will not be swallowed by the waters and therefore submerged?

It is therefore imperative to adjust to the new reality; to demonstrate new mental flexibility and plan for unexpected outcomes. After all, people have always refashioned reality to serve their own purposes.

In any case, the plot evokes some questions: Why did the fracture occur along the Cordillera, separating the Iberian Peninsula? Does this geographical location perhaps have a symbolic meaning? Nature seems to be sending humanity a message. But what exactly is it?

2 Pandemic Crisis in Europe: A Community Physically Divided

Saramago's novel can be used as a key to understand the pandemic crisis we are still experiencing. Italy was the first European country to be severely hit by the virus in January 2020. The first cases in Lombardy left the whole nation in suspense and in March, Conte's government implemented a national lockdown. The other European states closely monitored the Italian situation, but it would not remain an isolated case for long, as the virus spread rapidly throughout Europe.

The gravity of the situation led to restrictions on personal freedom being imposed throughout Europe to contain the numbers of infections and save lives. This catastrophe, unlike Saramago's story, has resulted in more than a million deaths in Europe to date. However, there are many parallels that seem to echo the central themes of the novel: the occurrence of an unpredictable, dystopian event, the fear of death, separation and isolation, the search for the causes as well as a solution, the uncertainty of the pandemic curve due to the many variants and variables, the role of scientists, and the doubts and fears of ordinary people.

The lockdown subsequently enforced in all affected countries polarized people, even within families. Friends, family members, colleagues, and acquaintances suddenly became a possible mortal threat. Relational unity was broken as in the novel. The same happened at the national borders of the European countries: Freedom of movement and residence, the symbol of European legacy, was suddenly arrested. What we truly shared globally is the risk of contagion. Today, as in the novel, a form of isolation remains a constant of the pandemic and it is still impossible to predict and control the speed of new infections, which have in no way ceased. We still do not know when the stone raft will stop, when we will be safe again, and when contact with others will no longer be something to fear. Despite the effectiveness of vaccines, many governments resorted to isolation measures during the highest peaks of contagion.

The pandemic has forced us to consider many crucial issues from a political, social, and economic point of view; to balance our fundamental rights (freedom and public health), to provide for the economic needs of those most affected, and above all to rethink the organization of health systems which were not prepared for this emergency. The prolonged suspension of manufacturing activities has worsened an already serious economic situation. Problems around employment have also worsened. Every European state has found itself adrift, casting about in the fog of uncertainty. Nobody has the privilege of immunity.

3 Europe as "Loving Mother": The Next Generation Plan

Despite the physical fracture, the European Union did not lose its sense of unity. Indeed, we can even say that this catastrophe has created new opportunities for the political and economic union of Europe. The preceding years of economic austerity seriously undermined any feeling of solidarity and the European institutions appeared disconnected from the concrete needs of millions of citizens in economic despair. One notable case in point was the Greek crisis, but there was also economic instability in Italy, Spain, and Portugal. Although it is not possible to delineate the reasons for that economic crisis here, we can nevertheless conclude that the European Union was not a "loving mother."

The pandemic, on the other hand, has generated a strong sense of cooperation and collaboration, and Europe has shown itself to be a "generous mother," eager to help and keep her children together, and thinking of the "next generation." The EU is applying the full flexibility of its fiscal rules to help its member states support their healthcare systems and businesses. The EU state aid rules have been loosened as never before so that governments can provide liquidity to the economy and preserve jobs.

To help the European Union recover from the economic and social impact of the pandemic a €750 billion one-off recovery fund, labelled *Next Generation Plan*, has been agreed on.[4] The recovery package will prioritize investments that go into digital and green transition. It is the largest stimulus package ever funded in Europe.[5] Furthermore, the European Council has approved a long-term EU budget for 2021–2027 that will stimulate growth and support citizens, businesses, and economies in the years to come. Overall, the multiannual budget and the recovery fund amount at least to €1,074.3 billion.[6]

Together with the €540 billion of funds already available for the three safety nets (for workers, businesses, and the member states), the comprehensive EU

---

4 European Council, "10 Things the EU is Doing to Fight COVID-19 and Ensure Recovery," (April 20, 2022), *Policies: COVID-19* <https://www.consilium.europa.eu/en/policies/coronavirus/10-things-against-covid-19/> (acc. May 30, 2022), n. pag.; Florian Dorn and Clemens Fuest, "Next Generation EU: Chancen und Risiken des Europäischen Fonds für die Wirtschaftliche Erholung nach der Corona-Krise," *Wirtschaftsdienst* 101.2 (2021): 78–81.

5 Riccardo Crescenzi, Mara Giua, and Giulia Valeria Sonzogno, "Mind the Covid-19 Crisis: An Evidence-Based Implementation of Next Generation EU," *Journal of Policy Modeling* 43.2 (2021): 278–297, 281.

6 European Council, "Recovery Plan for Europe," (n.d.), *Strategy: Priorities* <https://ec.europa.eu/info/strategy/recovery-plan-europe_en> (acc. May 30, 2022), n. pag.

recovery package amounts to €2,364.3 billion. The European Central Bank is mobilizing an additional €1,350 billion as part of its bond purchase program to help the governments during the crisis.[7]

Furthermore, EU countries have established a common framework for travel measures to safeguard free movement during the Covid-19 pandemic. They have agreed on common criteria to be followed in setting such measures and a common definition of risk areas.

From a health care perspective, four Covid-19 vaccines have already been authorized in the EU and vaccinations started on December 27, 2020, across Europe. The EU is coordinating a joint effort to secure the production of a sufficient quantity of safe and effective vaccines. In total, up to 4.6 billion doses of vaccines have been secured to date. The EU has also set up a common European stockpile of personal protective equipment and ventilators under the RescEU program that aims to strengthen the member states' disaster response preparedness and prevention measures by creating a dedicated pool of operational equipment at the Union level.

To secure jobs during the crisis, the European Union has introduced a support measure known as SURE (*Temporary Support to Mitigate Unemployment Risks in an Emergency*). It provides up to €100 billion in loans granted to the member states on favorable terms to help cover the costs of temporary national work schemes.[8] It amounts to €94.3 billion for nineteen member states.

Now more than ever the stability and prosperity of the European Union "hinges on its ability to provide timely and effective measures to repair the damage caused by Covid-19 and prepare a better future for coming generations."[9] It is the best way to combat the Euroscepticism felt by many dissatisfied EU citizens, left adrift on their stone rafts.

The evolutionary dynamics of the European integration process can open up new opportunities based on the events of the last two years. Europe has the chance to permanently redefine its political identity beyond the Coronavirus crisis, to go in a more explicitly solidarity-driven direction.

José Saramago's allegory tale helps us to understand that security is never guaranteed. In the novel, the fracture on the cordillera seems as absurd as the Coronavirus does today. Life can be disrupted by an unexpected turn of events, resulting in mass death and forcing people to take measures to survive. In order to counter any potential future threat, cooperation and joint effort are crucial.

7 European Council, "10 Things," n. pag.
8 European Council, "Recovery Plan," n. pag.
9 Crescenzi, Giua, and Sonzogno, "Mind the Covid-19 Crisis," 280.

Solidarity is a key concept in the modern political discourse. It is supposed to ensure the equal enjoyment of individual rights through social cohesion and integration, because it designates a bond of mutual support among people, and evokes, more or less, a wide range of social state protections to support the vulnerable in society. Solidarity is based upon the recognition of the other, upon the consideration of their full scope of needs, and aims to fully realize the ideal of an inclusive society.

Covid-19 has made Europe aware of this possibility. If we take the notion of solidarity seriously, the investment program to aid the most affected countries could represent a new form of integration that invests generously in the future for the good of Europe as a whole. There will be no peripheral countries in the new EU agenda.

Irina Wutsdorff

The Naturalization Process and Narrating *Where You Come From*: An Exploration of Saša Stanišić's *Herkunft*

Saša Stanišić's latest novel *Herkunft* (2019) is a literary text which, I believe, reflects the contemporary issues of migration politics in a very inspiring way. To explore why this is so, I will first comment upon the background of the author, before analyzing the title of the book, and finally, the book itself.

Saša Stanišić was born in former Yugoslavia, in the Bosnian town of Višegrad. Along with his parents, an ethnically mixed couple so typical of former Bosnia, he managed to escape from the Bosnian-Serb troops that were occupying the town and bringing to an end the multi-ethnic community that had dwelt there. He arrived in Germany as a fourteen-year-old boy and grew up in Heidelberg, where he also began his studies. After the war ended, Bosnian refugees were repatriated to their homeland, although the home they had left no longer existed, which, in addition to Bosnia in the form they had known it, pertained to the whole of the former Yugoslavia as well. Saša Stanišić somehow managed to convince an officer of the Alien Registration Office that, since he had begun to write, he would be able to make a living from it. Indeed, today he does, and he has become one of the most renowned writers in Germany. The 2019 German Book Prize is the most prestigious one he has so far received for *Herkunft*.

If you look up the term 'Herkunft' in an English dictionary, you will encounter several related meanings: 'origin, ancestry, provenance, descent, background, birth.' These are all encompassed by the term 'Herkunft.' However, it may be argued that the title of the English translation, *Where You Come From*, published in 2021, emphasizes more clearly than the German noun 'Herkunft' that the book in fact poses a question, a question for which there may be no single answer, but several ones – if any are to be found at all. In such a vein, Stanišić, instead of telling one chronological, coherent story, chooses to narrate a series of smaller vignettes of incidents which have happened, or could have happened to him and his family, as the boundary between fiction and reality is rendered deliberately fluid.

Herkunft is, as Saša Stanišić puts it himself, a mixture of essayistic, fictional, and biographical narration. I quote his own presentation of the book:

> *Where You Come From* is a book about the first coincidence in our biography: being born somewhere. And about what happens afterwards.

https://doi.org/10.1515/9783111075693-025

> *Where You Come From* is a book about the places that are my home, the ones in my memory and the ones I have invented. It is a book about language, moonlighting, youth and many summers. The summer when my grandfather trod on my grandmother's foot while dancing in such a way that I was almost never born. The summer when I nearly drowned. The summer when Angela Merkel opened the borders and which was very like the summer when I fled across many borders to Germany.
>
> *Where You Come From* is a farewell to my grandmother with her dementia. While I am collecting my memories she is losing hers.
>
> *Where You Come From* is sad because for me origin has got something to do with what I can no longer have.
>
> My biographic writings, also this text, are like the name on the doorbell of a man long since dead that I can no longer remember – an attempt to preserve something that used to be important. To preserve it, but also to develop it further in one's mind, to get to the bottom of it.[1]

The beginning of the novel is revealing in terms of the juridical question on the handling of migration and immigration. The short opening scene portrays the grandmother standing in the middle of a street, with cars slamming on their brakes all around her, as she calls out for a little girl she had just seen there, before she vanished; that girl being herself as an eleven-year-old girl. What follows this scene of dementia, of losing control over one's memories and the fluid boundary between imagination and reality, is the first full-length chapter of the book centred on the first-person narrator. This chapter is the starting point of his own remembering, of his narrating, of writing the book. When he applies for German citizenship – after several precarious years of living in Germany where he is merely tolerated – he must handwrite a formulated CV for the immigration authority. Thus, the chapter is titled, "To the Alien Registration Office." However, he has no idea where to start and what to write. Everything he thinks of seems to him either too impersonal or, conversely, too detailed and personal:

> Germans love bulleted lists. So I put in some bullet points along with some names and dates – "• Elementary school in Višegrad"; "• Slavic studies major in Heidelberg" – even though none of it felt like it had anything to do with me anymore. I knew the information was correct but I couldn't possibly leave it at that. I would never trust that kind of life.
>
> I started over. I wrote my date of birth again and described the rain [on that day] and how my grandmother Kristina, my father's mother, gave me my name. She took care of me a lot in my early years too, since my parents were studying (Mother) or employed (Father).[2]

---

1 Saša Stanišić, "*Where You Come From* Exposé," (n.d.), *Penguin Random House Verlagsgruppe* <https://foreignrights.penguinrandomhouse.de/edition/9783630874739> (acc. March 23, 2022), n. pag.

2 Stanišić, *Where You Come From* [2019], trans. Damion Searls (London: Jonathan Cape, 2021), 3; further references in the text, abbreviated as "WYCF."

Some of the biographical details which come to his mind might be misunderstood by the authorities: Unaccountably, he writes that his grandmother "was in the Mafia" and therefore had "a lot of time for children" or that his "grandfather Pero was a Communist, heart and soul and Party book"; nevertheless: "I erased the part about the Mafia. You never know" (WYCF, 3).

In another version, he attempts to describe a seemingly innocent childhood episode, in which he is sledding together with other children in his hometown. "I wrote: There's no such thing as a biographical narrative without childhood leisure activities" (WYCF, 5). However, there is no smooth, unimpaired recall, not even of the somewhat comical episode with Huso who "was nothing but an unemployed drunk who didn't brake before the ravine" and then turned out to be "sitting in his toboggan, which was caught in the underbrush halfway down the slope" (WYCF, 5). It is not possible to recall this moment, and the boys' shouting at Huso to keep going without also recalling Huso's subsequent violent fate during the war. The two memories are harshly juxtaposed: "Huso heaved himself out of the thicket and hurtled down the rest of the slope. It was unbelievable, we were over the moon, and Huso was shot in 1992, in his shack on the Drina, in his house of planks and cardboard" (WYCF, 5–6). In such a vein, the chapter's ending is somewhat consequent, when it ends – after two more attempts to fulfil the requirements of the Alien Registration Office – as follows: "I wrote: *Here's a number of things I had*" (WYCF, 6). A number of these things he no longer possesses, as one of his 'possessions' on the list "an unthinkable war" (WYCF, 13) – has destroyed them. "I had Yugoslavia – but not for long. Socialism was tired, nationalism was wide awake. Flags, each their own, in the wind, and the question in people's heads: What are you?" (WYCF, 7)

This link between these repeated attempts to establish a beginning, and the never-ending quest for 'Herkunft,' for where one comes from, on the one hand, and the repeated attempts to tell one's own story – or any story at all –, on the other hand, is laid bare in all its difficulty a few chapters later, when the letter to the Alien Registration Office is mentioned again:

> People occasionally ask me if I feel at home in Germany. I alternate between saying yes and saying no. They rarely mean it to be exclusionary. They justify the question, saying: "Please don't take it the wrong way, my cousin married a Czech."
>
> Dear Alien Registration Office, I was born in Yugoslavia on March 7, 1978, a rainy night. Since August 24, 1992, a rainy day, I have lived in Germany. I'm a polite person. I don't want anyone to feel uncomfortable just because I'm not Czech. [. . .]
>
> The story begins with a farmer named Gavrilo, no, with a rainy night in Višegrad, no with my grandmother who has dementia, no. The story begins with the world being set alight by addition of stories.
>
> Another one! Another one!

> I'll take more stabs at it and find a lot more endings. I know how I work. My stories just wouldn't be mine without digressions. Digression is my mode of writing. *My Own Adventure*. (WYCF, 32–33)

The chapter "To the Alien Registration Office," described above in some detail, is typical of the kind of narration that shapes the book: It alternates between memories, explanations, and short, recurring vignettes which have happened, or might have happened, to the narrator, coming back to him associatively and allowing him, as a mode of writing, to frequently digress. Above all, this narration is processual, as there is neither a clear starting point nor an end to it.

Consequently, the book does not have a traditional ending but allows the reader to "decide how the story should continue – you create your own adventure" (WYCF, 297). The structure of the closing section, "Dragon's Hoard," corresponds with one of the things he once had: "A mountain of books. In 1991, I'd discovered a new genre: *Choose your own adventure*. You as the reader decide for yourself how the story continues" (WYCF, 8). The reader is thus given two choices on how to proceed at the end of each sequence. Corresponding to its loose beginning, this book, which posits the existential question of "where you come from," does not have a fixed ending.

Paradoxically, it is an act of bureaucracy within the naturalization process that, for the first-person narrator, initiates the process of narration, of writing about his own "coming-from." At first glance it might seem incidental that the great novel we hold in our hands should lay bare all the absurdities of an immigration law which continues to be based on 'Herkunft,' on where you come from, on the coincidence of where you were born. Yet it does so by its very structure, by showing that there is neither a fixed point where you begin from, where you come from, nor a fixed point where you end at, where you belong to.

Part III: **Concerns**

Human Rights

The European Union's commitment to human rights is one of its most important principles, along with liberty, democracy, respect for fundamental freedoms, and the rule of law. This dedication is legally enshrined in Article 2 of the Treaty on European Union, which lists as the EU's fundamental values "human dignity, freedom, democracy, equality, the rule of law and respect for human rights, including the rights of persons belonging to minorities." The EU's commitment to human rights is not limited to its territory but extends to "its relations with the wider world" and includes explicit respect for the principles of the United Nations Charter (Art. 3). Firm adherence to human rights is also enshrined in the Charter of Fundamental Rights and the European Convention on Human Rights, to which EU Member States are required to be party (Art. 6). This protection is guaranteed not only for the domestic, but also for the external action of the Union (Art. 21). However, when the United Kingdom withdrew from the EU on February 1, 2020, these provisions were no longer binding for the UK. Both contributions in this section are thus dedicated to examining the legal implementation and protection of human rights in the UK before and after Brexit.

Whereas Lord Mance has an altogether favorable view on human rights protection in the given context and maintains that the "UK has, in summary, been a diligent applier and exponent of the Convention rights,"[1] Laura Zander highlights the discrepancy between the idealistic discourse of human rights in the UK and their actual application and realization in her contribution. This is especially visible in the respective hostile environment policy, but also, beyond that narrow setting, in some of the remaining EU nation-states. As Zander maintains in her contribution, instances of systematic human rights violations are not limited to the period following Brexit but had already been evident before the UK's withdrawal, a condition that becomes particularly striking in terms of citizenship and refugee policies.

While Mance emphasizes that the withdrawal agreement "committed the UK to remaining within the ECHR as a basis for future cooperation, and the EU-UK Trade Agreement likewise commits both parties to respecting human rights as a shared value and to respecting human rights treaties to which they are parties,"[2] Zander critically interrogates the adherence to these commitments for human rights protections, especially with regard to the questionable institution of indefinite detention of refugees in so-called Immigration Removal Centers. Whether laudatory or rather skeptical of British legal implementation and practice of human rights, the composite perspective of both contributions facilitates fresh

1 Lord Mance, this volume, 255.
2 Lord Mance, this volume, 256.

https://doi.org/10.1515/9783111075693-026

insights into the legal and literary negotiation of human rights that may ultimately also shed new light on the relationship between law and literature as such.

Jonathan Mance

Human Rights in UK and the Future of Europe

The Future of Europe Conference at the Villa Vigoni provided an excellent forum for a discussion on the British perspective on human rights. The United Kingdom (UK) has of course recently left the European Union (EU), but it remains a member of the Council of Europe and so party to the European Convention on Human Rights (ECHR) and has since 2000 incorporated the Convention rights into domestic law under the Human Rights Act of 1998.

Human rights reflect the importance which western philosophy and beliefs attach to individual liberty of action and thought, particularly in relation to state power, whether it be executive, legislative or even judicial. Human rights are an essential component of the rule of law. By that we refer to a separation, *de jure* or at least *de facto*, between the operation of the various elements of state. Without that separation individuals cannot be protected against abusive, misguided or unjust exercise of state power. The rule of law is fundamentally different from rule by law. There are regimes in the world where law and the judicial system are essentially tools of the legislative or executive branch. That may lead to rule by law, but it certainly does not involve the rule of law or protect human rights.

The protection of human rights is not of course novel in the UK. The UK played an important role in the drafting of the ECHR because it believed that it would very largely replicate rights already recognised as common law. It would be fallacious to regard Magna Carta, with its guarantee of fair trial by one's peers, as a direct progenitor of human rights for the whole population. It was basically a compact between the monarch and nobles. But it came symbolically to represent the idea of constitutionality and civil rights against an overwhelming executive in the early seventeenth century, largely through the remarkable proselytising of Sir Edward Coke, thorn in the King's flesh as successively Chief Justice of the Common Pleas and of the King's Bench and finally, after dismissal by the King, as a proselytising Member of Parliament.

The later events of the seventeenth century crystallised in the UK a constitutional settlement which exists in substance to this day, as any practitioner or student of the UK legal scene must recognise. The executive, in the form of the Crown, lost to Parliament, with the judiciary being a beneficiary in the form of guarantees of independence and tenure. Parliamentary supremacy remains the basic constitutional principle. There have been occasional judicial statements in recent times, suggesting that parliamentary supremacy is itself a legal construct, which might have

https://doi.org/10.1515/9783111075693-027

limits, e.g., if Parliament did something ridiculous, like purport to legislate against red-haired people, or abolished the right of judicial review. But so far the mutual respect among the different branches of state – like that of bees working together to construct a honeycomb, one judge has said[3]– has avoided any such direct clash.

Over the last half century, the judiciary has taken several steps in order to enforce human rights within the UK and to further ensure the division of power. The first was to develop a much more effective system of judicial review of executive and delegated (secondary) legislative activity, and extend this into areas of the royal prerogative (now exercised by the government) hitherto though immune from such review. Two recent striking examples are the two *Miller* cases about the need for parliamentary legislation to authorise a notice to leave the EU [4]and the illegitimacy of the PM's prorogation without reason of Parliament during the height of the debate over whether such legislation should be passed.[5] The second recognised a hierarchy of rights, with physical liberty and freedom from inhuman treatment being for instance at the top of the hierarchy. The third offered an interpretation of all legislation, primary or secondary, and executive acts with the presumption that the greater the infringement of individual rights, the less likely it is to have been intended or authorised.[6]

There were, however, still limits to this process of development of the rule of law and human rights. In the face of clear parliamentary intention, the courts remained powerless. But, because the UK was party to the ECHR, a disappointed litigant could go off to Strasbourg and get a judgment there against the UK government. This was embarrassing and it also deprived the UK courts of the opportunity to influence the European Court of Human Rights (ECtHR). Hence the Human Rights Act of 1998 (HRA) – a subtle piece of legislation, which makes the Convention rights part of domestic law, but with two particular features: First, it says no more than that UK courts must "take into account" decisions of the European Court of Human Rights (ECtHR) regarding their interpretation. So, in rare cases, the UK courts have been free to disagree with the ECtHR's decisions on the scope or meaning of the ECHR, and a real dialogue has been possible, with the ECtHR being free in return to modify its jurisprudence: witness the case of *Horncastle*[7]on use of hearsay evidence in

3 *Jackson v Attorney General* [2005] UKHL 56, [125] per Lord Hope.

4 *R (Miller) v Secretary of State for Exiting the European Union* [2017] UKSC 5.

5 *R (Miller) v The Prime Minister* [2019] UKSC 41.

6 *R v Secretary of State for the Home Department, ex p. Simms* [1999] UKHL 33.

7 *R v Horncastle* [2009] UKSC 14, refusing to follow the initial ECtHR decision in *Al-Khawaja and Tahery v The United Kingdom* (2009) 1 EHRR 49. In the later Grand Chamber decision in the latter case (applications nos. 26766/05 and 22228/06) the ECtHR did re-define its position in a manner going some, though not the whole, way to meet the Supreme Court's concerns.

criminal cases. In other areas, such as the extra-territorial application of human rights, e.g., in warlike operations in Iraq or Afghanistan, the UK courts, after initially resisting the ECtHR's rather extraordinary extension of the ECHR, eventually fell into line – not without some continuing concern at UK political levels. Second, it does not enable UK courts to strike down or invalidate primary legislation which infringes the Convention. All they can do is issue a declaration of incompatibility, leaving Parliament to decide by a speedy process whether and how far to adjust UK law. In practice, this has always been done (save with prisoner voting, where the UK maintains an absolute ban despite the ECtHR's modification of its jurisprudence in a way accommodating some of the UK government's objection).

In practice, the inability to invalidate primary legislation is not very important anyway. Much more important is the UK courts' obligation under the HRA "so far as it is possible to do so," to read and give effect to primary legislation and subordinate legislation in a way which is compatible with the Convention rights. That goes even further than the common law presumption mentioned earlier, and usually enables courts to avoid any clash between the meaning of legislation and human rights. UK courts are also free to develop the interpretation of Convention rights in areas within the UK's margin of appreciation, although the legislature's own choice will, very often at least, carry much weight with UK courts in deciding how far to go. Assisted dying is an ongoing area of discussion, which the courts have effectively left for decision by Parliament, which is currently considering a bill on the subject. The incorporated Convention rights have undoubtedly led to positive changes in UK law, which might not otherwise have been achieved – e.g., the removal of the executive right to set or extend the time spent in prison by offenders.

The UK has, in summary, been a diligent applier and exponent of the Convention rights, and has, I think, contributed strongly to the development of Strasbourg jurisprudence. But there is also no doubt that the Convention and the Strasbourg court were, for at least a time, the *bête noire* and an easy target for some. Politicians like power, and both the Convention system and the EU took power away from domestic politicians. The sense that Westminster was losing significance was undoubtedly one fear generating opposition to membership of the EU. Curiously, until seven or eight years ago the main objections voiced were to the ECHR and the ECtHR. The Conservative Party manifesto in 2014 included proposals for replacing the HRA, but these were quietly shelved and, in the lead-up to the EU referendum, sovereignty enthusiasts transferred their opposition to the Court of Justice of the EU itself. This became one of the features of the EU on which opponents of EU membership focused. The 2017 manifesto merely left open the possibility of some change in the relationship with Strasbourg after Brexit.

Is there any serious campaign or impetus to change our current relationship with the ECtHR or the Convention rights? On the face of it, it is difficult to see real scope for this.[8] The Political Declaration accompanying the 2018 EU Withdrawal Agreement committed the UK to remaining within the ECHR as a basis for future cooperation, and the EU-UK Trade Agreement likewise commits both parties to respecting human rights as a shared value and to respecting human rights treaties to which they are parties. Chapter 3 is even more specific in committing both parties to the ECHR and to giving effect to the Convention rights domestically – with a further provision that, if the UK withdraws from the ECHR, cooperation on law enforcement and security ceases, regardless whether the rest of the Agreement survives. Bearing in mind the post-Brexit ambitions of our present government in relation to "Global Britain" and perhaps especially bearing in mind our recent experience in relation to Afghanistan, one can question how far the UK would wish to cut itself off from cooperation on law enforcement and security. Finally, both parties must also deny certain benefits (relating to services and investment) to states denying human rights protection.

A yet further point is that human rights are hard-wired into the Northern Ireland Protocol, article 2(1) of which provides that there shall be no diminution of rights, safeguards or equality of opportunity in Northern Ireland as a result of Brexit. That protects both ECHR and EU rights. The UK is having enough problems in relation to the Protocol without, I suspect, wishing to attack that aspect also.

What the UK has of course lost, with Brexit, is the Charter of Fundamental Rights and its protection of human rights. The relationship between Luxembourg and Strasbourg rights is still generally a work in progress. Charter rights, interpreted and applied by the Court of Justice, are binding, inflexible rights, which give neither domestic courts nor a domestic legislature the right or power to disagree or qualify. Their effect, for example in relation to prisoner voting, could be politically sensitive. The UK has traditionally been cautious about EU initiatives in the area of justice. Even the UK Supreme Court has expressed sympathy for the view of the German Constitutional Court that some limits might be applied to the ambit of EU law in a domestic context. In the UK any such limit would have had to be found by implication in the European Communities Act of 1972, rather than in a written constitution. But what if, say, the Court of Justice had decided that jury trial was unacceptable? Would UK courts have enforced that? I doubt it. One

8 Since this talk was given, a new Minister of Justice, Mr Dominic Raab, has however spoken in alarmist terms on October 17, 2021, about the ECtHR "dictating things" and about a suggested need for a mechanism to "correct" its rulings, reserving particular criticism for the ECtHR's long-standing expansion of the concept of jurisdiction to bring many overseas troop operations within the scope of the Convention. In the writer's view, this view ignores the extent to which the ECtHR has over recent years respected and given effect to national jurisdictions' policies and choices.

may wonder therefore what the present UK government's attitude would have been, if we had remained members of the EU, to the extension of Court of Justice activity into areas such as the internal independence of the Polish legal system. I am not suggesting that this extension is either wrong or from a European perspective unwise. On the contrary, from a European legal point of view, the Court of Justice's defence of the supremacy of EU law appears inevitable. The German Constitutional Court's jurisprudence may have pointed a risky path down which Poland has followed. It could have been better if mutual respect and restraint had avoided any such clash of constitutional views – in areas where issues of identity and governance are at stake, and where state cooperation and public acceptance of the law are vital. Some relationships are better managed without bringing them to a legal head. But that of course requires respect and goodwill on all sides, which is not always present. At some point, a firm stand must be required.

Whatever the position in relation to EU rights, including those generated by the Charter, the present system for enforcing human rights under the ECHR, in Europe and domestically in the UK, appears to me to have a commendable flexibility which promotes the acceptability and sound application of the Convention rights, even if it means that they may not always have the scope and universality of effect that some might wish.

Laura A. Zander

A Host(ile) Union? Writing in Solidarity against a Hostile Environment

This prologue is not a poem
It is an act of welcome
It announces
That people present
Reject the terms
Of a debate that criminalises
Human movement
It is a declaration
This night in Shepherdswell
Of solidarity.[1]

It is with these words that the prologue of the first volume of *Refugee Tales* (2016) opens. This self-proclaimed *act of welcome* is said to *reject* the terms of a debate that criminalizes human movement and *declares* solidarity with refugees. The opening stanza of the prologue explicitly stages the first of a total of four volumes of *Refugee Tales* as a political intervention against the UK politics of indefinite detention and other inhumane asylum control practices. The understanding of solidarity as a remedy for such hostile politics was also enshrined in the subtitle of the original project, "A Walk in Solidarity with Refugees, Asylum Seekers and Detainees (from Dover to Crawley via Canterbury)."[2]

The *Refugee Tales* project, which has been ongoing since 2015, decidedly pushes the border between migratory literature and literary activism and can be understood as a new kind of aesthetic as well as political intervention aiming to change the politics of immigration detention in Britain. Over a period of seven years, the Gatwick Detainees Welfare Group has organized solidarity walks with refugees, asylum seekers, and immigration detainees, and has so far published four volumes of *Refugee Tales*. Written by acclaimed writers and poets, the latter

1 David Herd, "Prologue" in *Refugee Tales*, ed. Herd and Anna Pincus (Manchester: Comma P, 2016), v–x, v.

2 Herd, "Afterword: Walking with Refugee Tales" in *Refugee Tales*, 133–143, 133. As this list of the various groups of people affected by disparate instances of flight already shows, refugees are by no means a coherent group. I have therefore endeavored to apply the most precise term in each case, depending on whether the person concerned is referred to in her divergent role as refugee, asylum seeker, detainee, or migrating person. As an umbrella term to refer to the various forms of movement of heterogeneous groups such as refugees, migrants, or displaced persons, I use "subjects on the move."

https://doi.org/10.1515/9783111075693-028

two volumes also contain contributions by various detainees or asylees. In this way, in addition to archiving the stories in the four volumes, the project has been able to overcome some of the physical limitations imposed on refugees in the United Kingdom by indefinite detention in immigration removal centers, not only by allowing them to move through space by walking, but also by providing a stage for many of those affected and involved to tell their stories and to perform their otherwise silenced suffering on the occasion of the walks. Since most of the contributions were not written by the refugees whose experiences are depicted,[3] but are the product of collaboration between British-based writers and the refugees' testimony, they form a generic hybrid between life-writing and fiction, between autobiography and activism, which explicitly or implicitly addresses the narrative form and narratability of migration experiences.

The *Refugee Tales* outreach initiative has continuously sought to facilitate political change by rewriting the public discourse on the so-called "refugee crisis." While media portrayal in the UK as well as conservative and right-wing political forces have persistently attempted and, more often than not, unfortunately succeeded in portraying incoming migrants and asylees as a threat to be contained, the *Refugee Tales* individualize and rehumanize the respective individual experiences of various subjects on the move who have arrived in the UK. Apart from providing a space for sharing lived experience and simultaneously countering the criminalization of flight and solidarity efforts, as both appear essentially linked to illegality, the *Refugee Tales* outreach project is particularly significant in that it raises political awareness for human rights violations within and beyond UK borders. Consequently, the project offers a promising contribution in the context of an examination of human rights and their effectiveness and enforceability in the United Kingdom and the EU.

The Preamble of the Charter of Fundamental Rights of the European Union (CFR) underscores the spiritual and moral heritage upon which the Union is founded as the "indivisible, universal values of human dignity, freedom, equality and solidarity," putting particular emphasis not only on the principles of democracy and the rule of law, but also on citizenship of the Union as founded on those very values and constituting the EU as an area of freedom, security, and justice. This prominent reference to the right of human dignity is not restricted to the CFR. While human dignity is not explicitly named in the European Convention on Human Rights, the European Court of Human Rights frequently applies it in its rulings. It also features

3 These writers and poets serve as guardians of privacy, allowing the original storytellers to protect their true identities and remain anonymous while sharing their stories. It is not until the third volume of *Refugee Tales* that selected first-person narratives written by former detainees are presented. Their identities remain confidential, however, as initials replace their full names.

conspicuously in the Preamble of the Universal Declaration of Human Rights and various national constitutions, including that of Germany. It follows that even if the UK no longer feels bound by the EU Charter of Fundamental Rights after Brexit, the obligation to uphold human dignity and human rights under the UN Charter does not cease to apply. In contrast to this seemingly unambiguous legal status, post-Brexit literature tells a much more ambivalent and critical tale about human rights in the UK and the EU, presenting their treatment of refugees and migrants as undignified and inhumane. To make this point, there is a wide variety of textual examples available for study, but here I will focus on just a few. My rather eclectic selection is by no means exhaustive, but hopefully can reveal some of the most incisive portrayals of human rights violations and *undignified* policies in the UK. In addition to the before-mentioned *Refugee Tales* collection, Ali Smith's *Seasonal Quartet*, especially her novels *Spring* (2019) and *Summer* (2020), offers equivalent denunciation of the hostile politics of indefinite detention in immigration removal centers in the UK.[4] Olumide Popoola and Annie Holmes' collection of fictional refugee tales entitled *Breach* (2016) also portrays acts of hostility and solidarity in Calais' infamous "Jungle," as does Kamila Shamsie's 2017 *Home Fire*, which is inspired by the hostile treatment of citizens in present-day UK.

In the following discussion, I want to argue that hostile politics not only harm those who come to the Global North to seek protection, but that they also create a hostile climate that easily turns against those who have hitherto considered themselves citizens, a notion that becomes all to visible with so-called Brexlit.[5] To substantiate this argument, I will first examine the relationship between human rights and citizenship as well as provide a brief survey on UK human rights legislation before looking at the manifestation of British hostile politics in more detail. I will then review a selection of literary critiques of human rights violations in contemporary Britain, thereby exploring to what extent literature may be seen as an instrument to counter such ongoing violations. The question of the role and effect or rather efficacy of literature on law is certainly a pertinent one. In this context, Lyndsey Stonebridge cautions that the way in which literature is world-making

4 An earlier version of this essay included several passages from Smith's novels. However, due to Katharina Pink's comprehensive analysis of citizenship in this volume, the remarks seemed unnecessarily redundant, and I would like to direct readers to her article "Alternative Notions of Belonging: (European) Community and Citizenship in Ali Smith's *Seasonal Quartet*" in this volume instead, 313–337.

5 The term "Brexlit" has come to denote contemporary British fiction that critically examines the generational, political, and personal fractures that the referendum has created. Kristian Shaw, "BrexLit" in *Brexit and Literature: Critical and Cultural Responses*, ed. Robert Eaglestone (New York: Routledge, 2018), 15–30, 20. Cf. also Katharina Pink, this volume, 313–337; Sidia Fiorato, this volume, 73.

more often than not shapes the world in the interests of the powerful, and for this very reason, greater suspicion of naïve, banal, or excessive expectations of literature might be necessary.[6] To portray literature as the cultural wing of a politically impotent humanism, Stonebridge argues, is to disparage both human rights and writing, which can provide powerful and sometimes effective ideas and practices "of being moral and political in the world."[7] After all, one should not forget that literature can just as well be instrumentalized to re-inscribe discursive hierarchical structures. Ultimately, what is at stake is literature's subversive power, meaning whether literature might be able to induce political awareness and change, for instance by generating empathy and enabling moral judgments through reading processes, or whether it ultimately, albeit perhaps unintentionally, affirms established literary and political hierarchies. The discrepancy between legitimization through law and *de facto* injustice becomes particularly clear in contrast with literature, which demands and might potentially even bring about not simply empathy or compassion, but solidarity, and act as a powerful advocate for effective implementation of human rights law.

1 Human Rights and Citizenship

The crucial significance and, at the same time, limited effectiveness of human rights is perhaps most visible in the context of the global mobility of individuals and groups, whether through flight, displacement, or migration. Being nothing but human and thus legally reduced to the mere possession of human rights only seems to affirm that the dignity and freedom of the subject on the move can ultimately only be guaranteed by civic rights, as Hannah Arendt once feared.[8] On the one hand, every human being enjoys a right to mobility – as the right to emigrate and return freely to his or her home nation state – irrespective of nationality (Art. 13 para. 2 UDHR). The right of access to another state, however, is inseparably linked to citizenship; it is the only legal means to enable the exercise of the human right to mobility. There is a painful tension between an ideal, global, and universal claim to the validity of human rights and a geographically and personally limited legal reality, legal applicability, and legal enforceability of human rights. Bearing various implications with regard to inclusion as well as exclusion, citizenship is not only one of the determining factors that constitute perceptions

6 Lyndsey Stonebridge, *Writing & Righting* (Oxford: Oxford UP, 2021), x.
7 Stonebridge, *Writing & Righting*, 13.
8 Hannah Arendt, *The Origins of Totalitarianism* (New York: Harcourt, 1951), 296, 298.

of selfhood and otherness, but quite ironically seems to be the only legal means to practically enforce human rights, even if the enforcement of human rights should – in theory – depend on nothing but a notion of shared humanity. While globalization is exerting increasing strain on conventional notions of citizenship and challenging traditional or homogenous perceptions of national cultures, national borders remain very much in effect. Even though alternatives to territorial conceptions of citizenship have been suggested, such as cultural, multicultural, or transnational citizenships, or the extension of municipal "citizenship rights" for local, non-national residents, citizenship remains one of the principal factors for the enforceability of rights in general and human rights in particular.[9]

Citizenship and migration are not new phenomena, but they share a long history.[10] What was notoriously misconstrued as the 2015 "refugee crisis" has put renewed pressure on the ongoing debate about humanism, collective responsibility, and the feasibility of a hospitable society. The subsequent tensions of conflict and intolerance contest a new and increasingly dynamic perception of citizenship. Undoubtedly, the forging of a communal spirit necessarily seems to involve the forging of exclusion; consequently, exclusion becomes one of the main functions of citizenship as a form of belonging.[11] Notions of citizenship and belonging have therefore not only encompassed privilege but have become fortified *legally* by creating legal instruments for discrimination against non-citizens. In fact, not only does citizenship appear to establish a reciprocal relationship of duties and responsibilities between state and citizen, but citizenship as a "fundamental human right" grants "nothing less than the right to have rights."[12] This glaring discrepancy between ideal and reality in human rights discourse is reminiscent of Hannah Arendt's skepticism about the concept of human rights. In theory, these should be enjoyed by every human being by virtue of his or her mere existence,[13] but in fact, as Arendt feared in her 1951 *The Origins of Totalitarianism* and which still applies today, human rights can only be claimed by those who are also citizens.

9 For the historical development, current significance, and alternative models of citizenship, see Laura A. Zander, "Visions of Citizenship: 'The Strangers' Case' or 'What Would You Think to Be Thus Used?'" in *Citizenship, Law and Literature*, ed. Caroline Koegler, Jesper Reddig, and Klaus Stierstorfer (Berlin: De Gruyter, 2021), 45–65.

10 Mae N. Ngai, *Impossible Subjects: Illegal Aliens and the Making of Modern America* (Princeton: Princeton UP, 2004); Adam McKeown, *Melancholy Order: Asian Migration and the Globalization of Borders* (New York: Columbia UP, 2008); David Jacobson, *Rights across Borders: Immigration and the Decline of Citizenship* (Baltimore, MD: Johns Hopkins UP, 1996).

11 Peter Riesenberg, *Citizenship in the Western Tradition: Plato to Rousseau* (Chapel Hill: U of North Carolina P, 1992), xi, xvii.

12 Arendt, *Totalitarianism*, 297.

13 Cf. also Lynn Hunt, *Inventing Human Rights: A History* (New York: Norton, 2007), 20.

2 Human Rights in the UK

Since the history of human rights in the UK context is a complicated one, it might be helpful to provide a brief overview of the development of UK human rights legislation. The UK lacks a constitutional history of its own and harbors a long-held suspicion towards statutory guarantees of fundamental rights.[14] Sometimes the Magna Carta is invoked to compensate for the lack of a domestic constitutional tradition. However, the Magna Carta can hardly be considered a direct precursor of constitutional or human rights. Instead of conferring guarantees or fundamental rights for the entire citizenry, it was basically a concession by the king to his lords, guaranteeing the protection of church rights, the protection from illegal imprisonment, and access to swift legal remedies, while limiting feudal payments to the Crown.

The Magna Carta came to symbolize the idea of constitutionality and civil rights only in the late sixteenth and early seventeenth century, when jurists and historians such as Sir Edward Coke resorted to the Magna Carta to limit the divine rights of kings. The political myth of the Magna Carta and its protection of ancient personal liberties persisted well into the nineteenth century. In such a vein, Lord Denning, for instance, described it as "the greatest constitutional document of all times – the foundation of the freedom of the individual against the arbitrary authority of the despot,"[15] graciously overlooking the fact that it was neither a constitution nor a means of protection for the ordinary citizenry against despotic monarchs, but simply a treaty to regulate power between the king and his barons.[16]

In 2000, the European Convention on Human Rights (ECHR) was implemented by the United Kingdom into national law through the Human Rights Act of 1998 (HRA). Implementation by the HRA exhibits a certain reluctance to defer to the case law of the European Court of Human Rights. While the act requires the UK courts in Section 2 of the HRA to "take into account" the decisions of the European Court of Human Rights (ECtHR) in their interpretation, this rendering does not bind UK courts, but allows them to disagree with decisions of the ECtHR on the scope or meaning of the European Convention on Human Rights.[17] Moreover, the HRA does not allow the UK courts to overturn or strike down primary legislation that violates the Convention. They can only issue a declaration of incompatibility and leave it to

---

14 This is at least the case if a constitution is understood to be a uniform, written guarantee of certain fundamental rights.

15 Danny Danziger and John Gillingham, *1215: The Year of Magna Carta* (New York: Simon Schuster, 2004), 268.

16 Cf. also Lord Mance, this volume, 253.

17 This is the case, for instance, in *R v Horncastle and others* (Appellants) [2009] UKSC 14, in which the Supreme Court expressly diverted from Strasbourg case law relating to the right to a fair trial.

Parliament to decide in a fast-track procedure whether and to what extent UK law should be adapted.[18] Such a declaration of incompatibility does not impair the validity, operation, or enforcement of the law in question.[19]

Ultimately, the UK courts are not required under the Human Rights Act to read and apply primary and subordinate legislation in a way that is compatible with Convention rights. Under Section 3 of the HRA, they are only required to regard the Convention "so far as it is possible to do so"; under this provision, there is a deliberate acceptance of possible conflicts between domestic law and human rights. Although human rights protections are generally reliable, the United Kingdom under various governments has failed to uphold human rights in the past and has been criticized by the United Nations and other international bodies for discrimination, for instance for neglecting the rights of the disabled, migrants, or the unemployed. Despite this reluctance to fully enforce human rights and the UK's hesitancy about EU initiatives in the arena of justice, the Convention and the ECtHR have been a source of political discontent and have been repeatedly exploited by populist politics. Fears that Westminster would lose importance and power vis-à-vis the EU fueled opposition to EU membership; these very fears were later all too easily exploited for the EU referendum.

After Brexit, the United Kingdom continued to remain a member of the Council of Europe and thus a party to the European Convention on Human Rights. The 2018 EU withdrawal agreement was accompanied by a political declaration. In it, the UK committed to accede to the ECHR as a basis for future cooperation. The joint recognition and commitment to respect human rights also informs the trade agreement between the EU and the UK. This includes both parties' compliance with the human rights treaties to which they are parties. Furthermore, both parties undertake to respect the ECHR and to implement the rights of the Convention in their countries. Human rights are also firmly enshrined in the Northern Ireland Protocol. The rights, guarantees, and equality of opportunity in Northern Ireland must not be affected by Brexit (Art. 2 I). As a result of Brexit, however, the Charter of Fundamental Rights and the human rights protections contained therein are no longer applicable to the United Kingdom. Charter rights, as interpreted and applied by the ECtHR, are binding, inflexible rights that cannot be rejected or relativized by national courts or legislatures.[20]

---

18 One of the exceptions is the ban on voting rights for prisoners, where the UK's case law opposes the clear position of the ECtHR.

19 Alice Donald, Jane Gordon, and Philip Leach, *The UK and the European Court of Human Rights: Equality and Human Rights Commission Research Report 83* (Manchester: Equality and Human Rights Commission, 2012), 23.

20 See also Lord Mance, this volume, 253–257.

For the scope of my argument, it is of particular interest what this domestic implementation of human rights means for immigration law and asylum politics. The UN Special Rapporteur on contemporary forms of racism contends that international law, including international human rights law, protects a nation's sovereignty in that it entitles states to set their own immigration policy. However, as she maintains, "where the strategy for immigration enforcement is so overbroad, and foreseeably results in the exclusion, discrimination, and subordination of groups and individuals on the basis of their race, ethnicity, or related status, such a strategy violates international human rights law and undermines the government's stated commitment to racial equality."[21] It is particularly in view of the last ten years of the UK's notorious hostile environment policy that such a violation of international human rights law is palpable, as there is no development that has had a more significant impact on people detained indefinitely in the UK. The UK government – this much is clear – does not intend to revoke the hostile policy in the UK any time soon, but recently even expanded some of its policies in regard to immigration despite the fact that they are in clear violation of human rights standards and conventions. These policy extensions came in form of the new 2022 Nationality and Borders Act, at the same time as the Home Office explicitly stated its position on citizenship by claiming that "British citizenship is a privilege, not a right."[22]

3 Hostile Politics in the UK

Whereas the global mobility of people has increased, the empathy of the West towards migrants seems to have decreased. Many states have responded to the rise of the number of global migrants by abrogating their human rights obligations, whether by limiting the scope and space for incoming migrants, or by means of immigration policies applicable to refugees.[23] The term 'hostile environment' policy was coined by former Home Office Secretary, later Prime Minister, Theresa May, when she described her intentions for the 2016 Immigration Act in 2012: "The aim is

21 UN General Assembly, Human Rights Council, "Report of the Special Rapporteur on Contemporary Forms of Racism, Racial Discrimination, Xenophobia and Related Intolerance. Visit to the United Kingdom of Great Britain and Northern Ireland," A/HRC/41/54/Add.2, May 27, 2019, para. 56.

22 Qtd. in Haroon Siddique, "New Bill Quietly Gives Powers to Remove British Citizenship without Notice," (November 17, 2021), *The Guardian* <https://www.theguardian.com/politics/2021/nov/17/new-bill-quietly-gives-powers-to-remove-british-citizenship-without-notice> (acc. August 1, 2022), n. pag.

23 Fareda Banda, *African Migration, Human Rights and Literature* (Oxford: Hart, 2020), 130.

to create here in Britain a really hostile environment for illegal migration,"[24] May said, and indeed hostile it has been.[25] The explicit aim of the policy was to make life unbearable for those perceived to be unentitled to live in the jurisdiction, "to produce an environment in which personhood itself could hardly be sustained."[26] Many of the instruments introduced were deliberately aimed at making the life of the individual asylum seeker as uncomfortable as possible during the asylum process.[27] Concrete measures included the limiting of access for irregular refugees to services such as banking, health, and housing. The legislation to enforce this policy was based on two restrictive immigration acts in 2014 and 2016, respectively; they were strictly enforced by an operationalized regime and supplemented by high-profile campaigns. The *undignified* treatment of those within European borders has been variously directed against persons who hitherto considered themselves citizens. The 2013 "Go-Home" campaign by the British Home Office urged undocumented people to leave the UK voluntarily or to face detention or deportation. The hostile advertising campaign was widely distributed throughout the UK, and the government even deployed vans to spread the slogans more widely. Moreover, adverts were placed in "eight minority ethnic newspapers, postcards in shop windows, and leaflets and posters advertising immigration surgeries used by faith and charity groups" in order to bring the hostile message across.[28] In the same year, the Home Office posted a Valentines' Day tweet as a warning against illegal marriages: "#Rosesareredvioletsareblue, if your marriage is a sham we'll be on to you . . . #happyvalentinesday."[29] Even if this policy was purposefully directed against illegal immigrants only, it created a very hostile atmosphere for all residents of the UK. This was proven even more painfully on occasion of the 2018 Windrush scandal, an instance in which the government systematically discriminated against

---

24 Qtd. in David Herd, "Afterword: Calling for an End to Indefinite Detention" in *Refugee Tales*, Vol. II, ed. Herd and Pincus (Manchester: Comma P, 2017), 113–123, 115.

25 See also Katharina Pink, this volume, 328–329.

26 David Herd, "Afterword" in *Refugee Tales*, Vol. III, ed. Herd and Pincus (Manchester: Comma P, 2019), 183–194, 189.

27 Matthew Gibney, "Asylum Policy," (March 26, 2011), *The Migration Observatory at the University of Oxford* <https://migrationobservatory.ox.ac.uk/resources/primers/asylum-policy> (acc. August 1, 2022), n. pag.

28 Alan Travis, "'Go Home' Vans Resulted in 11 People Leaving Britain, Says Report," (October 31, 2013), *The Guardian* <https://www.theguardian.com/uk-news/2013/oct/31/go-home-vans-11-leave-britain> (acc. September 1, 2021), n. pag.

29 Qtd. in Sukhdev Sandhu, "*Homecoming* by Colin Grant; *The Windrush Betrayal* by Amelia Gentleman – Review," (September 29, 2019), *The Guardian* <https://www.theguardian.com/books/2019/sep/29/homecoming-colin-grant-windrush-betrayal-amelia-gentleman-review?CMP=gu_com> (acc. August 9, 2022), n. pag.

citizens with Caribbean heritage.[30] Despite the public outrage at the discoveries, reparations have been partial and unsatisfactory, and the effects of the hostile environment policy continue to be felt by minorities.[31] In consequence of such policies, there has been "a marked increase in suspicion of minorities, which has resulted in a reported increase in complaints about race discrimination and racial profiling."[32]

The 2019 report of the Special Rapporteur on contemporary forms of racism noted that the restrictive immigration policy had turned private individuals and civil servants into immigration officials, which directly resulted in heightened racial discrimination. The hostile immigration policy, according to the Rapporteur, turned places of safety and support, such as hospitals, banks, and private residences, into border checkpoints.[33] As everyday activities were 'illegalized' for the migrant, a constant atmosphere of fear has been created. While access to most basic needs such as health care is usually still provided, the right to social relations and movement within public spaces is often severely inhibited.[34] It probably comes as no surprise that the Rapporteur contrasted the draconian policies of the English government with that of the devolved states in the UK, highlighting policies and practices more compliant with human rights in Wales and Scotland.[35] As this very brief summary of the implementation of human rights in the UK clearly highlights, there was a palpable discrepancy between the European commitment to common legal principles and the respective national migration policies even before Brexit.

4 Writing against a Hostile Environment

So far, my argument has been limited mainly to legal and political perspectives of citizenship, human rights, and the infamous British hostile environment policy. From a legal perspective, this has revealed certain constructs of mutual rights and

30 See Amelia Gentleman, *The Windrush Betrayal: Exposing the Hostile Environment* (London: Guardian Faber Publishing, 2019).

31 UN General Assembly, Human Rights Council, "Report of the Special Rapporteur," para. 52.

32 Banda, *African Migration*, 132.

33 UN General Assembly, Human Rights Council, "Report of the Special Rapporteur," paras. 52–61.

34 Shahram Khosravi, *'Illegal' Traveller: An Auto-Ethnography of Borders* (Basingstoke: Palgrave Macmillan, 2010), 90.

35 UN General Assembly, Human Rights Council, "Report of the Special Rapporteur," paras. 58–59.

obligations between the state and each individual citizen, while also allowing for conclusions to be drawn about the operation of international agreements in a more general sense. A literary perspective, however, seems to provide generic insights into the underlying ideological conceptions from an individual point of view. What both legal and literary concepts have in common is that they make political arguments and negotiate the various forces and interests at stake, sometimes through similar and other times through divergent instruments. In doing so, law seeks – at least ideally – to constitute a reliable authority, a system that offers solutions to practical questions and provides a fixed yet sufficiently flexible structure that orders and manages the position of the subject of law vis-à-vis the state as well as other legal subjects. That this ideal is not always executed in the real world, especially in the context of human rights, has already become evident. Literature as criticism, in contrast, does not even attempt such a fixation, but – to quote Martin Kayman – moves quite deliberately in "the realm of ambiguity, paradox, provisionality, aporia, and postponement, not that of definitive judgments and propositions."[36] While the law seeks to provide a reliable set of rules, literature allows for the questioning and renegotiating of the complexity and opacity of the same relationships in the first place. Ultimately, at least ideally, literature enables a transcendence of personal experience and explores states of mind beyond individual moral codes and predetermined legal categories. Lynn Hunt, Richard Rorty, and Martha Nussbaum, among others, have asserted that literary texts provide intense and effective forms of empathy, and thus facilitate ethical and emotional subject-formation and education.[37] At the same time, literature should by no means be superficially misconstrued to warrant empathy. For one thing, literature can just as well be instrumentalized for the inscription of discriminatory or hierarchical power structures; for another, feelings of empathy are not automatically or necessarily translated into political action through the reading process. Accordingly, Sophia McClennen and Joseph Slaughter

---

36 Martin Kayman, "Law-and-Literature: Questions of Jurisdiction," *REAL Yearbook of Research in English and American Literature* 18 (2002): 1–20, 3.

37 Hunt, *Inventing Human Rights*; Richard Rorty, "Human Rights, Rationality, and Sentimentality" in *Wronging Rights? Philosophical Challenges for Human Rights*, ed. Aakash Singh Rathore and Alex Cistelecan (London: Routledge, 2011), 107–131; Martha Craven Nussbaum, *Cultivating Humanity: A Classical Defense of Reform in Liberal Education* (Cambridge: Harvard UP, 1997). In contrast, Joseph Slaughter criticizes what he calls a "sentimental model of reading" for its "tendency to become a patronizing humanitarianism that is enabled by and subsists on socioeconomic and political disparities." Joseph Slaughter, *Human Rights, Inc.: The World Novel, Narrative Form, and International Law* (New York: Fordham UP, 2007), 325. For a similar critique, see also Stonebridge, *Writing & Righting*, x.

concede that "as often as cultural forms make human suffering visible they distort perceptions in ways that make it possible to disenfranchise and abuse others"; contrary to elitist, western, humanist expectations, literature is not always helpful in order to "imagine others" and "often serves to underscore national and ethnic divisions."[38] In such a vein, in a 2019 essay on "The Banality of Empathy," Namwali Serpell cautions that the "empathy model of art can bleed too easily into the relishing of suffering by those who are safe from it."[39] Her criticism becomes even more acute when she labels the empathy model

> a gateway drug to white saviorism, with its familiar blend of propaganda, pornography, and paternalism. It's an emotional palliative that distracts us from real inequities, on the page and on screen, to say nothing of our actual lives. And it has imposed upon readers and viewers the idea that they can and ought to use art to inhabit others, especially the marginalized.[40]

Notwithstanding this critique, I would like to explore the potential of literature to facilitate empathy with the lives and thoughts of others by looking at a selected group of representations of human rights violations vis-à-vis an apparently homogenous and self-sufficient legal discourse. The question I would like to ask is, can the process of creating imaginary worlds, or the literary representation of non-fictional worlds, enable readers to de-normalize their surroundings in order to reinterpret them in new, radical, or even subversive terms, and thus to think and ultimately realize both politically and legally a rejection of inhumane laws as well as hostile policies, in order to instead embrace solidarity? The selected literary texts, so the central claim of this contribution, might ultimately be able to overcome the discrepancy between legitimization through law and *de facto* injustice, to become literature that acts as a powerful advocate for solidarity and effective implementation of human rights law; and perhaps at the same time they might also be able to bridge the discrepancy between the European commitment to common legal principles and the respective national migration policies.

---

38 Sophia McClennen and Joseph Slaughter, "Introducing Human Rights and Literary Forms; or, The Vehicles and Vocabularies of Human Rights," *Comparative Literature Studies* 46:1 (2009): 1–19, 6.

39 Namwali Serpell, "The Banality of Empathy," (March 2, 2019), *The New York Review of Books* <https://www.nybooks.com/daily/2019/03/02/the-banality-of-empathy/> (acc. July 31, 2022), n. pag.

40 Serpell, "The Banality of Empathy," n. pag.

5 Unwriting Human Rights Violations in the *Refugee Tales*

I'M A STRONG MAN.
Even for me this is too much.
I'm so tired enough is enough.
15 years of this.
15 years without knowing.
15 years if I can stay if I can start a life.
15 years neither here nor home.
15 years of corridors and doors and hours and years of working my case and hoping and waiting.
15 years of corridors and doors and years of hoping.
15 year of paperwork and casework and English and flawless prejudice.
15 years of compiling files speaking to solicitors going to court working my case reading the decision.
15 years of corridors and doors and hours and years of starting again.
15 years of working my appeal going to court reading the reports being moved again.
15 years of being moved and being moved. Another appeal another report.
15 years I work my case this judge rejects it. From service to service court to court city to city.
I work my case that judge rejects it.
It's so hard. I've tried for so long. What you've been doing to me here it's not human it's not right.[41]

This is how "The Voluntary Returner's Tale," published in the second *Refugee Tales* volume and written by Caroline Bergvall, begins. Those twenty-five initial lines of Bergvall's prose poem attempt to convey the hardships of the lived experience of indefinite detention and offer a powerful impression of the human rights violations suffered by the detainee and principal narrator of the story. The continuous repetition of the temporal span of the suffering experienced by the first-person narrator painfully underscores the plight of infinite suffering. The fractured rendering of the prose and textual repetitions clearly allude to a vicious as well as unbreakable cycle of mental distress experienced by the detainee, but also to the inability to create a coherent account of this experience, an experience ruptured by false hope and false promises that allows only one possible conclusion – the treatment suffered was neither "human" nor "right."

41 Caroline Bergvall, "The Voluntary Returner's Tale" in *Refugee Tales*, Vol. II, 63–72, 63–64.

A later section in "The Voluntary Returner's Tale" then serves primarily to illustrate the impossibility of a situation in which the detainees feel not so much like prisoners of the detention centers, but like prisoners of a vicious Kafkaesque legal cycle. Here they are subjected to a "sustained, systematic and brutal assault on every aspect of the life of the geo-politically vulnerable person," be it due to the incredibly narrow financial support of £5 per day or the fact that it is only provided in voucher form with a card that is not eligible for public transportation, while asylum seekers are forbidden to work and made to sign in regularly at the Home Office Registration Centres:[42]

> Then the detention centre is burned down. They have to put you somewhere, so they put you back in prison. "I am not a prisoner, I'm only a detainee," you tell them, but it takes four months before they release you. The first condition of your liberty is that you must be tagged. The second condition is that you have a curfew. The third condition is that you must report to the border authority three times a week. The fourth condition is that you cannot work. A return ticket to the place where you have to report is £24. You have to report three times a week. You cannot work. "Miss, life is hard," you tell me. "Life is hard."[43]

Until reforms are made, refugee removal policy in the UK will seemingly require decades-long incarceration in Kafkaesque uncertainty, as well as numerous failed attempts at removal or the systematic extraction from detention in the middle of the night. The unbearable temporal limbo many refugees suffer in detention, as this passage indicates, is mirrored by the dire economic pairing of insufficient economic support with a ban on employment once they are released and the deliberate *de facto* impairment of spatial movement by inhibiting their use of public transportation. In the above-quoted passage the *Refugee Tales* display, as do many others, how a respective asylee "becomes the victim of an arbitrary system (the Law) that often operates wilfully, thus abandoning subjectivity, voice and agency."[44] Subsequently, the *Refugee Tales* can be read as a collection of documented human rights violations, committed not only globally, but also within UK borders. Ultimately, the individual fates are set against a continuous backdrop of abuses against those who came to the UK seeking protection.

On more than one occasion, the *Refugee Tales* make explicit the connection between the hostile environment policy and the subsequent human rights violations in the UK, for instance when the UK is juxtaposed to France as an alleged proponent of human rights: "I am not sending you to France, your relative says.

42 Herd, "Afterword" in *Refugee Tales*, Vol. III, 186.

43 Olivia Laing, "The Abandoned Person's Tale" in *Refugee Tales*, Vol. II, 25–29, 27.

44 Cecile Sandten, "*Refugee Tales*: Asylum Stories and Walks as New Forms of Literary and Political Intervention," *Anglistik: International Journal of English Studies* 31.3 (2020): 121–136, 130.

'I'm going to send you to a country where they have human rights.'"[45] This perception of the UK as human rights advocate is debunked as a false promise, however, as Olivia Laing in "The Abandoned Person's Tale" reveals in no uncertain terms. Consequently, Laing feels compelled to respond forcefully and personally as do many of the writers of the *Refugee Tales*:

> I don't know when I have ever felt so ashamed. I think of you as a boy, running in the street, high on the notion that you can change your country, can make it better. You have not had a life. Your life has been wasted, thrown away. What has happened to you has happened here, on British soil. "I'm sorry," I say, but no words can help. What I would like to give you is time: 1303 weeks, 9125 days, 219,000 hours, a quarter century stolen from you.[46]

6 Hostile Politics against UK Citizens in *Home Fire*

The hostile treatment, not only of refugees but also of citizens in present-day UK, inspired Kamila Shamsie to write her novel, *Home Fire*. The text poses a "powerful reimagining of Sophocles' *Antigone*" recontextualized for contemporary Britain in the context of ISIS extremism.[47] Whereas the novel's intricate whole illustrates the painful conflict of competing loyalties to the law as well as loved ones, it also highlights the sense of unbelonging in terms of a precarious citizenship status. Due to his joining ISIS, Parvaiz's citizenship is revoked posthumously, and his body is taken to Pakistan, even after he has attempted to surrender at the British embassy. His twin sister Aneeka, Shamsie's British *Antigone*, who travels to Pakistan in the futile hope of retrieving his body, is in fact denied citizenship status without any recourse to legal action. Shamsie's fictional home secretary reveals the crude but simple elegance of his policy:

> There was no need to do anything so dramatic as strip her of her citizenship. She couldn't return to the UK on her Pakistani passport without applying for visa, which she was certainly welcome to do if she wanted to waste her time and money. As for her British passport, which had been confiscated by the security services when she tried to join her brother in Istanbul, it was neither lost nor stolen nor expired and therefore there were simply no grounds for her to apply for a new one. Let her continue to be British, but let her be British outside Britain.[48]

45 Laing, "The Abandoned Person's Tale," 26.
46 Laing, "The Abandoned Person's Tale," 29.
47 Katja Sarkowsky, "Expatriation, Belonging, and the Politics of Burial: The Urgency of Citizenship in Kamila Shamsie's *Home Fire*" in *Citizenship, Law and Literature*, 29–44, 31.
48 Kamila Shamsie, *Home Fire* [2017] (London: Bloomsbury, 2018), 230.

Their older sister Isma's citizenship status documented by her passport is not *legally* in question; her 'belonging' nonetheless is threatened as the airport interrogation in the novel's opening scene reveals:

> "Do you consider yourself British?" the man said. "I am British." "But do you consider yourself British?" "I've lived here all my life." She meant there was no other country of which she could feel herself a part, but the words came out sounding evasive.[49]

There is certainly a lot that could be said about airport security checks in the context of dignity. Even I, a privileged western white woman, must ask myself on a regular basis whether safe flights really require a degrading half-stripped, one-legged hop through airport security. Shamsie's portrayal of Isma's interrogation, is, however, *undignified* on a completely different level, as Shamsie depicts Isma's humiliating suffering through a three-hour interrogation process that eventually causes her to miss her flight despite her thorough preparation and packing. That is, Isma had carefully rehearsed the required answer to her position on "Shias, homosexuals, the Queen, democracy, the *Great British Bake Off*, the invasion of Iraq, Israel, suicide bombers" and "dating websites."[50] She had also "made sure not to pack anything that would invite comment or questions – no Quran, no family pictures, no books on her area of academic interest."[51]

Shamsie is certainly not the first author to choose an airport to depict the experience of exclusion, rigor, and humiliation at the spatial boundary to the legal space of the nation-state. This space, as Abdulrazak Gurnah's novel *By the Sea* also illustrates, is the site of the lived demarcation between those who are perceived as belonging and those who are considered illegal, alien, or at least undesirable.[52] Now, it may seem cynical to point out that in Gurnah's rendering, the object of such undignified treatment is indeed an asylum seeker, someone who has yet to prove his right to enter the country, a right to remain, whereas in Shamsie's portrayal in *Home Fire*, Isma *is* a citizen, someone who spent her entire life in the UK – but as the Home Office made so unmistakably clear, citizenship in the UK is not a *right*, but a *privilege*. In both *Home Fire* and Gurnah's novel, the border becomes much more than a spatial or political boundary: it becomes an instrument that not only disconnects people from one another but also an expression of a legally legitimized discrimination apparatus of the state. Exclusion on the basis of citizenship and a – if only supposedly precarious – citizenship status thus enables and justifies various forms of power abuse on the part of the state as well as the individual. The borders that

49 Shamsie, *Home Fire*, 5.
50 Shamsie, *Home Fire*, 5.
51 Shamsie, *Home Fire*, 3.
52 Cf. Abdulrazak Gurnah, *By the Sea* [2001] (London: Bloomsbury, 2002), 5–14.

are to be defended here seem to subsequently develop a momentum of their own that far exceeds the mere geographical demarcation of borders. Thus, Caroline Bergvall rightly asks in "The Voluntary Returner's Tale" about the limits of borders that no longer restrict themselves to the landscape, but come to divide people, identities, and the community:

> *Borders, are they drawn at a natural obstacle, at a temporary political boundary, at a set of shared language or languages, at preferred cultural or class or caste types, in a far more widespread and sinister way at preferred ethnic types, how far into a body do they reach, how far into a person do they go to keep them out, with what impeccably argued arguments is this person not worthy, not harmonisable enough, since that's what it's called: harmonisation.*[53]

While "The Voluntary Returner's Tale" more or less ends on this sinister note and fails to offer alternatives or comfort to either the reader or the narrator, the *Refugee Tales* as a whole, as well as some of the other texts selected for this contribution, do offer alternative endings. The following concluding discussion will thus address the question of whether, or to what extent, such literary interventions can indeed have an impact with regard to human rights violations and influence the law or the political as well as social behavior of the reader.

7 Writing Solidarity

In *Human Rights, Inc.*, Joseph Slaughter criticizes various depictions of human suffering resulting from severe human rights violations in literature of achieving nothing but a "heightened sensitivity to human misery and vulnerability and to the dignity and developmental potential of the human personality."[54] Is this really all these texts are capable of and, in effect, all they do? In his essay on the *Refugee Tales,* Jan Rupp concedes that "[w]hile it certainly cannot make up for the dim realities of immigration policy, the project nevertheless launches a powerful commentary, juxtaposing the practice of indefinite detention with an alternative vision of convivial culture."[55] On a similar note, Cecile Sandten states that "the stories and

53 Bergvall, "The Voluntary Returner's Tale," 71; emphasis in the original.

54 Slaughter, *Human Rights, Inc.*, 326.

55 Jan Rupp, "Writing Back to Brexit: Refugees, Transcultural Intertextuality, and the Colonial Archive," *Journal of Postcolonial Writing* 56.5 (2020): 689–702, 698. In his article, Rupp illustrates how the invocation of the colonial archive, almost in spite of itself, has served to encompass rather than marginalize refugees. This intertextuality is part of a larger cultural intervention, Rupp argues, to counter the disruptive logic and national retreat of Brexit with new modes and manifestations of solidarity, forms that inscribe subjects on the move in the process of writing back to Brexit.

the project practise a symbolic resistance, a 'writing back,' to the dominant state power and the established political and media discourses that tend to dehumanise migrants."[56] At the very least, it seems, the *Refugee Tales* are raising awareness about a policy that is so detrimental for those seeking refuge due to human rights violations within UK borders, only to find themselves in a different kind of predicament. But rather than simply collecting human suffering and invoking empathy or effect in order to prompt the readership to become politically active against such abuses, they also offer various acts of welcome, of people acting in solidarity to counter the hostile environment. Rather than merely forming a symbolic resistance, as Sandten writes, the project offers a factual resistance by challenging the dominant discourse about refugees, as being criminalized and at times illegalized, with a powerful counter-narrative.

To this day, *Refugee Tales* has not succeeded in abolishing indefinite detention, but it has succeeded in persuading countless individuals, politicians, and companies to take action against the law and demand an end to this continuous state of human rights abuse. Perhaps more significantly, the *Refugee Tales*, Smith's *Seasonal Quartet*, and Popoola and Holmes' fictional short story collection *Breach* provide a rhetoric of welcome, of solidarity. As all these texts not only depict violations of rights, but also contrast them with alternative, dignified patterns of behavior, the wrongfulness of the violation is not only pointedly contrasted, but other legal and social models are conceived and made possible, as becomes evident in the following passage of *Breach*:

> You survived the boat, you have been picked up by the coastguard. You survived the crazy people who want to keep their beach clean, free of refugees. They think refugees make their summer income leave through the back door. Tourism does not want to see any dead bodies floating onto the sand. A man told me this. That man spat in front of my feet. I didn't understand him. That is how I met Calculate. He translated it with his funny Arabic. I didn't spit back. I just nodded. And smiled.
>
> I would never talk to strangers like that in my country. My first lesson in this Europe. But there are others who have a different view. Tourism or not, there is war. People are fleeing. They feel it is their duty. One of those gave me a backpack. She was waiting at the street that runs to the beach. She said there were clean clothes inside. And some food. There was also a note, a postcard written by a child. It said, *Welcome*. And, *We hope that you will be happy and that you will be with family and friends. Safe.*[57]

---

56 Cecile Sandten, "*Refugee Tales*," 127–128. Sandten also writes that the project aims also at transforming the historical English landscape into a hospitable space – in palpable contrast to May's hostile environment policy (126).

57 Olumide Popoola and Annie Holmes, "Counting Down" in *Breach*, ed. Popoola and Holmes (London: Pereine P, 2016), 9–26, 13–14; emphasis in the original.

In this passage, the realm of fiction is more than an imaginary space devoted to debating potential agency and experience; it is also a space for negotiation, that is, a space in which values are submitted to negotiation.[58] The above-quoted section presents the reader with two alternatives, that of hostility and that of hospitality, and invites her to weigh and evaluate both options in order to position herself in relation to the situation described and the accompanying conflict of values. I began this contribution with David Herd's prologue to the original *Refugee Tales* volume and I want to conclude here with another section of that very same prologue.

> But this prologue is not a poem
> It is an act of introduction
> Bathes every veyne in swich licour
> And all the introduction can do
> Is set the tone
> Albeit the tone
> Is everything
> And the tone is welcoming
> And the tone is celebratory
> And the tone is courteous
> And the tone is real
> And every step sets out a demand
> And every demand is urgent
> And what we call for
> Is an end
> To this inhuman discourse.[59]

In both passages, it becomes all too clear that it is *we* who have the choice. This is the consequence of the hierarchy, the power imbalance that border politics and the reliance on citizenship to enforce human rights entails. The question of the possible applicability of human rights depends – so much I hope has become clear in this article – not only on the conceptualization of human rights, but above all on our understanding of ourselves as host nations which have in effect legally decreed that asylum is not a privilege, not a question of hospitality, but a question of humanity and respect for human dignity. The literary texts selected for this contribution offer – imaginatively – an alternative sphere where the discrepancy between legal legitimacy and virtual injustice

58 Peter Schneck, "Das Recht der Entrechteten: Literatur und die Erfindung der Menschenrechte" in *Sprache, Flucht, Migration: Kritische, historische und pädagogische Annäherungen*, ed. Radhika Natarajan (Wiesbaden: Springer, 2019), 447–470, 459.
59 Herd, "Prologue," x.

can indeed be overcome, where solidarity is offered as a first, necessary, and ultimately potent cornerstone for effective implementation of human rights.

8 Postscript

In these post-Brexit times, it might be tempting to denounce the British hostile politics as UK-specific, as policies the remaining countries of the European Union had not adopted before the split and would be even less likely to adopt following it; these countries could perhaps even pride themselves on maintaining a comforting distance from the hostile policies of the former empire after its resentful departure from the Union. Unfortunately, however, there is no doubt that at least some of the remaining EU countries are creating similar, if not the same, hostile practices. Apart from various hostile EU border politics within and beyond European borders, this certainly holds true for the debatable German institution of anchor centers for refugees or the willfully misguided investigation of the NSU murders, recently dramatized by various theaters all over Germany on occasion of the trial's tenth anniversary.

What is it then that actually unites the European Union in this post-Brexit era? Is it indeed a set of common values, as the CFR so persuasively claims? Or does the discrepancy between the European commitment to common legal principles and the respective national migration policies ultimately prevail? More than seventy years after Hanna Arendt constituted 'human rights' as the right to have rights, perhaps what is needed is a different angle or a shifting view. What could be more telling of the identity formation of a political union founded upon the universal value of human dignity than to judge it by its treatment of those who may be unwelcome, of those who are illegal, of those it tends to fear? In my view, the European Union can evolve from hostile to hospitable only if the persons who are rendered absolutely vulnerable as subject to our law's immense power are granted equal access to the law's protections.

Migration

Historically, Europe has been uniquely affected by migration, displacement, and flight, movements which have repeatedly changed the political, social, or religious borders of the continent. Europe's ancient founding myth also imagines the territory as a sphere of up- and re-rooting; Phoenician princess Europa was abducted by a love-crazed Zeus in the form of a bull, who in turn was fleeing his jealous wife, Hera. Since its mythologically inspired eponymous origins, Europe has consisted of and self-identified with processes of transformation, dislocation, and re-constitution. The name Europe is therefore not primarily the proprietary appellation of a continent, but it instead conceptualizes a space created by processes of separation and annexation, rather than through the identification with something prior as 'inherent' or 'essential.' From the perspective of migration and its preeminent impact in the shaping of the continent, Europe is itself a migrating concept.

Both contributions in this section negotiate the issue of migration: in the case of Thomas Gutmann, in view of a possible non-discriminatory rendering of citizenship politics, and in Matteo Nicolini's, in the equally topical context of climate change.

With respect to globalization and "global horizons," Gutmann makes a convincing argument in favor of more "fluid concepts of national citizenship rights," which are not "contained within national borders."[1] Yet, while the European Union has extended the right to move and reside freely (including the free movement of labor) to EU citizens and the entire territory of the Union, it otherwise adheres to traditional notions of citizenship, "fortifies its external borders as a 'Fortress Europe' and allows migrants attempting to reach Europe to drown *en masse* as it closes its borders and scales back its rescue services."[2]

In contrast, Nicolini's cross-disciplinary investigation brings together a non-fictional literary genre, i.e., climate-change pop science, with climate change as a non-legal variable that triggers change in the legal spectrum, a fact that raises concerns about the ability of state policies and legal patterns to address the current ecological crisis. In this context, he demonstrates how the global supply chain mobilises mass migration while migrants become integrated economically, not ethically, and how the EU border policies secure EU borders externally to make it increasingly difficult for all refugees to enter, including those who have to flee due to climate change.[3] Ultimately, both contributions challenge the tricky distinction between internal and external mobility, and question whether global issues do not call for global solutions to end the present state of discrimination and promotion of inequality in the context of migration and enforced mobility.

---

1 Thomas Gutmann, this volume, 288.
2 Thomas Gutmann, this volume, 289.
3 Matteo Nicolini, this volume, 301.

https://doi.org/10.1515/9783111075693-029

Thomas Gutmann

Europe, Non-Discrimination, and Migration

1 European Non-Discrimination Law

Four years ago, the European Union Agency for Fundamental Rights and the Council of Europe published their latest edition of the *Handbook on European Non-Discrimination Law*,[4] highlighting the impressive body of case law developed by the European Court of Human Rights and the Court of Justice of the European Union in the non-discrimination field.[5] The prohibition of discrimination is established in Article 14 of the European Convention for the Protection of Human Rights and Fundamental Freedoms, which guarantees equal treatment in the enjoyment of the other rights set out in the Convention. The Council of Europe's European Social Charter (revised 1996) contains a provision prohibiting discrimination and providing protection from discrimination through a clause covering grounds such as race, color, sex, language, religion, political or other opinion, national extraction or social origin, health, association with a national minority, birth, or 'other status' (Article E). According to Article 2 of the Treaty on European Union, the non-discrimination principle is one of the fundamental values of the Union. Article 10 of the Treaty on the Functioning of the European Union requires the EU to combat discrimination based on sex, racial or ethnic origin, religion or belief, disability, age, or sexual orientation. To date, European Union non-discrimination directives prohibit all forms of discrimination based on race or ethnic origin in a number of areas and all forms of discrimination in employment and occupation based on religion or convictions, disability, age, and sexual orientation. The *Handbook* stresses that the principle of non-discrimination is of outstanding importance because it affects the enjoyment of all other human rights: "The aim of non-discrimination law is to allow all individuals an equal and fair prospect to access opportunities available in a society."[6]

4 European Union Agency for Fundamental Rights and Council of Europe, *Handbook on European Non-Discrimination Law* (Luxembourg: Publications Office of the European Union, 2018).
5 This chapter continues an idea that was developed in the following essay: Volker H. Schmidt and Thomas Gutmann, "National Citizenship and Categorical Inequality: Philosophical and Sociological Perspectives," *People on the Move: Migrants, Refugees, and Citizenship Rights*, ed. Massimo La Torre, spec. issue of *Rechtstheorie* 51.1 (2020): 89–97.
6 *Handbook on European Non-Discrimination Law*, 11.

https://doi.org/10.1515/9783111075693-030

2 The Normative Dynamics of Western Modernity

In this way the development of the principle of non-discrimination not only serves as a historical justification narrative for the European legal identity,[7] but as the engine and core of the normative dynamics of Western modernity, which is to be found in the institutionalization of egalitarian Normative Individualism within the legal system. The implicit, but pivotal notion of modern normative discourse beginning in the seventeenth century is that every person has an individual "right to equality of respect and concern."[8] The first derivation from this principle of equal freedom for all is that everyone has a right not to be legally discriminated against. The premise of egalitarian individualism is that all human beings are born free and equal, thus shifting the burden of proof to those insisting on inequality, to those who claim that different groups of people constitute qualitatively different types of human beings who cannot be judged by, or treated according to, the same standards.

Given an individual right to equality of respect and concern, all legal discrimination requires justification. Thus emerges a generalized expectation of inclusion and equal respect for all, the violation of which is deemed discriminatory and hence requires a strong, case-specific justification rather than being merely taken for granted. However, under conditions of normative modernity, such justifications are increasingly hard to come by, hence the delegitimization of categorical inequalities and the call for remedial action whenever and wherever they occur. This idea would inaugurate a coherent, consequential, and directed process which we cannot but analyze as the unfolding of a principle. As far as it actually unfolds in the real world, the right to equal respect and concern resists *all* practices defying its realization; its logic is egalitarian, aiming at the inclusion of all persons within its ambit.

The bundle of rights advocated by the first generations of liberals in the eighteenth and nineteenth centuries was much more limited than that which, two hundred years later, came to comprise the UN Universal Declaration of Human Rights. The liberals of the time pleaded for the civil and political rights of a *citoyen*, a status for which only a small fraction of the population was assumed to qualify. The large majority of humankind was thus excluded: the poor and the propertyless classes, women and children, in most cases also non-Caucasians, non-Europeans, non-Christians, as well as numerous others who were either

7 For the concept of a "justification narrative" [*Rechtfertigungsnarrativ*], cf. Rainer Forst, *Normativität und Macht: Zur Analyse sozialer Rechtfertigungsordnungen* (Berlin: Suhrkamp, 2015), especially ch. 3 in its translation as Forst, *Normativity and Power: Analyzing Social Orders of Justification* [2015], trans. Ciaran Cronin (Oxford: Oxford UP, 2017).

8 Ronald Dworkin, *Taking Rights Seriously* (Cambridge: Harvard UP, 1977), 181.

deemed dependents (and hence by definition ineligible) or otherwise found to be lacking. The history of the notion of human rights, which was originally confined to white, male, free, heterosexual, and economically independent citizens, is a history of its continuous, if gradual, and often painful extension.[9] We are witnessing and promoting the progress of a historical learning process[10] which is still far from being completed.

Egalitarian Normative Individualism is the *normative* reason for why modern society can tolerate a great deal of gradual inequality, but no form of categorical discrimination. Without sugar-coating the often brutal consequences of disparities in wealth and power that exist even in EU countries, it is easy to see that categorical discrimination is unique. While a tolerance of gradual inequality is compatible both with modern society's structural mode of organization and its ideational foundations, modern society cannot accommodate persistent categorical inequalities, which have been rendered historically obsolete and are fundamentally at odds with our society's image of itself.[11]

Though most of the exclusions initially seemed self-evident to people at the time, the inclusionary logic of the human rights discourse went against them from the outset. 'Aren't women human beings too?' Well, yes but . . . – and here is where the trouble inevitably starts. What could one possibly say to defend the curbing of women's (or some other category's) rights? Since the liberal case for freedom and equality implied that those subject to (legal) norms should be both their putative authors and addressees, the reasons brought forward by any would-be defector had to be publicly presentable and universally acceptable, and they had to be reasons that nobody could reasonably reject. As it turned out, such reasons do not exist. Categorical inequality proved indefensible. Thus, over time, one bastion of (legal) discrimination after another fell. It might take decades, even centuries of struggles for a new social category to be admitted to full membership of a political community, but eventually the walls of exclusion had to come down. So, despite their distinctness, most categorical inequalities share

---

9 "The translation of the first human right into positive law gave rise to a legal duty to realize exacting moral requirements, and that has become engraved into the collective memory of humanity." Jürgen Habermas, "The Concept of Human Dignity and The Realistic Utopia of Human Rights," *Metaphilosophy* 41.4 (2010): 464–480, 476.

10 Jürgen Habermas, "Equal Treatment of Cultures and the Limits of Postmodern Liberalism," *Journal of Political Philosophy* 13.1 (2005): 1–28, 8; Thomas Gutmann, "Constitutionalism and the Justification of Norms," *Diritto e Questioni Pubbliche* 16.1 (2016): 28–38.

11 Volker H. Schmidt, "Gradual and Categorical Inequalities" in *Worlds of Difference*, ed. Saïd Amir Arjomand and Elisa Reis (London: Sage, 2013), 252–270.

two commonalities: first, their delegitimization; and second, their widespread legal abolishment, at least in the world of liberal democracy.[12]

3 Citizenship as an Exception?

One important exception to this, however, is citizenship, the exclusionary effects of which are both widely recognized and backed by law. Citizenship is a rule-based status position, a form of categorical inequality, since it is a form of feudal-like[13] "birthright attribution": "[T]he vast majority of the global population has no way to acquire membership except by circumstances of birth. To the extent that citizenship is a valuable resource, it is currently secured on the basis of a morally arbitrary set of criteria."[14] However, citizenship-based exclusions continue to be far more widely accepted than other kinds of categorical inequality which were historically no less firmly held to be justified.

The categorical distinction between citizens and strangers (or foreigners) is built not only into the basic structure of the modern state, but into the modern state system as well. The power to admit or exclude aliens is inherent to sovereignty and essential for any political community,[15] or so we are told. As such, the categorical distinction between citizens and strangers/foreigners is central to the "segmentary organization" of the world political system,[16] from which it cannot be easily detached and which affords it globally recognized legitimacy. Citizenship "cages" (Michael Mann) the entire world population within circumscribed territorial spaces, both serving to justify ownership stakes and additionally functioning as a regime of "forced immobility"; in this latter capacity, it "contributes decisively to perpetuating vast social inequalities in life chances."[17]

Exclusion on the basis of citizenship, an ascribed status, continues to be taken for granted as natural – just as other ascribed categorizations that are now widely

12 Rogers Brubaker, *Grounds for Difference* (Cambridge: Harvard UP, 2015), 22.

13 As Carens writes: "[C]itizenship in Western liberal democracies is the modern equivalent of feudal class privilege – an inherited status that greatly enhances one's life chances. [. . .] Like feudal birthright privileges, restrictive citizenship is hard to justify when one thinks about it closely." Joseph Carens, *The Ethics of Immigration* (Oxford: Oxford UP, 2013), 226.

14 Ayelet Shachar, *The Birthright Lottery: Citizenship and Global Inequality* (Cambridge: Harvard UP, 2009), 4, 7, 17.

15 Joseph Carens, "Aliens and Citizens: The Case for Open Border," *The Review of Politics* 49.2 (1987): 251–273, 251.

16 Brubaker, *Grounds for Difference*, 22.

17 Brubaker, *Grounds for Difference*, 20.

regarded as dubious (such as race or gender) were before their de(con)struction. These systems based on birthright are, however, neither apolitical nor neutral.[18] Citizenship assigns and freezes in place inequality of position and opportunity in the world political system; a disadvantage which is then passed on to subsequent generations, thus forming the basis of inherited privilege or disadvantage. Birthplace and parentage are natural contingencies and hence are arbitrary from a moral standpoint.[19] People ending up with the "wrong" citizenship through the accident of birth are bound to a subordinate position in a "global structure of unequal positions"[20] which thwarts their opportunities from the very start.

Should citizenship be considered "special," then? Do we have good reasons for treating it differently to other forms of categorical discrimination? Are there functional reasons for doing so? Yes, national citizenship *does* help to preserve "some degree of bounded membership" and imagined community "as a source of security, continuity, and identity."[21] However, open borders do not render democratic self-governance impossible, and there is no reason to claim that the "self" in self-determination and self-governance should be defined by the privileged to protect them from changes in the *demos*.[22] Moreover, we do not think that there really exist constitutive ties in a strong and communitarian sense in our pluralistic, liberal societies today which could be threatened by a weakening of the notion of national citizenship. We can change our identity narratives, and they will still be chain novels. Nor is the functionality of legal systems threatened by the opening of borders. Robust legal institutions (which are also a prerequisite for any meaningful model of global citizenship) can still be upheld with permeable borders and fluid notions of citizenship. In any case, this will be the next question to answer as we continue to build European law upon the principle of non-discrimination and inclusion.

---

18 Shachar, *The Birthright Lottery*, 10.

19 John Rawls, qtd. in Carens, "Aliens and Citizens," 261.

20 Brubaker, *Grounds for Difference*, 21.

21 Shachar, *The Birthright Lottery*, 164.

22 Shachar, *The Birthright Lottery*, 139–140. For the circularity of the argument from democratic self-governance, cf. Hillel Steiner, "Hard Borders, Compensation, and Classical Liberalism" in *Boundaries and Justice: Diverse Ethical Perspectives*, ed. David Miller and Sohail H. Hashmi (Princeton: Princeton UP, 2001), 79–88.

4 Global Society and Global Citizenship

Throughout the twentieth century, the terms 'society' and 'nation-state' were essentially used interchangeably. That made some sense as long as the territorial boundaries of the state were more or less coextensive with the boundaries of society's systemic operations – as long as economies were first and foremost national economies; as long as politics, science, education, medicine, the arts, and just about every other system of society were largely national endeavours, which they had only become in the nineteenth century after sustained efforts by the state to nationalize them.[23] Today, the situation is different. Society's subsystems increasingly project global horizons for their operations, constituting a *de facto* global society and establishing a supranational regulatory regime which directly or indirectly shapes the living conditions of (almost) every human being.[24] Thus the notion of "unity of society," which can only be preserved by closing borders, is inadequate, since, strictly speaking, there is no such thing as a national society any longer. Unequal life chances in different parts of the world are determined to a significant extent by the daily operations of a world-encompassing society and its (often enough highly contested) system of governance.

If these inequalities are found to be unfair, then justice requires that the rules which generate them be changed. However, in keeping within the conventions of methodological nationalism, mainstream philosophy continues to delimit the scope of justice by the boundaries of the nation-state, with citizenship serving as the central lever for grounding demands of justice. But if there is reason to believe that society itself has gone global, then so too must justice[25] and citizenship. Global citizenship and fluid concepts of national citizenship rights are the necessary conceptual counterparts to a societal reality which can no longer be contained within national borders, nor be adequately governed by national institutions and/or actors (alone). Moreover, if principles of justice are to be applied to a community of global, rather than national, citizens, then their reach too must be globalized. Global justice is the inevitable corollary of a globalized society, for which a societal exterior has simply ceased to exist. Thus citizen rights become global rights and the normative case for restricting them to the national level

23 Saskia Sassen, *A Sociology of Globalization* (New York: Norton, 2007).

24 Volker H. Schmidt, *Global Modernity: A Conceptual Sketch* (Basingstoke: Palgrave Macmillan, 2014).

25 Volker H. Schmidt, "Global Modernity, World Society and Global Justice: Preliminary Thoughts" in *Positivität, Normativität und Institutionalität des Rechts*, ed. Aulis Aarni, Thomas Hoeren, Stanley L. Paulson, Martin Schulte, and Dieter Wyduckel (Berlin: Duncker & Humblot, 2013), 73–83.

collapses. The latest wave of globalization that began around the turn to the 1980s has effectively rendered obsolete the nation-state-based model of citizenship by giving rise to the emergence of a world society. The model of the nation-state posits a congruity between the state, territory, and citizenship. This model treats mobility within the nation-state as normal. Mobility between nation-states, on the other hand, is understood as anomalous,[26] although mobility is an intrinsic dynamic of societal modernization.[27] The European Union has extended the right to move and reside freely, including the freedom of movement for workers, to EU citizens and the entire territory of the Union (Articles 10 and 45 of the Treaty on the Functioning of the European Union), but otherwise sticks to the model, fortifies its external borders as a "Fortress Europe" and allows migrants attempting to reach Europe to drown *en masse* as it closes its borders and scales back its rescue services.

It is precisely this model that lends credibility to a system of tightly controlled borders which routinely excludes billions of noncitizens from the territories of wealthy countries. Yet, if the forces of globalization have undermined this model's normative foundations, then such exclusion is no longer justifiable. Instead, the borders have to be torn down, opened up to all global citizens who request entry, because in a truly global society the distinction between internal and external mobility dissolves, evaporates into thin air.

5 A Thought Experiment

Assuming that it transpires, upon thorough investigation and deliberation, that the reasons mobilized in support of territorial (citizenship-based) exclusions are indeed as weak and untenable as the ones which were historically utilized in defence of other kinds of categorical inequality,[28] can we therefore continue to uphold the practice? We think we can, but only at considerable cost. To explain why this is so, let me end this paper with a thought experiment: In this hypothetical scenario, once we have liberated ourselves from the demands of consistency in one case, we figure we might as well do the same in other cases. Thus, if we can freely discriminate against foreigners/noncitizens, then why not also discriminate

26 Brubaker, *Grounds for Difference*, 132.

27 Cf. Wilbur Zelinsky, "The Hypothesis of the Mobility Transition," *Geographical Review* 61.2 (1971): 219–249; Robert Woods, Martin Cadwallader, and Wilbur Zelinsky, "Zelinsky, W. 1971: The Hypothesis of the Mobility Transition. Geographical Review 61, 219–249," *Progress in Human Geography* 17.2 (1993): 213–219.

28 Cf. Carens, *The Ethics of Immigration*; David Miller, *Strangers in Our Midst: The Political Philosophy of Immigration* (Cambridge: Harvard UP, 2016); Shachar, *The Birthright Lottery*.

against women, blacks, homosexuals, etc.? Or to put it differently, if we can get away with acts of xenophobia, then what should possibly prevent us from being sexist, racist, and homophobic if and when it suits our interests?

By today's standards, this is admittedly an extreme scenario. It does, however, shed light upon a dilemma we face if we are to take the premises of our normative commitments, of egalitarian individualism, and the human rights logic, seriously. Sexism, racism, homophobia, and xenophobia are all practices that no present-day liberal would openly embrace. The conventional understanding of xenophobia refers to the ill-treatment of noncitizens after they have legally or illegally crossed the borders of a given country. To prevent such a situation, we may simply grant them negative rights of non-interference which protect their physical and psychic integrity while under "our" jurisdiction. Most liberals would unambiguously support this. However, in a world society the notion of xenophobia assumes a new meaning. In this much more expansive definition, xenophobic behavior begins with the very erection of borders, and the first act of xenophobia is to forcibly prevent anyone from crossing them. The only way to avoid such a situation would be to grant all of humankind virtually unlimited mobility. If this is the price to be paid for consistency, however, then some of us may well have second thoughts about it. It is probably for this reason that, for the time being, territorial exclusions are far more widely accepted (if not actively endorsed and lobbied for) than any other type of categorical exclusion.

The logic of egalitarian individualism is almost inevitably subversive. Critics of liberalism have, on occasion, historically been more aware of this subversive logic than the liberals themselves. For instance, in a review of John Stuart Mills' works published in 1866, a conservative critic claimed that the famous thinker "cannot help claiming the suffrage for the Negro – and the woman. Such conclusions are the inevitable results of the premises whence he started."[29] They are indeed. Mill himself, as has been frequently noted, was far from consistent in the conclusions he personally drew from these premises, and so he could at once be sympathetic to the cause of women's emancipation and simultaneously be an ardent defender of British colonialism. Similar inconsistencies pervade the work of liberals to the present day. They (and by extension most of us) are still reluctant to fully accept the conclusions of the premises to which they (we) ostensibly subscribe. We preach the inviolability of human rights, but when the consequences appear to be "too" radical, too demanding, too uncomfortable, then we quickly back down, maintaining the case in question is "different," and thus the human rights criteria do not really apply. They do,

29 Qtd. in Eric J. Hobsbawm, *The Age of Capital: 1848–1875* (London: Abacus, 1977), 251.

however, apply to the matters of citizenship and territorial (citizenship-based) exclusions.

Ultimately, the question is: Do we really have better reasons than the noble classes of the *ancien régime* to justify our non-deserved privileges? I do not think so. For the reasons sketched, we should not think that the Rawlsian answer provided by Ayelet Shachar, namely, to impose a tax on the hitherto “untaxed inherited property” of citizenship in the name of global distributive justice, is the adequate response to “the archaic mechanism of conferring citizenship by virtue of birthright.”[30] Financial redistribution in favor of those who are less fortunate in their citizenship assignment (namely, distributing revenues from citizenship taxes to specific projects designed to improve the life chances of children in the world's poorest countries) is not enough. The structural incompatibility of *global* social and economic systems, on the one hand, and *territorial* citizenship-based exclusions, on the other hand, call equally for open borders and fluid concepts of citizenship. Therefore it seems high time to add another chapter to our European justification narrative; one called ‘non-discrimination.’

30 Shachar, *The Birthright Lottery*, 3.

Matteo Nicolini

"Is There Still Such Thing as a Safe Space?" States in Times of Global Migration and Climate Change

1 Winning Arguments and State Failures

In *Untying the Sovereign State* (1988), the postmodernist scholar Richard K. Ashley provides an unusual approach to the nation state. Rather than labelling it as *the* "organizing principle" of modern politics,[1] he highlights its unique role in a world system characterised by the "*absence of an orderer*" capable of "enforcing rational global designs."[2]

Ashley's "*condition of anarchy*" is boosted more by the fragmentation of national identities than by the lack of an international government. Fragmentation has given rise to a competition regarding which state is better at arranging its own politico-legal order within the mayhem of the international community. States cultivate their own *horti conclusi* through narcissistic exercises in political superiority. Like in a global contest, they compete seeking to demonstrate that their "well bounded order of politics"[3] is the safest space in the world.

This essay reappraises these assumptions by locating them *in a time of migration and climate change*. I do not intend to revise the general theories of state in modern politico-legal thought. Yet, I understand they are useful when examining state narcissism in an age, like ours, where the idea of borders is being undermined. In transcending them, displaced refugees and mass migration add fuel to the transnational effects of globalisation. Likewise, climate change has spill-over effects triggering transformative changes within national orders.

Among the tools supplied by legal theory, the expression "safe normative space" is particularly fitting for my purposes. Richard Mullender elaborated it as regards Stanley Fish's book *Winning Arguments* (2017).[4] As Fish explains, "arguments may sweep away politico-legal frameworks, or normative worlds, we make and inhabit

1 James Anderson and Liam O'Dowd, "Borders, Border Regions and Territoriality: Contradictory Meanings, Changing Significance," *Regional Studies* 33.7 (1999): 593–604, 594.
2 Richard K. Ashley, "Untying the Sovereign State: A Double Reading of the Anarchy Problematique," *Millennium* 17 (1988): 227–262, 227.
3 Ashley, "Untying," 238.
4 Richard Mullender, "There is No Such Thing as a Safe Space," *The Modern Law Review* 82.3 (2019): 549–576.

https://doi.org/10.1515/9783111075693-031

and that invest our lives with a sense of significance and security."[5] To put the metaphor aside for a moment: political communities are threatened by arguments, which are the socio-climatic consequences of climate change. The well-defined order of politics provides the winning arguments protecting us against these. Borders recreate a "safe oasis" within which the disturbing arguments prompted by climate change and migration might be neutralised and brought "to an end."[6] This is exactly what a safe place is. In critical geopolitics, Geraoid O'Tuathail called this fencing process "geo-graphing."[7] Safe spaces are thus construed as politico-legal discourses with a good dose of ideological motivation. Mullender terms this type of space "a normatively appealing, enduring, but not entirely safe politico-legal space."[8] The state is *safe*, inasmuch as it insulates us from the insurgent social, migratory and ecological catastrophe. It is also *safe* because, like in a walled garden, borders shield us from contexts populated with disturbing arguments, doubts and other existential threats. These are slyly kept in the background, together with the socio-climatic consequences of the environmental crisis. Yet, doubts persist and insinuate into safe spaces, making their whole politico-legal construction creak like ice under our feet. That is, in Mullender's words, they are "not entirely safe."[9] This definition deserves to be explored, and this is what this essay intends to do. Echoing that of Mullender's, indeed, my title rhetorically turns his legal theoretical predicament into a research question.

The question requires a change of mood in addressing the state in a time, like ours, when climate change is undermining our long-established legal taxonomies. It challenges political authority, causing what I term *state failures*: nation states have failed to address the tensions it triggers because they still apply traditional legal paradigms without formulating innovative responses. Rather, they normalise ecological issues, making them fit into their legal frameworks. This reveals a disjuncture at the heart of our taxonomies, which reflects the mainstream legal discourse in climate change-related issues.[10] The same idea of safe space acts inconsistently when it comes to addressing them. On the one hand, it prevents the

5 Mullender, "There is No Such Thing," 550; see Stanley E. Fish, *Winning Arguments: What Works and Doesn't Work in Politics, the Bedroom, the Courtroom, and the Classroom* (New York: Harper Collins, 2017), 3, 120.

6 Fish, *Winning Arguments*, 3; Mullender, "There is No Such Thing," 551.

7 Geraoid O'Tuathail, *Critical Geopolitics: The Politics of Writing Global Space* (Minneapolis: Minnesota UP, 1996).

8 Mullender, "There is No Such Thing," 550.

9 Mullender, "There is No Such Thing," 550.

10 See Matteo Nicolini, "Law, the Humanities and Political Incertitude in a Time of Climate Change," *Legalities: The Australian and New Zealand Journal of Law and Society* 1.1 (2021): 91–115. See also Nicole Rogers, *Law, Fiction and Activism in a Time of Climate Change* (New York: Routledge, 2022).

effects of global warming, cordoning off its arguments; on the other, it convinces us that there are no real alternatives to the politics of the safe oasis. Ultimately, its winning argument is that *there is not such a thing as safe space* when mitigating the environmental catastrophe that we are provoking.

The paper adopts a cross-disciplinary stance to answer its research question. It draws arguments from a non-fictional literary genre, i.e., climate-change pop-science. Prompted by the insurgent ecological crisis, this genre comprises essays, pamphlets, letters and other writings related to the outcomes of our burning the planet, which convey a convincing "callout to the public [. . .] in response to climate and ecological emergency."[11] Through a cross-disciplinary approach, I shall assess how climate change acts as a non-legal variable triggering transformation in the legal spectrum, also raising concerns about the ability of state policies and legal patterns to confront the current ecological crisis.

2 The State, a Not Entirely Safe Place

We assume that the state is *safe* because it possesses the "border" argument. Enclosure follows a process of demarcation which resonates with the creation of a walled garden – whose walls, in the case of islands, are made of water. In *Richard II*, indeed, Shakespeare labelled England a "sea-wallèd garden"[12] which several "bad migrants" are now trying to reach by illegally crossing the Channel in the aftermath of Brexit.[13] Thanks to bordering-winning arguments, there is no room left for the threats caused by the insurgent environmental catastrophe.

Shakespeare also employs the metaphor of the garden to embed a politico-legal discourse made up of imagined geographies. Winning arguments do not automatically exclude loopholes in their texture. Like in our distressing time, Richard II's "commonwealth" and "government" are menaced by several threats; there are "too-fast-growing sprays / That look too lofty in" them, and "noisome weeds [. . .] without profit suck the soil's fertility." The political community is besieged like

11 Emma Thompson, ed., *Letters to the Earth: Writing to a Planet in Crisis* (London: Collins, 2020), 6; further references in the text, abbreviated as "LE." For more on climate-change pop-science, see Matteo Nicolini, "The 'Passing Away' of Our Environmental and Political Tales: Politico-Legal Incertitude in a Time of Climate Change" in *Citizenship, Law and Literature*, ed. Caroline Koegler et al. (Berlin: De Gruyter, 2021): 129–150.

12 William Shakespeare, *Richard II* [1597], in *The Oxford Shakespeare: Richard II*, ed. Anthony B. Dawson and Paul Yachnin (Oxford: Oxford UP, 2011), 3.4.42.

13 Maya Goodfellow, *Hostile Environment: How Migrants Became Scapegoats* (London: Verso, 2020), 240–246; further references in the text, abbreviated as "HE."

"herbs swarming with caterpillars."[14] Challenged by variables with "the power to unsettle existing certainties," safe spaces lose their "accents of infallibility"[15] and become "vulnerable to the assaults" of the winning arguments of climate change.[16] That is why Mullender labels safe spaces as "normatively appealing, enduring," adding that they are "not entirely safe."[17] Not *entirely safe* means that security is a *relative* concept, as risks are inherent to every human venture. *Fortuna* (i.e., the goddess of chance) may intervene and work against our safe spaces. As an adverse fate, she stirs climate change with disquieting arguments.

Take, for example, the non-fictional literary texts that make up climate-change pop-science. They all address the ecological crisis after the fashion of an apocalyptic lexicon. *The Uninhabitable Earth* points to "climate horrors," "sufferings" and "deprivation."[18] *This Is Not A Drill*[19] is oversaturated with either the term "extinction" or ones of its associated lexical items (ND, 7, 30, 78). *Inheritors of the Earth* mentions "human-created mass extinction."[20] All these books are suffused with the ideas of "climate and ecological emergency" and "collapse" (ND, 9; LE, 5; UE, 155),[21] as well as of the "ecological and political devastation" prompted by climate change (UE, 172), which "promises to transform everything we thought we knew about nature, including the moral infrastructure of those tales" (UE, 150).

The breakdown of our communities is caused by the disruption of our physical world. Evidently, "[t]here is No Planet B."[22] The chapter headings of *The Uninhabitable Earth* are revealing: our environments will be rendered un-survivable by "Heat Death," "Dying Oceans," "Freshwater Drain," "Unbreathable Air" and "Plagues of Warming." Geographic scenarios are now reaching the tipping point with loss of water, "carbon emission into the atmosphere" (UE, 101) or "the melting of the glaciers" (ND, 37). Winning arguments have deserted us. As we thought

14 Shakespeare, *Richard II*, 3.4.35, 3.4.36, 3.4.34, 3.4.46–47.
15 Alasdair Macintyre, *After Virtue: A Study in Moral Theory*, 2nd ed. (London: Duckworth, 1985), 17.
16 Richard Sennett, *Building and Dwelling: Ethics for the City* (London: Penguin, 2019), 268; further references in the text, abbreviated as "BD."
17 Mullender, "There is No Such Thing," 550.
18 David Wallace-Wells, *The Uninhabitable Earth: A Story of the Future* (London: Allen Lane, 2019), 198, 200, 192; further references in the text, abbreviated as "UE."
19 Extinction Rebellion, *This Is Not A Drill: An Extinction Rebellion Handbook* (London: Penguin, 2019); further references in the text, abbreviated as "ND."
20 Chris D. Thomas, *Inheritors of the Earth: How Nature Is Thriving in an Age of Extinction* (London: Allen Lane, 2018), 117; see also 173; further references in the text, abbreviated as "IE."
21 Kate Aronoff et al., *A Planet to Win: Why We Need a Green New Deal* (London: Verso, 2019), 3; further references in the text, abbreviated as "PW."
22 Mike Berners-Lee, *There Is No Planet B: A Handbook for the Make or Break Years* (Cambridge: Cambridge UP, 2019).

that "wealth was a shield against the ravages" of climate change, we kept on "mortgaging the ecological future of the planet" and building "our way out of nature" (UE, 51, 54, 71). We allowed its "cruelest impacts" to affect the less-developed countries (UE, 54). Capitalism deepens "inequalities of wealth and power" which are both "tightly linked to the challenge of confronting climate change."[23] Thus, the "world's suffering will be distributed as unequally as its profits" (UE, 121).[24]

Another disturbing argument concerns the "transformation *of* the political" caused by climate change (CL, 28). For example, several towns have been defined by "waterways" and "watery edges" (BD, 271). Owing to rising sea levels, "water has become a destructive as well as a functional and a scenic material," whose "malign threat" will affect them. "Built at the edge of the seas," coastal cities like New York, Mumbai or Rio will "risk episodic flooding" – if not be completely underwater (BD, 272). Likewise, small islands "face the risk of becoming practically uninhabitable" and "entirely underwater" with economic consequences that point to both their submersion and the "loss of [their] territory."[25]

Human-related consequences are also distressing; climate change may "unleash as many as a billion migrants by 2050" (UE, 133), boosting the "movement of people across borders, the mixing of bodies and places, and the reconfiguration of labour markets."[26] The threats of war will also be creeping into the texture of the walled gardens; "climate-displaced people will be both numerous and threatening to global security."[27]

A plethora of distressing arguments challenge our safe oases. State borders become blurred. Ours has become a "Human-Altered World" (IE, 29), where the melting bonds of political communities make us navigate "an entirely new social and political structure" (UE, 167). Hence, "Is There Still Such Thing as a Safe Space?"

---

23 Geoff Mann and Joel Wainwright, *Climate Leviathan: A Political Theory of Our Planetary Future* (London: Verso, 2018), 34: further references in the text, abbreviated as "CL."

24 Among legal scholars, see Katharina Pistor, *The Code of Capital: How the Law Creates Wealth and Inequality* (Princeton: Princeton UP, 2019), 23.

25 Rafael Leal-Arcas, *Climate Change and International Trade* (Cheltenham: Edward Elgar, 2013), 46, 51.

26 Andrew Baldwin, "Pluralising Climate Change and Migration: An Argument in Favour of Open Futures," *Geography Compass* 8.8 (2014): 516–528, 516. See also Roman Felli, *The Great Adaptation. Climate, Capitalism and Catastrophe* (London: Verso, 2021), 115.

27 Carol Farbotko et al., "Climate Migrants and New Identities? The Geopolitics of Embracing or Rejecting Mobility," *Social & Cultural Geography* 17.4 (2016): 533–552, 534. See also Gregory White, *Climate Change and Migration: Security and Borders in a Warming World* (Oxford: Oxford UP, 2011); Jon Barnett, "Security and Climate Change," *Global Environmental Change* 13.1 (2013): 7–17.

3 How Not to Address Climate Change: State Political Failures and "Constitutional Violation"

One of the winning arguments deployed by states is not to address climate change issues. They often exhibit *relaxed political tactics* towards it with the aim of preserving the capitalism-nation-state nexus and limiting "climate liability – for oil companies, for governments, for nations" (UE, 168).

In *The Code of Capital* (2019), Katharina Pistor explains why this occurs. Economic globalisation holds a particular fascination *also* for states, which "are not neutral when it comes to whose interests in an asset shall be given priority"; the prospect of benefitting from capital gains is "more likely to find their blessings than claims that assert self-governance or seek to ensure environmental sustainability."[28] To preserve the capitalism-nation-state nexus, we must carry on purchasing and consuming, even on the brink of ecological collapse. Consequently, climate change and its disturbing arguments must be kept out of our sight. Too much sensate, deep knowledge and conscious understanding of the catastrophe may cause a drop in commerce, threaten the collection of commodities and reduce profits.

"Normal politic has failed us" granting "access to government by big business" and bringing "the whole planet to the brink of ecological disaster" (ND, 22–23). *This Is Not A Drill* frontally challenges state authority because of its failure to tackle the distressing argument related to climate change, namely, migration, and the tensions that arise from environmental issues.

The way global warming is altering the organising themes within political communities may be properly understood by referring to what I have termed "state failures." This is patent in how we have removed restraints to greenhouse emissions. Under the 2015 Paris Agreement, the 2021 Glasgow Climate Pact, and the 2022 Sharm el-Sheikh Implementation Plan the increase in global average temperature should be limited to "well below 2°C above pre-industrial levels."[29] "Influenced by corporate lobbyists," the signatories to the 1997 Kyoto Protocol and the 2009 Copenhagen Accord established an emission trading system, thus commodifying carbon dioxide, i.e., the principal greenhouse gas.[30] This scheme

28 Pistor, *The Code*, 23.

29 Art. 2.1(a) of the 2015 Paris Agreement; Part IV (Mitigation) No. 15 of the 2021 Glasgow Climate Pact; Part I (Science and Urgency) No. 15 and Part IV (Mitigation) No. 11 of the 2022 Sharm el-Sheikh Implementation Plan.

30 See "Introduction: Climate Change – Developments in the Law," *Harvard Law Review*, 135.6 (2022): 1524–1543, 1528.

favours "big emitters" (i.e., nations which are the largest CO_2 contributors[31]) and non-country actors, such as international aviation and shipping located outside the scope of the Paris Agreement.[32] Failures like these cause what *Climate Leviathan* denotes the "principle failure":

> [The] Paris Agreement does not keep fossil fuels in the ground, but this does not mean it will not set the foundation for adaptation on a burning planet. On the contrary, the so-called "failures" of Paris are enabling, and part of, a crucial adaptation, the adaptation of the political. (CL, 38)

This also explains why the 2021 draft of the Glasgow Climate Pact "coals down" our hopes of limiting greenhouse emissions.[33]

These failures raise concerns as to the legitimacy of the current political obligation. To support the economic interests of economic sectionalities, sovereign states have used their winning arguments to ignore the geographical and socio-cultural contexts within which the bonds of communities and the mobility-climate change nexus take place. If availability of resources is reduced, and "our fragile web of life [. . .] poisoned and broken" (ND, 6), then the political obligation becomes unsustainable. *This Is Not A Drill* suggests that "[e]very parliament, state legislature and local authority [need] to declare a climate and ecological emergency," following the lead of more than twenty-five countries and more than 1,000 local councils throughout the world (ND, 22). The UK House of Commons was the first one to declare:

> an environment and climate emergency following the finding of the Inter-governmental Panel on Climate Change that to avoid a more than 1.5°C rise in global warming, global emissions would need to fall by around 45 per cent from 2010 levels by 2030, reaching net zero by around 2050.[34]

Several other countries followed suit.[35]

The capitalism-state nexus has marginalised climate change issues in political negotiations. This triggers a further failure, namely, "that of state authorities to

---

31 Art. 17 of the 1997 Kyoto Protocol. On such commodification, see Michael Watts, "Commodities" in *Introducing Human Geographies*, ed. Paul Clok et al. (Abingdon: Routledge, 2014), 391–412, 406–407.

32 See Vesselin Popovski, ed., *The Implementation of the Paris Agreement on Climate Change* (Abingdon: Routledge, 2019).

33 See Glasgow Climate Pact, Part IV (Mitigation) Nos. 17 ("rapid, deep, and sustained reductions in global greenhouse emissions") and 20 ("accelerating efforts towards the phase-out of unabated coal power and inefficient fossil fuel subsidies"); Part III (Energy) No. 8 of the 2022 Sharm el-Sheikh Implemation Plan reiterates this "urgent need."

34 House of Commons, "Hansard May 21, 2019," Vol. 659, Columns 317–318.

35 A comprehensive list of climate emergency declarations is available at <https://climateemergencydeclaration.org/climate-emergency-declarations-cover-15-million-citizens/> (acc. May 13, 2022).

create the law that was wanted" by the political community, i.e., a law which should be firmly rooted in a sustainable compactual agreement. The "readiness on the part of the state authorities to allow" the private international investors to "make a considerable part of the law" discloses state opportunism towards these contentious topics.[36] This also explains why Extinction Rebellion has recently declared the same "bonds of the social contract [. . .] to be null and void":

> When Government and the law fail to provide any assurance of adequate protection, as well as security for its people's well-being and the nation's future, it becomes the right of its citizens to seek redress in order to restore dutiful democracy and to secure the solutions needed to avert catastrophe and protect the future. (ND, 1–2)

Finally, this resonates with Johannes Althusius's idea of gross "constitutional violation," entailing a general callout to the public when there is any "egregious," "chronic," "persistent," "pervasive," "wilful," "intentional" or "widespread" "breach of a ruler's constitutional duties."[37] There are hints of *abusus potestatis publicae* when a ruler "violates, changes, overthrows, or destroys" the fundamental law and people's rights. When such abuses disrupt "the natural laws and rights" (i.e., the environmental context) on which the constitutional framework is based, the state is also "chronically [neglecting] the sick, the poor, and innocent."[38]

4 Migration and Climate Change: New Arguments in Favour of Borders

The concept of gross constitutional violation supplies a strong argument against the role of nation-states in our distressing age. Not only are the herbs of our walled gardens swarming with doubts and threats, but in failing us states no longer represent "such thing as a safe place."

In a time of ecological distress, the capital-state nexus must work out new winning arguments to persuade us that the state is still a safe place. The capital-state nexus contrasts our doubts through a new process of persuasion, convincing us that we can quietly live in our walled gardens and carry on purchasing, consuming and sustaining the economic cycle. In these places, we have commodities

36 Alan Watson, *Failures of the Legal Imagination* (Philadelphia: U of Pennsylvania P, 1988), 87, 96.
37 Johannes Althusius, *Dicaeologicae libri tres, totum et universum jus, quo utimur methodice complectentes* (Heidelberg 1617), I.113.9–17. Qtd. in John Witte, Jr., *The Reformation of Rights: Law, Religion, and Human Rights in Early Modern Calvinism* (Cambridge: Cambridge UP, 2007), 201.
38 Althusius, *Dicaeologicae*, I.113.1–3, I.113.8–9, 13.

shipped and "recollected in tranquillity."[39] The resilience of capitalism in a time of climate change represents an enthralling organising theme for state communities.

This is apparent as regards migration. The global supply chain needs labour to work. Capital uses several arguments to convince prospective workers to migrate to the places in which it produces. These arguments are convincing since they give migrants the illusion of taking part in the global distribution of workers, who are attracted by the pursuit of happiness and the perspective of improving their (and their family's) standard of life. The global supply chain mobilises mass migration from the Global South towards the Global North with a "promise of growth [that] has been the justification for inequality, injustice, and exploitation," with more wounds to heal "in the near climate future" (UE, 166).

Under the aegis of the UN, two Global Compacts were signed in 2018, namely, The Global Compact for Safe, Orderly and Regular Migration (GCM) and the Global Compact on Refugees (GCR).[40] The GCM acknowledges that migration has been "part of the human experience throughout history"; it also terms it "a source of prosperity," whose "positive impacts can be optimized by improving migration governance." The signatories also acknowledge that both instruments are "complementary international cooperation frameworks," because "migrants and refugees may face many common challenges and similar vulnerabilities."[41]

There is something treacherous in such sanctification of global mobility. The narrative of prosperity and progress hides a new winning argument: the safe oasis is promised only to those living in the walled gardens, leaving to those taking part in the global supply chain the mere illusion of pursuing happiness through migration.

When economic migrants legally (and sometimes illegally) cross the fences of our *hortus conclusi*, they enter the walled garden, into which (as well as into its supply chain) they become integrated. Our notion of integration, though, is economic, not ethical. It is functional only to production and consumption of commodities.

What do these migrants expect from us? Integrated in our safe spaces economically, they must comply with the following rules: they must take part in the supply chain; like us, they must spend their stipends (their share in the global wealth) on the commodities they produce to sustain the economic cycle; finally, after having

39 William Wordsworth, "Preface" [1802] in *Wordsworth and Coleridge: Lyrical Ballads, 1798 and 1802* (Oxford: Oxford UP, 2013), 95–115, 96–97.

40 Resolution adopted by the General Assembly on December 19, 2018, UN Doc A/RES/73/195 (January 11, 2019) Annex: Global Compact for Safe, Orderly and Regular Migration. Report of the United Nations High Commissioner for Refugees (13 September 2018) UN Doc A/RES/73/12 (Part II) Global Compact on Refugees.

41 Paras. 3 and 4 of GCM. See Elizabeth G. Ferris and Katharine M. Donato, *Refugees, Migration and Global Governance: Negotiating the Global Compacts* (Abingdon: Routledge, 2020), 100–122.

worked in our safer places, they must retreat from them. The last requirement is also known as the NIMBY (Not In My Back Yard) factor, which reflects what has been termed as the "Global Apartheid."[42] As consumers, shareholders and entrepreneurs, we turn workers into *something servient* to the comfort zones of capitalist economies. Again, our motto revolves around the maximisation of financial returns and the idea of the safe space: the quieter the space, the safer it is, and the higher the returns are.

In his *Reimagining Britain*, the Archbishop of Canterbury Justin Welby highlights how economic integration makes communities (even parish communities) "resistant to outsiders and reluctant to sponsor diversity if there is any possibility that it will diminish housing values or be perceived as a risk to the aesthetics of that community"; there is no "diversity, or mixing, no valuing of difference, no sight of the poor."[43] This sharply contrasts with the biblical (and Christian) mandate.

Ultimately, gentrification recreates a safe space whose community is homogenous, "expensive" and "exclusive." In Welby's words, "the balance of property values and influence of location" are extremely "materialistic" and point to the "economic maximization" of investments in housing.[44] The presence of outsiders makes the space diverse and no longer exclusive, that is, less expensive if housing prices drop because of the *mixité*. That is why Western states have reproduced the "racially marginalised hierarchies" between the metropolis and its colonies within their urban areas. As a result, migrants are located into cordoned-off "periphractic spaces," which constrain immigrants "in terms of location and their limitation in terms of access – to power, to (the realization of) rights, and to goods and services."[45]

Spatial marginalisation triggers a "really hostile environment for [allegedly] illegal immigrants" (HE, 2),[46] i.e., a by-product of "heightened border measures that restrict migration, measures that play well with anxious electorates and hawkish politicians"; states disavow "the West's complicity in the wider social,

---

42 Yajaira Ceciliano-Navarro et al., "Reflections on Anti-Immigration Narratives and the Establishment of Global Apartheid" in *Beyond Borders: The Human Rights of Non-Citizens at Home and Abroad*, ed. Molly Katrina Land et al. (Cambridge: Cambridge UP, 2021), 94–110.

43 Justin Welby, *Reimagining Britain: Foundations for Hope* (London: Bloomsbury, 2018), 145.

44 Welby, *Reimagining Britain*, 146.

45 David Theo Goldberg, "'Polluting the Body Politic': Race and Urban Location" in *The Legal Geographies Reader: Law, Powers, and Space*, ed. Nicholas Blomley et al. (Oxford: Blackwell, 2001), 69–76, 71, 72.

46 The so-called "hostile environment immigration" policy was coined by the then UK Home Secretary Theresa May. See James Kirkup and Robert Winnett, "Theresa May Interview: 'We're Going to Give Illegal Migrants a Really Hostile Reception,'" (May 25, 2012), *The Telegraph* <https://www.telegraph.co.uk/news/0/theresa-may-interview-going-give-illegal-migrants-really-hostile/> (acc. July 30, 2020).

political and economic conditions that contribute to the migrations the West seeks to secure."[47] Whilst praising the economic benefits of global mobility and the protection of migrants' rights, "politicians work together across borders to make it more difficult for people to move, while capital is allowed to flow freely" (HE, 35).

Take the EU policies related to migration and refugeeism. On the one hand, they are strongly inclusive but, on the other hand, EU treaties and legislation are overpopulated with references to external borders. Schemes such as Frontex are "the culmination of the process of securitization of the EU external borders," whereas the European Border Management (EBM) has "multiple dimensions": it encompasses several methods of "border checks and surveillance," which make it hard for migrants to access the EU.[48] Indeed, EU citizenship complements national citizenship, which means that third-country nationals residing within its borders are, in principle, excluded from it. To make the EU a safer space, it has been "necessary to draw a line between insiders and outsiders, between 'us' and 'them.'"[49] What is walled is not the border, but the space where the integration process takes place; the EU thus establishes "a unitary basis for exclusion rather than a coherent set of criteria for inclusion."[50] Evidently, the "principle of solidarity and fair sharing of responsibility," which underpins the Area of Freedom, Security, and Justice laid down by the Treaty on the Functioning of the EU, is a privilege reserved for EU citizens, whereas third-country nationals must merely be treated fairly when they try to access the EU.[51]

Included but marginalised, migrants enter irredeemable conveyances with the capitalism-nation-state nexus and bear the costs of politico-legal marginalisation. Migrants – even climate-induced ones – accept to "subject themselves" to this organising principle and its "authority by their own consent and voluntary act"; within our wealthy communities, they accept these "unnatural" structures and strictures of authority, for "they realize that without them [. . .] even their most basic rights will mean little."[52]

---

47 Baldwin, "Pluralising," 521.

48 On the so-called "Fortress Europe," see David Delaney, *The Spatial, the Legal and the Pragmatics of World-Making* (Oxford: Blackwell, 2010), 153.

49 Serhii Lashyn, "The Aporia of EU Citizenship," *Liverpool Law Review* 42 (2021): 361–377, 364.

50 Jaqueline Bhabha, "'Get Back to Where You Once Belonged': Identity, Citizenship, and Exclusion in Europe," *Human Rights Quarterly* 20 (1998): 592–627, 604.

51 Article 80 TFEU. See Violeta Moreno-Lax, *Accessing Asylum in Europe: Extraterritorial Border Controls and Refugee Rights under EU Law* (Oxford: Oxford UP, 2017), 31, 34; see also Andrew Burridge et al., "Polymorphic Borders," *Territory, Politics, Governance* 5 (2017): 239–251, 242.

52 Witte, *The Reformation*, 183–184.

5 The Force of Arguments and Our Egalitarian Misery

There is a further argument the capital-state nexus uses to convince us that we still live in safe places. The force of this argument lies in its egalitarianism and universalism: every community must confront climate change, which we can tackle by adopting a global-response strategy. This response is supplied by global capital, which operates at a transnational scale. To favour the smooth flow of goods and services across frontiers and national legal systems, global markets approach territories and borders through the application of generalisations and "global-business-as-usual" strategies.

Yet, these strategies are unlikely to "produce predictable outcomes as laboratory experiments might."[53] Like cross-border economic interests, ecological concerns are also shared by transnational communities; but, unlike economic interests, our concerns are extremely concrete. Beyond the global law, there are communities. Climate change is certainly an international, cross-border and domestic phenomenon. As a transnational phenomenon, it transcends borders; but it is also a concrete concern striking indiscriminately on a territorial basis.

Global-business-as-usual strategies lead us to fall prey to Hayek's "synoptic delusion." It certainly gives us the illusion that, from a central standpoint, we can access all the information we need to respond effectively to our ecological problems. In Hayek's opinion, though, this is the "characteristic error" of those who underestimate "concrete facts," such as the complexities of our environmental crisis. Besides this, the "synoptic delusion" replaces the social reality we seek to regulate with "a surveyable whole of all data" and arguments complemented by the capital-state nexus. This prevents us from tackling climate change with a more nuanced and contextual approach, leaving us intoxicated by "the sense of unlimited power" that arises from the global strategy of ecological adaptation.[54]

Such a synoptic delusion, I assume, reflects a kind of egalitarian misery, which is the paradigm of adaptation.[55] We have deceived ourselves, assuming that bracketed within the winning arguments of the nation-state is the winning

---

53 Cinnamon Carlarne and Daniel Farber, "Law beyond Borders: Transnational Responses to Global Environmental Issues," *Transnational Environmental Law* 1.1. (2012): 13–21, 19.

54 See Friedrich A. Hayek, *Law, Legislation and Liberty*, Vol I, *Rules and Order* (London: Routledge & Kegan Paul, 1973), 14, 8, 14–155. I owe this set of reflections on Hayek's predicaments to Richard Mullender; see Richard Mullender, "Negligence, Public Bodies, and Ruthlessness," *Modern Law Review* 72.6 (2009): 961–983, 973.

55 On the concept of "egalitarian misery," see Richard Mullender, "On the French Revolution and the Programmatic Imagination: Hilary Mantel on Law, Politics, and Misery" in *Law and*

argument of capitalism and the "progress" of our time. We know that the world is on fire. To be honest, we do not really care a straw about it. The decline is a misery; it sounds so egalitarian because it consumes all our lives in our safe spaces. Yet, the wealthy will decline in better spirits than the lowly and marginalised.

6 But . . . Is There Still Such Thing as a Safe Space? Concluding Remarks

Let me conclude by providing a methodological answer to my initial research question. I understand that legal theory supplies us with several instruments that, in broadening our perspective, allow us to avoid the synoptic-delusion syndrome.

My answer is methodological because the synoptic delusion has accents of infallibility that also percolate through academia. Paraphrasing Jeanne Gaakeer, we tend to tackle climate change by sticking to our "disciplinary islands," whose dams preclude "new academic insights and societal impact" and accept arguments related to it that are external to such islands.[56] It does not come as a surprise, then, that the self-referential attitude of scholars insulated within "disciplinary boundaries, intuitively presumed or authoritatively drawn,"[57] reflects the fragmentation of the general theory of state into differentiated *horti conclusi*. What is certain is that we feel safe when we do research within our disciplines.

Although "disciplinary islands" are eulogised within mainstream academic circles, I think that sticking to them runs counter to the very idea of scientific research. We should remain open to the exchange of ideas and opinions, and arguments, whether alluring or disturbing. We cannot assess climate change only by picking up winning arguments and discarding the distressing ones as if they were in watertight compartments. Quite the opposite; they mutually interact. When doing research, we must accept that other disciplines provide alternative readings of our safe places. Like borders, our disciplinary arguments are vulnerable to the assaults of arguments stemming from different areas of knowledge. A methodological change is therefore required, as well as the change in mood I mentioned above. If we intend to deal with climate change and its transnational concerns, we must engage in cross-disciplinary investigations.

Imagination in Troubled Times: A Legal and Literary Discourse, ed. Richard Mullender et al. (Abingdon: Routledge, 2020), 133–156, 153.

56 Jeanne Gaakeer, "Interdisciplinarity 3.0: The Hub of the Universe or Fantasy Island?" *Pólemos*, 14.2 (2020): 319–336, 322.

57 Gaakeer, "Interdisciplinarity 3.0," 322.

In this article, I have adopted a cross-disciplinary stance to address the politico-legal consequences of climate change by focusing on how literary outputs convey our transnational ecological concerns. With its variety of approaches and styles, climate-change pop-science has assisted me in evaluating how global warming is concretely altering the organising themes within political communities. When referring to the threats posed by climate change, they have supplied arguments to critically assess the idea of comfort zones, borders and one-size-fits-all mitigation solutions. This has also meant *being subversive*, also addressing the ecological crisis through arguments capable of disturbing the safe spaces created by the capital-state nexus. Being subversive runs counter to the idea of normalisation of ecological and climate concerns in politico-legal studies.

This pattern of cross-disciplinarity also challenges the "paradigm of biological decline" predominant "among ecologists, environmentalists and conservationists"; without denying the environmental threats, ecological biodiversity also responds "by evolving" to the changes caused by anthropogenic drivers (IE, 30, 117). This entails reframing our methodological attitude in a time of climate change. We should shake off the "pessimism-laden, loss-only view" of our future, the narrative of decline as well as the idea that adaptation is the sole type of progress of our time (IE, 9).

Climate change and migration should be confronted throughout a variety of new arguments, as well as legal responses. *A Planet to Win, On Fire, The Case for a Green New Deal* and *Planet on Fire* advocate for a new foundation of our political bonds.[58] We should pluralise the debate when addressing the distributive effects of climate change and contrasting the neo-colonial segregation practiced in Western communities. This might be fostered by "new regulatory practices" and new "forms of governance," such as public participation or legislative frameworks whereby decision makers stir the law simply by adjusting "existing legal processes to accommodate changing environmental or social condition."[59]

Is the state still a safe place? To a certain extent, it is, provided that we turn the walled garden into a public sphere where safety is guaranteed by openness, inclusion and courage of tackling all arguments, even the most distressing ones. We must therefore remain vigilant and keep the door of the walled garden open to a constant conversation with the rest of the world. Also, we must accept that

---

58 Aronoff et al., *A Planet to Win*; Naomi Klein, *On Fire: The (Burning) Case for a Green New Deal* (London: Penguin, 2019); Ann Pettifor, *The Case for the Green New Deal* (London: Verso, 2019); Mathew Laurence and Laurie Laybourn-Langton, *Planet on Fire: A Manifesto for the Age of Environmental Breakdown* (London: Verso, 2021).

59 See Joseph Wenta et al., "Enhancing Resilience and Justice in Climate Adaptation Laws," *Transnational Environmental Law* 8.1 (2019): 89–118, 113, 108.

ecological threats are part of our relatively safe communities. In so doing, we can recreate the state as a safe space. The adoption of a cross-disciplinary perspective involves unceasing conversations with all societal forces and arguments, whose callouts to the public in response to climate and ecological emergencies stretch our thinking into the future.

Citizenship

The crucial significance of citizenship for society within Europe as a whole, but also for the legal status of the individual, can hardly be overestimated in principle, but it becomes particularly acute in the context of migration and human rights, both of which were discussed in the previous sections. The special rights and obligations resulting from a citizenship status endow the individual with the necessary effective and legal agency, but their absence all too often renders the individual powerless and legally unprotected, a lack that is unfortunately more often than not insufficiently compensated for by human rights – allegedly universally applicable –, an ideal that seems to be rarely realized in practice.

Katharina Pink's contribution explores the inequalities of current citizenship legislation in the UK and offers Ali Smith's *Seasonal Quartet* as a fictional inquiry into alternative notions of citizenship based neither on territory nor nationality but rather on community as "an alternative, affective notion of belonging and citizenship: a post-territorial, trans-generational bond formed by empathy and dialogue based on a common acknowledgement of values and responsibilities that can serve to unite individuals as well as nations."[1] Pink's reading of Smith's *Seasonal Quartet* as BrexLit addresses current crises and concerns in the context of Brexit, migration, and the EU as she embeds her literary analysis within the legal framework of current British politics.

In a similar vein, Jayana Jain suggests that the violent politics of inclusion and exclusion are often not made visible in citizenship laws; Jain therefore offers a selection of Rohingya poetry to highlight the violence and trauma of the marginalized migrants. Jain's contribution further aims at deconstructing the Eurocentric perspective on migrants and refugees that more often than not pays too little attention to the deplorable situation of people beyond the borders of the continent. To counter such a limited view, Jain maintains that the Rohingya poems may both facilitate and become part of the global legal discourse on citizenship rights. As a result, these poems not only allow insights into the plight of the Rohingyas, but also a fresh approach to a view of Europe from the periphery that transgresses received, increasingly encrusted perspectives and conveys an alternative point of view.[2] Both contributions then set citizenship legislation against humanist ethics, conventional perspectives on Europe against alternative ones, and negotiate how both law and literature might operate in and be instrumentalized to facilitate a better citizenship regime – one more just, equal, and humane.

---

1 Katharina Pink, this volume, 337.

2 Jayana Jain, this volume, 339–352.

https://doi.org/10.1515/9783111075693-032

Katharina Pink

Alternative Notions of Belonging: (European) Community and Citizenship in Ali Smith's *Seasonal Quartet*

Ali Smith's "ultra-of-the-moment seasonal quartet," composed and published "at breakneck speed,"[3] received a lot of attention for its extraordinary contemporaneousness which enabled the four novels – *Autumn* (2016), *Winter* (2017), *Spring* (2019), and *Summer* (2020) – to chronicle in real time the often-unforeseeable developments in Britain during an epoch of political upheaval, social turmoil, and an unprecedented global pandemic. All four of the subtly interconnected novels self-consciously respond to current and emergent events, touching on public discord, social media, migration, COVID-19, British politics, Brexit, and the EU.

Immediacy of composition was part of the initial intention for the tetralogy – "a kind of keeping the novel novel project,"[4] as Smith put it – that aimed to return to one of the basic qualities of the novel, because "the novel as a form is always about time, and [. . .] the name we've given to the novel form also means new, something new, something so new it's news."[5] Smith sought to explore "how closely to contemporaneousness a finished book might be in the world, and yet how it could also be, all through, very much about stratified, cyclic time"[6] by reflecting emerging history in the cyclicity of the seasons. As a result, the novels record events as they are unfolding, embedding them within the broader context of British and European history as well as within the cycle of natural growth and decline.

Autumn, the first instalment of the quartet published in the wake of the Brexit referendum 2016 and occupied with its fallout, invokes as a recurring motif the seasonal falling of the leaves[7] in its more lyrical passages, leaving

3 Alex Preston, "*Spring* by Ali Smith Review – Luminous and Generous," (March 19, 2019), *The Guardian* <https://www.theguardian.com/books/2019/mar/19/spring-ali-smith-review> (acc. February 28, 2022), n. pag.

4 Qtd. in Claire Armitstead, "Ali Smith: 'This Young Generation Is Showing Us that We Need to Change and Can Change,'" (March 23, 2019), *The Guardian* <https://www.theguardian.com/books/2019/mar/23/ali-smith-spring-young-generation-brexit-future> (acc. February 28, 2022), n. pag.

5 Qtd. in Eric K. Anderson, "Ali Smith on *Autumn*, Brexit, and the Shortness of Life," (October 12, 2016), *Penguin Features* <https://penguin.co.uk/articles/2016/ali-smith-on-autumn> (acc. January 19, 2022), n. pag.

6 Qtd. in Anderson, "Ali Smith on *Autumn*," n. pag.

7 See, for instance, Ali Smith, *Autumn* [2016] (London: Penguin, 2017), 192–193; further references in the text, abbreviated as "A."

https://doi.org/10.1515/9783111075693-033

ample room for innuendo and wordplay revolving around Britain's decision to leave or not to leave the EU. As symbols of decay and potential rebirth the autumnal leaves recall the cyclical nature of things, with their seasonality implying repetition and continuity even in the face of desolation – be it within nature, the nation, or the bloc.

Short-listed for the Booker Prize 2017, *Autumn* was also hailed as "the first significant post-Brexit novel"[8] and a "post-Brexit masterpiece."[9] As such, it formed part of what has come to be called "BrexLit,"[10] i.e., contemporary British fiction which, succeeding the pre-Brexit trend of British Eurosceptic fiction, critically reflects the generational, political, and personal fault lines that the referendum wrenched open in a no longer United Kingdom. A whole cascade of similar works had begun to flood the market by the end of 2017 – some of them by such established authors as Ian McEwan,[11] Mohsin Hamid,[12] Amanda Craig,[13] and Zadie Smith.[14] Through the prism of Brexit, they all seek to address crucial current issues, whether it be the migration crisis, climate change, the spread of xenophobic nationalism, or the threats posed by populism and social media. Smith's *Quartet*, however, interweaves politics and aesthetics in a rather unique fashion, constantly intertwining reality and fiction, past and present, individual memory and collective history, as well as references to contemporary phenomena and canonical texts. What also sets the series apart from other Brexit-informed titles is the collage-like, fragmented structure of its narratives that jump back and forth through space and time, moving between different time frames and events occurring simultaneously in different places. As one of the protagonists of *Winter* puts it: "That's one of the things stories and books can do, they can make more than one time possible at once."[15] Contemporary political events such as the Windrush Scandal, the Grenfell

8 Kristian Shaw, "BrexLit" in *Brexit and Literature: Critical and Cultural Responses*, ed. Robert Eaglestone (New York: Routledge, 2018), 15–30, 20.

9 Sophie Gilbert, "Ali Smith's *Autumn* Is a Post-Brexit Masterpiece," (February 15, 2017), *The Atlantic* <https://www.theatlantic.com/entertainment/archive/2017/02/ali-smiths-autumn-is-a-post brexit-masterpiece/516660> (acc. January 19, 2022), n. pag.

10 This is a term coined by Kristian Shaw; see Shaw, "BrexLit."

11 McEwan's novel *Nutshell* (London: Jonathan Cape, 2016) already subtly explored his anti-Brexit mindset which shows itself in full in his satirical Brexit novella *The Cockroach* (New York: Anchor Books, 2019).

12 Mohsin Hamid, *Exit West: A Novel* (London: Penguin, 2017).

13 Amanda Craig, *The Lie of the Land* (London: Little, Brown Book Group 2017).

14 Zadie Smith, "Fences: A Brexit Diary," (August 18, 2016), *The New York Review of Books* <https://www.nybooks.com/articles/2016/08/18/fences-brexit-diary/> (acc. May 31, 2022), n. pag.

15 Ali Smith, *Winter* (London: Hamish Hamilton, 2017), 224; further references in the text, abbreviated as "W."

Tower fire, the murder of Batley MP Jo Cox, or the overcrowding of Immigration Removal Centres in Britain are thus pitched against political events of the past, as for instance the Profumo Scandal in 1963, nuclear protests at Greenham Common in the 1980s, or the internment camps of World War II.

What connects all these histories, characters, and places are the recurring ecopoetic descriptions of the seasonal cycle, infusing the reader with resignation and hopefulness alike as they seem to deny the linear progress of human history, suggesting inevitable cyclic repetition instead. In this kaleidoscopic vision of history, the current state of the nation seems “a mere continuation of historical moments of migration, movement, and Othering that return, just like the seasons, to a different time and space.”[16] This notion is made explicit in *Winter*, Smith’s post-referendum Christmas Carol: “Solstice, she said. You said it. Darkest days ever. There’s never been a time like this. Yes there has, he said. The solstices are cyclic and they happen every year” (W, 58). The seasonal theme can also be taken, quite literally, as a comment on the so-called ‘Brexit Season’ which already at that point appeared to evince a vicious cycle with its never-ending cross-party negotiations, deadlines, and ultimatums that time and again led to stand-off, postponement, and a weary sense of déjà-vu. As such, it marks a

> dystopic, never-ending “season” of disorientation, disconnection and division: of the UK from the EU, of different factions from inclusive ideas of nation and cosmopolitanism, of families and communities subjected to a continuous bombardment of factional fantasies and international misinformation by global media.[17]

Chronicling these seasons in Britain, Smith’s novels, for all their pastiche and metafiction, represent a latter-day variant of the Condition-of-England Novel – and self-consciously so. Smith opens her first instalment with an ironic, much quoted adulteration of the famous opening sentences of *Tale of Two Cities* (1859) by Charles Dickens, *the* chronicler of the British condition: “It was the worst of times, it was the worst of times. Again” (A, 3).

The reference to Dickens’ classic about the French Revolution – a “season of Light” and of “Darkness,” a “spring of hope” and “a winter of despair,” as the original quotation continues – once more implies that the seemingly unprecedented age of upheaval may merely represent one more season in the long European history of

16 Birte Heidemann, “The Brexit Within: Mapping the Rural and the Urban in Contemporary British Fiction,” *Journal of Postcolonial Writing* 56.5 (2020): 676–688, 685.

17 Eleanor Byrne, “Autumn, Winter, Never Spring: Brexit Season,” *Open Arts Journal* 8 (2020): 83–94, 84.

crises: the worst of times, *again*.[18] Just as *Tale of Two Cities* was one of many such efforts by British writers to process and deal with the revolution's still reverberating impact on British culture in the nineteenth century, Smith's *Seasonal Quartet* is one of the many efforts of BrexLit to come to terms with the volatile political present. But Smith does so in real-time, in the manner of Dickens in his other novels: "the concept was always to do what the Victorian novelists did at a time when the novel was meant to be new. Dickens published as he was writing *Oliver Twist*. He was still making his mind up about the story halfway through."[19]

Despite Smith's particular penchant for Charles Dickens, with *Winter* repeatedly invoking *A Christmas Carol* and some of the quartet's characters seeming to "jump right out of" the latter's literary imagination,[20] the intertexts by Dickens are by no means the only ones. Every single one of the quartet's novels converses consciously with an aptly chosen Shakespeare play which is usually named in a respective epigraph. Beyond those two fixpoints from the pantheon of British authors, the *Seasonal Quartet* is teeming with allusions to 'classic' representatives of English literature (John Keats, Katherine Mansfield, Aldous Huxley, Sylvia Plath, etc.), world literature (such as Ovid and Rainer Maria Rilke), as well as popular culture (such as Charlie Chaplin and Elvis Presley). Consequently, *Autumn*'s aforementioned opening not only plays on Dickens' famous quote but also represents a tongue-in-cheek allusion to William Butler Yeats' much-plundered "The Second Coming" (1920), an enigmatic poem prophesying doom and destruction. In its third verse Yeats famously states "Things fall apart; the centre cannot hold" to which Smith tersely responds: "That's the thing about things. They fall apart, always have, always will, it's in their nature" (A, 3). This time round, it is the European Union, the British nation and society, families, memories, and other things, formerly taken for granted, that are in the process of disintegration.

Despite this intertextual farrago, Smith keeps returning to a certain Dickensian ductus. At a later point in the novel, she once more resorts to the oxymoronic style of the opening paragraph of *Tale of Two Cities* to describe the shockwaves the Brexit referendum sent through the nation:[21]

18 In "Autumn, Winter, Never Spring," Byrne argues that "[f]or *Autumn*, Dickens' earlier novel operates as a point of orientation for Smith's engagement with another national political turmoil in the present, and a lesson in the ways that past events replay and return in the imaginary lives of the present" (85).

19 Qtd. in Armitstead, "Ali Smith," n. pag.

20 Cf. Jean Huets, "Things Fall Apart: On Ali Smith's 'Autumn' and 'Winter,'" (January 16, 2018), *The Millions* <https://themillions.com/2018/01/on-ali-smiths-autumn-and-winter.html> (acc. January 27, 2022), n. pag.

21 At an even later point she quotes Dickens' famous words literally and connects them to topics at the heart of her novel: "*It was the best of times, it was the worst of times, it was the age of wisdom, it was the age of foolishness, it was the epoch of belief, it was the age of incredulity, it was*

> All across the country, people felt it was the wrong thing. All across the country, people felt it was the right thing. All across the country, people felt they'd really lost. All across the country, people felt they'd really won. All across the country, people felt they'd done the right thing and other people had done the wrong thing. All across the country, people looked up Google: *what is EU?* All across the country, people looked up Google: *move to Scotland.* All across the country, people looked up Google: *Irish passport applications.* (A, 59; emphasis in the original)

Just like Dickens who wrote to process the traumatic impact of the French Revolution on British culture – "not from a place of geographical and historical safety but, instead, from an apprehension of the volatile political present"[22] – so Smith recycles these words to grapple with her own volatile present. The unfolding events, incidentally, fit her general thematic preoccupations: "I found, as Brexit started to happen round us all, that what I'd been writing was already about divisions and borders and identities and, yes, slightly more historic parliamentary lies."[23] Indeed, borders, passports, as well as questions of citizenship and asylum have played a significant role in Smith's oeuvre from 2010 onwards with her novel *There but for the* (2011) openly engaging with the specific politics of immigration. Even prior to that, her short story "The Art of Elsewhere," published in her recent short story collection *Public Library and Other Stories* (2015), but originally composed for the Edinburgh International Book Festival 2010, explores a utopian country named "Elsewhere" that has neither borders nor passports: "Elsewhere there are no borders. Elsewhere nobody is a refugee or an asylum seeker whose worth can be decided about by a government."[24] Her short story "The Detainee's Tale," originally published 2015 in support of the Refugee Tales Project,[25] forms part of a new kind of literary and political intervention to change

---

the season of Light, it was the season of Darkness, it was the spring of hope, it was the winter of despair, we had everything before us, we had nothing before us. The words had acted like a charm. They'd released it all, in seconds. They'd made everything happening stand just far enough away. It was nothing less than magic. Who needs a passport?" (A, 201–202; emphasis in the original).

22 Sally Ledger, "From the Old Bailey to Revolutionary France: The Trials of Charles Darnay" in *Charles Dickens,* A Tale of Two Cities *and the French Revolution*, ed. Colin Jones, Josephine McDonagh, and Jon Mee (Basingstoke: Palgrave, 2009), 75–86, 78.

23 Qtd. in Anderson, "Ali Smith on *Autumn*," n. pag.

24 Ali Smith, "Elsewhere" in *Public Library and Other Stories* (London: Hamish Hamilton, 2015), 129–32, 132.

25 *Refugee Tales* is an outreach project of Gatwick Detainees Welfare Group that calls for an immediate end to the UK's policy of indefinite detention by sharing the tales of people held in immigration detention and those who work with them. For five years the project has organized walks in solidarity with refugees, asylees, and immigration detainees and has by now published four volumes of *Refugee Tales*, edited by David Herd and Anna Pincus, and written by various

the policies on immigration detention. In it, the narrator raises the question which, in the current epoch of crises concerning immigration, refugees, and EU border policies, seems more pressing than ever: "What kind of a life are we living on this earth when a photocopied piece of paper can mean and say more about your life than your life does?"[26] In *Autumn*, protagonist Elisabeth asks the same question, when trying to prove her identity in a doctor's surgery – a question that ultimately proves central to the novel: "So what does a piece of paper prove, exactly, in the end?" (A, 106).

Despite these valid objections, pieces of paper form the central part of the legal processes involved in all life-changing situations, be it birth, death, marriage, or – politically most pertinent these days – at the border where the line between citizen and alien is drawn. But even beyond that, as the various struggles in the context of legal identification in *Autumn* make clear, possessing the right piece of paper is often required to be "on the inside" of the law, i.e., to participate in the legal rights of a citizen of the EU, such as the right of abode, the freedom of movement, as well as the right to work and to own property.

This status, however, has altered drastically for the British, who, after Brexit will no longer by default be afforded the legal rights of EU citizens. There is a new anxiety surrounding Britain's national identity which is thrown into stark relief in *Autumn* when Elisabeth Demand repeatedly attempts to apply for a passport in a post office. First, the dour clerk informs her that her name – indeed a telling pun on the French phrase *du monde* – is spelled like that of "people from other countries" (A, 22), which raises concern; second, her hair is too close to her face which, to make matters worse, is the wrong size, falling short by five millimetres – a seemingly absurd objection. Nevertheless, her application ultimately gets shelved with the remark "HEAD INCORRECT SIZE," suggestively annotated in "a box next to the word *Other*" (A, 25). At her second attempt at the same post office she is once again 'diagnosed' with her hairline being too low and her eyes too small. After "sliding the pictures of Elisabeth up and down inside a transparent plastic chart with markings and measurements in different boxes printed all over it," the clerk reaches a verdict: "Your eyes don't fit with the permissible regularity inside the shaded area [. . .]. This doesn't line up" (A, 108). Elisabeth's objections that this is the natural symmetry of her face, and

novelists, poets and people who have been through the process of flight, asylum seeking, and detention. Ali Smith is one of these novelists and also acts as patron of the project.

26 Ali Smith, "The Detainee's Tale by Ali Smith: 'I Thought You Would Help Me,'" (June 27, 2015), *The Guardian* <www.theguardian.com/books/2015/jun/27/ali-smith-so-far-the-detainees-tale-extract> (acc. February 2, 2022), n. pag.

that otherwise her passport photo would not actually look like her, are dismissed as irrelevant. Stipulations are to be met.

This entire process is chillingly reminiscent of the racial phenotyping carried out in the Third Reich – an association Smith carefully threads in in the preceding chapter describing a dream of Daniel Gluck, Elisabeth's 101-year-old friend. It is him she wants to visit in a nursing home, which is why she was required to get her passport renewed in the first place. The novel keeps skipping back and forth between the various memories of this German-English centenarian, recalling how, as a child, Elisabeth found a father figure in him, how he lost the love of his life to cancer and his sister Hannah in World War II. It is primarily due to these interspersed recollections of his long life that the tumultuous present depicted in the novel seems a mere continuation of historical moments of migration, Othering, and upheaval in Europe. Just a couple of pages before Elisabeth's frustrating visit to the post office, his dreams carry him back to a past train ride through Germany of the 1930s where, not long before the anti-Semitic Nuremberg Laws, he once overheard other passengers discussing "the necessity of developing a scientific and legal means of gauging exactly who's what" (A, 99). The trick, they say, is to record physical statistics, such as the space between eyes and ears, as well as the proportions of nose and forehead: "The measurement of parts of the body, most especially of the features of the head area, can tell you quite succinctly everything you need to know. Eye colour, hair colour, the sizing of foreheads. It's been done before, but never so expertly" (A, 100). With that last remark of it having been done before, Smith takes one further step backwards in history and traces this infamous system of phenotyping back to the racial anthropometry of colonial times – once more emphasizing the revenant nature of history.[27]

So ultimately, in their soulless profiling of a fellow citizen the postal clerks stand in a long ignominious tradition, evoking besides the archetypal "ruthless immigration officer who reveals a post-referendum political rhetoric that challenges notions of belonging and national identity. If you don't fit the (racial) frame of what is stipulated as 'UK citizen,' then your life in Britain will bristle with obstacles."[28] Elisabeth is lectured accordingly when she appeals to the clerk's common sense and eventually ends up mocking the absurdity of these stipulations. Witticism, she is told (off), is not a wise idea if she wants to obtain this document required to be allowed to leave Britain's shores: "Will get you. Nowhere" (A, 23).

---

27 See also Birte Heidemann, "The Brexit Within: Mapping the Rural and the Urban in Contemporary British Fiction," *Journal of Postcolonial Writing* 56.5 (2020): 676–688, 685.
28 Heidemann, "The Brexit Within," 683.

While thus flaunting the absurdity and alienating power of bureaucracy in Kafkaesque fashion, these scenes also seem to prefigure a post-Brexit future. After all, Elisabeth's efforts to obtain a passport represent the attempt to establish an identity in relation to a superordinate entity, namely, the British nation state which in turn mirrors Britain's own need to establish its identity with relation to the superordinate entity of the EU.[29]

In the end, despite the admonitions during the application process that one "can't joke about passports" (A, 20), the passport Elisabeth finally receives looks much like a joke to her:

> Her mother points to the words European Union at the top of the cover of the passport and makes a sad face. Then she flicks through it. What are all these drawings? she says. This passport has been illustrated like a Ladybird book. A Ladybird book on acid, Elisabeth says. (A, 195)

This depiction of the material reality of this crucial 'piece of paper' once more underlines the absurdity of a textual object granting not only personal identity, but also legal status and, ultimately, human dignity. According to Elisabeth's mother, it looks like a children's book, a silly attempt to depict a UK national identity, replete with Scottish pipers, "ethnic stereotype dancers" (A, 196), and the token woman in a silly hat. It is merely a "ridiculous thing that passes for a passport" (A, 196). Yet, as the novel unfolds, it repeatedly highlights the fact that one needs these ridiculous things to access all kinds of places and resources. Although in the UK there is no legal obligation to possess and carry a government-issued identity card, the reality is, that without proper ID a lot of state services are inaccessible. This can be seen in Elisabeth's struggle to get medical assistance at her mother's medical practice. She is turned down because she only has her expired passport and library card without her current address or photograph on her, but none of the documents so often required in these cases – a utility bill, for instance. Using one of them as proof of identity is indeed standard procedure in the UK when one opens a bank account or seeks medical care from the NHS. Frustrated, Elisabeth argues quite correctly that it is "perfectly easy to mock up a bill and print it out. To pretend to be a person, Elisabeth says. And what about all the people doing scams? How does having your name on a piece of printed-out paper make you who you are?" (A, 105).

Indeed, incidents of identity scammers outwitting the witless, automated system figure repeatedly in the *Seasonal Quartet*. In *Autumn*, Elisabeth has been receiving bank statements for a certain Anna Pavlova for years, despite repeatedly informing the bank that there never was a person of that name residing at her

29 Johannes Wally, "The Return of Political Fiction?" *Arbeiten aus Anglistik und Amerikanistik* 43.1 (2018): 43–86, 78.

address. In *Summer*, the house of protagonist Richard Greenlaw's mother is forcefully entered by a bailiff, locksmith, and two security men, because a scammer using her address had failed to pay his bills to the electricity provider SA4A POWER. Her protestations prove useless – it is all in the paperwork:

> They forced your door? [. . .] And entered your house without permission? They wouldn't let me in into my own house, his mother says. I live here, I said. Who are you? They said was I Mrs Nureyev. Nobody of that name lives here, I said. How long have you lived here? they said. Since round about the time you were born, I said. They showed me letters they had copies of, saying a Mr R Nureyev lived here. They told me they were replacing our meters with prepay meters because Mr Nureyev hadn't paid his bills for over a year.[30]

This breach of the inviolability of the home shows how easy it is to play the system and override or appropriate the rights of other citizens. Even after showing them her own balanced power account and calling the SA4A customer service with a phonebot verifying her customer ID, they refuse to leave the premises and continue to install the new meters – technically an act of property damage. To make them stop it takes yet another piece of paper, namely, the deed to the house. This crucial document, however, is issued to her ex-husband causing the intruders to evict her out of her own house:

> The bailiff and the SA4A man literally blocked the door, I mean stood in the doorway and blocked it with their arms. Finally, but only when they'd finished what they were doing, they accompanied me into my own house again and waited on either side of me while I went through the bureau and got the house deeds out and showed them our name. And they said, you're clearly not a Mr Jeffrey Greenlaw, and threw me out of my own house. So I called Jeff. But even when he came round and showed them his passport they refused to remove their new meters and put the old meters back. (S, 104–105)

This seemingly trivial episode is rather alarming as it exposes a citizen's inviolable rights as rather frail fictions that depend entirely on documents and their (correct) validation by the system. In the aforementioned episodes, all it takes to bar a citizen from basic state services such as the NHS is an expired passport and the "wrong face" when applying for a new one; all it takes for breaching the inviolability of a citizen's home and property is a fake electricity account that passes as valid within an automatized administration system.

In *Summer*, the theme of faked IDs resurfaces, albeit in an entirely different and more menacing context. It tells the story of Daniel's sister Hannah Gluck who during World War II lived in occupied France and worked for the resistance,

30 Ali Smith, *Summer* [2020] (London: Penguin, 2021), 104; further references in the text, abbreviated as "S."

supplying Jews with forged passports to flee the country. In this case, the right piece of paper and its validation by a superordinate, oppressive system is a matter of life and death. The names and identities used for these documents Hannah gleans from graveyards, more specifically from the tombstones of children who have died young:

> This is a good source. It's not completely safe but birth and death certification are usually held in different lists, often in different drawers or cabinets, sometimes even in different buildings if you're lucky. [. . .] Hannah Gluck is more than Hannah Gluck. At the moment she is Adrienne Albert, seamstress. Adrienne Albert died at eighteen months old, in Nancy, in 1920, of Spanish influenza. [. . .] But here she is, regardless, living and breathing and as warm as any living flesh and blood, though just a touch younger than it says on her papers, and today she's trawling a graveyard and looking to resurrect other lives like her own. (S, 199–200)

This scene is remarkable both for its symbolic setting and for highlighting the dual existence humans lead in such systems: as entities of flesh and bone as well as entities on paper – the latter of which can be tampered with, killed off, and born again with immediate effects on the former. Targeting this legal avatar is usually one of the first integral steps in a systematic persecution of unwanted groups or minorities. In Nazi Germany, invalidating and withdrawing passports was one of the earliest measures taken against the Jewish population, denying them basic civic and human rights, which effectively dehumanized them. By stripping them of the status of legal personae, the path to their elimination was paved.[31]

Rather than just dwelling on the atrocities of the Nazis, however, Smith is careful to highlight the universality and reciprocity of it all. In *Summer*, she goes on to show how, across the English Channel, legal and national identity also become a crucial issue. Whilst Hannah Gluck risks her life saving innocents from deportation, her German father and brother, who have been living in England for most of their lives, are deported and imprisoned in a UK German Internment Camp on the Isle of Man.

Once again, it is possession of the right papers that decides their fate. Daniel's father is a 'German Englishman,' growing up in England from infancy and making his fortune there. Yet, as far as his papers are concerned, he is German. Due to his hybrid national status he has been interned before by the British, for nearly six years in World War I, but had trusted his status as a *de facto* Englishman afterwards and never gotten his papers: a serious mistake – as he of all people should have known.

31 Cf. Daniela Carpi, "Dehumanizing the Enemy: How to Avoid Human Rights" in *Literature and Human Rights: The Law, the Language and the Limitations of Human Rights Discourse*, ed. Ian Ward (Berlin: De Gruyter, 2015), 101–112, 101.

When he finally did go to get them issued it was too late. The war had already begun and a general fear of resident aliens from Germany had started to spread. Surprisingly, despite his past incarceration by the British that has left him maimed in body and soul, Daniel's father never loses faith in British decency and level-headedness. He is convinced that England has learned from the atrocities of World War I and will not repeat past injustices:

> It's different this time. It's a different place, now, England, his father says. Its better self has come to the fore. [. . .] They know about fairness now, and why to go to war, and what happens when you do. They know about newspapers that lie for money. They know you don't put innocent people in prison. The British are just. They're practical. They're forbearing. They're not childish. They're calm, they're civilized now. They'll put it right. We'll be out of here in no time. See if I'm wrong. (S, 165–166)

While Daniel's father was right in 1940 – they are released shortly after – this scene nevertheless brings into question whether his appraisal of Britain's better nature still rings true today. After all, the recurring flashbacks to Europe during World War II, with their various accounts of xenophobia, deportation, and death, unfailingly point towards the tumultuous political present of the novels, in particular to the current rise of the extreme right and the new populist and nationalist strain in European politics.[32]

In *Summer*, teenage protagonist Robert Greenlaw reflects on these tendencies in British politics and their potential to lead to unthinkable transgressions of historical dimensions. He perceptively apprehends the dangers posed by the current government with a Prime Minister like Boris Johnson who hides behind spectacle, flaunted simplicity, and clownish naivety whilst pursuing a ruthless and often enough undemocratic agenda:

> Yesterday the blond beast prime minister tried, like the Americans, banning some journalists and not others from being let into Downing St. [. . .] All the journalists boycotted the dividing of them into two. But that won't last. Robert Greenlaw admires above all the adviser of the prime minister, who knows how to style politics so that it doesn't look like politics any more, who knows full well that Stalin and Hitler were possible even though everyone in old-style politics looks aghast when anyone suggests it's possible to act the ways they did.

32 By way of example, during his imprisonment Daniel has a curious encounter with a ten-year-old local boy approaching the fences of the camp. The boy tells him that *The Daily Mail*, the most popular British tabloid back then, is boasting how "enemy aliens" are "getting a sea air holiday" on the Isle of Man with "sugar and milk and eggs" for breakfast and "more money than we've got and hot water and coal" (S, 149). This scene openly recalls the xenophobic narratives of the present where British citizens with a low-income have long since been pitched against immigrants seemingly reaping all the benefits inaccessible to the former.

> The people in charge in England right now are geniuses of manipulation.
> Robert Greenlaw is in awe of their performance of callousness.
> He is in awe of how they get away with talking about patriotism with all the fervour of 12 year olds – Robert Greenlaw still aspires to it a bit, though he's now 13 and recognizes its pre-adolescent ventriloquisms.
> It is all just more genius.
> Prime minister, consciously dishevelled. Styled. [. . .]
> It is a brilliant subterfuge to look like he doesn't know what he's doing and to make people like him for it. (S, 54–55)

These deliberations by thirteen-year-old Robert seem to echo – in reverse – some of the assessments by Daniel's father eighty years ago. The England of today is a nation marked by a public sphere gorged on populist ethno-nationalist and far-right discourse, by a media culture constantly bombarding the populace with news of the latest scandals and crises, and a lack of reliable leadership. Instead of displaying civilized calm, forbearance, and fairness in the face of the adversities of a globalized world, public discourse in Britain has resorted to a state of permanent agitation, xenophobia, and a child-like insistence on what used to be one's prerogative. Politics has turned into a spectacle with its agents resembling showmen rather than statesmen, and a prime minister posturing as a "clown king,"[33] always carefully dishevelled. Robert accordingly closes his musings with the dry observation that "this is the dawn of a new era, a caricature kind of an era" (S, 56). Charlotte, in *Winter*, likewise comments on how in Britain "pre-planned theatre is replacing politics" with the public constantly being "propelled into shock mode, trained to wait for whatever the next shock will be, served up shock on a 24 hour newsfeed [. . .]. It's like walking in a blizzard all the time just trying to get to what's really happening beyond the noise and hype" (W, 57–58).[34]

Nevertheless, these caricatures in the eye of a constant storm of scandals and global crises must not be dismissed as ineffectual. Clowns, ultimately, are transgressors and Johnson's quizzical posturing indeed seems to serve as a subterfuge: a smokescreen behind which fundamental changes to general policies and laws

---

33 Cf. Edward Docx, "The Clown King: How Boris Johnson Made It by Playing the Fool," (March 18, 2021), *The Guardian* <https://www.theguardian.com/news/2021/mar/18/all-hail-the-clown-king-how-boris-johnson-made-it-by-playing-the-fool> (acc. February 12, 2022), n. pag.

34 In *Autumn*, Elisabeth's mother likewise voices her exasperation with this permanent shock mode of the public: "I'm tired of the news. I'm tired of the way it makes things spectacular that aren't, and deals so simplistically with what's truly appalling. I'm tired of the vitriol. I'm tired of the anger. I'm tired of the meanness. I'm tired of the selfishness. [. . .] I'm tired of the violence there is and I'm tired of the violence that's on its way, that's coming, that hasn't happened yet. [. . .] I'm tired of lying governments. I'm tired of people not caring whether they're being lied to anymore. I'm tired of being made to feel this fearful" (A, 57).

are being set on their way. Johnson's attempted breach of the right to freedom of expression and free press – by trying to cherry-pick the journalists allowed to enter Downing Street – is just one of several undemocratic dealings of his government that go against the Human Rights Act and, by extension, against the European Convention on Human Rights (ECHR). The administration under Johnson has introduced several new pieces of legislation with constitutionally far-reaching consequences: changes to policing, surveillance, judicial review, as well as new policies concerning citizenship and immigration – all of which fundamentally strengthen state power at the expense of democratic civil and basic human rights.[35]

There is, for one, the Police, Crime, Sentencing and Courts Bill,[36] which effectively bans protest in England and Wales and authorizes the police to shut down all demonstrations prone to cause "serious disruption." Merely participating in a protest and making noise would be enough to meet this condition and face substantial fines or even prison sentences. Then there is the Nationality and Borders Bill[37] that further hardens Britain's already abrasive immigration policy, criminalizing asylum seekers who take unauthorized routes to the UK: refugees who arrive by boat, for instance, could face up to four years in prison, regardless of the legitimacy of their claim for asylum. According to a provision of this bill, not even British citizens would be safe, as it would allow the government to strip dual nationals of their British citizenship without notice. Thus, in effect, certain citizens, despite being born and brought up in the UK and having no other home (like Daniel's father), effectively remain alien residents. Their status as citizens becomes precarious and contingent. Several basic human rights and freedoms of the Human Rights Act – which are granted to citizens, foreigners, and refugees alike – are threatened by these statutes alone. In fact, the HRA itself is in danger, due to a proposed reform which has been pending since David Cameron took office and has taken on new momentum under Boris Johnson. Officially it strives for independence from Strasbourg's jurisdiction – *taking control back*, once again – but in effect it would complicate enforcing human rights whilst making it easier for the government to, for instance, deport foreign nationals and dismiss their claims of mistreatment. Ali Smith has strongly opposed these efforts to 'scrap' the HRA, as the rhetoric went, in order to replace it with a British Bill of Rights:

---

35 Cf. Joe Griffin, "UK Introducing Three Laws that Threaten Human Rights, Says UN Expert," (June 24, 2021), *The Guardian* <https://www.theguardian.com/law/2021/jun/24/uk-introducing-three-laws-that-threaten-human-rights-says-un-expert> (acc. February 12, 2022), n. pag.

36 The Police, Crime, Sentencing and Courts Bill was introduced to Parliament on March 9, 2021; it received Royal Assent and became an Act of Parliament on April 28, 2022.

37 The Nationality and Borders Bill was introduced to Parliament in July 2021; it received Royal Assent and became an Act of Parliament on April 28, 2022.

> our own Human Rights Act is right now coming under attack. The government keeps calling it Labour's Human Rights Act. It's not. It's ours. It was a cross-party formation. It belongs to all of us. They want to replace it with a British bill of rights, as if all nationalities are equal, but some are more equal than others.[38]

Human rights law must transcend national borders and citizenship; it must apply to all humans on European soil or it leaves migrants stateless and refugees open to violations of their basic rights and liberties.

Yet, this is exactly what seems to be happening, as Smith shows in *Spring* with her extensive depiction of the British Immigration Removal Centres (IRC), where putative illegal immigrants and asylum seekers are detained indefinitely, without charge, and under inhumane conditions. *Spring* explores the hidden world of these detainment centres, showing the destructive effects of UK's immigration policy on enforcers and detainees alike. In the novel, they are run by SA4A, a private service provider that figures in all four books as the omnipresent agent of state power and a proxy to real companies like G4S or Serco. In *Spring*, SA4A does the 'dirty work' for the state, policing and detaining immigrants in the UK. One of the protagonists, Brittany Hall, is a Detainee Custody Officer (DCO) at one of its immigration detention centres in London and her work there has already begun to take a dehumanizing toll on her. She has become numb to her own life and to the lives and sufferings of the "deets" in her charge:

> Here are some things Brittany Hall learned in her first two months as a DCO at a UK IRC:
>
> – What privacy meant. (It meant she wasn't a deet.)
> – What effect an official report about an independent inspection of the centre had on the place: it meant there was a new water cooler installed in the visits room.
> – How there were 30,000 people detained in this country at any one time, and that was the level of interned deets across detention estate that kept SA4A salaries stable. [. . .]
> – How to choose which deets to speak to, who to ignore.
> – How to talk weather with other DCOs while they're holding someone in headlock or four of you are sitting on someone to calm him.
> – How to say without thinking much about it, *they're kicking off. We're not a hotel. If you don't like it here go home. How dare you ask for a blanket.* The day she heard herself say that last one she knew something terrible was happening, but by now the terrible thing, as terrible as a death, felt quite far away, as if not really happening to her [. . .].

38 Ali Smith, "Celebrating HG Wells's Role in the Creation of the UN Declaration of Human Rights," (November 20, 2015) *The Guardian* <www.theguardian.com/books/2015/nov/20/ali-smith-celebrates-hg-wells-role-creation-un-declaration-of-human-rights> (acc. February 12, 2022), n. pag.

> *Detention is the key to maintaining an effective immigration system*
> HO
> *Nobody is detained indefinitely and regular reviews of detention are undertaken to ensure that it remains lawful and proportionate*
> HO HO HO[39]

The cynicism and callousness of Brittany – aptly nicknamed 'Britannia' by a co-worker – can be understood to reflect the mental state of her homeland in recent years. The crassly caustic slogans, followed by the sarcastic "HO HO HO" refer to maxims of the Home Office (HO) claiming that all detention is necessary and lawfully exercised with a "realistic prospect of removal within a reasonable period."[40] Many immigrants, however, have been detained "for years, years and years" (SP, 135). It seems, the British have forgotten after all that "you don't put innocent people in prison" (S, 166), for that is what these centres amount to, as the book leaves in no doubt.[41] Perhaps they are even worse than prison, because their often traumatized, ill and/or violent detainees are crammed together into small cells designed for short-term detention where they can be held indefinitely.[42]

In fact, the UK is the only country (formerly) in the EU not to have a maximum detention time for immigrants in its ten detention centers – which contravenes Article 5.1. of the ECHR, i.e., the Right to Liberty and Security – and thus makes these prolonged detentions unlawful. What is more, according to the European Council, asylum seekers may not be detained for the sole reason of seeking international protection or having entered or stayed in a country irregularly. With regard to the condition of their detention, they must be treated with dignity and due respect for their

---

39 Ali Smith, *Spring* [2019] (London: Penguin, 2020), 165–167 (emphasis in the original); further references in the text, abbreviated as "SP."

40 See the "General Instructions on Detention published by the Home Office for the Home Office staff from 14 January 2022" <https://assets.publishing.service.gov.uk/government/uploads/system/uploads/attachment_data/file/1046288/Detention_General_instructions.pdf> (acc. February 15, 2022), n. pag.

41 Just like UK's German internment camps during the World Wars, these British IRCs are concerned with the detainment of perceived enemy aliens for an unspecified amount of time and under degrading conditions. In *Summer*, Smith will set out to align the IRCs with that 'tradition,' highlighting once more the recurrence of these seasons of xenophobia. The quartet thus illustrates how "Britain's perennial refusal to grapple with its past has set the nation on a dizzying path of tragic repetition." Natasha Hakimi Zapata, "Antidotes to Brexit, COVID-19, and Other Afflictions in Ali Smith's Seasonal Quartet," (November 30, 2020), *Los Angeles Review of Books* <https://lareviewofbooks.org/article/antidotes-to-brexit-covid-19-and-other-afflictions-in-ali-smiths-seasonal-quartet/> (acc. May 31, 2022), n. pag.

42 See also Diane Taylor, "Worse than Prison: Life inside Britain's 10 Deportation Centres," (October 11, 2018), *The Guardian* <https://www.theguardian.com/uk-news/2018/oct/11/life-in-a-uk-immigration-removal-centre-worse-than-prison-as-criminal-sentence> (acc. February 14, 2022), n. pag.

rights; that is, not be subjected to degrading treatment. This, however, is clearly not the case, as media coverage and inspection reports of recent years have shown. Not even detention centres for female asylum seekers – typically survivors of rape, human trafficking, torture, and other horrific violence – are any better. In *Spring*, Brittany describes "The Wood," a fictional proxy to Yarl's Wood, UK's main detention centre for women, as the worst of all:

> The Wood, everyone knows, is rough on the women there, like living in a shower room with a bunch of strangers. Worse, the body searches. The assaults that never make it to report. The story goes, rapes. Course there are. Brit had heard it, they'd all heard it. No smoke. Plus, the women who'd been sex-trafficked across the world and ended up at the Wood all swore it. Detention there was worse than any of the rest of what had happened to them. (SP, 143)

Despite such outrageous, inhumane dealings on British soil, which have been brought to light thanks to whistle-blowers, numerous press reports and human rights watch organizations, there has been little public outcry to speak of. This general lack of indignation and empathy in the face of gross injustice and misery on the British public's doorstep may well be considered a corollary of years of far-right, nationalist propaganda exploiting the fear and discontent of a populace struggling with the challenges of globalization and economic change. Populist politicians then skillfully stoked and exploited the growing xenophobia to promote their Brexit agenda. In 2016, for instance, UKIP leader Nigel Farage unveiled a poster of a long line of refugees – most of them young men of color to invoke the Orientalist cliché of the black male perpetrator – that read, "Breaking Point: the EU has failed us all." Consequently, the influx of Syrian refugees in 2015/16 did not arouse public empathy, but rather anxiety and anger, reinforcing the decision of many Britons to leave the EU.

But even before that, a larger ideological shift could be detected in the UK, intensifying from 2010 onwards when Theresa May began her tenure as Home Secretary. Her implementation of the 'hostile environment' policy in 2013/14 paved the way for such blatantly racist campaigning and left its own traces in the public consciousness through the notorious deployment of vans reading, "In the UK illegally? Go home or face arrest." They were part of a state-run campaign to induce failed seekers of asylum and undocumented migrants to voluntarily leave the country by making them constantly aware of the "near and present danger of their being arrested."[43] This imminent threat was emphasized by a flashy text box

43 Home Office, "Operation Vaken, Evaluation Report – October 2013," <https://assets.publishing.service.gov.uk/government/uploads/system/uploads/attachment_data/file/254411/Operation_Vaken_Evaluation_Report.pdf> (acc. February 16, 2022), 2, 5.

on the vans that boasted: "106 arrests last week in your area." This culture of open intimidation and menace from an official state organ can well be said to have legitimated and fuelled racist hostilities. Empathy for the hardships of refugees in turn became effectively stifled, not least because moral, ethical, and religious institutions remained silent. As Iris, one of the protagonists in *Winter*, asks: "what kind of vicar, what kind of church, brings a child up to think that words like *very* and *hostile* and *environment* and *refugees* can ever go together in any response to what happens to people in the real world?" (W, 233; emphasis in the original).

With the government and the church alike failing to act as moral compasses, the scandals and humanitarian disasters of the last few years, in which time and again the poor and stateless were victimized, have attracted comparably little public scorn. Take, as an illustrative case, the disastrous fire in the decrepit Grenfell Tower, which killed more than seventy people – many of whom were immigrants and refugees reliant on public housing; or the Windrush scandal which saw several thousand Commonwealth citizens, who had immigrated from the Caribbean countries before 1973 and had been living, working, and paying taxes in the UK for decades, wrongly detained, denied legal rights, and even deported by the Home Office.[44] Neither public outcry nor any official reckoning ever followed these scandals, as Paddy laments in *Spring*:

> Oh, I understand Brexit, she'd said. So many people angered into democracy for all the reasons. What I don't understand is Windrush. What I don't get, can't get my head round, is Grenfell. [. . .] Common wealth, she said. What a lie. Why hasn't there been an outcry the size of this so-called United Kingdom? Those things would've brought down a government at any other time in my life. What's happened to all the good people of this country? Compassion fatigue, Richard said. Fuck compassion fatigue, she said. That's people walking about with dead souls. (SP, 66–67)

This modern-day lack of compassion is the black hole all four novels seem to orbit. The very first pages of the quartet's first instalment, opening with Daniel's dream vision of tourists "holidaying up the shore from the dead" (A, 12), confront the reader with a post-Brexit landscape where "a new kind of detachment" (A, 54) pervades all social interactions.[45] In the following, Smith addresses several reasons for

44 For more details on the Windrush scandal, see Huon Wardle and Laura Obermuller, "'Windrush Generation' and 'Hostile Environment': Symbols and Lived Experiences in Caribbean Migration to the UK," *Migration and Society* 2.1 (2019): 81–89.

45 See also the beginning of *Summer*: "Everybody said: so? As in *so what*? As in *shoulder shrug*, or *what do you expect me to do about it*? or *I so don't really give a fuck*, or *actually I approve of it, it's fine by me*. [. . .] It got fashionable around then to act like you didn't care. It got fashionable, too, to insist the people who did care, or said they cared, were either hopeless losers or were just

this vacuum, one of them being the digital age: all the outrage and compassion so conspicuously missing in the face of these real-life tragedies seem to be otherwise engaged and worn out by the internet, by 'shitstorms' on social media and the proverbial cat video. In *Spring,* fake online obituaries of people that never existed draw more sympathy than dead refugee children being washed up on Europe's shores. This emotional outpouring online is, of course, being monetized by a young Cambridge graduate. His start-up posts the obituaries and photos of these allegedly dead people, their gravestones, their families, pets, and possessions on a website which then harvests and sells the data of its commiserating visitors. The reactions from the public have been overwhelming: "They'd been truly moving, he said, deeply personal and responsive, real cries from the heart. A picture of a bicycle or a guitar that had 'belonged' to a 'dead' person could move strangers all over the world to tears" (SP, 100). Simultaneously, all this triggering of emotions in the virtual realm leads to a certain coarsening towards real suffering. However, it is not merely cathartic sympathy that is reaped online. In *Summer*, teenage protagonist Robert is addicted to playing ABUSEHEAP, a computer game with the objective of torturing various victims as creatively as possible in order to get them to give up information without dying in the process of their cruel mistreatment. (S, 57–60). While the emotional capacity of the younger generation is outworn by such perverted simulations, the older generation has taken refuge in nostalgia for the good old days or an all-encompassing apathy. In *Winter*, Art's mother Sophia comes to represent this stance in an exemplary fashion:

> Sophia had been feeling nothing for some time now. Refugees in the sea. Children in ambulances. Blood-soaked men running to hospitals or away from burning hospitals carrying blood-covered children. Dust-covered dead people by the sides of roads. Atrocities. People beaten up and tortured in cells. Nothing. (W, 29–30)

Sophia has seemingly lost all capacity to commiserate. Instead, she has internalized the selfish fears and xenophobic misgivings instilled into the public by the nationalist discourse of the past decades. Her attitude, 'walking about with a dead soul,' is challenged by Lux, a homeless Croatian girl hired by her son Art to pose as his girlfriend during his Christmas visit. This mysterious girl ends up forming a surprisingly close connection with Sophia, though they could not be any more different. Sophia Cleves, a successful 'pro-establishment' businesswoman, represents

showing off. [. . .] I could spend my whole life listing things about, and talking about, and demonstrating with sources and graphs and examples and statistics, what history's made it clear happens when we're indifferent, and what the consequences are of the political cultivation of indifference, which whoever wants to disavow will dismiss in an instant with their own punchy little *so*?" (S, 3–5; emphasis in the original).

"a modern-day Scrooge"[46] and the Brexiteer's refusal to accept more flexible ways of living with others, whilst Lux is the bearer of visions for a more equitable, compassionate future: the literal bright light in the dark season of post-referendum winter.

With child-like simplicity she asks Sophia what was so wrong with people fleeing from war zones and wanting better lives for themselves and their children: a fundamentally relevant question that exposes the general heartlessness of criminalizing such natural human motivations. Her empathetic point of view is immediately rebutted by Sophia with arguments infused with the nationalist hegemony of 'us vs. them': "You mustn't be naive [. . .]. They're coming here because they want *our* lives" (W, 206; emphasis in the original). Lux, however, remains undeterred by such threatening possibilities, asking the questions that strike at the heart of the European migration crisis which younger generations are about to inherit:

> But what will the world do, though, Mrs Cleves, Lux says, if we can't solve the problem of the millions and millions of people with no home to go to or whose homes aren't good enough, except by saying go away and building fences and walls? It isn't a good enough answer, that one group of people can be in charge of the destinies of another group of people and choose whether to exclude them or include them. Human beings have to be more ingenious than this, and more generous. We've got to come up with a better answer. (W, 206)

Borders, as Lux makes clear, are not only key battlegrounds over the question of national belonging, but also over ethical questions of human equality and generosity. In this context, the most critical border may not be the border policed by guards and crossed with a passport, but the ideological, dichotomic border between citizen and migrant, between self and other.[47] It is this conceptual demarcation with its inherent practice of Othering that leads to the term 'asylum seeker' not simply being descriptive of legal status, but also value laden and negative. Immigration and citizenship have come to be about status in the sense of

46 Harriet Baker, "A Living Thing," *Women: A Cultural Review* 30.1 (2019): 100–103, 101.

47 Bridget Anderson, *Us and Them? The Dangerous Politics of Immigration Control* (Oxford: Oxford UP, 2013), 2: "as has been observed ever more frequently in recent years, borders are not simply territorial, but they reach into the heart of political space. Together with their associated practices, and in particular, laws and practices of citizenship, they may be more usefully analysed as producing rather than reflecting status, as creating specific types of social, political, and economic relations."

worth and honor: A non-citizen becomes a foreigner from whom one's nation, resources, and values must be protected.[48] However, in the face of the globalizing phenomena of diaspora and displacement – and considering the "contemporary European situation where mass migration has cancelled the idea of known borders"[49] – a new, more cosmopolitan notion of community and citizenship is needed. In *Winter*, Lux espouses this philosophical idea by repeatedly alluding to Shakespeare's *Cymbeline*, which serves not only as intertext for the novel but as analogy for the mindset of the British and European population:

> the people in the play are living in the same world but separately from each other, like their worlds have somehow become disjointed or broken off each other's worlds. But if they could just step out of themselves, or just hear and see what's happening right next to their ears and eyes, they'd see it's the same play they're all in, the same world, that they're all part of the same story. (W, 201)

Cosmopolitanism is based on the idea that all human beings are members of a universal community, regardless of national identity, religious affiliation, ethnicity, or place of birth. They all share the same privileges and obligations, based solely on their common humanity. From this, cosmopolitanism deduces "the normative claim that political boundaries and national identities are morally arbitrary and that all human beings should be held as the primary units of moral worth, as if they were equal citizens of a universal political community."[50] The notion that borders are an arbitrary and predominantly metaphorical institution is also articulated in *Spring*, by twelve-year-old Florence who, like Lux, is a childlike harbinger of hope for a brighter future. Like Lux she bears a telling name, promising the 'bloom' of spring after a long dark winter.

On the train to Scotland, Florence muses on the nature of border crossings, imagining alternate conceptions of borders and belonging. She travels in the company of Brittany who has taken a strange liking to the unusual girl she met at the

48 See also Didier Bigo, "Security and Immigration: Toward a Critique of the Governmentality of Unease" *Alternatives* 27 (2002): 63–92, 71: "*Migrant*, as a term, is the way to designate someone as a threat to the core values of a country, a state, and has nothing to do with the legal terminology of foreigners. [. . .] Immigration is now problematised in Western countries in a way that is very different from the distinction between citizen and foreigner. It is not a legal status that is under discussion but a social image, concerning [. . .] the 'social distribution of bad'" (emphasis in the original).

49 Daniela Carpi, "The Ambiguous Nature of Citizenship" in *Citizenship, Law and Literature*, ed. Caroline Koegler, Jesper Reddig, and Klaus Stierstorfer (Berlin: De Gruyter, 2021), 241–252, 241.

50 Garrett Wallace Brown, "Cosmopolitanism," (n.d.), *Oxford Reference* <https://www.oxfordreference.com/view/10.1093/oi/authority.20110803095641459> (acc. February 18, 2022), n. pag.

train station and who – unbeknownst to Brit – is on her way to be reunited with her mother, an escaped IRC detainee.

> What if, the girl says. Instead of saying, this border divides these places. We said, this border *unites* these places. This border holds together these two really interesting different places. What if we declared border crossings places where, listen, when you crossed them, you yourself became doubly possible.
>
> You're being naive, Brit says. In so many ways.
>
> I'm twelve, the girl says. What do you expect? But listen. Just say. Say. Instead of having to prove who you are with a paper booklet or by showing a screen your eye or the print in your finger or the information about your face. Instead, you could prove who you are by what you *see* with your eyes and by what you *make* with your hands and –
>
> And by the faces you can make with your face, Brit says. There'd be all-out war. (SP, 196–197, emphasis in the original)

In Florence's vision, borders are not mechanisms of exclusion and restriction, but metaphors of connection and gateways of possibility. When crossing them, rather than becoming eligible or illegal, one becomes *doubly* possible. Identification, in turn, becomes a matter of seeing the world through somebody else's eyes and acknowledging their deeds and abilities – in other words: It becomes a matter of empathy and unprejudiced recognition. Brittany, just like Sophia in *Winter*, dismisses these ideas as naive, arguing that the resulting diversity of people allowed to enter would lead to hatred and war. Pitched against hopeful young Florence, the SA4A officer not only represents Britain's nationalist mindset and its hostile refugee removal policy, but also the older generation in general which, since the days of Margaret Thatcher, has been taught to be hard-headed and distrustful of the idea of community or one's own empathetic impulses. As Smith puts it in *Autumn*:

> *it's not just that we've been rhetorically and practically encouraging the opposite of integration for immigrants to this country. It's that we've been rhetorically and practically encouraging ourselves not to integrate. We've been doing this as a matter of self-policing since Thatcher taught us to be selfish and not just to think but to believe that there's no such thing as society.* (A, 111–112; emphasis in the original)

In Smith's *Seasonal Quartet*, a potential healing or reformation of this selfish worldview comes through friendship and empathetic exchange which, tellingly, does not take place amongst blood relations but in the context of unusual bonds that are being formed between strangers of different generations and origin. Each novel features such an unlikely, yet deep connection: Daniel and Elisabeth in *Autumn*, Lux and Sophia in *Winter*, Brittany and Florence in *Spring*, as well as Richard and Charlotte in *Summer*, to name only the most prominent ones. There is a rare kind of kinship at work in their relationships, one based on compassion and sincerity. Even those characters that seem trapped in numbness and isolation like Sophia or Brittany, find that their hardened shell is softened by a persistent offering of empathy and care. Using their stories synecdochally, Smith writes against a society built upon division, reminding the reader that it is the absence of that kind of empathetic exchange which has caused and is perpetuating it: "It has become a time of people saying stuff to each other and none of it actually ever becoming dialogue. It is the end of dialogue" (A, 112).

Dialogue and debate, however, are at the heart of any functioning community and democracy. Where dialogue ceases, prejudice and discord thrive. So, as in her previous novels *Hotel World* (2001) and *The Accidental* (2005), Smith evokes a "'community of strangers' that is able to mediate between the cosmopolitan imperatives of universal care and respect for particular difference," reminding us that there is "a universality to this ethical stance that is not limited to a particular historical moment."[51] It could be argued that, on a political level, the historical moment for this stance has come and gone with the founding of the European Union and Britain's decision to leave it. After all, scholars have championed the EU as "the first international organization which begins to resemble the cosmopolitan model"[52] and a "valid attempt to reconcile existing tensions between national and cosmopolitan forms of belonging and identification."[53] Indeed, even though EU policy makers rarely allude to cosmopolitanism and eschew its terminology, they habitually refer to Europeans as cosmopolitans.[54] What is more, their legislative frameworks, transnational ventures, and trade agreements translate cosmopolitan's ideological concepts into actual practices. But there has also been criticism that this cosmopolitan project has failed, especially with regard to the top-down bureaucratic mechanisms of the EU which brought forth a "deformed cosmopolitanism," fuelled by "egoism of the member states, economic self-interest and the asymmetries in influence on political decisions."[55]

It is this egoism and economic self-interest which drove the 'Leave' campaign of nationalist Brexiteers opposing the cosmopolitan dimension of the EU. Likewise, conservative politicians view cosmopolitanism in a pejorative sense, with it primarily denoting a lack of national identification and solidarity. This can be observed in

51 Alice Bennett, "'This Ridiculous Thing That Passes for a Passport': Seeking Asylum in Ali Smith's Fiction," *Contemporary Women's Writing* 12.3 (2018): 322–337, 324.

52 Daniele Archibugi, "Principles of Cosmopolitan Democracy" in *Re-imagining Political Community: Studies in Cosmopolitan Democracy*, ed. Daniele Archibugi, David Held, and Martin Köhler (Cambridge: Polity P, 1998), 198–228, 219.

53 Shaw, "BrexLit," 16.

54 Cf. Chris Rumford, "Introduction" in *Cosmopolitanism and Europe*, ed. Rumford (Liverpool: Liverpool UP, 2007), 1–15, 4.

55 Ulrich Beck and Edgar Grande, *Cosmopolitan Europe* (Cambridge: Polity P, 2007), 20.

Theresa May's anti-cosmopolitan statement in October 2016, the infamous dictum of which figures as the epigraph for *Winter*: "But if you believe you're a citizen of the world, you're a citizen of nowhere. You don't understand what the very word 'citizenship' means."[56] For May, the term obviously provides the basis for the crucial distinction between citizen and alien; that is, a person with or without rights. Giving up this exclusivist conception of citizenship in favor of a cosmopolitan approach would have robbed post-Brexit policy making of its very foundation.

In spite of such setbacks, the EU, as "international example of cosmopolitan democracy,"[57] has paved the way for new diversified notions of citizenship, expanding the narrow view of citizenship as something closely connected to nationality and territory. Since the 1990s, scholars have increasingly developed "segmented citizenships pertaining to practices and fields of practice (e.g., environmental or cultural citizenship); to identities and subject positions (e.g., queer, gendered, and ethnic/racialized citizenship); or scope of application (e.g., cosmopolitan, global, diasporic, or transnational notions of citizenship)."[58] Most of these concepts are less concerned with state borders, but rather with a global web of responsibilities and rights involving various ethical, political, and social decisions. They are rooted in universal liabilities that may concern the environment, trade, crime, and the protection of human rights, calling for corresponding "acts of citizenship."[59] Rather than being divided by national borders, civic community is connected through problems pertaining to humanity at large. Its citizens indeed become 'doubly possible' – as well as doubly responsible:

> Cosmopolitan citizenship and good international citizenship stress the need for compassion towards all other members of the human race, for assuming personal or collective responsibility for, among other things, the global environment, and, in some formulations, for risking the lives of co-nationals in military efforts to end or prevent serious human rights violations abroad.[60]

Humanitarian and ecological obligations replace shared nationality or self-interest, forming the basis for the civic duty to avoid and compensate for harm and injustice done to fellow man or nature. This obligation is not merely a moral one, based on

---

56 Theresa May, "Theresa May's Conference Speech in Full," (October 5, 2016), *The Telegraph* <https://www.telegraph.co.uk/news/2016/10/05/theresa-mays-conference-speech-in-full/> (acc. February 28, 2022), n. pag.

57 Cf. Carpi, "Ambiguous Nature," 246.

58 Katja Sarkowsky, "Expatriation, Belonging, and the Politics of Burial: The Urgency of Citizenship in Kamila Shamsie's *Home Fire*" in *Citizenship, Law and Literature*, ed. Koegler, Reddig, and Stierstorfer (Berlin: De Gruyter, 2021), 29–44, 29.

59 Cf. Engin F. Isin and Greg M. Nielsen, eds., *Acts of Citizenship* (London: Zed Books, 2013).

60 Andrew Linklater, *Critical Theory and World Politics – Citizenship, Sovereignty and Humanity* (Abingdon: Routledge, 2007), 7.

an individual's humanity, but a political one, predicated on a person's status as citizen of a community of shared values.

As mentioned before, this alternative conception of affiliation based on common beliefs and duties has already been implemented to a certain degree on the macro level of the EU. From its inception, the European Union has been a community of shared values, the membership in which has never been about access to markets and funds, economic performance, and regulatory standards alone; it has always been about "embracing the values that inform EU policies, such as transparent and accountable governance, human rights protection, and resolution of social conflicts."[61] However, dissenting EU members like Hungary, in their refusal to adhere to the quota of refugees they should shelter, and Britain, in its leaving the bloc, seem to have forgotten about these core principles of solidarity and common destiny that inherently inform the Union.[62]

Ali Smith's tetralogy chronicles this prevalent erosion of values and solidarity within the local, national, and international community, hinting at a potential remedy. With her insistence on compassion and tolerance towards others and especially *the* other, Ali Smith's tetralogy seems to call for a 'grassroot movement' that cultivates a kind of community building severed from questions of birth, generation, ethnicity, and nationality. Instead, it is based on a stance of compassion and tolerance towards 'the stranger' – in whatever guise they may be encountered: be it a homeless youth, a secluded old neighbor, a bitter old lady, a ragged refugee, or their jailor. This sympathetic attitude and acknowledgement of one's shared humanity and responsibility represent an act of citizenship in a globalized, interconnected world for "it's the same play they're all in, the same world" (W, 200).

As a kind of *affective* world citizenship, it seems an adequate response to all the political boundary-making that habitually uses affect and emotions to reinforce difference and protectionist thinking in the populace. Official discourses, practices, and policies of all kinds have since long mobilized, regulated, and reproduced emotions such as "unease, anger, empathy, (mis)trust, (dis)respect, love, and hate toward an imagined 'us' and 'others'"[63] for their respective political agendas. And last but not

---

61 Cvete Koneska, "The Vanishing European Dream: The Double Crisis of Migration and European (Dis)Integration" in *A European Crisis – Perspectives on Refugees, Solidarity, and Europe*, ed. Timofey Agarin and Nevena Nancheva (Stuttgart: ibidem, 2018), 149–168, 160.

62 The remaining EU countries can be accused of similar attitudes and policies that lack in solidarity and humanity. Germany, for instance, implemented equally problematic anchor centres for refugees and keeps refusing to grapple with its history of violence towards immigrants and asylum seekers, as could be observed in the wilfully misguided investigation of the NSU-murders. (Cf. Laura Zander, this volume, 278).

63 Cf. Bilgin Ayata, "Affective Citizenship" in *Affective Societies*, eds. Jan Slaby and Christian von Scheve (Abingdon: Routledge, 2019), 330–339, 334.

least, voters of the Brexit referendum have just rewarded a 'Leave' campaign that was predicated on specific affective reactions to immigrants as 'other.' This kind of "governing through affect"[64] that targets, designs, and utilizes the 'affective subject' and its conduct within the community, must be met with a poise of affective citizenship that is rooted in the ideas of shared humanity, community, dialogue, and compassion. A poise that supersedes the indifference, inertia, and compassion fatigue which apparently has been a widespread reaction to the emotional overstimulation through politics, the media, and social media.

Hence, in *Spring*, formerly suicidal protagonist Richard finds feelings of true purpose and belonging where he least expected them: on Culloden battlefield – the place of the last battle on English soil – where, after his life-changing road trip with Florence and Brittany, he is producing an independent documentary called *A Thousand Thousand People*. It is about the "Auld Alliance," a countrywide underground group dedicated to helping refugees escape or avoid detection and detention. It is a true grassroot movement with people heeding the call of "the stranger's case,"[65] helping unwelcome immigrants how and where they can: "Countrywide we're trying to change the impossible, to move things an inch at a time all those thousands of miles towards the possible, and believe me, there are a thousand thousand people [. . .] ready to help" (SP, 275). They fail in the case of Florence's mother, but they do, in a way, save Richard who, forlorn after a failed marriage, the estrangement from his only child, and the death of his best friend and true love Paddy, had been ready to end his life. Documenting and thereby partaking in their selfless endeavor gives him a feeling of true belonging that is not rooted in nationality or family, but rather in a shared sense of (in)justice and responsibility:

> This project's making me feel, all right. It's making me feel very all right. I'm spending all this time in a place I don't know, and I feel like I'm home. I meet people all the time who are risking themselves and they fill me with their confidence. I don't belong, they know I don't, I know I don't. But I feel like I do. What I feel is welcome. (SP, 287)

The protagonists of all four novels experience such potentially transformative encounters, finding kinship and belonging in unexpected places and with unlikely people. Their stories promote an alternative, affective notion of belonging and citizenship: a post-territorial, trans-generational bond formed by empathy and dialogue based on a common acknowledgement of values and responsibilities that can serve to unite individuals as well as nations.

---

64 Anne-Marie Fortier, "Proximity by Design? Affective Citizenship and the Management of Unease," *Citizenship Studies* 14.1 (2010): 17–30, 27.

65 Cf. William Shakespeare, *Sir Thomas More* [c. 1591–93], in *The Arden Shakespeare*, ed. John Jowett (London: Bloomsbury, 2011), 6.153–155.

Jayana Jain

Poetry from the Camps: Deconstructing Eurocentric and Colonial Remains in Citizenship Laws

1 Introduction: Citizenship Laws and Colonial Legacies

As an exercise of state sovereignty, citizenship laws often mask the violent politics of inclusion and exclusion through the legal language of necessity and rationality. In the post-colonial societies of South and Southeast Asia, the concept and practices of citizenship accompany the idea of nation-building based largely on colonial legacies.[1] By replacing the pre-colonial frameworks where multiple and shifting identities often co-existed without the fear of losing one's membership in a polity, the British colonial administration in India and Myanmar established its rule based on the European Enlightenment model. Such a model aimed to achieve homogenous sovereignty using divisive and cartographical approaches for territorial demarcation, and exclusionary categories that labeled colonized subjects based on caste, class, ethnicity, and religion.[2] As this process led to the creation of a hierarchy between the colonized subjects and the colonialists, it also mandated the creation of a homogenous majority and the marginalization of minority communities within the colonies. Post-independence, when the rights of the post-colonial citizens were determined through a newly formed constitution, colonial vestiges within the law cathected the space of the minority citizens as the Other, to the point of overwriting their histories. Such a categorization and exclusion of minorities based on parameters such as religion, ethnicity, and civilizational superiority gradually led to the creation of the "marginal" and "stateless" communities in post-colonial states such as India and Myanmar.[3]

In the case of the Rohingya Muslim minorities of Myanmar, several events that occurred during the pre-colonial period, the colonial rule in Burma, and the post-

1 Meghna Kajla and Nasreen Chowdhory, "The Unmaking of Citizenship of Rohingyas in Myanmar" in *Citizenship, Nationalism and Refugeehood of Rohingyas in Southern Asia*, ed. Chowdhory and Biswajit Mohanty (Singapore: Springer, 2020), 51–70, 57.

2 Ratna Kapur, "The Citizen and the Migrant: Postcolonial Anxieties, Law, and the Politics of Exclusion/Inclusion," *Theoretical Inquiries in Law* 8.2 (2007): 537–569.

3 Kamal Sadiq, "Postcolonial Citizenship" in *The Oxford Handbook of Citizenship*, ed. Ayelet Shachar, Rainer Bauböck, Irene Bloemraad, and Maarten Vink (Oxford: Oxford UP, 2017), 1–24.

https://doi.org/10.1515/9783111075693-034

independence nation formation of Myanmar, have led to their statelessness and persecution at the hands of the Burmese military.[4] Settled as traders who navigated their way from Arabia and Persia to the Arakan region of present-day Myanmar via the Bengal coastal belt, the Rohingya Muslims have a distinct "spatial identity"[5] that can be traced to as early as 3000 BC. Although their interactions with the Hindus in British India and the Rakhine Buddhists in Myanmar were limited, given the geographical challenges posed by the Arakan Yoma mountains, they had peacefully coexisted as a multicultural entity until the seventeenth century.[6] However, in the eighteenth century, to ensure Buddhist purity for the Rakhines and cut down the rising Islamic influence in Burma, the Buddhist ruler Bodawpaya of the Konbaung dynasty conquered the Arakan Kingdom. As a result, the Arakanese Rohingya Muslims were forced to migrate to the Bengal region of British India. Around this time, the colonial British administration provided refuge to the Rohingya Muslims in the Cox Bazaar region of present-day Bangladesh. Assigned as "wastelands" for the Rohingya Muslims arriving from the Rakhine state in the eighteenth century, Cox Bazaar is a result of the imperialistic strategy of Captain Hiram Cox, an officer of the East India Company between 1797 and 1799.[7] Built to trap the Rohingya refugees in a "*choky*"[8] (prison), the Cox Bazaar has become symbolic of the claustrophobic lives of the Rohingyas who, to date, continue to grapple with the perilous conditions of the refugee camps. It was also during and after the building of these camps in the late eighteenth century that tensions rose between the Burmese Kingdom and the British colonial forces who had been trying to gain control over the Arakan region. After the three Anglo-Burmese wars, Myanmar became a British colony in 1886, and the rift between the Rohingya Muslims and the Rakhine Buddhists continued to deepen. Later, in the year 1942, when the Japanese army invaded Burma to assist the Burmese nationalists in their fight for an independent Myanmar, the Rohingya minorities allied with the British.[9] This further escalated the animosity between the Rohingya Muslims and

---

4 Shamna Poyil, "National Identity and Conceptualization of Nationalism Among Rohingya" in *Citizenship, Nationalism and Refugeehood of Rohingyas*, 31–50, 41.

5 Parvathy Rajeev and Devi. K, "Re-Presenting the Rohingya Genocide through Literature: A Study of Exodus: Between Genocide and Me by Mayyu Ali as an Alternate History," *Annals of the Romanian Society for Cell Biology* 25.6 (2021): 9042–9051, 9043.

6 Rajeev and K, "Rohingya Genocide," 9043.

7 James Byrne, "Introduction: A New Rohingya Poetics" in *I am a Rohingya: Poetry from the Camps and Beyond*, ed. Byrne and Shehzar Doja (Todmorden: Arc Publications, 2019), 13–19, 13.

8 Byrne, "Introduction," 13.

9 Kaveri, "The Politics of Marginalization and Statelessness of the Rohingyas in India" in *Citizenship, Nationalism and Refugeehood of Rohingyas*, 71–96, 76; further references in the text, abbreviated as "PM."

the Burmese Buddhist nationalists, thus "radicaliz[ing] the independence movement against foreigners and Muslims" (PM, 76).

In 1947, after gaining independence from British colonial rule, the Buddhist majority took control of the institutional and judicial structures of Myanmar to construct a homogenous nation. As a result, religious ethnic minorities such as the Rohingya Muslims were marginalized in the post-colonial nation's imagination. Although Myanmar's first constitution of 1947 recognized them as citizens, the 1948 Citizenship Law imposed specific criteria on the Rohingyas in order for them to attain full citizenship.[10] At this juncture, the practice of 'Othering' the Rohingyas had been institutionalized, and the subsequent amendments to the constitution reinforced the idea of the Rohingyas as the 'dangerous Other' to Myanmar's sovereignty. In the 1982 constitution of Myanmar, in an effort to definitively prescribe the rights of full citizenship, the foundation of the "national race" was laid down, and 135 ethnic groups were identified as part of the collective called *taingyintha*, (the sons of the soil) who, crucially, settled in Myanmar before 1824.[11] Despite the historical evidence of the Rohingyas' early settlement in Myanmar, they were excluded from the official list of ethnic groups. Later, the constitution of 2008 addressed the political community of Myanmar as a "national race" instead of citizens, thereby emphatically excluding the Rohingyas, who eventually became *de facto* stateless (NF, 199, 206). Thus, a brief historical account of the Rohingya Muslims of Myanmar from the pre-colonial to the post-colonial period attunes to the fact that "the socio-historical constructs [. . .] became 'legal' factors, hence dictating distinctions made and hierarchies established between ethnicities, and leading to a jurisprudentially crowned construction of belonging versus foreignness" (NF, 204). In her study on the Rohingya exodus, Nergis Canefe observes, "[w]hat is unique about the Rohingya issue is the legalized nature of the crisis from the very onset" (NF, 204). She uses the term "lawfare" or "the coercive use of legal instruments and in particular, the constitution" to describe the atrocities committed by the post-colonial Myanmar government on the Rohingyas (NF, 204).

Considered "one of the gravest human rights violations and humanitarian crises of our times," the vulnerable situation of the Rohingyas cannot be investigated merely through the lens of its colonial history and the post-colonial laws of Myanmar. Both the predominantly West-controlled international laws concerning refugees in 1951, and the post-colonial citizenship laws of Myanmar's neighboring

10 Nergis Canefe, "New Faces of Statelessness: The Rohingya Exodus and Remapping of Rights" in *Citizenship, Nationalism and Refugeehood of Rohingyas*, 197–216, 205; further references in the text, abbreviated as "NF."

11 Nasreen Chowdhory and Biswajit Mohanty, "Contextualizing Citizenship, Nationalism and Refugeehood of Rohingya: An Introduction" in *Citizenship, Nationalism and Refugeehood of Rohingyas*, 1–30, 23.

countries such as India must first be examined. While the years from 1945 to 1951 narrate a trajectory of both the disintegration of Europe and the rise of the European movement, in South Asia they mark the birth of decolonized and independent statehood with concomitant civil wars, increasing numbers of refugees, and stateless communities. Born out of the Refugee Convention of 1951, the definition of a "refugee" was framed from a Eurocentric perspective and none of the South Asian nation-states became a signatory to the Convention.[12] Even though "the largest refugee-generating phenomenon was the partition of the South Asian subcontinent in 1947 where, by a conservative estimate, fifteen million people were displaced," the Refugee Convention did not outline any specific provisions for the refugees of partition (FW, v). However, some of the South Asian countries such as India adopted the Western principles of non-refoulement to ensure justice for the refugees. While this was a critical step during the partition, according to Paula Banerjee, with the changes in the Northern gaze, in the context of the Rohingyas, the "South Asian attitude to refugees [became] analogous to European attitude to the African refugees" (FW, v). Building on her proposition, this study argues that, in the "post-9/11 context"[13] of the struggles of migrants and refugees in the West and India, there is also the need to scrutinize the Islamophobic frames of recognizing and differentiating migrant subjectivities. Although immigration policies and citizenship laws in India, Myanmar, and the European nation-states demonstrate varying degrees of multiculturalism that emerged in distinct historical contexts, they indicate a mutual false perception of threat emanating from nation-states with a Muslim majority and a hesitancy toward the integration of Muslim migrants.[14] For instance, in the European multicultural context, Germany's post-2010 foreign policies concerning immigrants and refugees have been suspected of "wilful neglect," exhibiting the nation's "threshold of tolerance."[15] In the South Asian multicultural context, India's 2019 Citizenship Amendment Act[16] (CAA) specifically seeks to exclude Muslim migrants. Applying the law selectively works to effectively bar migrant Muslim minorities such as the Rohingyas from the neighboring country of India. In her study on the stateless Rohingyas in India, Sahana Basavapatna rightly points out, in the post-2014 Hindutva political reality of India, the "image of the Rohingya is unenviable:

12 Paula Banerjee, "Foreword" in *Citizenship, Nationalism and Refugeehood of Rohingyas*, v–vii, v; further references in the text, abbreviated as "FW."

13 Jayana Jain, *Thinking Past 'Post-9/11': Home, Nation and Transnational Desires in Pakistani English Novels and Hindi Films* (London: Routledge, 2021), 121–122.

14 Michael Dusche, *Identity Politics in India and Europe* (New Delhi: SAGE, 2010), 139.

15 Rita Chin, *The Crisis of Multiculturalism in Europe* (New Jersey: Princeton UP, 2017), 124, 136.

16 Ministry of Law and Justice, "Citizenship Amendment Act 2019 (No. 47 of 2019)" in *The Gazette of India Extraordinary* (New Delhi: Government of India P, 2019), 1–3.

foreigner, Muslim, stateless, suspected Bangladeshi national, illiterate, impoverished . . . and the other . . . "[17]

Today, despite the intervention of some international NGOs in the Cox Bazar's refugee camps in Bangladesh, the everyday hardships of the Rohingyas remain at the periphery of global attention and outside the ambit of international legal systems. Often, in national and international courtrooms alike, the Rohingya refugees become mere case studies, whose appeal for citizenship and the right to belong are studied, cited, and discarded once their utility is over. It is in this context that this study turns to literature written by the Rohingyas, as it provides an important platform for narrating the violence accompanying the implementation of state citizenship laws. Considering that both law and literature cross-pollinate as modes of representation and act as catalytic agents in addressing the problems of migrants and refugees, excavating marginalized perspectives of law within literature becomes an urgent endeavor. Such an endeavor is useful, however, as a means of mapping the historical oppression of present-day migrant communities and exposing the ways in which colonial legacies and Eurocentrism masquerade and continue to discursively inform the post-colonial present of Myanmar and India that have become increasingly hostile to Muslim immigrants and refugees. Considering that *I am a Rohingya: Poetry from the Camps and Beyond* (2019) is the first English-language anthology of poetry written by Rohingya poets, it demands attention from both literary critics and legal experts. To understand, for instance, how Rohingya poetry aids in the questioning of neo-colonial practices within the current citizenship and migration laws of post-colonial nation-states such as Myanmar and India, it is crucial to underline their common thematic concerns and literary strategies. Equally important is the simultaneous study of the specific political, cultural, environmental, and literary contexts in which the poems were composed.

2 Rewriting History and Asserting the Rohingya Identity

The unabated state-sponsored persecution of the Rohingyas in Myanmar and the denial of basic rights such as the right to access food, shelter, and education have created a condition of precarity and extreme anxiety. This has further stifled the

17 Sahana Basavapatna, qtd. in Sudipta Datta, "'The Rohingya in South Asia – People without a State' Review: No Place to Call Home," (November 24, 2018), *The Hindu* <https://www.thehindu.com/todays-chapter/tp-features/tp-bookreview/noplace-to-call-home/article25589238.ece> (acc. November 11, 2021), 4.

abilities of the Rohingyas to think, articulate, and respond to the historical human rights violations practiced upon them. Moreover, under the repressive rule of the Myanmar government and censorship regulations, the very act of questioning or attempting to signal their oppression to a wider audience has become even more challenging. In such a context, the arrival of an anthology of Rohingya poetry denotes not only the Rohingya poets' dauntless resistance to their historical silencing, but also an attempt to explore literature's potential in challenging the lawfare of the Burmese state. According to the Rohingya poet Mayyu Ali, "[w]riting for Rohingya people is activism [. . .]. [It] is a battle between trying to survive and raising the voices of the people who are counted as forgotten in the world."[18] As he emphasizes the importance of writing his poetry in English to communicate with a large international audience,[19] his poems force readers to confront their own complacency, and hear the sound of their own silence regarding the dehumanization of the Rohingyas.

Emerging as an outcome of teaching and creative writing workshops conducted by James Byrne and Shehzar Doja in the Cox's Bazar refugee camps, *I am a Rohingya* is also a reflection of the Rohingya participants' tuition from the workshop discussions on the modernist works of T.S. Eliot, Mina Loy, and Tomas Tranströmer.[20] Although the workshops provided the educational, intellectual, and aesthetic contexts through which the anthology of poems came into being, the methodology of introducing predominantly West-centric works and literary styles to the Rohingyas raises doubts about a form of academic imperialism in practice. In times when we actively strive to decolonize our teaching methodologies and university curricula, it would arguably have been better to have encouraged the Rohingyas to engage in a creative dialogue with the literature of the colonized regions, or to reflect upon their own hardships, while questioning how and why literature from the West has become canonical. However, considering the lack of reading resources and denial of education, the workshop was effective in familiarizing the Rohingya poets with the use of literary strategies and devices such as lyric, collage, ekphrasis, metaphor, and repetition. It was also successful in developing the poets' sense of imagery and the surrounding soundscape as they began to write down their untold narratives with the aim of instigating great change. As Mayyu Ali observes, "[t]here are a million Rohingya, each of us has an oral history. Each one of us has trauma. I want a new generation to write for themselves."[21]

---

18 Ali, qtd. in Byrne, "Afterword: An Interview with Mayyu Ali" in *I am a Rohingya: Poetry from the Camps and Beyond*, 74–79, 76.

19 Ali, qtd. in Byrne, "Afterword," 75.

20 Byrne, "Introduction," 14.

21 Ali, qtd. in Poppy McPherson and Simon Lewis, "In Exile in Bangladesh, a Bittersweet Revival of Rohingya Culture," (May 8, 2019), *Reuters* <https://www.reuters.com/article/uk-myanmar-rohingya-culture-idUKKCN1SE02N> (acc. January 11, 2022), 6.

All poems in the anthology reflect on the confined life of the Rohingyas in Myanmar and the Cox's Bazar camps, from witnessing how their statelessness was institutionalized, to the horrors of state-sponsored persecution, and genocide. At the same time, by using anonymized identities and prefixing them with the pseudonym "Ro," for instance, "Ro Pacifist,"[22] "Ro Mehrooz,"[23] "Ro B.M. Hairu,"[24] the poems assert pride in the Rohingya identity. As they reveal how their systematic ethnic cleansing and denial of citizenship rights led to their dehumanization and the suppression of their voice, they shed light on the imperfect tools of language and its failure to communicate their history. The poem "Mother Arakan" underlines this failure of language and that of the people who have systematically neglected or suppressed the voice of the Rohingyas. The poet contemplates, "everywhere there is speech – but no one speaks (about us)."[25] In the poem "Too Much Bitterness," the poet Yar Tin struggles "to make rhymes out of gunshots," and "to make poetry out of death and destruction."[26] As the poet reflects on the burden that words and speech have to carry in describing the trauma of his fellow Rohingyas, he questions the patronizing intent and implications of the workshop that made him "use another's tragedy as pages for my poetry" (TB, 61).

The collected poems of the Rohingya survivors also underline the historical fragmentation of their identities and respond to the categories and labels that have often been used to describe them in the mainstream media. By employing metaphors in poems such as the "pet,"[27] "cut bud"[28] and "a fly in the kitchen buzzing on the boundary of a blind wall,"[29] the poets reflect on the dehumanized and ruptured identities of refugees and immigrants who are often described patronizingly as "the twenty-first century's white man's burden"[30] or represented as a "nuisance."[31] Often interpellated as the "boat people,"[32] "the world's most oppressed people" (TB, 61),

22 Ro Pacifist, "Give Me a Chance to Restart this Life" in *I am a Rohingya*, 36–37.
23 Ro Mehrooz, "Night-Blooming Jasmine" in *I am a Rohingya*, 71.
24 Ro B.M. Hairu, "Behind Life" in *I am a Rohingya*, 43.
25 Anonymous, "Mother Arakan" in *I am a Rohingya*, 70.
26 Yar Tin, "Too Much Bitterness" in *I am a Rohingya*, 60–61, 60; further references in the text, abbreviated as "TB."
27 Ali, "That's Me, A Rohingya" in *I am a Rohingya*, 23–25, 23.
28 Ro Mehrooz, "The Cut Bud" in *I am a Rohingya*, 27.
29 Zaki Ovais, "Someone I'm Afraid of" in *I am a Rohingya*, 33.
30 Tamas Wells, *Narrating Democracy in Myanmar: The Struggle Between Activists, Democratic Leaders and Aid Workers* (Amsterdam: Amsterdam UP, 2021), 62.
31 "Editorial: Rohingya Refugees Deserve Far Better," (January 24, 2013), *Arab News* <https://www.arabnews.com/editorial-rohingya-refugees-deserve-far-better> (acc. November 11, 2021), 1.
32 Byrne, "Contributors" in *I am a Rohingya*, 80–83, 80.

and "orphans,"[33] the Rohingyas remain unaccepted in their homeland as their identities float alongside the shores of the river Naf that flows between the borders of Western Myanmar and Southeastern Bangladesh. In Zaki Ovais's poem "Water,"[34] the speaker reveals that as the Rohingyas squeeze aboard boats on the river Naf, despite the abundance of water around them, they lack access to clean drinking water. Even in other poems, as the speakers demand their fundamental rights to clean water, food, and shelter, they underline how the denial of these basic rights or "the discriminated minutes" has turned their life "into years."[35] The description of the Rohingya refugees' enduring pain and hopelessness also reflects the spatio-temporal politics of discriminatory state laws through which human lifespans are cruelly cut short: "a whole lifetime turns into ash with a blink of any eye" (BP, 30).

Alongside the water poems, the translated transcriptions of the river songs in the anthology act as historical and present-day vessels of the individual and collective experiences of the Rohingyas that remain lost in Myanmar's legal and fictional texts. Passed down from generation to generation through folk tradition, the songs reflect the shared histories, cultures, and oral traditions of Myanmar and Bangladesh. They reflect the precariousness of the Rohingyas' fate, their fears and underlying anxieties that are often intertwined with the capricious and unpredictable river Naf. Embedded in a "modern poetic frame," folk songs such as Ro Mehrooz's "Night-Blooming Jasmine"[36] are also songs of yearning, reflecting the Rohingyas' rich cultural heritage and their homing desires. Corresponding to Doja's 2019 hope that the Rohingya folk songs act as a "catalyst for more research," this study proposes that their folk songs should be considered as vital historical archives that challenge the hegemonic narratives of the past and offer a retelling of their suppressed trauma. They are a valuable resource for studying those marginalized literary traditions and songs of resistance that echo the unjust practices of the state and the relentless struggles of "one of the most persecuted communities in the world."[37]

In other poems such as RO B.M. Hairu's "Behind Life,"[38] the use of parenthesis as a subtext becomes an effective strategy to represent the suppressed life of the Rohingyas; a life of restricted movement, curfews, relentless firings, and endless lootings. The parenthesis also acts as a literary device to supplement the

33 Maung Hla Shwe, "An Orphan" in *I am a Rohingya*, 34.
34 Zaki Ovais, "Water" in *I am a Rohingya*, 58.
35 Yar Tin, "About Those Born into this Place" in *I am a Rohingya*, 29–31, 30; further references in the text, abbreviated as "BP."
36 Ro Mehrooz, "Night-Blooming Jasmine," 71.
37 Byrne, "Introduction," 18.
38 Ro B.M. Hairu, "Behind Life," 43.

metanarrative of the nation's history with expressions of the silenced, the unsaid, or the unspoken of. Such a paradigm reflects the resilience of the Rohingya refugees and their refusal to accept their fates as mere pawns of Myanmar's colonial and post-colonial history. The repeated use of second-person pronouns and interrogative style in several other poems also underlines the need for the world to accept responsibility and blame for the suppressed histories of violence committed against the Rohingyas. The poet asks, "what do you feel when you see your birthplace bald-headed?," "what do you feel when you see your sister raped?," and "what do you feel when you see your home burnt down?"[39] In another poem, "Being Rohingya," Ro Anamul Hasan demands to know, "we all wear human organs, am I not the same as you?"[40] Such rhetorical questions throughout the anthology not only fill the readers with indignation but also encourage them to be weary of those legal lenses that categorize and label humans, thus determining their right to belong or not belong to different regions of our shared planet.

3 Poetry as a Testament to "Lawfare"

I am a Rohingya is also deeply concerned with the lawfare of the Burmese military or the state-sponsored torture committed against the Rohingyas that led to the denial of their fundamental rights to food, clothing, shelter, citizenship, and education. It engages with issues of kidnapping, human trafficking, rape, physical violence, and deaths that have become an everyday reality for the Rohingya refugees fleeing from Myanmar and those currently being confined in the Cox's Bazar camps. In the poem "Birth," Yasmin Ullah presents the "complex case" of the Rohingyas.[41] She begins by describing her birth in the global context of the challenging environmental conditions and the political wars fought across the world, especially in Myanmar. She then attacks the UN Charter of 1942 and its failure to maintain global peace. She questions the irrational political, religious, cultural, and economic fears of the nations that deny or restrict the entry of immigrants and refugees, as she emphasizes that the Rohingyas "weren't looking for riches nor to exert their power over anyone" (BT, 49). The poet is appalled that, even though the Rohingyas only wanted "to work hard and survive," the Myanmar government failed to protect their economic rights: "labour of jobs, barely paid / the pennies

39 Maung Hla Shwe, "My Arakan" in *I am a Rohingya*, 46–47.

40 Ro Anamul Hasan, "Being Rohingya" in *I am a Rohingya*, 40–41, 40.

41 Yasmin Ullah, "Birth" in *I am a Rohingya*, 49–55, 55; further references in the text, abbreviated as "BT."

we made snatched" (BT, 49). Other poems in the anthology also attest to the systemic forms of discrimination encountered by the Rohingyas at the hands of the Buddhist nationalists. For instance, the poem "About those Born into this Place" exposes the Islamophobic nature of the Buddhist nationalists of Myanmar and the discrimination against the Rohingya Muslims for practicing their religion: "the gates of the mosques that embodied peace, / are dressed in giant locks" (BP, 29). As the poem depicts the absence of secular and democratic practices in Myanmar, it exposes the authoritarian, fundamentalist, cruel, and genocidal nature of the Myanmar government that neither assured the Rohingyas a fair trial, nor guaranteed them any civil rights in a secular environment (BT, 50).[42] Instead, for many of the Rohingyas, the torture inflicted by the state has been the "longest-running mind movie"[43] about suicidal thoughts, as they witnessed their babies thrown into bonfires, sisters trafficked, and brothers kidnapped (BT, 51). With no assurance of a birth certificate upon being born or of a funeral after death,[44] the lives of the Rohingya refugees remain devoid of subjectivity and agency as they are subjected to "limit experience"[45] with no right to citizenship or full political membership of a nation-state. Gradually, with no choices or free will left, the Rohingyas were "pushed to the lowest of the low," and despite the erosion of their culture, they self-identify as Rohingyas "so they won't lose the last glimpse of history and its triumphs" (BT, 50).

In the poem, "They're kind killers," Mayyu Ali presents the reader with a testimony of torture in a female voice who has been robbed, raped, and brutally killed. As the poem implicates the reader in this violence for being ignorant or silent about it, "the world is too brave to watch us being killed,"[46] it underlines how Rohingya refugee women have endured the worst of circumstances in the patriarchal and prejudiced society of Myanmar. As bearers of progeny and victims of sex trafficking, women often find their bodies transformed into a locus of violence.[47] Challenging the abuse of women and attacking the callousness of a world that took "over half a century to take notice" of their enduring pain, the Rohingya female poet Thida Shani urges the reader to collectively scream:

---

42 Ali, "That's Me a Rohingya," 23–25.

43 Ali, "A Rohingya Refugee" in *I am a Rohingya*, 64.

44 Ali, "That's Me a Rohingya," 23–25.

45 In their study on the Rohingya genocide in literature, Parvathy Rajeev and Devi. K build on Foucault's concept of "limit experience" or "that point of life which lies as close as possible to the impossibility of living" to reflect on the dissociated identities and the existential crisis of the Rohingyas ("Rohingya Genocide," 9048).

46 Ali, "They're Kind Killers" in *I am a Rohingya*, 44.

47 Rajeev and K, "Rohingya Genocide," 9048.

Scream to save lives
Scream to save dignity
Scream to save humanity
No matter who he or she is
Young or old, Palestinian, Yemini, Syrian, Kashmiri or even a Rohingya.[48]

In synchronicity with the sensory imagery that evokes an alarming soundscape, the poem "About Those Born into this Place" refers to "hearts cracking," "bitter whispers," "uncertain sobs," and "blood-scented oxygen" in Arakan where they "kill and bury" the Rohingyas "under the treasure of human rights"[49] (BP, 30). As the poem laments the absence of both justice and the guarantors of human rights in Myanmar, it raises significant issues: What exactly does the treasure of human rights consist of? For whom is it? Who owns it? Finally, how is it to be distributed or shared? Considering that human rights is itself a contested concept accused of Eurocentrism and an inherently Western framing[50] the poem ruminates on the role of the Rohingya refugees in the global discourse on human rights. In the absence of a "scope of friendship"[51] between the Myanmar government and the Rohingyas and the ongoing silence of the international community concerning the Burmese military's brutal killings of the Rohingyas, one wonders how the "complex case" of the Rohingyas will be resolved. How can we ensure their "safe repatriation and proper rehabilitation?"[52] According to the Rohingya poet Yasmin Ullah, "the case might easily be solved," "if we all just brush up on our empathy" and wear the lens of humanity that makes Rohingyas appear "wholesome," "human," and "not so different from you" (BT, 55).

4 Thinking Planetarity: Decentring the West

Oh, weather, my question to you,
as one of many genocide survivors is why-
why in this treeless, shadeless refugee camp,

why like the Myanmar government,
do you still set us on fire?[53]

48 Thida Shania, "Save Me" in *I am a Rohingya*, 45.
49 Pacifist Farooq, "My Life" in *I am a Rohingya*, 32.
50 Sebastian Bonnet, "Overcoming Eurocentrism in Human Rights: Postcolonial Critiques – Islamic Answers?" *Muslim World Journal of Human Rights* 12.1 (2015): 1–24, 1.
51 Ro Mehrooz, "The Cut Bud," 27.
52 Ali, qtd. in Byrne, "Afterword," 79.
53 Azad Mohammed, "Misfortune" in *I am a Rohingya*, 48.

In the above poem "Misfortune," the poet laments the loss of trees and flowing streams in the golden Arakan. By doing so, he addresses the environmental precarity induced by the civil and international wars and the everyday violence meted out by humans upon the planet's natural resources. The poet then describes how the Western world takes for granted the "assortment and abundance of fruits" or uses "umbrellas for rain," "jackets for cold," and "sunglasses for heat," while the Rohingyas mourn how their golden Arakan has become a "hell," "bloodstream," and "battleground" full of "limp and lifeless" skin devoid of such privileged protection (BP, 29).[54] In another poem, "About Those Born into this Place," the speaker questions the colonial legacy and the West's hegemony in the discourse on the ownership rights of our planet's natural resources: "we who don't own mountains, the ocean, / the earth, the wide plains, / don't own anything" (BP, 29). Likewise, in the poem "Give Me a Chance to Restart this Life," Ro Pacifist depicts a world of unimagined vulnerabilities and brutalities as the reader is transported to an "ash of villages burnt down over decades" and the once "lush green motherland" is now "scorched by fire."[55] Using juxtaposition, the poet asks the reader to compare the seasonal changes and the quality of air over the years between his village and other parts of the world. This directs the poet to evoke a sense of planetarity and collective responsibility towards the environmental damage done to the Arakan region. More significantly, it reminds the readers of the similarities between the predatory behavior of the colonial masters who captured the land and the exterminatory acts of the Burmese military soldiers who built the "NaTaLa"[56] after bulldozing the Rohingya villages.[57] The poem "Memory of Torture"[58] even compares the "inhumanity" and the bigoted nature of the "969" Buddhist monks with that of the British colonialists who enslaved minds and burned down the rich heritage of Myanmar.

In addition to addressing the colonial and post-colonial mistakes in Myanmar that changed the fate of the Rohingyas, poems such as "Being Rohingya"[59] and "The Unfamiliar Home"[60] accuse the global media of suppressing or neglecting

54 Ro Anamul Hasan, "Being Rohingya" in *I am a Rohingya*, 40–41, 41.

55 Ro Pacifist, "Give Me a Chance to Restart this Life" in *I am a Rohingya*, 36–37, 36.

56 They refer to the "new structures" including the "three military bases in Maungdaw and Buthidaung townships, helipads, fencing, roads, extensions of non-Rohingya (NaTaLa) villages, and even a refugee processing center." Angshuman Choudhury, "Will Rohingya Refugees Ever Be Repatriated to Myanmar?" (April 5, 2018), *The Diplomat* <https://thediplomat.com/2018/04/will-rohingya-refugees-ever-be-repatriated-to-myanmar/> (acc. January 24, 2022), 2.

57 Ro B.M. Hairu, "Behind Life," 43.

58 Ahtaram Shine, "Memory of Torture" in *I am a Rohingya*, 62.

59 Ro Anamul Hasan, "Being Rohingya," 41.

60 Ullah, "The Unfamiliar Home" in *I am a Rohingya*, 68–69, 68.

the pogroms against the Rohingyas. While the media allots a considerable amount of screen time to Western countries' "architecture, buildings and landscapes," the poet wonders why none of the Rohingya issues "makes it to the cover of magazines."[61] Likewise, international organizations are also charged with doing little to provide donations and humanitarian protection to the Rohingya refugees, as the poet claims:

> I saw on television they had rescued a man.
> Many navy boats, helicopters.
> But not one wooden boat was sent to rescue
> Thousands of us drowning in the river.[62]

In a study on the national and international politics of marginalization of the Rohingyas, Kaveri argues that "no human emergency becomes an emergency until it hits the European borders" (PM, 90). In the case of the Rohingyas, providing humanitarian assistance has been a strategy of the developed nations of the West "to restrict such population from migrating and entering their borders," "fulfil their participation in global politics," and "get away from the real issue" (PM, 90). In the South Asian context, although the Indian government came forward with humanitarian aid and relief operation *Insaniyat* (humanity) for the Rohingya refugees in Bangladesh, "it remained mute on the crisis" (PM, 90). Instead, the Ministry of External Affairs of India even refrained from using the term "Rohingya" and their operation "can be seen as de-incentivizing Rohingyas entering into India" (PM, 90). Today, even though formal legal status has been conferred to some of the Rohingya refugees who fled from Myanmar to Bangladesh, and millions of euros are being donated by the EU to Cox Bazar's refugee camps, their citizenship remains poised along the axis of inclusion and exclusion. Given that the starting point of post-colonial citizenship laws is always, and continues to be, exclusive, Eurocentric, and discriminatory,[63] Rohingya poetry questions what degree of relevance, if any, the colonial remnants in the citizenship laws still carry today. As Tin's poem poignantly asks: "For the right to live as humans, among humans, what else must we give up?" (TB, 61).

---

61 Ullah, "The Unfamiliar Home," 68.

62 Ro Anamul Hasan, "Being Rohingya," 41.

63 Kenneth Nunn, "Law as a Eurocentric Enterprise," *LAW & INEQ* 15.2 (1997): 323–371, 323.

5 Conclusion: Migrant Bodies at the Borders in Search of Optimal Legal and Policy Outcomes

While a Eurocentric narrative of citizenship places emphasis upon securing and militarizing the nation, in the decolonizing perspective of Rohingya poetry, the bestiality of the state's efforts to maintain security in Myanmar and beyond is questioned. Although the Rohingya poets do not directly hold Britain's colonial laws and policies as responsible for their present plight, they nevertheless challenge the "colossal colonial errors"[64] embedded within the national and international laws that fail to offer them adequate protection. The poems in the anthology force the readers to reflect on what remains in today's citizenship laws that can lead to the inhumanity of people condemned to beg at the borders of their homeland. Instead, the irreparable losses of human lives that result from the failure of such laws outrage the very justice supposed to be accorded through them. In this context, *I am a Rohingya* acts as a significant body of literary work that sheds light on the Rohingya refugees' histories and everyday realities while resisting the Eurocentric and colonial constructions of their past and present-day genocide. The anthology acts as a testimony to Burmese lawfare and aspires to become a part of the global legal discourse on citizenship rights and belonging. Ultimately, it calls for the "tentative beginnings of the language of the imprescriptible time," or the "time where claims of justice are imperishable."[65] In seeking just provisions or optimal legal and policy outcomes, the poems demand the "ear of love" and "the heart of justice" that believes "as much as we [Rohingyas] are victims, there is potential in our social contribution" (BT, 54). Certainly, as the poet Yasmin Ullah claims, "there is more to being Rohingyas than exodus" (BT, 54).

---

64 Rajeev and K, "Rohingya Genocide," 9044.

65 In her elaborate study on the poetics of political transition in Myanmar, Catherine Renshaw builds on the French philosopher Vladimir Jankélévitch's concept of time to suggest how Myanmar poetry represents different modes of time depending on the nation's political transition. For her, while the earlier poems of Myanmar composed during the period of military rule represent "irreversible time," the poems, written after the period of dictatorship reflect the poetics of 'irrevocable time.' However, her study claims that "Myanmar still lacks a poetics representing time's third domain: imprescriptible time – 'the time of jurisdiction, redress for crimes against humanity and the imperishable claims of justice.'" Catherine Renshaw, "Poetry, Irrevocable Time and Myanmar's Political Transition," *International Journal of Transitional Justice* 14 (2020): 14–34, 14, 16.

Digital Self-Determination

In its legal, political, and economic emergence and formation, modern Europe is arguably the result of globalization processes, creating an expanding sphere of competition, conflict, and antagonistic interests and concerns, but also cooperation and co-dependence. One of the central elements of the narratives that a globalized and globalizing Europe has wrapped around its persistent aspirations to 'own the world' and shape the globe in its own image is the idea of self-determination based on free will and personal liberty – securing a space of individual productivity and creativity within the larger political economies of national or transnational systems.

The most recent form of globalization processes is inherently connected to and radicalized by digitalization and the reach of international intellectual property regulations – this makes the question of what a "digital" Europe should look like an urgent one, not just as a cultural challenge to traditional notions of creative invention, authorship, and cultural productivity, but as an eminent challenge also to the political and economic stability and sovereignty of democratic societies and the privacy rights of individuals.

In this section, both contributions deal with the difficulties and dangers arising from a digitalized world, albeit in different settings and forms. In this regard, Peter Schneck explores copyright issues and law cases in times of globalization and digitalization with the example of the Netflix series *The Billion Dollar Code*, which depicts the legal case between Google and Art&Com (located in Berlin). Schneck sets forth why the series does not simply present a struggle between two understandings of copyright, but instead "dramatizes an internal tension between individualized and de-individualized, i.e., incorporated forms of creativity, a tension which is inherent to and characteristic of a global system of creative production based on digital technologies and computer programming."[1] Johannes Ueberfeldt, on the other hand, presents and analyzes the SF novel *Der Würfel* in order to show how European science fiction, like Moini's book, is relevant to questions of independence, data security, digital self-determination, and geopolitical power dependencies; he thereby presents the dangers of AI and highlights "Europe's hesitant approach to these technologies that might ultimately endanger Europe's integrity and political self-determination."[2] He sees a necessity "to create a legal framework that protects humanity from the misuse of these technologies and preserves the freedom and self-determination of the individual."[3] Ultimately, both contributions indicate that technical progress always entails new risks and challenges that need to be legally addressed. Both literature and culture seem to offer a particularly promising

1 Peter Schneck, this volume, 370.
2 Johannes Ueberfeldt, this volume, 385.
3 Johannes Ueberfeldt, this volume, 385.

https://doi.org/10.1515/9783111075693-035

space for debate in which new solutions and possibilities for the imaginative recreation and reproduction of Europe as an act of "digital self-determination" can be fruitfully imagined, envisioned, and negotiated.

Peter Schneck

Creativity Incorporated: Google, Netflix, and the Global Copyright Sphere

1 Introduction

In 2014, the Berlin-based *Designagentur* Art&Com (one of the first companies in Germany in the 1990s offering digital communication design solutions to large businesses and corporations) filed a lawsuit against Google in the U.S. The central claim was that Google had infringed on the intellectual property rights of Art&Com by essentially copying the underlying programming for the visualization and rendering of geo-data in an application that Art&Com had allegedly patented in 1996 as "TerraVision" – and which Google had used to launch its *Google Earth* viewer in 2004 to great acclaim.[4]

The suit was rather unsuccessful and eventually died in a federal appellate court (in Delaware) in 2017 – and it would have most likely been forgotten by most IP lawyers and the public at large (and probably rightfully so) if Netflix had not picked up on it, funding a German production of the story behind the court case in 2021 entitled *The Billion Dollar Code*.[5] The four-part mini-series is remarkable in more than one sense, and not just because it became somewhat of a cult hit, resonating equally with social media audiences and critical reviews in mainstream newspapers both in Germany and the U.S. The series clearly tapped into current European debates about the increasing power and legal purchase of global corporate social media networks – and while Google is the most visible in the specific context of the narrative, it is obviously not the only one referenced. Facebook, Amazon, and Twitter are likely contenders as targets of the critical comments on surveillance capitalism which frames and underlies the series' fictional rendering of the particular law case.

What is most interesting, however – especially from the perspective of law and culture in Europe –, is the way in which the series uses a rather specific legal form characteristic of U.S.-American lawsuits and pre-trial preparations, the

4 *Art+Com Innovationpool v. Google LLC,* United States Court of Appeals Federal Circuit No. 1:14-cv-00217-TBD (2017); *ArtCom Innovationpool v. Google Inc.*, U.S. District Court District of Delaware. Civil Action No. 14–217-RGA (2015). For a description of the system, see Yvan G. Leclerc and Steven Q. Lau, "TerraVision: A Terrain Visualization System," Technical Note No. 540 in *SRI International* (April 1994), 1–20.

5 *The Billion Dollar Code*, dir. Robert Thalheim, script Oliver Ziegenbalg, Netflix, 2021.

https://doi.org/10.1515/9783111075693-036

deposition. This serves as the major representational space in which the narrative of the plaintiffs is both elicited and contested at the same time. Even though there are equivalents in European and also German legal procedure – e.g., the *Eidesstattliche Erklärung* (an *affidavit*) – it is less known and rarely encountered in the filmic or cultural representation of court cases.[6] One of the central sources of the narrative energy and contest at the heart of the plot can then be seen in the attempt to adapt a European cultural narrative to a U.S.-American legal format – and in the very resistance to this adaptation. While the story appears to simply reproduce certain presumptions and cultural prejudices from the European point of view regarding the ideological underpinnings of U.S.-American legal culture, it may also, and more profitably so, be read as a critical commentary on the way in which national narratives about cultural creativity are constructed to obscure – in a strategic way – the degree of factual complicity between European and American narratives of globalization. This reading may go well beyond the conscious intentions of the creators of the mini-series, but critical overreaching in this respect is almost inevitable. It is inevitable precisely because *The Billion Dollar Code* attempts to wrap up several contending *cultural* narratives within an overall logic of legal deliberation and conflict resolution. One aim of the following discussion is to identify and interpret the role of the various narratives which the series tries to integrate and synthesize.

Moreover – and this is an aspect most likely lost both on most viewers and reviewers of the series – the deposition in the narrative is merely a rehearsal, which means it is neither the trial itself nor a deposition proper instigated on behalf of opposing counsel. Although the trial itself features prominently in the last of the four installments of the series, the character of the deposition as a "mock" stage has certain advantages for the scripting and the dramatic options of the overall narrative, most of all because it introduces a meta-discourse or "meta-trial" situation or space. This "space" is characterized above all by a constant telling and retelling of stories of origin and moments of creative invention, which then are debated and re-arranged according to their strategic potential for the upcoming trial. That is, the series "stages" the act of legal storytelling – or more precisely, it stages the act of "creating" legal narratives about creativity.

In other words, the series is as much about a certain law case involving an intellectual property dispute as it is a more general reflection about the law's

---

6 At least not in classical court room drama *à la* Hollywood. It is, however, a much more common format in more contemporary TV series, such as *The Good Wife* or *Suits*. The reason is simply that these series focus so much on the practices of law firms defending their clients and less on the actions of individual lawyers or judges in the court room, which are as integral to the trial action.

conceptions of creativity within the context of the globalization of cultural production and property. The reflection is staged as a *cultural* struggle, a contest between two distinct cultural attitudes towards copyright, creativity, and corporate globalization – this struggle is made most obvious by the different attitudes of the German plaintiffs in contrast to the representatives of the U.S.-American global tech giant. Moreover, within the legal team which presents the plaintiffs and rehearses the deposition, the two sides are also represented, namely, a German lawyer sympathetic to the stories of the original inventors of the "billion dollar code" and her American colleague, who plays the *advocatus diaboli*, putting the stories of the German creators in doubt over and over again.

As I will argue, however, it would be a thorough misunderstanding to interpret the conflict which the series presents merely in cultural terms. In fact, such a misunderstanding falls prey to the strategic force of the staged difference between distinct copyright cultures (German or European versus U.S.-American or global), whereas the real conflict is *within* an already existing global corporate copyright sphere. What marks this sphere is the gradual and inevitable de-individualization of creativity, the economic erosion, and conglomerate dissolution of the romantic ideal of individual authorship which, in *The Billion Dollar Code*, nevertheless takes aesthetic centerstage in the very moment it loses its legal viability. The series therefore does not present just one exemplary narrative, nor does it make merely one exemplary case for intellectual property; in fact, it attempts to negotiate a number of historically related narratives and cases to find a new synthesis between economic interests and cultural legitimacy.

In the following, I would like to extract and interrogate the various "narratives of intellectual property" which *The Billion Dollar Code* weaves into each other and around itself. In a rather revealing and also symptomatic manner, the series presents both a mythical narrative of the global incorporation of creativity and copyright and a surprisingly realistic assessment of the corporate investment in that mythical narrative. In consequence, the law – especially in its capacity to engender narratives and "create" legitimate authors – is the most crucial medium for instituting and negotiating the cultural legitimacy of a global copyright sphere.

2 The Copyright Wars: Europe v. America

In his massive comparative history of copyright regulation in Europe and the U.S., *The Copyright Wars*, historian Peter Baldwin has argued that current debates surrounding the expanding purview of intellectual property rights, and especially in regard to cultural production and knowledge production, are far from unprecedented. Even though the excessive propertization of cultural production today is linked to processes of technological and legal globalization, and as such appears much more radical and potentially threatening for the public sphere, Baldwin observes that the basic tension or conflict has been the same since the advent of modern copyright and author's rights for at least two centuries. For Baldwin, the challenge inherent in modern copyright was and is the same for all nations that have established complex legal frameworks to outbalance the mutual interests that govern the political economy of cultural creativity and knowledge production in general.

Baldwin identifies three major players whose interests have to be taken into account and regulated by the respective copyright laws: authors, disseminators, and the audience (i.e., the public);

> all must be kept content: the author productive, the disseminator profitable, and the audience enlightened. [. . .] If the authors become too exacting, the audience suffers. If the disseminators are greedy, or the audience miserly, culture and eventually the public domain dessicate. But within these extremes there is much room for adjustment. Will copyright laws take as their first task protecting authors? Or will they consider the audience and the public domain also as important? Seen historically, that has been the fundamental choice faced as copyright developed in the Anglo-American world and in the major continental European nations, France and Germany. [. . .] The choice between them has never been either/or but always a question of emphasis, a positioning along a spectrum. And yet the battle between these views has also been what the Germans call a *Kulturkampf*, a clash of ideologies and fundamental assumptions, that has stretched back well over two centuries.[7]

Quoting Baldwin at length is worthwhile since his interpretation of the tension between the American and European "copyright ideologies" and the stakes invested in the struggle between the two systems is helpful in revealing the main fault lines in the "transatlantic" struggle about the "uses" of cultural production within the political economy of capitalist democracies of Western provenience. As Baldwin rightfully points out, the need for a careful balance between the interests of the three major players is due to the fact that both political legitimacy and economic productivity are indispensable ingredients of the specific political systems and their link to a specific mode of production.

Cultural production has thus become the central field of negotiating the convergence but also the conflict between economy and politics in modern democracies. In other words, in this particular historical perspective, copyright regulation from its original inception onwards has always been an essential legal instrument of democratic governance in both the European and the Anglo-American context.

7 Peter Baldwin, *The Copyright Wars: Three Centuries of Trans-Atlantic Battle* (Princeton: Princeton UP, 2014), 14.

The major conflict, as Baldwin sees it, lies in the different perspective on the field of cultural production as such. While in the Anglo-American system, creative artists and writers are essentially seen as producers who participate in the political sphere via their contractual relations to the disseminators, in the European system, the creative person is a self-determined individual whose creations are the most exemplary and ideal venue to enter the public sphere as a political agent.

It is this conflict that *The Billion Dollar Code* highlights and responds to above all. In a curious, but also rather consequential move, the drama presents the technical inventors – the coders – as the true creative artists and the artists as visionary entrepreneurs. In doing so, it stresses a line of reasoning which has been increasingly put forward over the last decades in which the true creative artists of the digital age are those that follow and enhance the affordances offered by digital technologies for human practices of creation and innovation.

However, the opposition or even antagonism between the romantic artist and the disruptive tech inventor is simply more bait for the specific reading the series is aiming at, investing in clear-cut distinctions which make for good drama and cultural identification and, in the process, also completely obscure the fact that these distinctions no longer apply.

3 Art, Technology, and Creative Industries: Tradition v. Disruption

It is curious, if not a bit scandalous, that Baldwin's history of three centuries of transatlantic copyright battles does not discuss nor even mention an earlier important study of that same history by Swedish IP scholar and cultural historian Eva Hemmungs Wirtén.[8] Writing in 2004 – ten years before Baldwin – Hemmungs Wirtén discusses the same dynamic, i.e., the shifting priority of interests in the U.S.-American cultural and legal attitude towards copyright. Like Baldwin, Hemmungs Wirtén acknowledges that the U.S. has changed its attitude towards international copyright considerably from the nineteenth to the twentieth century, and she acknowledges that this change was in clear favor of the business interests of authors and disseminators over the interests of the public domain. The "tremendous historical shift" of the U.S. position in regard to "international intellectual property rights," Hemmungs Wirtén writes in a 2003 article preceding

8 Eva Hemmungs Wirtén, *No Trespassing: Authorship, Intellectual Property Rights, and the Boundaries of Globalization* (Toronto: U of Toronto P, 2004).

her book, "recasts the nation from being a developing or importing one, to being a developed and exporting one."[9] While this resonates with Baldwin's central argument about the fateful investment in author's rights being detrimental to the public interest, Hemmungs Wirtén's argument comes to rest on an explicit counter-metaphor. Whereas Baldwin speaks of the "Europeanization" of copyright in regard to the changed attitude of U.S.-American cultural producers and legislators, Hemmungs Wirtén in contrast sees the contemporary expansion of authorial and corporate interests as a clear instance of unrestrained "Americanization." Indeed, as the "relentless pursuit of ownership" in her article's title implies, her argument takes the U.S. attitude towards cultural production and creativity very much as an outgrowth of U.S.-American political and economic culture within the context of excessive globalization. For Hemmungs Wirtén – and again in contrast to Baldwin – the complete reversal of the U.S. position in regard to international copyright from the late nineteenth to the late twentieth century has to be seen within the context of rights, most specifically within the context of participation in culture and access to cultural resources:

> Intellectual property rights are important because they safeguard what makes the wheels of the information society turn: culture, information, knowledge, or, in other words, resources "of the mind." Making these rights into explicit policy is however a fairly new phenomenon in the U.S., and it is precisely the structural sea change of the global economy that made it possible. Interconnected, technology-driven, and above all, knowledge based, this economy was stimulated by products it had or could manufacture plenty of [. . .] and subsequently, U.S. companies were likely to benefit from the deregulation of global markets and the increase of transnational trade.[10]

There are two aspects worth considering in contrasting the two "histories" of European-American copyright relations and attitudes presented by Baldwin and Hemmungs Wirtén. First of all, they point to a shared understanding, even an agreement, in regard to the threat which a fully commercialized global system of cultural production presents to the public sphere as an essential element of a democratic society. Secondly, however, they diverge in their assessment of the *cultural* characteristics or dimension of the very same process they are describing. One key observation, which may help to understand the surface contradiction and the deeper complicity of the two positions, can be found in Hemmungs Wirtén's succinct remarks about the inherent dialectics invested in the justification of specific political economies of copyright and cultural creativity: "While

9 Eva Hemmungs Wirtén, "Life, Liberty and the Relentless Pursuit of Ownership," *American Studies in Scandinavia* 35.2 (2003): 85–94, 88–89.
10 Hemmungs Wirtén, "Relentless Pursuit," 89.

intellectual property rights are increasingly global, the analysis of this fact tends to relapse into an interpretation based on national or domestic experience."[11]

At first glance, *The Billion Dollar Code* thus merely seems to affirm both Baldwin's narrative of transatlantic "copyright wars" and Hemmungs Wirtén's more nuanced account of the increasing globalization of intellectual property regimes predominantly driven by U.S-American interests – but in fact it does much more than that. Indeed, the Netflix series presents a symptomatic case study revealing the sheer generative, or even creative potential of the legal and narrative image the cultural industry of the twenty-first century weaves around itself. Looking a bit closer and in more detail at the various tales of globalization which *The Billion Dollar Code* ties together, it will become obvious that the narratives of struggle and domination, with their neat and stereotypical identification of American versus European interests and ideals, are not competitive but rather complementary versions of a larger story – the *grand recit* of the global copyright sphere.[12]

4 Digital Globalization: Corporate Productivity v. Individual Authorship

As already mentioned, the main narrative sphere or dramatic "theater" in which the story of *The Billion Dollar Code* unfolds is characterized by a particular legal format, the deposition. Depositions are accepted means of discovery and pre-trial litigation, and they may be used by opposing counsel to explore the knowledge of witnesses to prepare for in-court questioning. The purpose of a deposition and its difference from trial interrogation can be described as follows:

> The deposition is taken at the request of opposing counsel for the purpose of discovering what a witness knows and how this may impact their case. Because it is generally conducted by the opposing counsel, the process of asking questions is called cross examination. Unlike questions asked at trial, questions asked during a typical deposition may pursue avenues

11 Hemmungs Wirtén, *No Trespassing*, 145.

12 The term refers to Lyotard's famous observation of the failure and breakdown of the essential narratives of Western modernization, thereby affirming the critical and elegiacal impulses of the postmodern moment – and yet at the same time highlighting the potential reaffirmation of such narratives in the age of corporate creativity and digital globalization. Jean-François Lyotard, *The Postmodern Condition* (Madison: U of Wisconsin P, 1984). For the specific function and rhetoric of such "narratives of globalization," see Néstor García Canclini, *Imagined Globalization* (Durham: Duke UP, 2016).

> suggested by each answer, and questions may be asked in a way that does not present an organized synthesis of the witness' knowledge.
>
> At trial, however, witnesses are examined by their own attorney first; thus, there is an opportunity to logically and completely present the testimony. On cross examination, the attorney who took the deposition will attempt to use information from the deposition to limit or constrain the earlier testimony.[13]

This format, already rather specific in its function of providing or eliciting (or even forcing) evidence for the actual trial by way of recorded oral examination *before* the trial, is even more peculiar in the series because here the deposition is a *staged* deposition arranged by the lawyers who represent the plaintiff (Art&-Com) in preparation for the trial. Only in the final installment does the narrative eventually move into the sphere of the trial, i.e., the theater of justice itself. This is clearly meant to be read as a process of development or even adaptation of European sentiments and notions of justice towards accepting and realizing U.S.-American professional practices and standards of adjudicative justice.[14]

Repeatedly and insistently, the German inventors of Art&Com are reminded of the significant particularities of the American jury trial, specifically pointing out that they need to adjust their "stories" to the expectations of the jury and the adversarial logic of contested narratives which dominates the American legal system. This particular "emplotment" of enlisting useful elements of biographical storytelling while ignoring others is constantly reflected upon, with the result that the narrative seems to be "doubling down" on its own content, strategically investing in adapting the factual and biographical to the conditions of legal storytelling.

This self-reflexive doubling of the narrative situation, which could be described as a "cultural narrative in search of a legal narrative," allows the plot to branch out into competitive versions of the same basic narrative, literally exploring and discussing different modes or strategies of emplotment for the sake of a story which is historically and legally "true." As it turns out, the true "history" of globalization is a matter of conflict and struggle between various versions of the same narrative seen and constructed from different perspectives. What makes *The Billion Dollar Code* so interesting is that it attempts to reveal and, at the same time, obscure the ways in which this globalization narrative has been constructed

---

13 Beatrice Crofts Yorker, "Providing Deposition Testimony in a Legal Case," *AAOHN Journal* 42.12 (1994): 601–606, 602.

14 The preparation and adaptation culminate in a lesson with a trial coach shortly before the trial. Here the plaintiffs are being coached what to say and how to say it in court. When Juri Müller (one of the major protagonists [see section below]) in the trial sticks to the script, the trial coach is shown as approving; when Müller appears to veer away, however, he has to be brought back "on track" as it were by his former colleague.

and reconstructed by the law. In fact, the law, and crucially in its most modern, diversified form as intellectual or immaterial property law, assumes the central narrative agency in the actual "case" that the series tries to argue. Not in terms of the law, however, but to culture at large: the case about the legitimate appropriation and presentation of the world itself.

This is a tall order, to be sure, but the legal struggle presented and staged in *The Billion Dollar Code* is wrapped into resonant and interwoven narrative layers which translate the U.S. versus Europe "copyright wars" into a larger (indeed global) struggle between corporate power and productivity on the one hand and individual creativity and freedom on the other. This is largely the effect of the format of the deposition which strongly individualizes the plaintiff side by focusing on the narratives of the two major German protagonists, the former art and design student and founder of Art&Com, Carsten Schlüter, and the computer programmer and former hacker, Juri Müller, who wrote the code for TerraVision.[15] The deposition forms the legal stage for their biographical narratives, and thus the scenes of the interrogation by the legal team are interspersed with anecdotal fragments from their past. These come in the form of short clips in which the plaintiffs' testimonies come alive as narratives in their own right, namely the retelling of a particular moment in the history of digital culture and media incorporation in the 1990s in a specific location, a recently re-united Germany and its new, also re-united capital, Berlin.

On the one hand, this allows the story to locate the origin of the case historically in a period of political transition from a communist to a democratic system, which, at the same time, is marked by a moment of economic opportunity and transformation with the aggressive capitalization on the ruinous state of the East German economy as well as the expanding corporate push towards digital media and communication technologies. This nexus between political and economic moments of disruption literally creates a space of invention in which technological creativity becomes situated and has to be calibrated between artistic and

15 The narrative shifts between the deposition (the abstract legal sphere) and the biographical narratives (the concrete "authentic" historical sphere), cast with different actors for each sphere, visually marking the passage of historical and biographical time between the late 1990s and 2017 (presumably the time of the fictional jury trial which concludes with the appellate decision). This adds to the individualization of the testimonies of the plaintiff side. The narrative structure is inverted in the presentation of the defendant side (i.e., Google), which is presented in the legal sphere of the deposition by proxy only by the critical lawyer before it can become fully individualized – again only in the legal sphere with the appearance in court of the "individual" antagonist, Brian Anderson, whose testimony eventually convinces the jury to reject the plaintiff's claim.

commercial values and interests.[16] In this perspective, the very name of the design agency, Art&Com, is both a historically correct index of that space of innovation emerging between old and overcome notions of artistic creation and new forms of computational creativity as well as a programmatic expression of the synthesis of artistic creation, commercial interests, and the investment characteristic of the process of digital globalization. But Art&Com also hints at the important emerging interface between aesthetics and communication technologies especially prevalent from the 1990s onwards in the intensive discussions of interface design as artistic modulations, i.e., creations in their own right.

Moreover, and maybe even more effectively, the historical and political situatedness and the recalibration of creativity in the context of digital globalization allows the story to gradually transform the case from a patent case to a copyright case, changing its legal narrative, as it were, by the emphatic individualization and historization of its cultural and political narrative. The difference between patent and copyright as two related, but distinct, legal forms of securing and protecting intellectual property rights is worth noting as it has a particular importance for the singular effects of the narrative, but it also may help to reveal the rather different readings of the case the narrative attempts to reconcile.[17]

While patent law and copyright law are often regarded as similar in kind, albeit different in the degree of protection they offer for intellectual property, there remain two major distinctions in regard to the normative and technical aspects of the two formats. One aspect refers to the functionality / non-functionality distinction between inventions which are subject to patent or copyright protection; another aspect refers to the privilege/rights distinction, i.e., the distinction between

16 This "space" of invention is represented in the story in the flashbacks from the 1990s, but also at the end as an actual space, a kind of undeveloped wasteland in the center of Berlin where the young Schlüter and Müller meet to share beer and *Döner Kebab* (a signature street food of the time) and talk about the digital future of the globe and their visualization models. The space was made possible by the fall of the Berlin Wall, but only for a short time before the vast strip of wasteland which the Wall had occupied was appropriated and incorporated by the architecture of global media companies, e.g., Sony. This clearly alludes to the development and restructuring of the Potsdamer Platz area from a space of confrontation between capitalist and communist systems to a "globalized" incorporated space.

17 The following discussion focuses on U.S. patent and copyright law and the debate about software programs as protectable works – a rather complex and convoluted debate that can only be touched upon by citing exemplary positions characteristic for the U.S.-American legal system. Yet the debate itself and the differences between patent and copyright protection can be found in other systems as well. The examples taken from the U.S. legal context may also be found in other legal contexts, e.g., EU law and its reaction to the protection of software programs.

the different ways in which the rights vested in patent and in copyright protection are claimed and come into effect. Thus, while both patent and copyright law are meant to provide "an incentive for the creation of works desired by society and recognizing in some fair and just way the efforts of their creators" thereby "insuring a broad public domain that permits later inventors and authors to build on the existing foundation to advance technology and culture for the overall benefit of society," they are also "radically different," as Dennis S. Karjala has pointed out:

> Patents must be narrowly claimed and protection is narrowly limited to the claim. Patents must be approved by administrative authorities, must involve a "nonobvious" and not simply a normal engineering advance, and remain valid for twenty years from filing. Copyrights, on the other hand, come into existence automatically, with no requirement that the rightsholder specify precisely which aspects of her work are protected and which are not. The work need only be "original" in the sense of being the intellectual work product of the author and not "novel" or "new" in any absolute sense.[18]

This distinction refers to the parallel historical emergence of patents and copyright as licensing instruments; the first clearly remained to be viewed as a privilege granted by a higher authority, while the second gradually developed to be understood as a (natural) right (of creators of individual works) under a specific protecting statute. In other words, whereas patents were "created rights," copyright "developed into something more than a mere privilege. It became an inherent right."[19]

But there is another, even more crucial reason why patents and copyright are seen as different forms of protecting creative inventions, and this regards the degree of functionality, or in other words, how the "product" or result of individual creativity is seen in its "usefulness" for the public good. As Karjala warns, functionality as such is not to be confused with usefulness, because then there would be no difference between the subject matter of patent versus copyright protection. But there are different degrees of usefulness embedded in the U.S. copyright clause. While many works are protected by copyright because they are useful, "there is a subcategory of 'usefulness' that has generally be excluded from copyright protection [. . .] if [the work] performs some utilitarian (or useful) task *other than* to inform, entertain, or portray an appearance to human beings."[20] From this

18 Dennis S. Karjala, "The Relative Role of Patent and Copyright in the Protection of Computer Programs," *John Marshall Journal of Computer and Information Law* 17.1 (1998): 41–74, 44, 45.
19 Edward C. Waterscheid, "Inherent or Created Rights: Early Views on the Intellectual Property Clause," *Hamline Law Review* 19.1 (1995): 81–106, 84.
20 Karjala, "Protection of Computer Programs," 46.

perspective (inscribed in U.S. law), "patents protect creative, *functional* invention; copyright protects creative, *nonfunctional* authorship."[21]

Within the context of functionality and usefulness, software programming presents a particular challenge – a challenge which serves as another narrative impulse and produces a hidden or rather unobtrusive narrative layer in *The Billion Dollar Code*. The retelling of the real patent case in terms of a copyright case is not so much a deliberate or merely strategic dramaturgic ploy as it is an unconscious reaction to the legal (mis-)interpretation of software authorship in a series of decisions in U.S.-American courts and in copyright acts since the mid-1970s. These decisions and acts basically inscribed into law an understanding of software programs as "means of expression" in the same way as works of literature. When Congress passed the 1980 Copyright Act it "endorsed the notion that the same principles that apply to traditional literary works should govern computer programs."[22]

Obviously, from the perspective of mere functionality, a computer program (which is the subject matter in need of protection) is "produced for the purely functional purpose of causing a computer to perform a particular task or set of tasks. Computer programs are, in short, technology – the technology for using computers."[23] They may thus be protected by patent law but need not be protected by copyright. However, from the perspective of copyright law, software *programming* (hence the *practice* of creating the program) may be regarded as a highly individualized form of expression and creative achievement, as a defender of the copyright view on software programming emphasizes:

> Computer programs and other more traditional literary works, and the processes by which they are created, are quite similar. Computer programs, like other literary works, are expressive. The imagination, originality, and creativity involved in writing a program is comparable to that involved in more time-honored literary works [. . .]. Moreover, programming entails a significant degree of individuality. Just as no two novelists independently would compose the same detailed plot of the downfall of a tragic hero, or the travails of star-crossed lovers, or the consequences of making a pact with the devil, no two programmers independently would design a program that enabled the computer to solve highly intricate problems with the same structural details, let alone precisely the same set of instructions.[24]

Both legal precedent and statutory legislation in U.S. patent and copyright law would thus provide for a reading of *The Billion Dollar Code* as a consequent and

21 Karjala, "Protection of Computer Programs," 45; emphasis in the original.

22 Arthur R. Miller "Copyright Protection for Computer Programs, Databases, and Computer-Generated Works: Is Anything New since CONTU?," *Harvard Law Review* 106.5 (1993): 977–1073, 983.

23 Karjala, "Protection of Computer Programs," 42.

24 Miller, "Copyright Protection," 983, 984.

rather plausible translation of the legal and cultural underpinnings of the case – yet comparison to the actual trial documents in no way supports this reading. On the contrary, it clearly shows that the series does not follow the reasoning of the appellate court nor the reasoning of the jury trial.

A close look at the final decision reveals that the reasoning of the law is predominantly based on patent law considerations and premises – copyright issues or concerns are glaringly absent, especially in regard to questions of individuality, authorship, or originality. The appellate court does not look at the program as a "literary work," i.e., the outcome of *individual* creativity – it instead looks at the different versions of the program from the perspective of a longer, continuous process of corporate productivity. That process is marked by a rather de-individualized form of invention in which programs are ideas and technological tools which are exchanged and optimized by various corporate teams. Indeed, the fluidity and dynamics inherent in this process of corporate creativity completely render the question of individual originality and authorship irrelevant; at least in the perspective of U.S. patent law, programming is a collective work, and there can be no infringement because the essential elements of the code were widely known before Art&Com claimed a patent for their version of TerraVision.[25]

While *The Billion Dollar Code* retells the patent case from the perspective of copyright, as it were, it does not pitch a European perspective on creativity and authorship against an American one. Indeed, as a closer look at the legal reaction to software programming since the 1970s shows, the individualized copyright / authorship perspective and the incorporated patent perspective offered competing, sometimes even overlapping, venues for claiming protection for creative work opening a sphere where creative authorship and corporate productivity could be

25 The appellate decision is full of technical details which clearly refer to the functionality of the program but never refer to the originality of the program itself. In affirming the decision of the lower court (which was the outcome of a jury trial), the appellate court also affirms the reasoning which convinced the jury. The major point in the reasoning was that what Art&Com claimed as innovative and new in their patent regarding their visualization program had indeed been already used and shared by other programmers before that time – among them individuals who worked for Art&Com and others who ended up working with Google. The decision in both cases was based on *patentability*, which is a status required for the work to be patented. The court argued that the program elements in question had already reached that status when their functionality was proven (and shared) in public. This means that even though Art&Com claimed a patent for their program before Google claimed one for Google Earth, the essential code elements had been used and proven fully functional before either patent came into effect. There is no infringement then, because both patents have the same point of origin (at least in regard to the code elements which Art&Com claimed as original).

seen as complementary claims, as a most useful and fully functional form of incorporated authorship and creativity.

The Netflix series therefore does not simply stage a struggle between two distinct *cultural* understandings of copyright and authorship; instead it pointedly dramatizes an internal tension between individualized and de-individualized, i.e., incorporated forms of creativity, a tension which is inherent to and characteristic of a *global* system of creative production based on digital technologies and computer programming. That tension has been rather effectively negotiated and reconciled by IP law and its transnational purview in the process of the ever-increasing global propertization of individual creativity, expression, and productivity. While the narrative achieves its dramatic effects mostly by individualizing the opposing parties of the case, there can be no doubt that there would be no case without the law of intellectual property and the corporate lawyers who bring these cases forward. The conflict between individual claims for originality and corporate claims for IP protection is acknowledged and dramatized in a sphere that is itself fully incorporated. The series does not hide this fact; indeed, it turns it into an essential narrative device by using the deposition form as the major structural element for eliciting, arranging, and finally reconstructing the "true" story of creative invention and original authorship.

5 Owning the World: Access v. Control

In the global copyright sphere, the fate of creative authorship as the most truly individual and original form of expression is at stake – at least, that appears to be the central argument of the reconstructed narrative of globalization which *The Billion Dollar Code* presents. Told by two German protagonists but elicited and re-arranged by U.S.-American lawyers within the context of U.S.-American law, the narrative does not come about by itself, but it is rather "re-discovered" with the help of the legal form by which it turns from historical and biographical memory into witness account and testimony; that is, admissible legal evidence. In the most obvious moment of rearrangement, the narrative brought about by legal storytelling counterfactually "wins" the case. In a completely fictionalized conclusion, the triumphant plaintiffs Art&Com return to their Berlin headquarters to celebrate their victory, a scene which viewers unfamiliar with the case and its outcome most likely will accept and even welcome as a rather plausible and justified decision, thereby affirming the persuasive power of the legal narrative which the series spins. But here the narrative outruns itself and reveals itself *as fiction* by coming to a complete halt, by literally stopping the filmic representation, first by slowing down, freezing, and eventually reversing the sequence of images, running the scene of celebration backwards to return to the real trial and its actual outcome.

The final rearrangement which is meant to "reveal" the reason for the actual decision is no longer part of the legal narrative constructed with the help of the deposition. It belongs completely to the sphere of dramatic performance as an individual act of creative fiction and an act of deception. In the dramatic climax, the programmer antagonist, Brian Anderson, supposedly the "inventor" of Google Earth, testifies before the jury (a completely fictionalized scene and irrelevant to the final decision). The performance of the surprise witness is framed in the series' narrative by the voice of Carsten Schlüter, who announces Anderson's testimony by pointing out that Anderson should have truthfully admitted that "Google Earth would have been impossible without TerraVision," but what Anderson then actually says on the stand is presented directly to the spectators, who become part of the jury, as it were. The Google programmer then delivers a pathetic speech about how and why he "created" Google Earth to bring together people from all over the world in peace and harmony, regardless of their country of origin – to create a utopian space without borders and conflicts that anyone can inhabit by simply using the program. This not only contradicts (by obvious omission) the statement about the true originality of TerraVision versus Google Earth, but the very pathos of the speech and the utopia of free access and peaceful globality also amounts to an act of blatant appropriation. For it was exactly the dream of universal access to the globe (in its visual form) which prompted the efforts of the younger and more idealist Schlüter to create a form of public art enhanced by technology, and which also affected the hacker and activist temperament of the younger Müller when he started to program what would eventually become TerraVision. The Google witness thus appropriates a particular discourse or version of globalization as the increasing reconciliation of aesthetic and political universality and equality.

This particular ending – exposing the underlying strategic deceitfulness of Google's global vision (which originally stated "Do no evil") – refers back to the very beginning of the series, which shows some documentary footage of, among other things, demonstrations against globalized forms of data appropriation and identity propertization by surveillance capitalism. As a corporate narrative in its own right, *The Billion Dollar Code* thus stages itself as yet another critical globalization narrative at the intersection of art and commerce, dressing up the patent case as an example for a far more universal and political struggle between creative citizenship and corporate disenfranchisement. It certainly does not make Netflix a more democratic enterprise, but it may help to obstruct the fatal state of incorporated creativity with the soothing balm of resistance and the continuing myth of individual authorship and freedom of creative invention. In a final act of resistance, Müller hacks a playlist in the American club where they meet for a farewell drink with their German-American lawyer. When they are driven out of the club by the angry owner, Schlüter and Müller make their way home on foot, while the lawyer enters a driverless minivan to get to the airport on her way to the next copyright or patent case, prepared to spin yet another narrative about the global copyright sphere and the fate of individual authorship.

Johannes Ueberfeldt

Freedom, Human Dignity, and Digital Self-Determination: European Perspectives in Speculative Fiction

> Firstly, science fiction can be *enjoyed* as art, and secondly, it can be employed to *think* of things and conditions that would have remained unthought-of without it.* – Dietmar Dath

1 Introduction

We live in a time that challenges human rights – not only within the digital realm, but digital self-determination is also closely related to fundamental human rights.[1] Given the mounting problems surrounding web anonymity, lack of encryption (in the case of web communication), Internet censorship, phishing, and other types of fraud, ransomware, hacking, etc., the digital space and digital self-determination have become increasingly endangered. In addition to this, artificial intelligence and machine learning continue to evolve, which could eventually lead to mass surveillance and totalitarian control problems of a kind that are, as yet, only known from works of science fiction. Most of these science fiction[2] visions – not counting space operas like *Star Wars*[3] – are rather dystopian,[4] presenting a bleak technology-driven future.[5] In contrast to notions of utopia, which represent a place of future

1 See, e.g., Michelle Bachelet, "Human Rights and Democracy in the Digital Age," (April 25, 2022), *United Nations: Media Center* <https://www.ohchr.org/en/statements/2022/04/human-rights-and-democracy-digital-age> (acc. May 1, 2022), n. pag.

2 Science fiction will be abbreviated as "SF" in the following.

3 *Star Wars*, dir. George Lucas, Lucasfilm Ltd., 1977.

4 Although the terms 'science fiction' and 'dystopia' are not interchangeable, there is a great deal of intersection between the SF and dystopian genres.

5 SF, in contrast to other fantastical genres, has a closer relationship to reality, since the depicted world is compatible with the known natural laws of our world, or suggests a higher scientific plausibility. Cf. Roland Innerhofer, "Science Fiction" in *Phantastik: Ein interdisziplinäres Handbuch*, ed. Hans Richard Brittnacher and Markus May (Stuttgart: Metzler, 2013), 318–328, 318.

* My translation: "Man kann Science Fiction erstens als Kunst *genießen*, und man kann mit ihr zweitens Dinge und Verhältnisse *denken*, die ohne sie ungedachte bleiben müssten." Dietmar Dath, *Niegeschichte: Science Fiction als Kunst- und Denkmaschine* (Berlin: Matthes & Seitz, 2019), 21.

https://doi.org/10.1515/9783111075693-037

happiness, in dystopias, an undesirable place is presented.[6] Its function is to warn of current developments that could lead to an undesirable future.[7] While most modern dystopian texts convey an American perspective, or present a Western view but exclude Europe as a setting, it is in fact precisely Europe's future that is thrown into uncertainty, both economically and politically.[8] Bijan Moini's SF novel *Der Würfel*[9] conceives a dystopian future from the European perspective; one that is on a superficial level carefree, since mankind has traded self-determination for secured prosperity, but nevertheless addresses issues relevant to contemporary European politics.

The purpose of this essay is not to examine the social value of prognostic literature in general and SF specifically,[10] but to show why European science fiction like Moini's book is relevant to questions of independence, data security, digital self-determination, and geopolitical power dependencies.

In the following article, I will first introduce SF as a concept and a theory, using literature and film examples to help provide an understanding of its functions and perspectives. Subsequently, after a short plot summary of *Der Würfel*, I will explore its special status and its distinctiveness in relation to traditional SF. Lastly, I will discuss the implications for Europe's future.

2 The Prognostic Function of SF

As indicated above, SF does not deal with real conditions, and the bleak vision of the future it often presents, created by the harmful potentiality of unregulated technologies and developments, are perhaps unlikely to materialize in reality – or, in Dietmar Dath's words: "Science fiction tells stories of incidents that have never happened and never will happen. It is tremendously improbable that the imagination will fathom something in world-adequate density of detail

6 Cf. Peter Kuon, "Utopie/Dystopie" in *Phantastik*, 328–335, 334.

7 Kuon, "Utopie/Dystopie," 334.

8 This uncertainty is rooted in the questionable unity of the European Union (including the rightward shift of some European governments), the increasing economic dependence on the dominant U.S. and Asian systems, as well as the threatening loss of political and economic power when human rights concerns are voiced.

9 The title can be translated as *The Cube*, or maybe, rather, *The Die* (the German title is ambiguous). Bijan Moini, *Der Würfel: Roman* (Zurich: Atrium, 2018). Further references in the text, abbreviated as "DW."

10 On the one hand, there is presently not enough space for such a task; on the other hand, it has already been written about by many other authors.

that subsequently becomes real."[11] Nevertheless, although SF literature seems quite irrelevant to the real world, it should still be read, because preventing potential hazards today may become impossible in the future.

According to Stanisław Lem, all literature has three functions: (i) an informative, (ii) a didactic, and (iii) an entertaining function. SF literature additionally offers a prognostic function,[12] which is fulfilled by enriching the narrated world (*diegesis*) with an imagined element, which Darko Suvin calls *novum*.[13] This *novum* is the missing variable in the real world, which turns the exposition into an experimental arrangement and the *narratio* into a thought experiment.

In most cases, the *novum* is – not surprisingly for the genre – a scientific device, an invention that results in sidestepping our current knowledge of the world to bring about a vastly different future. Still, the most shocking examples are prognostic visions displaying different iterations of AI-controlled societies, posthuman life, or other extrapolations based upon our current processing in a digitized world.

Since the days of early SF, novels and short stories such as the works of Jules Verne or H.G. Wells – for the early German SF, most notably Kurd Lasswitz – have not only invested their futuristic diegetic worlds with technical advancements and new opportunities, but also with technical or environmental threats. Ironically, most technological advancements are not intrinsically hazardous but only become so by human misuse – often through creating artificial sentient beings that end up outperforming human beings. George Orwell's *Nineteen Eighty-Four*[14] is the most obvious example of this technology-driven totalitarianism.

In some stories, however, it is not solely due to human carelessness – or plain stupidity – alone, but another intelligence (albeit often man-made) that, after attaining consciousness, threatens society by attempting to enslave or obliterate humanity. Various examples of these narrative schemes can be found in the history of literature and pop culture. From a German perspective, Fritz Lang's film *Metropolis* and the homonymous literary template by Thea von Harbou[15] come to mind. In Michael Crichton's biotechnological thriller *Jurassic Park*[16] (and

11 My translation: "Science Fiction erzählt Geschichten von Vorkommnissen, die nie geschehen sind und nie geschehen werden. Es ist ungeheuer unwahrscheinlich, dass die Fantasie etwas in weltadäquater Detaildichte errät, das anschließend wirklich wird." Dath, *Niegeschichte*, 14.

12 Cf. Stanisław Lem, *Phantastik und Futurologie: 1. Teil* (Frankfurt a.M.: Insel Verlag, 1977), 10.

13 Cf. Darko Suvin, *Poetik der Science Fiction* (Frankfurt a.M.: Suhrkamp, 1979).

14 George Orwell, *Nineteen Eighty-Four: A Novel* (London: Secker & Warburg, 1949).

15 Thea von Harbou, *Metropolis* (Frankfurt a.M.: Ullstein, 1984).

16 Michael Crichton, *Jurassic Park* (London: Arrow Books, 1991).

its even more popular movie adaptation by Steven Spielberg[17] which, although toned down in violence and cultural pessimism, is still frightening) biologically engineered dinosaurs threaten mankind as a result – naturally – of human greed. To cite another popular example, in the *Terminator*[18] universe, the original man-made threat is not the singular eponymous killer machine named T-800 (famously played by Arnold Schwarzenegger), but the neural net-based artificial intelligence 'Skynet,' which has gained self-awareness and, in response to humans trying to deactivate it, retaliates with a nuclear strike that wipes most of humanity from the Earth.

Most of these works, and especially the Hollywood movies – an exception being Fritz Lang's *Metropolis* –, only show U.S.-based developments or planetary catastrophes from an American point of view. Moreover, most of them depict a solely dystopian scenario, which, while displaying the positive intentions of the failed research or development, respectively, do not present the viewer with an ambiguous outcome that shows both the positive and negative results – or allow the viewer to evaluate the situation themselves.

In Bijan Moini's novel, both aspects matter. Regarding the aforementioned perspective, the setting is Europe, and more specifically, Germany. The rest of the world is mentioned, and here the special role of Europe is already apparent as it is completely under AI control. The Europeans fear being pulverized between the U.S. and Asian hegemonies. Regarding the ambiguity of technological developments, the novel exhibits a future of prosperity, without unemployment or poverty, but with a basic income generated by the work of artificial intelligence. To an extent, Moini reinterprets Orwell's vision of the modern technological paradigm and the contemporary demands of a post-work society[19] and adds a legal focal point. In the following, the ideology underlying the novel and its legal implications will be explored.

3 *Cubism*: Both Sides of the Coin

The dystopian SF novel *Der Würfel* is set in the not-too-distant future, perhaps some fifteen or twenty years ahead of our present. The reader is asked to imagine a Germany where digitization has actually been implemented – to an unimaginable

17 *Jurassic Park*, dir. Steven Spielberg, Universal Pictures, 1993.

18 *The Terminator*, dir. James Cameron, Cinema '84, 1984.

19 It builds on the socialist idea of total work automation for the greater good. See, e.g., Andy Beckett, "Post-Work: The Radical Idea of a World without Jobs," (January 19, 2018), *The Guardian* <https://www.theguardian.com/news/2018/jan/19/post-work-the-radical-idea-of-a-world-without-jobs> (acc. May 1, 2022), n. pag.

degree of perfection. The country is controlled by an omnipotent algorithm: The "cube"[20] (or the die) enables people to live a carefree life. The most intimate data is exchanged for the prosperity of all, which is called *cubism*[21] in an AI-governed pseudo-utilitarian totalitarian system.[22] One benefit of this is that the system pays everyone a basic income and, thanks to pervasive surveillance, crime is reduced to near zero. To achieve this outcome, the cube collects every person's most intimate data. Predictability, enabled by Big Data, has thus become the greatest good. The book follows the twenty-eight-year-old protagonist, Taso, who is struggling within a system that has rendered him a misfit, unwilling to contribute to this prescribed self-abandonment. Taso lives in a city where his every step is watched, analyzed, and archived; where reality and simulations are difficult to differentiate. Even before the change of government, the so-called "Referendum," Taso had been a member of the anti-cubist movement, making him a so-called 'juggler'[23] – as he tries to conceal every part of his life, his true identity including his thoughts and feelings from the *cube*. In situations where he cannot escape the AI-driven total surveillance, he randomizes his actions with die rolls and coin flips.

The aforementioned premise of the novel is the fact that technology has two sides to it. Technological progress may come at a cost that is not immediately apparent at first – or remains concealed by compelling yet elusive promises. In such a vein, the citizen becomes transparent, has very little agency, but nevertheless receives economic security, a basic income, and the assurance that they do not have to fear crime. To make matters worse (or perhaps better), the novel not only presents us with both sides of the coin but contrasts Taso's fight against the cube with characters whose lives have considerably improved through cubism; people who used to suffer in our pre-cubist system and thus fear the demise of cubism.[24]

---

20 Both meanings of the German term *Würfel* (English "cube" *or* "die") are of relevance. The die throwing element of randomness explains the main protagonist's intention to remain unpredictable to the algorithm; *Würfel* as a geometric shape is frequently used in architecture as well as describing artificial intelligence's real-world embodiment. Ironically, both extensions are juxtaposed in the novel: the ordered geometry of the AI and the randomized subversion methods of the countermovement.

21 *Kubismus* in the German original.

22 On a side note, although the novel may not primarily be categorized as 'cyberpunk,' it covers many topics of this subgenre. Cyberpunk is both a SF subgenre, aesthetic style (and to a degree a political stance) and deals with political and social problems. Above all, it depicts the fusion and/or coexistence of humans and technology. Cf. Jiré Emine Gözen, *Cyberpunk Science Fiction: Literarische Fiktionen und Medientheorie* (Bielefeld: transcript, 2012).

23 *Gaukler* in the German original.

24 This is a common argument in the debate over data security, because poor people, it is argued, are able to use free services that would not be free without Big Data.

As we have seen above, as a work of SF, the book provides a prognostic picture. It objectifies and concretizes abstract concepts such as encryption, digital surveillance, filter algorithms, or machine learning. With respect to the prognostic function of SF that Lem describes in *Phantastik und Futurologie*, novels like *Der Würfel* might operate as a playtest (experimental setup) presenting a possible future that humanity might wish to pursue or prevent. By pointing out the possible dystopian outcomes, the novel provides its readers with the ideas and tools to control technology in a more beneficial way, without any harmful side effects. Particularly with regard to law, the novel illustrates how dichotomized the idealism of the individual and the true consequences of AI implementation really are.

4 Squaring the Law

As we have seen, the novel illuminates the potential uses and imminent threats of contemporary technical and social developments. Besides the dystopian implications (and its European perspective), the book fascinates in particular when being looked at from the perspective of law and literature. Both its author Bijan Moini and his protagonist Taso are lawyers by profession. Moreover, the aforementioned issues around digital self-determination are, in reality, legal considerations – presented in a fictional futuristic *diegesis*, which is not so far removed from the world we live in right now,[25] when one extrapolates contemporary data protection issues. The novel presents us with what might well transpire to be the next step in the ongoing development of our society. Regarding the practical work of a lawyer, the novel introduces a data-driven automatization of the legal system, resulting in a degradation of human personnel. Analogous to the overall passivity of consumerist behavior, the diegetic lawyers lack basic professional agency, occupying the last soon-to-be-closed gaps of an otherwise omnipotent artificial intelligence. The following example is intended to illustrate this shift in legal competence and capacity:

> Taso booted his work software "Insta-Supervision." When he had started law school ten years ago, he had imagined his future work differently. He had dreamed of passionate pleadings and thrilling witness hearings, of justice and exciting stories from real life that he

25 Besides, it is placed in Berlin and some of the buildings described in the novel exist already there today, which creates a realistic effect. According to Rottensteiner, the diegetic vision can be described as a 'secondary world' with authentic ties to our real world. Cf. Franz Rottensteiner, *Erkundungen im Nirgendwo: Kritische Streifzüge durch das phantastische Genre* (Passau: Erster Deutscher Fantasy Club, 2003).

> would tell or about which he would judge. [. . .] But then "Instalaw" was launched. The program decided legal disputes ad hoc: From smart recordings and all the other data on the cube, it determined what had happened and passed judgment. (DW, 74)[26]

"Instalaw" as a name serves two purposes (and attacks the legal system on two fronts). First, the law is not an act of negotiation anymore, but a positivist equation that can be evaluated at any time. The assumed benefit is transparency. Every person knows at any time the consequences of violating the law. But on a sublevel, this transparency is a mere illusion, because the only thing known is the penalty; the basis for it and the way it is calculated are hidden.[27] The second benefit is efficiency: The algorithms' runtime outperforms the sluggish judicial systems; this saves costs and results in immediate investigation of the crime and direct response to the criminals,[28] but – in combination with the first point – simplifies the procedure from a discursive to a static, normative one. Although the chance of a wrongful conviction is massively reduced (without being ruled out completely), legal action against a specific conviction becomes near impossible. The consequence is that people are pushed out of the legal system. The hierarchy matrix relegates them below the AI, which is why they are then guarded and punished without direct access to the legal system.

Not only is each individual tracked and analyzed by the cube to a ridiculous degree, but they are then evaluated and accounted for using a so-called 'PRED score,' which measures the predictability of individual behavior. Social status is contingent on the quantity and coherence of data collected about each person. This means that the "Instalaw" system might not even be relevant in the diegetic future, because crimes may be countered before they happen, with criminals being imprisoned or terminated before they can harm society, resulting in a law and order setup known from SF *dieges*es such as that, for example, in *Minority Report*.[29]

26 My translation: "Taso startete seine Arbeitssoftware 'Insta-Supervision.' Als er vor zehn Jahren mit dem Jurastudium begonnen hatte, hatte er sich seine künftige Arbeit anders vorgestellt. Er hatte von leidenschaftlichen Plädoyers und aufreibenden Zeugenvernehmungen geträumt, von Gerechtigkeit und spannenden Geschichten aus dem prallen Leben, die er erzählen oder über die er urteilen würde. [. . .] Dann aber wurde 'Instalaw' eingeführt. Das Programm entschied Rechtsstreite ad hoc: Aus Smartsaufnahmen und allen anderen Daten des Würfels ermittelte es, was passiert war, und fällte ein Urteil."

27 This is how Big Data companies like Google operate nowadays. They offer a service that is seemingly for free use without explaining the basis of calculation and data storage. The algorithm (the capital of these companies) is guarded like a state secret.

28 It thus massively reduces criminality regarding the directly mediated causality of potential crimes.

29 The idea suggests itself that such a system could also react by uniformally eradicating any human danger, which in turn would be equivalent to the aforementioned Skynet structure in the *Terminator* franchise.

After highlighting the connections and problems between the dis- or hyperfunctional legal system and an AI beyond human control, as well as a possible downward spiral of rights protection, I want to turn to the second significant element of the novel, the specifically European perspective. Before, however, I discuss the latter, the questions must first be answered to what extent this scenario would be conceivable in our world, and to what extent Taso's subversion strategies have real-world counterparts.

5 Is *Cubism* a Real Threat?

In view of the implications of a totalitarian Big Data intelligence and its ramifications in terms of law and digital self-determination, the burning question is: Are we at the very beginning of this transition to open data and transparent citizens, or are we already in the middle of it? To put it another way: Is this novel still SF or has it already become reality?

One problem currently is that the more data is stored, the more transparent the citizens become and the more difficult it will be to ensure future data protection. Or, to rephrase, the more difficult it will be to return to a point in time before Big Data. An additional problem is that the novel paints a world where power is still in the hands of the state agencies – steered by parliament or AI. But in our reality, data is stored by private corporations.[30] It would be an impossible task to erase all the data stored by just one nation. Moreover, from a European perspective, the people of Europe are losing their self-determination twice over, as the majority of the so-called 'data kraken' are non-European, which renders the situation much more complex and less specific in reality. We are not dealing with one isolated cube structure that stores our data, but with many such structures. This process is less conspicuous, less transparent, and ridiculously complex.

What the novel does manage to do, however, is make abstract concepts and techniques concrete. In *Der Würfel*, virtual entities are given a diegetic topographical equivalent. The digital world is becoming increasingly complex, and even digital natives run the risk of losing their grip on data security, of becoming desensitized. A good example is the picture of the "Cryptocenter," which denominates a building where people can go to disguise their identity. This is a concretization of technical strategies that are available today, but in a more abstruse form: Secure search engines, VPNs (virtual private networks), or the TOR project are all examples of privacy and security tools for web anonymity. In this sense, then, the book provides

30 The novel ignores today's increasing power shift from nations to multinational corporations.

implicit examples of strategies to lower everyone's PRED score today. You may rest assured that something like this – even if invisible to us – already exists today.

The novel also outlines the impact of advanced digitization on legal practice and literary production. We have already discussed the opportunities and pitfalls of algorithm-based legal practice in which human consideration and reflection are no longer required – or at least rendered not as effective and fast as the cube's artificial intelligence. But the novel also presents us with a concept of literature in the age of ruling AI; one in which narratives are generated algorithmically, tailored to each subject. In this diegetic world, the people do not read or see anything that might challenge them. They only experience the things that the algorithm expects will be most appealing to them. The novel describes a form of literature that people do not have to work through, but is ready-made entertainment for them. We are already witnessing this concept, broadly speaking, in what the media and streaming services selectively offer to us on the Internet, where users are specifically presented with content that they are assumed to favor according to their previous viewing patterns. Significantly, Taso's brother Peter works as a programmer for the so-called 'storytelling algorithms':

> Peter didn't like to talk about his work. His programming was classified, he had once said. Taso only knew that his brother was devising storytelling algorithms for a company that produced individual movies. Most of the entertainment industry now consisted of movies, series, books, music, or games of the indie genre. [. . .] Photorealistically animated, they corresponded entirely to the users' preferences and moods. The characters mostly resembled once-popular actors to give the simulations the illusion of real movies. This way, everyone could always see, hear, read, and play exactly what they felt like, without having to choose for themselves. (DW, 26)[31]

The fact that Moini transposes his two professions (lawyer and writer) into two diegetic figures and arranges them in opposition to each other makes the law and literature discourse even more intriguing. Literature is – like law – AI-processed, which means that the procedures in both systems (literature and law) are quite similar: Stored user data is functionalized to calculate both the reception to the

31 My translation: "Peter sprach nicht gern über seine Arbeit. Seine Programmiererei sei geheim, hatte er mal gesagt. Taso wusste nur, dass sein Bruder Storytelling-Algorithmen für ein Unternehmen schrieb, das individuelle Filme produzierte. Der größte Teil der Unterhaltungsindustrie bestand mittlerweile aus Filmen, Serien, Büchern, Musik oder Spielen des Indi-Genres. [. . .] Fotorealistisch animiert entsprachen sie ganz der Vorliebe und Stimmung der Nutzer. Die Figuren glichen meist einst beliebten Schauspielern, um den Simulationen die Illusion echter Filme zu verleihen. So konnte jeder stets genau das sehen, hören, lesen, spielen, wonach ihm der Sinn stand, ohne selbst auswählen zu müssen."

literature and the probability of lawbreaking. Ultimately, one wonders what effect this will have on human rights.

The most obvious legal provision in this context is Article 19 of the United Nations Universal Declaration of Human Rights. It states: "Everyone has the right to freedom of opinion and expression; this right includes freedom to hold opinions without interference and to seek, receive and impart information and ideas through any media and regardless of frontiers."[32] Obviously, free expression is not possible in a totalitarian system governed by an omnipotent AI. In addition to the possible punishment of citizens with differing views, an unconscious restraint due to the knowledge of total surveillance is likely. Finally, Big Data would presumably also make it possible to find dissenters even without them giving explicit cause.

Furthermore, the book vividly exemplifies violations of human dignity. The protagonist, Taso, is fully aware of the problem:

> The cube bereaves us, humans, in small steps of no less than our dignity. And by that, I mean *all* people. We are losing control of our own fate, and becoming mere disruptive factors in a world formula that we do not understand. The free subject is abolished, and made the object of a higher power. (DW, 338)[33]

This relates to the first article of the draft proposal for a Charter of Fundamental Digital Rights of the European Union which states: "Human dignity remains inviolable in the digital age. Human dignity must be respected and safeguarded. No technological development may be allowed to encroach upon it."[34] The article explicitly prohibits any technological appropriation of basic human rights. Human autonomy and a dignified life would be impossible with systems like the PRED-score, total surveillance, and the algorithmic calculation of legal issues by "Instalaw." Ultimately, the novel reflects on the role of Europe in this state of tension between law, literature, individual autonomy, self-determination, as

---

32 United Nations, "Universal Declaration of Human Rights – English," (n.d.), *United Nations: Human Rights* <https://www.ohchr.org/en/human-rights/universal-declaration/translations/english> (acc. May 1, 2022), n. pag.

33 My translation: "Der Würfel raubt uns Menschen in kleinen Schritten nicht weniger als unsere Würde. Und damit meine ich *allen* Menschen. Wir verlieren die Herrschaft über unser eigenes Schicksal, werden zu bloßen Störfaktoren in einer Weltformel, die wir selbst nicht verstehen. Der freie Mensch wird abgeschafft und zum Objekt einer höheren Macht."

34 Cf. Bucerius Lab, "Draft Proposal for a Charter of Fundamental Digital Rights of the European Union," (September 19, 2019), *Digital Charter Initiative* <https://medium.com/digital-charter/draft-proposal-for-a-charter-of-fundamental-digital-rights-of-the-european-union-40b18ff72ad1?source=user_profile> (acc. May 1, 2022), n. pag.

well as national and international politics. In the novel, Europe is depicted as a plaything of the more powerful nations of the U.S. and China.[35]

6 What Will Become of Europe?

The author Bijan Moini also contributed to the book *Jeder Mensch* by Ferdinand von Schirach – an argument for the renewal of the European Charter of Fundamental Rights, which was much discussed after its release.[36] The authors' collective call for six new fundamental European rights.[37] Let us here focus on numbers two and three: respectively, the right to digital self-determination and the rights of people concerning AI systems that are increasingly implemented in autonomous decision-making algorithms: "Everyone has the right to know that any algorithms imposed on them are transparent, verifiable, and fair. Key decisions must be taken by a human being."[38] Is such phrasing really adequate to address the problem? Or is it too abstract to have any effect? Indeed, there have been many more complex suggestions with more precise formulations, such as the proposal for a Charter of Fundamental Digital Rights (2018). However, the most common objection is that the technical jargon has become far too complex for the average, not so tech-savvy citizen. That is why von Schirach's deliberately simple proposal is so compelling – and, in combination with literary examples, well illustrates why Europe as a unique digital realm is at stake.

The novel's diegetic geopolitical situation is structured in a way that a free Europe faces danger from two outside systems: First, the totalitarian system from the East and second, the capitalist system from the U.S. Both threats are magnified by the AI's performance. Human dignity and freedom are core values at the heart of the European Convention on Human Rights, along with equality and solidarity – and for good reasons at that, even if the policies of European states and even of EU member states often fail to meet the obligations arising from these rights.

35 In the novel, Cubists and Harmonists (the name of the Asian totalitarian group) also fight for the African continent.

36 For a discussion of the book, see, e.g., Heinrich Wefing, "'Endlich unser Europa,'" (March 31, 2021), *Die Zeit* <https://www.zeit.de/2021/14/ferdinand-von-schirach-jeder-mensch-eu-politik-klimaschutz-google-facebook> (acc. May 1, 2022), n. pag.; Ingolf Pernice, "'Jeder Mensch,'" (April 4, 2021), *Frankfurter Allgemeine Zeitung* <https://www.faz.net/einspruch/ferdinand-von-schirachs-jeder-mensch-zukunftsweisend-17280803.html> (acc. May 1, 2022), n. pag.

37 The new articles can be found, as translated into various languages at Stiftung Jeder Mensch e.V., "Eine neue Utopie für Europa," (2022), *Home Page* <https://jeder-mensch.eu> (acc. May 1, 2022).

38 Stiftung Jeder Mensch e.V., "Eine neue Utopie," n. pag.

However, the right to digital self-determination has hitherto not been addressed in EU legal documents, although it will prove increasingly important to forge a way to protect our freedom and right to self-determination in the digital world.

We must be prepared, not only as individuals but also as a society, on both the European level and on an international level, to meet the challenges to our freedom, our right to self-determination, and even to the very conditions for human dignity, for equality and solidarity, as well as the challenges that emerge from the ongoing development of data harvesting, digital surveillance technologies, and artificial intelligence.

Currently we only have Article 7 of the Charter of Fundamental Rights, which guarantees "respect for private and family life," as well as "home and communications," and Article 8 on the Protection of Personal Data, including "the right of access to data which has been collected concerning him or her, and the right to have it rectified."[39] In addition we have the General Data Protection Regulation of 2016 which spells out this right to the protection of personal data and has forced online service providers to rethink the way they do business with the data they gather from and about their users.[40] To understand the implications of the emergence of data-driven economic and political superpowers is an unprecedented challenge. Perhaps SF can help us shine a light to see what is really at stake. Often, changes come about incrementally, so that one hardly notices what is happening. However, imaginative literature has the power to lay out the consequences in detail for us to see and reflect upon.

7 Conclusion

In this article, I have described the potential future problems faced by our society with regard to digital rights, and provided various examples of literature in which these issues have been explored. As mentioned at the beginning, SF literature has a prognostic and thus also a culturally reflective function. This function sometimes involves reflecting upon rights and, as in the case of the book under discussion, reflecting upon literature. Moini's novel, in particular, is an example of SF literature

39 Cf. European Union, "Charter of Fundamental Rights of the European Union," (October 26, 2012), *EUR-Lex* <https://eur-lex.europa.eu/legal-content/EN/TXT/?uri=CELEX:12012P/TXT> (acc. May 1, 2022), n. pag.

40 Cf. European Parliament and Council of the European Union, "International Cooperation for the Protection of Personal Data," (n.d.), *General Data Protection Regulation* <https://gdpr-info.eu/art-50-gdpr> (acc. May 1, 2022).

that not only functions dystopically, but also casts future technologies such as AI in an ambivalent light. Opportunities and possibilities are considered alongside possible dangers. At the same time, however, it is precisely Europe's hesitant approach to these technologies that might ultimately endanger Europe's integrity and political self-determination. It seems crucial to create a legal framework that protects humanity from the misuse of these technologies and preserves the freedom and self-determination of the individual. We have seen that concepts introduced by SF literature are increasingly becoming reality and that legal systems must respond to these new technologies so as not to jeopardize the rule of law.

This gives rise to a variety of pertinent follow-up questions that cannot be answered satisfactorily in the limited space of the present article but will remain crucial in the current debate on freedom, human dignity, and digital self-determination: Does Europe as a concept and bastion of digital self-determination still have a future at all? Or is globalization in the digital space moving too fast? How can Europeans resist liberal data policies and the shift of power to multinational corporations? Indeed, is it even necessary? Are stricter regulations needed in AI development? Should more European science fiction literature be read to gain a better understanding of Europe's position and potential future realities? Is SF literature a good testing ground to establish a legal framework for future technologies, or do fictional scare scenarios simply foment groundless paranoia?

Epilogue

Julia Cimafiejeva

My European Poem

This poem should be written in English.
This poem should be written in German.
This poem should be written in French,
In Swedish, in Spanish, in my adorable Norwegian,
Maybe in Finnish, Danish and Dutch.
Baltic languages should decide for themselves.
No Belarusian version for the poem,
No Russian version for the poem,
No Ukrainian version for the poem.
The rest are your choice.
This poem should be written in the languages
Of human rights organizations,
Of those multiple expressed concerns
By European politicians.

So
Shall I get used to the thought
That I could be taken to prison
By the men wearing black,
By the men in plain clothes,
By the men with four fat letters
On their fat black backs?
Otherwise, my country
Won't gain any freedom.
And it could not work anyway,
As usual.

Shall I take it calmly that I
Could be beaten and ultimately
Found guilty for that
Because (They would say)
I cried antistate slogans like "Freedom!"
Or "Release all political prisoners!"
Though I would not need to cry them out at all
(Like my Facebook friends and thousands of
Someone else's friends)
In order to be arrested or beaten.
I won't have to cry anything,
I won't have to do anything,
Just stand silently, just be.
I know I have to get used to that thought

https://doi.org/10.1515/9783111075693-038

Just in case, because it's so likely to happen.
(Oh, my! I haven't yet saved those numbers to contact
in case of detention.)

I can't say that in Belarusian,
I can't say that in Russian,
I can't say that in Ukrainian,
Only in English: I am afraid,
Only in German: Ich habe Angst,
Only in Norwegian: Jeg er redd.
That's enough, for other variants,
Please, use Google translate.
The translations should be
more Or less accurate. These are not
Those strange Eastern European languages
With their funny Cyrillic letters.

I'm afraid
Like you would be in my place,
If you lived in a country that is not free
Where they've had the same president
For 26 (!) years. Oh, my god! More than
Two thirds of my life I've spent
Under the power of a madman
Whom I've never voted for!

Sorry, it's a long poem,
Because it's a long story,
I spent more than two thirds of my life
Under the power of the man
I've never voted for,
Who harassed and suppressed and killed
(They say).

And when I come to the literary festivals abroad,
And when I speak English
I try to tell the complicated history of my country
(When I am asked)
As if I am another person,
As if I am like all those European poets and writers,
Who do not have to get used to the thought
That they could be arrested and beaten
For the sake of their country's freedom.
As if my ugly history is just a harsh story
That I can easily cut from *The Anthology of*
Modern European Short Stories because

It's too long,
And too dull.

When I tell it in English,
I want to pretend that I am you,
That I don't have that painful experience
Of constant protesting and constant failing,
That nasty feeling of frustration and dismay.
I want to pretend that I have a hope,
Because when I tell it in Belarusian
I realize, we all realize, there is none
We can look forward to.

So, forgive me my nagging in a half-broken English,
My Eastern European never-ending complaints,
As having read the books you've read,
I still want to have a hope,
I still believe I have a right for a hope,
That beaten hope that builds its nest
On my roof and sings
Its songs in Belarusian
(Not in Russian).

August 5, 2020

List of Contributors

Dominik Brodowksi is Professor of Criminal Law and Criminal Procedure at Saarland University, Saarbrücken, Germany. He focuses on European criminal law, criminal justice and digitalization, constitutional criminal justice, and the foundations and frontiers of criminal justice. Dominik Brodowski holds a Dr. iur. from the University of Tübingen, an LL.M. from the University of Pennsylvania, and was granted *venia legendi* for Criminal Law, Criminal Procedure, European and International Law, IT Criminal Law and Economic Criminal Law by Goethe University Frankfurt. He is a senior fellow at the Carol and Lawrence Zicklin Center for Business Ethics Research, The Wharton School, University of Pennsylvania, and was Visiting Professor at the University of São Paulo Law School, Campus Ribeirão Preto.

Paola Chiarella is Associate Professor in Philosophy of Law at the Department of Law, Economics and Sociology of the University of Catanzaro, Italy. After earning a master's degree in Law with *summa cum laude* and submitting an honors thesis at the University of Catanzaro, she also obtained a PhD in Theory of Law and Legal and Economic Order (PhD with scholarship) at the same university. She is author of several monographs and essays, including, most recently, *Twisting the Tail of the Cosmos: costellazioni filosofiche nella teoria di Oliver Wendell Holmes* (2022); *Domus aurea: abitare in pandemia tra diritti e privazioni* (2022); *Il patriottismo razionale di Richard Price nella stagione delle rivoluzioni* (2021); *Il diritto comprensivo e l'altruità del corpo: alcune riflessioni sul fine vita* (2020); and *El malestar de la laicidad: algunas reflexiones sobre el caso italiano* (2020).

Julia Cimafiejeva is a Belarusian poet, writer, and translator. She is also one of the founders and editors of the Belarusian literary magazine *PrajdziSvet*. Her poems have been translated into German, English, Swedish, and many other languages. Her poetry collections *Zirkus* and *Der Angststein* were published in German translation in 2019 and 2022; in 2022, her book *Minsk: Die Stadt, die ich vermisse*, featuring photographs and poetic texts, appeared in Germany in both German and Belarusian. She has participated in literary festivals in many European countries. Her diary about life in Belarus at the time of the protests was published in multiple languages; in Germany, the book appeared in 2021. In 2020, she had to leave Belarus due to political repression.

Walter Cohen is Professor of English at the University of Michigan and Professor Emeritus of Comparative Literature at Cornell University; at the latter institution he spent many years in university administration. He is the author of *Drama of a Nation: Public Theater in Renaissance England and Spain* (Cornell UP, 1985), *A History of European Literature: The West and the World from Antiquity to the Present* (Oxford UP, 2017), and dozens of articles. In addition, he is one of the editors of *The Norton Shakespeare* (3rd ed. 2017). His current projects include the languages of Jewish literature, the continuity of African literature from Ancient Egypt to the present, the formative influence on literary history of ecological catastrophe, the increasingly neglected function of social class and economic inequality in literary study, and, conversely, the impact of language and literature on social change.

Tetyana Dagovych was born in Ukraine (Ukrainian SSR) and spent one year in Belarus as a child. She received her master's degree in Slavic Studies from Dnipro State University, then studied Romance Philology and Philosophy at the University of Münster, where she received her master's in Philosophy of Science. She has worked as a lecturer for Ukrainian and Russian at the University of Bochum. Since 2020, she has been a doctoral candidate at the Collaborative Research Center (SFB

https://doi.org/10.1515/9783111075693-039

1385) "Law and Literature" at the University of Münster and is working on her PhD thesis on literary devices in defense closing arguments of Russian lawyers between 1864 and 1917. She has also published articles on law in the dramaturgy of Lesya Ukrainka.

Sidia Fiorato is Associate Professor of English Literature at the University of Verona. Her research interests include law and literature with a specific focus on the legal thriller, literature and the performing arts, adaptation studies, the fairy tale, Shakespeare studies, and gender studies. She is a member of ESSE (European Society for the Study of English), AIA (Associazione Italiana di Anglistica), AIDEL (Associazione Italiana Diritto e Letteratura), CUSVE (Centro Universitario di Studi Vittoriani e Edoardiani), and Skenè Research Center. Her publications include *Il Gioco con l'ombra: Ambiguità e metanarrazioni nella narrativa di Peter Ackroyd* (2003), *The Relationship Between Literature and Science in John Banville's Scientific Tetralogy* (2007), and *Performing the Renaissance Body: Essays on Drama, Law and Representation* (edited volume with John Drakakis, 2016). She is a member of the Advisory Board of the journal *Pólemos: Journal of Law, Literature and Culture*.

Melanie Foik studied Eastern European History, Slavonic Studies, and German Studies in Münster and Krakow. Various study and research trips also took her to Warsaw, Prague, Lviv, and Moscow. She spent a year in Chernivtsi as a DAAD language assistant before joining the Institute for Slavonic Studies as well as the Department of History at the University of Münster as a research assistant. In 2020, she completed her doctorate in Eastern European History with a thesis on the health services of the Polish People's Republic. Since then, she has been working as a research fellow in the subproject "Literary Forms of European Legal Culture in Poland, Russia and Ukraine" at the Collaborative Research Center (SFB 1385) "Law and Literature" at the University of Münster. In her current postdoctoral project, she is researching representations of crime, policing, and criminal justice in Polish literature from the second half of the nineteenth century to the present day.

Thomas Gutmann is Professor for Civil Law, Philosophy of Law, and Medical Law and Co-Director of the Research Institute for Philosophy of Law at the University of Münster. He serves as Co-Editor of the *Encyclopedia of Law and Literature* for the Collaborative Research Center (SFB 1385) "Law and Literature" at the University of Münster. His main fields of interest are legal theory, practical philosophy, theory of society, private law, medical law, and ethics.

Jayana Jain completed her Ph.D. in English and Cultural Studies at the University of Münster. She was a recipient of the DAAD scholarship and EU's Marie Curie Fellowship to conduct research on South Asian diasporic literature and films. She has also served as a research fellow and lecturer at the University of Munich (LMU) and the University of Münster. Her first published monograph, *Thinking Past "Post-9/11": Home, Nation and Transnational Desires in Pakistani English Novels and Hindi Films*, traces the multiple origins and shifts in national xenophobic policies after 9/11, and discusses the role of literature and film in negotiating multiple modalities of political and cultural belonging. Alongside South Asian literature and film, she is interested in diaspora and migration studies, legal cultures, digital media and politics, and gender and disability studies.

Nicola Kramp-Seidel, PhD, is a research fellow in the subproject "Rhetorical Strategies in Jewish and Islamic Legislative Texts" at the Collaborative Research Center (SFB 1385) "Law and Literature" at the University of Münster. Her research areas focus mainly on Jewish law in different eras, especially the study of Jewish responsa in the Middle Ages and Modern Era and codification literature in the Middle Ages. Her first monograph (PhD), *Isaak Alfasis Kodifizierung des talmudischen Rechts im Sefer ha-Halakhot* *zum Traktat Pesachim*, analyses one tractate of the code "Sefer ha-Halakhot" written by Isaak Alfasi (eleventh century). Her second monograph focuses on the decision-making process as well as the presentation and visibility of decisions in responsa written by Salomon Adret (thirteenth century). In further publications, she analyses the semantics of decision-making and the patterns of argumentation, tropes, and stylistic devices in responsa.

Massimo La Torre is Professor of Legal Philosophy at the Magna Græcia University of Catanzaro, Italy. He received his Ph.D. from the European University Institute in Florence and studied Law and Political Science at the University of Messina and at Johns Hopkins University, Bologna Center. He has held numerous professorships and visiting professorial fellowships at European universities, and he was a fellow of the Alliance Française, the Consiglio Nazionale delle Ricerche, the British Council, and the Alexander von Humboldt Foundation. In 2009, La Torre was honored with the Research Award of the Alexander von Humboldt Foundation. He is Associate Editor of *Ratio Juris: An International Journal of Jurisprudence and Philosophy of Law*. His latest monograph is *Il diritto contro se stesso: Saggio sul positivismo giuridico e la sua crisi* (Olschki, 2020).

Kathrin Löhr studied History, German Philology, and Political Science in Münster and Lyon. Since 2020, she has been a PhD student at the Collaborative Research Center (SFB 1385) "Law and Literature" at the University of Münster. She is participating in research in subproject A03 "Das Recht der Erfahrungsseelenkunde: Der Pitaval als Milieu- und Prozessliteratur zwischen 1730 und 1840." In addition to literature of the early modern period with a focus on Germany and France, her main interests are German exile literature and the cultural life and cultural politics of the GDR.

Lord Jonathan Mance is former Deputy President of the Supreme Court of the United Kingdom. He represents the United Kingdom on the Council of Europe's Consultative Council of European Judges (2000). He currently chairs the International Law Association and the Lord Chancellor's Advisory Committee on Private International Law. He is a member of the Judicial Integrity Group and of the seven-person panel set up under the Treaty on the Functioning of the European Union to give an opinion on candidates' suitability to perform the duties of Judge and Advocate-General at the European Court of Justice and General Court. He served on the House of Lords European Union Select Committee from 2007 to 2009. In 2008, he led an international delegation for the same Group and the Swedish Foundation for Human Rights, reporting on the problems of impunity in relation to violence against women in the Congo. Lord Mance is a founding member of the European Law Institute.

Pier Giuseppe Monateri is Professor of Law at the University of Torino. He is a member of the International Academy of Comparative Law (New York), l'Accademia delle Scienze (Bologna), and la Société de Législation Comparée (Paris). His most recent publications include *Dominus Mundi: Political Sublime and the World Order* (Hart 2018) and *Advanced Introduction to Comparative Legal Methods* (Edward Elgar 2021).

Matteo Nicolini, PhD, is Associate Professor of Public Comparative Law, Department of Law, University of Verona (Italy). He is also Visiting Lecturer at the Newcastle University Law School (UK), and External Partner of the Center for the Study of Law in Theory and Practice (LTAP) at Liverpool John Moores University (UK). He has held teaching and visiting appointments at the Universities of Stellenbosch, Barcelona, Valladolid, Tübingen, Lille, UNED (Madrid), Alberto Hurtado (Chile), and Innsbruck. He is the author of several works, including *Law, Territory and Conflict Resolution: Law as a*

Problem and Law as a Solution (Brill, 2016) (editor with Francesco Palermo and Enrico Milano); *Law and Imagination in Troubled Times: A Legal and Literary Discourse* (Routledge, 2020) (editor with Richard Mullender, Thomas D.C. Bennett, Emilia Mickiewicz); *Comparative Constitutional Justice* (Eleven, 2021) (with Silvia Bagni), and *Islands in Geography, Law, and Literature: A Cross-Disciplinary Journey* (De Gruyter 2022) (with Chiara Battisti, Sidia Fiorato, Thomas Perrin). His last monograph is titled *Legal Geography: Comparative Law and the Production of Space* (Springer 2022).

Katharina Pink is Senior Lecturer in English Literature at the University of Munich (LMU). Her thesis *Identitas Oriens* (Ergon 2014) formed part of the interdisciplinary DFG research project "Encountering the Other: A Poetics of British Travel Writing" funded by the Excellence Initiative of the German Research Foundation (DFG). Since 2009, she has been a lecturer at the Chair of Modern Literature, University of Munich, where she received tenure in 2016. She is co-editor of *Romanticism and Knowledge* (wvt, 2015) as well as author of the biography *Charlotte Brontë – Zwischen Anpassung und Rebellion* (WBG/Lambert Schneider, 2016). More recently, she has published essays on "Romantic Discontent and its Discontents" *(Romanticism and the Forms of Discontent*, wvt, 2017) as well as on "Cross-Cultural Narratives of Travel in the Age of Globalization" (*East-West Dialogues*, Peter Lang, 2021).

Norbert Oberauer received his PhD at the University of Freiburg im Breisgau, with a thesis on the concept of taklīf (religious obligation) and its theological, legal, and social dimensions in Islamic thought. He continued his academic career as a research assistant at the University of Bayreuth, where he obtained his *Habilitation* (postdoctoral thesis) with a study on *waqf* (Islamic religious endowments) in Zanzibar under colonial rule. Since 2010, he has been a professor for Islamic studies at the University of Münster with a special focus on Islamic law. His main fields of research include Islamic contract law, Islamic legal hermeneutics, *waqf*, and the history of Islamic law in general.

Silvia Reuvekamp is Professor of German Philology with a focus on Medieval Literature at the University of Münster. Her research interests include intersections between narratology and anthropology, negotiations between vernacular literature and learned knowledge from theology, philosophy and law, as well as the semantics of literary form.

Alberto Scerbo is Full Professor in Philosophy of Law at the Department of Law, Economics and Sociology at the University of Catanzaro, Italy, and coordinator of the professors of the Italian Society of Philosophy of Law. He is a member of the Scientific Committee of the Research Center *Constitutional Law and Political Institutions* and a member of the academic staff of the doctoral degree in Legal and Economic European Order of the University of Catanzaro. He is the author of several monographs and essays, including, most recently, *Dal nulla all'essere: diritto e potere nella pittura di Goya* (2018), *L'infinita vanità del tutto: Sul politico e giuridico nel pensiero di Leopardi* (2019), *La questione del sergente Grischa: un esperimento letterario sul confronto tra umanità del diritto e disumanità del potere* (2021), *La porta stretta del processo: Gide e le angosce del giudizio* (2022), and *A partire da G.F. Puchta: Intorno alla filosofia del diritto italiana nel XIX secolo* (2022).

Peter Schneck is Professor and Chair of American Literature and Culture at Osnabrück University, and currently the director of the Institute for English and American Studies. After studying American Studies, Media and Communication Studies at the Free University Berlin and Yale University, he received his Ph.D. at the FU Berlin. Between 1997 and 2006, he taught at the Amerika-Institut at the University of Munich (LMU) where he concluded his *Habilitation* (postdoctoral thesis). Publications include *The U.S. and the Questions of Rights* (Heidelberg 2020; co-ed); *Rhetoric and Evidence: Legal Conflict and Literary Representation in American Culture* (Berlin, 2011); as well as articles on cognitive poetics, literature and visual art, media history, cultural studies, and law and literature. Since 2019, he has been leading a research group at Osnabrück University on the formation of literary property within the Collaborative Research Center (SFB 1385) "Law and Literature," hosted by the University of Münster and funded by the German Research Foundation (DFG).

Alfred Sproede (*1951) was a student of Slavic and Romance Studies, Philosophy, and East European History (in Frankfurt a.M., Paris, and Konstanz, 1969–76) before working in Moscow as a dyestuff representative for Hoechst Chemicals AG (1976–78) and completing his PhD on Andrei Platonov's fiction in 1982 (Konstanz). From 1983 to 1990, he worked at the Slavic Department at Fribourg CH and for a project on Roman Ingarden (Swiss Research Foundation). He then served as Visiting Assistant Professor at Duke University, Durham, NC (Slavic Department, Graduate Program in Literature; Jan.–Sept. 1991), and at Oldenburg University, Germany (1991–94). After his *Habilitation* (postdoctoral thesis) on Renaissance poet Jan Kochanowski (Fribourg CH 1993), he served as a Full Professor at Halle (summer term 1995) and the University of Münster (1995–2017; Slavic and Baltic Studies). Later appointments include Visiting Professor at Harvard University (spring term 1998) and at Jagiellonian University, Cracow (Feb.–Apr. 2001); and Guest Lecturer at Università degli Studi Milano (Apr. 2016). He has been a Member of the North Rhine-Westphalian Academy of Sciences, Humanities, and the Arts since 2015. His research interests include modern Polish, Russian, and Ukrainian literatures, Renaissance and Baroque culture, and Eastern European social and legal philosophy.

Johannes Ueberfeldt, M.A., studied Philosophy, German Studies, and Cultural Poetics at the University of Münster and is currently working on the subproject "An Anthropology of Crime: On the Discursive Interferences between Poetics, Morals, Law and Medicine in German Crime Stories of the 19th Century" at the Collaborative Research Center (SFB 1385) "Law and Literature" at the University of Münster on the topic "Legal Figurations: Social Anthropology and Criticism of Justice in the Crime Narratives of J. D. H. Temme." His research interests include film theory, literary media and cultural semiotics, and crime literature. Selected publications include "Slow Cinema – Echtzeitästhetik des kontemplativen Kinos" in Stephan Brössel and Susanne Kaul (eds.), *Echtzeit im Film: Konzepte – Wirkungen – Kontexte* (Paderborn 2020) and "Der Mensch im Zeitalter seiner technischen Reproduzierbarkeit: Black Mirror als Meta-Anthologie und innovierender Serialisierungsprozess" In Kilian Hauptmann, Philipp Pabst, and Felix Schallenberg (eds.), *Anthologieserie: Systematik und Geschichte eines narrativen Formats* (Marburg 2022, with Sebastian Berlich).

Martina Wagner-Egelhaaf studied Germanics and History at the University of Tübingen. In 1997, she received her PhD with a dissertation on "Mystik der Moderne: Zur visionären Ästhetik der deutschen Literatur im 20. Jahrhundert" from the University of Tübingen. After her dissertation, Martina Wagner-Egelhaaf worked as a postdoctoral researcher at the University of Konstanz, where she completed her *Habilitation* (postdoctoral thesis), "Die Melancholie der Literatur: Diskursgeschichte und Textfiguration" in 1994. From 1995 to 1998, she was Professor for New German Studies with a focus on the Theory of Literature and Rhetoric at the University of Bochum. Since 1998, she has been working as Professor for Modern German Literature at the University of Münster. Her fields of research include German literature from the eighteenth century to contemporary literature, literary theory and rhetoric, autobiography research, and literature in relation to religion, politics, and law. Martina Wagner-Egelhaaf has held Visiting Professorships in the USA, in China, and in Japan.

Irina Wutsdorff holds the Chair of Slavic Studies at the University of Münster. Her research interests include Slavic literatures in comparative perspective, literary theory as well as the relationship of literature to the other arts. She received her doctorate at the University of Potsdam (*Bachtin und der Prager Strukturalismus: Modelle poetischer Offenheit am Beispiel der tschechischen Avantgarde*. Paderborn: Wilhelm Fink 2006). She was Junior Professor of Transcultural East Central European Studies at the University of Tübingen, where she wrote her postdoctoral thesis on the interaction of literature and philosophy in Russian culture. Her comparative research interests include Czech and German-language literature of Prague modernism(s) (*Prager Moderne(n): Interkulturelle Perspektiven auf Raum, Identität und Literatur*, eds. Manfred Weinberg, Irina Wutsdorff, and Štěpán Zbytovský, Bielefeld: transcript 2018). The handbook *Central and Eastern European Literary Theory and the West*, (Berlin: De Gruyter), edited by Irina Wutsdorff, Schamma Schahadat and Michał Mrugalski, will be published in 2023.

Laura A. Zander is a postdoctoral research fellow at the Collaborative Research Center (SFB 1385) "Law and Literature" at the University of Münster, which is funded by the German Research Foundation (DFG). Laura holds an M.A. in English Literature and Linguistics and both state examinations in Law after completing her postgraduate judicial service traineeship. After receiving her PhD by the Faculty of Language and Literatures at the University of Munich (LMU), she worked as a lecturer in the English Department. She also worked as a research assistant and taught at the Faculty of Law at the Universities of Munich, Frankfurt, and Saarbrücken for a master's program in Digital Forensics. Publications include *Writing Back / Reading Forward: Reconsidering the Postcolonial Approach* (Berlin 2019) as well as articles on law and literature, gender and postcolonial studies, and both South African and Caribbean literature.

Index

https://doi.org/10.1515/9783111075693-040

Printed and bound by CPI Group (UK) Ltd, Croydon, CR0 4YY
13/09/2026
14961092-0004